THE CENTURY PSYCHOLOGY SERIES

The Stream of Behavior

CONTRIBUTING AUTHORS

Louise Shedd Barker
Roger G. Barker
Harold R. Dickman
Arthur J. Dyck
Clifford L. Fawl
Paul V. Gump
Vera P. John
Nehemiah Jordan
Fritz Redl
Maxine Schoggen
Phil Schoggen
Helen Simmons
James E. Simpson
William F. Soskin

The Stream of Behavior

EXPLORATIONS OF ITS STRUCTURE & CONTENT

Edited by

ROGER G. BARKER

DIRECTOR, MIDWEST PSYCHOLOGICAL FIELD STATION
UNIVERSITY OF KANSAS

New York

APPLETON-CENTURY-CROFTS

Division of Meredith Publishing Company

633-1

Library of Congress Card Number: 62-18400

PRINTED IN THE UNITED STATES OF AMERICA

E05920

ACKNOWLEDGMENTS

IT IS A SOURCE OF SATISFACTION and encouragement to the authors of *The Stream of Behavior* that so many persons, identified in the reports by pseudonyms only, agreed that more must be known about the conditions and consequences of everyday life and willingly co-operated as subjects, and as associates of subjects, in the pursuit of this knowledge. Scientists who investigate behavior under the natural conditions of life owe a special debt to the people they study, and the authors wish to express their sincere appreciation for the part played by all those who contributed in this essential way to the research reported here.

The research received financial support from a number of sources. All of the studies benefited from grants made to the Midwest Psychological Field Station of the University of Kansas (a) by PHS research grants MH-6 and M-1513 from the National Institute of Mental Health, Public Health Service, and (b) by the University of Kansas Research Fund.

The work presented in Chapters 1, 3, 4, 5, 6, 7, and 8 was done primarily with the financial assistance of the two agencies named above; additional support was provided as follows: The research of Phil Schoggen and Helen Simmons (Chapters 3 and 4) was aided by grants from the Graduate School, University of Oregon, and the U.S. Office of Vocational Rehabilitation (RD 714–61). Clifford L. Fawl's study (Chapter 6) was assisted by a dissertation-completion fellowship awarded the author in 1958 by the Social Science Research Council. The investigations of Roger G. Barker, Louise Shedd Barker, and Maxine Schoggen (Chapters 7 and 8) received grants from the Carnegie Corporation of New York and the Ford Foundation; some of the writing and analyses were done while Roger G. Barker was a Fellow of the Center for Advanced Study in the Behavioral Sciences. The studies involving disabled children (Chapters 3, 4, and 6) were supported by the Association for the Aid of Crippled Children and by the Carnegie Corporation of New York.

The research of Paul V. Gump, Phil Schoggen, and Fritz Redl (Chapter 9) was sponsored by the School of Social Work, Wayne State University and aided by PHS research grant M-550 from the National Institute of Mental Health, Public Health Service. The study of William F. Soskin and Vera P. John (Chapter 12) was assisted by PHS research grants M-701 and M-3321 from the National Institute of Mental Health, Public Health Service.

Many people in addition to the authors had a part in the preparation of the volume. Dr. Thomas F. Nichols and Dr. Lois M. Stolz were valued consultants in connection with a number of the investigations. The following assistants performed essential ratings and computations: Margaret Ashton, Sylvia A. Dyck, Wallace Friesen, Guney Kozacioglu, Richard Lawless, William LeCompte, Eleanor Hall Mikesell, Edwin Willems, Karl Zangerle, and Harold Zender.

The authors of particular chapters acknowledge special obligations to these persons:

ARTHUR J. DYCK (Chapter 5). Dr. J. S. Kounin provided helpful advice and stimulation during the early stages of the research, and Dr. C. L. Fawl contributed substantially to the study by means of his cogent criticisms, his encouragement, and his assistance in marking agreement checks. An indispensable aid was Sylvia A. Dyck who shared the tasks of analyzing and recording data.

CLIFFORD L. FAWL (Chapter 6). The influence of Professor Martin Scheerer on the nature of the study is gratefully acknowledged, as is, also, the contribution of Arthur J. Dyck to whom the author is immeasurably indebted for the generous performance of services both big and little.

ROGER G. BARKER, LOUISE SHEDD BARKER, and MAXINE SCHOGGEN (Chapters 7 and 8). The studies profited greatly from the co-operation of Mr. F. Barraclough, Mr. R. Oliver, Mr. C. M. Turner, Mr. H. L. Streator, and Mr. R. L. Taylor who not only opened schools in Yorkshire and Kansas, but provided essential and timely aid and encouragement. For help in selecting the books analyzed in the study, the authors are indebted to Ruth Gagliardo, Director of Library Services, Kansas State Teachers Association; to Mildred L. Batchelder, Executive Secretary, American Library Association of Libraries for Children and Young People; to F. Phyllis Parrott, Children's Librarian, Reading, Berkshire; and to Joan Butler, Herfordshire County Library. Hermina Nichols rendered important assistance in rating the data from the books.

PAUL V. GUMP, PHIL SCHOGGEN, and FRITZ REDL (Chapter 9). Sincere appreciation is extended to the personnel of University Boys' Camp, and to Maxine Schoggen, Ted Goldberg, and Brian Sutton-Smith who served as observers.

NEHEMIAH JORDAN (Chapter 10). The help and co-operation of Dr. Fritz Redl, Dr. Harold L. Raush, and Mrs. Florence W. Glaser were essential for the completion of this investigation.

JAMES E. SIMPSON (Chapter 11). Encouragement and help were received from Dr. Anthony J. Smith, Dr. Riley W. Gardner, Dr. Gardner Murphy, and Dr. Mary E. Simpson.

WILLIAM F. SOSKIN and VERA P. JOHN (Chapter 12). The authors are deeply indebted to Mr. Paul Doty of Bell Telephone Laboratories, who was a graduate student at the time of this study, not only for his remarkable achievement in designing and constructing the apparatus used, but also for his inestimable services in erecting the receiving station and supervising all technical phases of the pilot run.

The preparation of the manuscript was the work of Marjorie Elkinton Reed, Isla Herbert, Maxine Mize, Dorothy Streator, Ruth Finley, Gwendolyn Willems, LaVelle Anderson, and Barbara Patrick.

It is a pleasure to express the sincere appreciation of the authors of *The Stream of Behavior* for these generous contributions to their scientific endeavors.

R.G.B.

CONTENTS

The Stream of Behavior

I went to work to learn the shape of the river; and of all the eluding and ungraspable objects that ever I tried to get mind or hands on, that was the chief.

MARK TWAIN
Life on the Mississippi

CHAPTER 1

The Stream of Behavior as an Empirical Problem

ROGER G. BARKER

TEMPORAL ASPECTS OF BEHAVIOR are among the most compelling in experience and among the most easily measured of all of behavior's unnumbered characteristics. Despite the saliency of the time dimension however, little is known about the actual arrangement of behavior along its temporal axis. The studies reported in this volume attempt to push forward on this frontier; they are all empirical approaches to the stream of behavior and they have had to cope with some common problems.

Behavior Units and Behavior Tesserae

Innumerable parts of the behavior stream have been identified and described, encompassing such diverse phenomena as an alpha wave, a maze-learning trial, and a psychotic episode, a five-minute segment of behavior, a game of marbles, and an answer to a pollster's question. The stream of behavior can be divided into an infinite number of parts. These countless parts of the behavior continuum are of two types so far as their origin along the time dimension is concerned.

One type, here called *behavior units,* consists of the inherent segments of the stream of behavior. The boundaries of behavior units occur at those points of the behavior stream where changes occur independently of the operations of the investigator. Alpha waves, psychotic episodes, and games of marbles are behavior units. Behavior units enter psychology when investigators function as transducers, observing and recording behavior with techniques that do not influence its course. When a child is observed to sit on a rock (Lewin, 1935, p. 83), to refuse to say "Please" (Stern, 1938, p. 499), or to make a "house" (Isaacs, 1933, p. 168) in the ordinary course of his life without instigation or direction by the observer, behavior units are observed.

The other parts of the behavior stream may be appropriately called *behavior tesserae.* Tesserae are the pieces of glass or marble used in mosaic work; they are created or selected by the mosaic maker to fulfill his artistic aims. Similarly, behavior tesserae are fragments of behavior that are created or selected by the investigator in accordance with his scientific aims.

Maze-learning trials, five-minute segments of behavior, and answers to pollsters' questions are behavior tesserae. They occur when there is feedback between the investigator and the behavior stream. When an investigator directs a subject to "Define orange," "Tell me what you see on the card," "Judge which of these weights is the heavier," he destroys the natural units of the behavior stream and imposes behavior tesserae in their place. Behavior tesserae are produced by experiments, tests, questionnaires, and interviews, i.e., by all methods that require the subject to undertake actions at the behest of the investigator. Behavior tesserae are produced, too, by research methods which divide the behavior continuum into predetermined time periods or number-of-occurrence segments. In these cases, the beginning and the end points of the selected parts of the behavior stream are established by the technical requirements of the investigator, and they coincide only by chance with the inherent units of the behavior continuum. When an investigator tallies the occurrence of aggressive behavior in a sample of one-minute observations of a child (Walters, Pearce, & Dahms, 1957), or records a child's first fifty utterances during a period of observation (McCarthy, 1930) he disregards the intrinsic structure of the behavior stream and selects parts from it which fit his research design.

Behavior units are natural units in the sense that they occur without intervention by the investigator; they are self-generated parts of the stream of behavior. Behavior tesserae, on the other hand, are alien parts of the behavior stream in the sense that they are formed when an investigator, ignoring or dismantling the existing stream of behavior, imposes or chooses parts of it according to his own preconceptions and intentions. Heyns and Lippett (1954, p. 375) have made the distinction between natural and imposed behavior elements and Jenny (1958) and Barker and Barker (1961) have used the term tessera in ecological contexts.

Research methods which ignore or destroy existing structures and select or create new ones are standard techniques and of greatest value in most sciences. Chemists, biologists, and geologists grind and macerate, compound, synthesize, and rearrange their substances in order to make important analyses. The imposition of alien tesserae upon the material of a science is dramatically illustrated by the way geographers and geometers divide the surface of the earth. About one hundred years ago, geodetic surveyors came to eastern Kansas with measuring rods and a plan. They divided the landscape into the surprising lattice of geometric squares shown in Figure 1.1. These are geographical tesserae. They are true and useful regions, but they had no existence until the surveyors came with geometry and a design in their heads and staked out the section boundaries. The tesserae, themselves, tell nothing directly about the topography of this part of the earth.

In addition, however, to structure-ignoring and structure-destroying research methods, all sciences devise tender, sensitive, nondestructive techniques for exploring the natural units of their phenomena. Here we find X-ray analyses, electrical, magnetic, and resonance techniques, and photographic recording (von Hippel, 1956; Weiskopf, 1961). A primary concern of geographers, geologists, and oceanographers is, precisely, with the naturally occurring, unrearranged surface of the earth. A map of eastern Kansas showing both the natural and the imposed structure of this part of the earth's surface is presented in Figure 1.2. Here, the rectangular sections (geometers' structures) have been superimposed upon the water-cut valleys of the area (nature's structures).

The identification and description of the natural entities or events of a science, and of their relevant contexts or environments, and the incorporation of these into a unified system of concepts constitutes the ecological side of science. The ecological side of science is important for a number of reasons, one being the elucidation of tesserae, themselves. Knowledge of tesserae alone divorced from the natural units of the intact system, is incomplete knowledge, for the natural and the contrived systems of units inevitably generate interaction phenomena. This interaction occurs through two influence channels: The intact system provides the raw material and the context with which the operations of creating and maintaining the tesserae must contend, and with which the dynamic processes of the tesserae, themselves, must come to terms. Even in the case of so precisely contrived a system as geometry, and such a static, natural system as the earth's surface, an interaction is evident in the superimposed maps of eastern Kansas: the rough terrain of the area made it impossible to establish and/or maintain some section lines prescribed by the geometrical model. This is shown by those roads which deviate from the grid in conformity with the terrain; these are now, in most cases, the boundaries of deviant, irregular geographical tesserae.

At about the time the surveyors came to Kansas, scientific psychologists moved into the field of behavior, and began staking off alien tesserae on its surface. In this task they were tough-minded like the surveyors; they allowed few natural features of the behavioral terrain to interfere with the structures imposed by their experiments, tests, questionnaires, and interviews. They imposed a geometry upon behavior, a geometry grounded upon the axioms of experimental design and statistical methods, a geometry which reveals nothing directly about the behavioral surface upon which it is imposed. Tesserae have dominated psychological research over the ensuing years.

Some phases of behavior stream ecology have not been neglected. All systematists of psychology are concerned implicitly or explicitly with the temporal dimension of behavior; they refer to behavior's "patent continuities" (G. Allport, 1937, p. 5), to its "continuous and connected process" (Ladd, 1898, p. 136), to its "orderly, continuous whole" (Dewey,

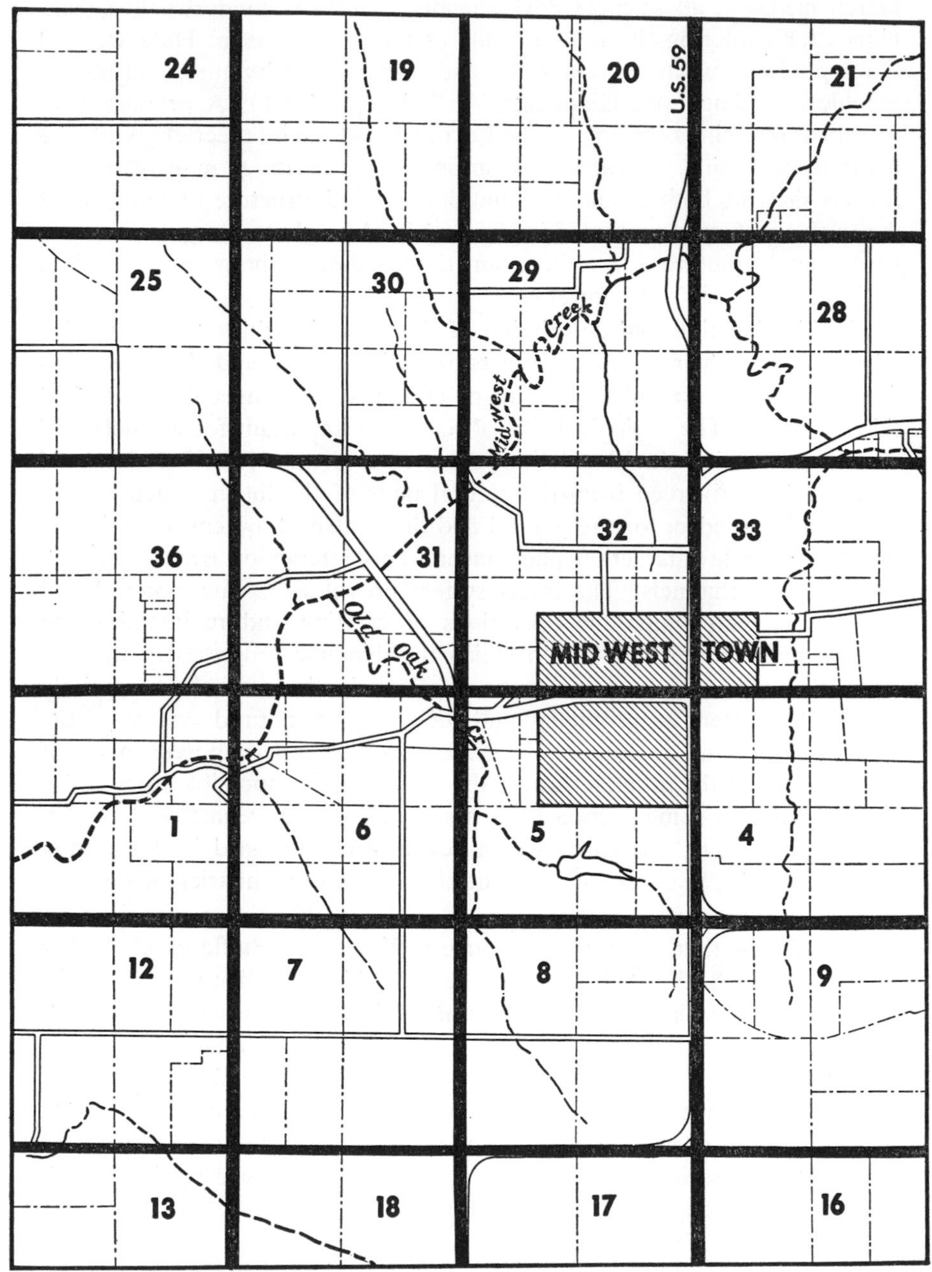

FIGURE 1.1

Area of Eastern Kansas Showing Imposed Structure (Geographical Tesserae)

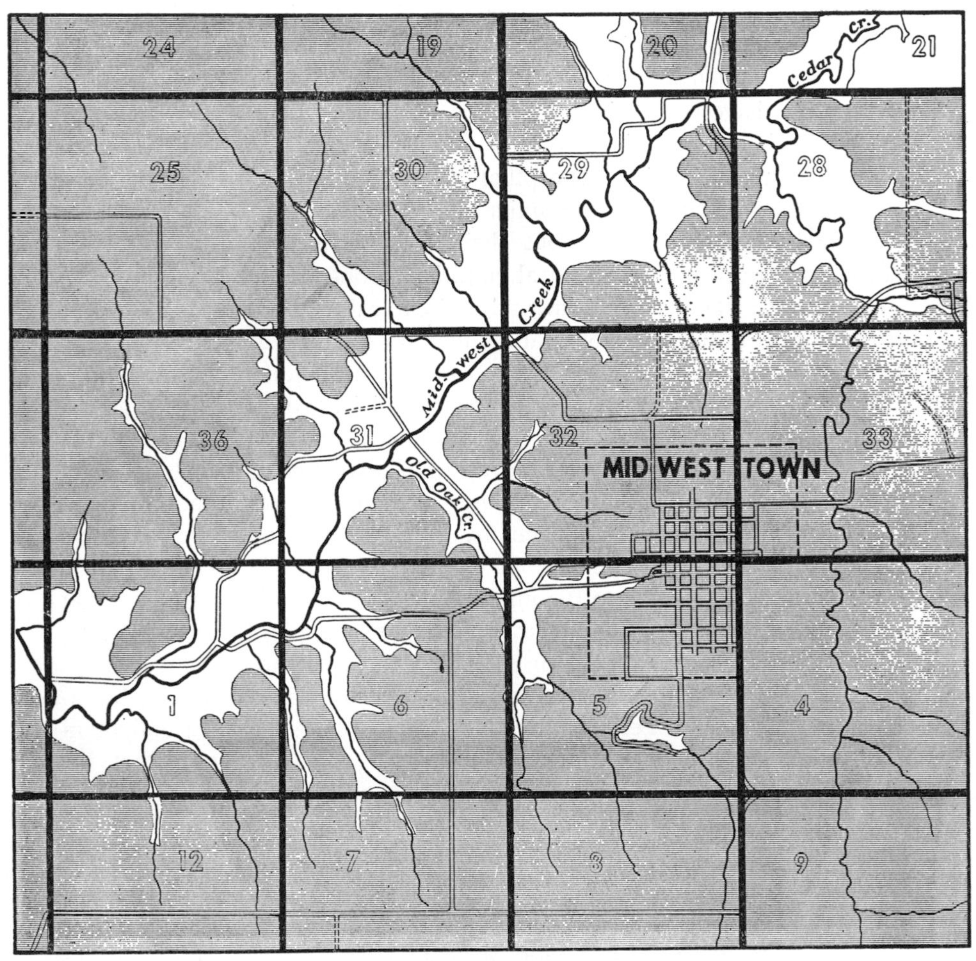

FIGURE 1.2

Area in Eastern Kansas Showing Natural and Imposed Structure

1891, p. 86), to its "continuous, flowing activity" (Stern, 1938, p. 78), to its "ceaseless movement" (Watson, 1924, p. 161), to its "organized process extending through time" (Angyal, 1941, p. 348), to its "sequential character" (Leighton, 1959, p. 18), to its "continuous change" (White, 1952, p. 328). Such statements are usually in the nature of axiomatic assertions; empirical data regarding the actual arrangement of behavior in time are seldomly offered or sought. Many systematists give a fundamental place to the building blocks, to the units, of the behavior stream; Murray (1959), Parsons (1959), Muenzinger (1939), Tolman (1932), Millet et al. (1960), for example, have emphasized the problem of behavior stream units. For these and other systematists we have studied, the selected units are constructs, with greater or less conceptual elaboration, defined within the context of a theory. The behavior units may be illustrated, or they may be experimentally demonstrated, but their disposition within the behavior stream is not presented as a central empirical problem.

Many of the standard experimental and clinical methodologies recognize the importance of the behavior continuum and its natural units in an oblique way. The view is widespread that the course of behavior is such a complicated unstable phenomenon when unrestrained by experimental controls, that it is not amenable to ordering in lawful ways, and that it is one source of the unfortunate variability of the results of experiments and tests. Recommended ways of handling this source of behavior perturbation are to eliminate behavior stream influences by ever stronger and more pervasive controls, and when this is impossible, to discount them via error estimates. There is another approach to the unreliability of tests and experiments that is congruent with ecological endeavor; see, for example, Sidman (1960), and Raush, Dittmann, and Taylor (1959b). In this approach, the sources of the variability of experiments and tests are seen as phenomena to be investigated, themselves. Perturbations become possible sources of enlightenment rather than sources of error only. This approach holds that the anomalies of behavior tesserae which arise from interaction with units of the behavior stream will never be understood by eliminating their sources without understanding them, or by making allowance for them by means of distribution statistics.

Empirical psychology, like systematics and methodology, has not entirely disregarded the stream of behavior. Wright (1960) analyzed the methods used in a sample of 1409 studies of child and adolescent behavior published in the 68-year period 1890–1958 and found 110 "observational" studies in the sample, i.e., studies resting "upon direct observation . . . of naturally occurring things and events" (p. 71). Not all of these were ecological studies of the natural parts and context of the behavior stream. In fact Wright reports that while among the 110 studies "some with an ecological aim can indeed be found. . . . They are uncommon" (p. 78). Nonetheless, Wright's survey provides evidence that the behavior stream has received some attention from investigators, and since his review a number of important investigations have been reported (Raush, 1959; Raush et al., 1959a, 1959b, 1960). It is interesting to note, that the amount of attention is negatively related to subjects' ages. Of 643 studies of preschool children 104 (16 per cent) were observational studies, while three of 430 studies of adolescents (0.7 per cent) used observational methods. The proportion surely declines further among studies of adults. In fact, investigations only marginally related to the behavior stream and its natural units have been discovered. Here fall periodic self-reports (Sorokin and Berger, 1939), analyses of personal documents (G. Allport, 1942), case studies (White, 1952), time and motion studies by industrial engineers (Barnes, 1958) and by home economists (Muse, 1946). The references cited here are illustrative; no one has undertaken the major task of discovering, reviewing and summarizing the scattered literature on the stream of behavior. Indeed this has been, and perhaps it is still an impossible task. Before it can be done effectively, sensible limits of the vast range of tangentially related studies must be established. The fact is evident, in any case, that ecological studies of the behavior stream while not entirely absent are meager indeed. Psychology is surely one of the few sciences that has little more knowledge than laymen about the occurrence in nature of many of its phenomena; of talk, of fear, of problem-solving efforts (and their successes and failures), of laughter, of frustration, of being disciplined, of anger, of achievement, of co-operation, of play, of being teased. . . .

The Taxonomy of Behavior Units

The tedious and difficult task of identifying, describing, and classifying behavior units is an essential part of stream of behavior research. Taxonomy must proceed hand in hand with more dynamically and theoretically oriented studies, for the kinds of behavior units in the behavior stream are of fundamental significance for dynamical and theoretical problems. If behavior units differ quantitatively on a limited number of dimensions, as do ripples on the surface of water, the behavior stream is a fundamentally different phenomenon than if there are a number of "qualitatively" different types of behavior units, with many replications of each type, as is true of the cells of an organism. It is of utmost importance to establish criteria for reliably identifying the "same" behavior units, and an essential part of this problem is to discover more than superficial identities. Here is a research problem requiring, in the first place, careful analytical and descriptive studies of individual behavior units.

Although only a beginning has been made, some features of the taxonomic problem are beginning to become clear. Much of what was known prior to the studies reported here come from the original work at the Midwest Psychological Field Station (Barker, 1960; Barker et al., 1950, 1951, 1955; Barker & Wright, 1949, 1951a, 1951b, 1955; Barker & Barker, 1961; Dyck, 1958; Fawl, 1959; Schoggen, 1951, 1954; Simpson, 1956; Wright & Barker, 1950a, 1950b; Wright et al., 1951, 1955).

There are, at the present time, two grounds for identifying and classifying behavior units. One ground is their structural-dynamic characteristics; the other ground is their material-content properties. These two bases for identifying and classifying behavior units are illustrated in the following specimen record.

Brett Butley, 7 years 2 months of age on July 5, 1957, was a member of the Upper Infants Class of the Yoredale County School. The morning "break" occurred at 10:30. After having a glass of milk supplied by the school, and peeling an orange he had brought from home, Brett wandered into the school yard where much very noisy activity was in progress: Some nine-year-old girls were running about trailing long strips of aluminum foil, boys the same age were administering the Yorkshire Bumps to any of their mates they could catch, a vigorous game of chain tag charged helter-skelter over the crowded yard, and four of Brett's classmates played a quiet game of cricket in one corner. Here is the record:

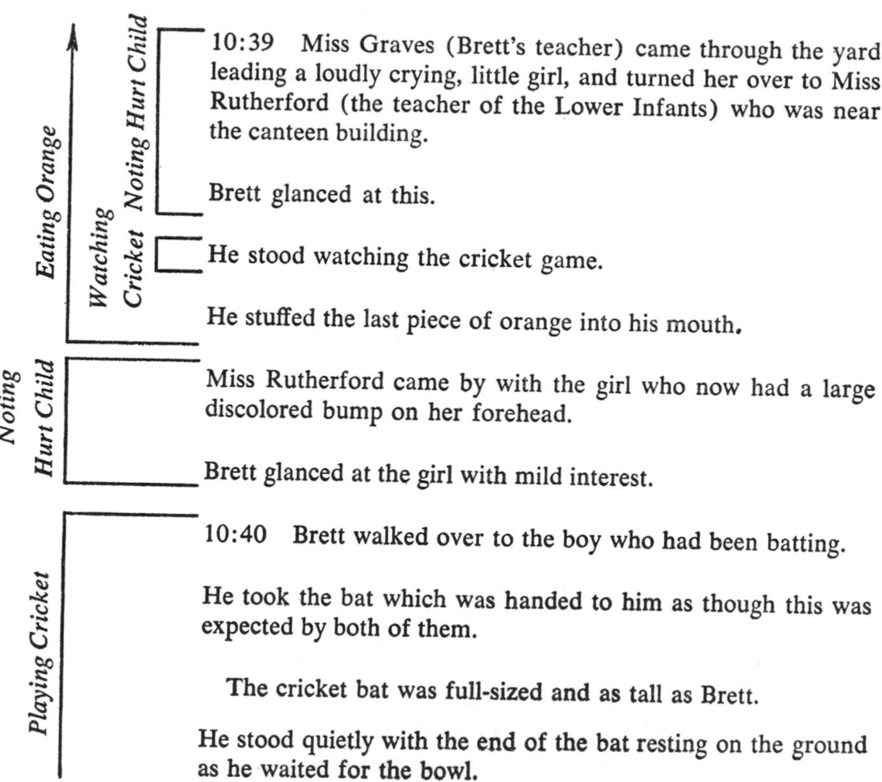

Eating Orange
Watching Cricket
Noting Hurt Child
10:39 Miss Graves (Brett's teacher) came through the yard leading a loudly crying, little girl, and turned her over to Miss Rutherford (the teacher of the Lower Infants) who was near the canteen building.
Brett glanced at this.
He stood watching the cricket game.
He stuffed the last piece of orange into his mouth.
Noting Hurt Child
Miss Rutherford came by with the girl who now had a large discolored bump on her forehead.
Brett glanced at the girl with mild interest.
Playing Cricket
10:40 Brett walked over to the boy who had been batting.
He took the bat which was handed to him as though this was expected by both of them.
The cricket bat was full-sized and as tall as Brett.
He stood quietly with the end of the bat resting on the ground as he waited for the bowl.

Playing Cricket

Orin bowled.

Brett struck at the ball rather awkwardly and failed to hit it.

It was difficult for Brett to swing the bat.

The ball was thrown back to Orin and he bowled again.

This time Brett succeeded in hitting the ball.

It went a short distance and was thrown back to Orin.

Waiting for Boys to Move Away

Six of the boys playing chain tag came rushing arm in arm through the edges of the cricket game and disrupted it momentarily.

The cricket players including Brett waited patiently, watching the tag game.

Orin bowled.

Brett made a hit. He seemed mildly pleased.

The ball was returned to Orin and he bowled to Brett.

Brett tried but failed to hit.

A group of bigger boys, 12-year-olds, came out for their break.

Playing Cricket

10:43 Orin bowled to Brett.

Brett hit the ball energetically.

One of the big boys reached out and caught the ball as it was thrown to Orin. The big boy then bowled rather gently to Brett.

Brett tried but missed.

The big boy evidently intended to bowl, and Orin moved to the batter's position. Orin took the bat from Brett.

Watching Cricket

Brett appeared to make no objection.

10:44 Brett stood passively with his fingers in his mouth watching as the game continued.

This is a segment of Brett's behavior which, however, continued minutes, hours, days, even years, before and after the actions described. The question to be determined is whether this is one or several units of Brett's behavior continuum, or if it is a behavior tessera, i.e., an arbitrary behavior fragment containing no complete behavior unit. The analyst of the record identified the units marked along the record, namely, Eating Orange (the terminal part of a long unit that overlapped with a number of previous units), Noting Hurt Child, Watching Cricket Game, Noting Hurt Child, Playing Cricket, Waiting for Boys to Move Away, Watching Cricket Game (the beginning of a unit that extended beyond this part of the record).

Were the decisions of the analyst correct?

It is obvious that the analyst performed the task of unitizing Brett's record in terms of a structural-dynamic behavior unit, for the behavioral content varies widely within units. Within the unit Playing Cricket, for example, there were intervals when Brett was quiet, when he was energetic, when he failed, when he succeeded, when he was pleased, and when he was patient. Each of these was a naturally occurring part of Brett's behavior stream, and could, legitimately, have been identified as a behavior unit. In fact, however, the units identified in Brett's specimen record have as their common feature behavior that is directed throughout the course of a unit toward a single end-state or goal without regard for the nature of the goal or for the kinds of behavior that occur between the beginning and the end of the unit.

A further complication of the taxonomic problem is evident in Brett's record. The structural-dynamic units identified are of a particular "size," even though the record reports structural-dynamic units of other sizes. For example, the record reports that Playing Cricket was made up of the subordinate, directed behavior units: walking to the wicket, taking the bat, waiting for the bowl, striking at the ball, hitting the ball, etc. These might legitimately have been identified as units of Brett's stream of behavior, but they were omitted; the analyst considered them to be subparts of the more inclusive structural-dynamic unit Playing Cricket.

Here, then, are glimpses of the untidy taxonomic problem. How does one approach such complex phenomena? The aim of the research must be to discover units that will help to bring order to the innumerable data the behavior stream provides. This has to be accomplished on the frontier of knowledge where guidance by pre-established facts and hypotheses is necessarily minimal, and where investigation must follow the canons of discovery rather than those of scientific verification. The problem is to unriddle both facts and theories. On the frontier, a pluralistic, open-minded, empirical, prototheoretical approach is the only one possible. To ward off discouragement it is well to keep in mind that a process which follows a course of development, as is true of scientific understanding, does not display in its early stages the characteristics of its late stages. Walking is a much better answer to the locomotion problem than creeping, but creeping is right for a one-year-old. The most complete understanding of the logical and technical requirements of good research methodology and theory construction will not save investigators of the behavior stream from primitive searching and thinking at the present time. This is inevitable. And it is not serious if the primitive theories and methods keep investigators close to the reality of the stream of behavior, and encourage freedom of intellectual movement within a flexible conceptual system.

Structure of the Stream of Behavior

Entities and events of many sorts are arranged in circumjacent-interjacent series: cells, organs, and organisms; words, sentences, and narratives form such series. Brett's specimen record reports a number of enclosing-enclosed structures, where small structural-dynamic units are enclosed within larger units. Playing Cricket encloses walking to the wicket, taking the bat, waiting for the bowl, etc. We know, furthermore, that more detailed records, such as sound recordings, psychophysiological records, and slow motion film, would reveal many other structural-dynamic parts of each of these units, even to the level of precise muscle and neural responses (Pittinger et al., 1960). And, it is equally true that a longer, more comprehensive, panoramic record of Brett's behavior would reveal grosser units: engaging in recess activities and participating in the arithmetic lesson, for example. These facts point to a fundamental structural feature of the behavior stream: behavior units occur in enclosing-enclosed structures; small units form the components of large units, and these in turn are incorporated into still larger units. Within these kinds of structures there are persisting problems for most sciences, and the stream of behavior is no exception. The number of levels within an including-included series, the terminal levels of the series, the types of units at each level, and the nature of the couplings between the units on the different levels are the foci of important empirical and theoretical issues; see, for example Miller et al. (1960).

By no means, however, do behavior units occur only in circumjacent-interjacent assemblies. They also occur singly, as discrete behavior entities, and in chains of interlinked units. Furthermore the behavior stream is not a single current upon which behavior units pass single file, either separately, in chains, or in enclosing-enclosed structures. In the short record of Brett Butley's stream of behavior there is in some places a single current of behavior units, and in other places dual, parallel channels. A study of a great number of records of the behavior stream analyzed in terms of behavior episodes has revealed the kinds of currents of behavior episodes shown in Figure 1.3 (Barker & Wright, 1955, p. 286), and illustrated by three concrete records in Figures 1.4 and 1.5. Only a small portion of the total complexity of the behavior stream is shown in these figures, for they do not include other sizes of structural-dynamic behavior units than behavior episodes, nor units defined in terms of material-content criteria.

Dynamics of the Behavior Stream

The units of the stream of behavior are not independent and static like a course of stepping stones; they are interdependent to various degrees. It is an important problem of the behavior stream research to discover the degree and nature of this interdependence. Enclosing-enclosed structures are doubtless of crucial importance here, for the concepts and theories appropriate for entities on one inclusiveness level inevitably differ from those that are apposite for entities on other levels, yet the different levels are linked within the same structures. The "laws" which govern organs differ from those which govern cells or organisms, they are incommensurate; yet organs are constrained, often in empirically predictable ways, by the cells of which they are made and by the organisms of which they are parts. The same is true of words, sentences, and narratives; of electrons, atoms, and molecules; of individual children, school classes, and schools. This is the transboundary paradox, the inside-outside problem as Floyd Allport (1955) has called it. It is concerned with the fact that across the boundaries which separate incommensurate systems there are regular and uniform causative relationships. How can it be that a gas molecule behaves according to the laws governing molecular motion and simultaneously according to the entirely different laws of the jet of gas of which it is a part (Gamow, 1958, p. 198)? How can it be that the explanations of the movement of a train of wheat across the Kansas plains by an economist (a scientist of circumjacent structures); and by an engineer (a scientist of interjacent entities) are both true, both operative in a predictable way upon the train, but as utterly incommensurate as the price of wheat in Chicago and the horse power of the engine? This inside-outside problem has already caused trouble along the stream of behavior. Some systematists have been at pains to point out the lack of univocal connections between such enclosing-enclosed units as actions and actones and molar and molecular actions; others have argued that small units (S-R units, for example) are the fundamental elements of behavior (Skinner, 1938; Murray, 1959).

Unfortunately, there is not one boundary problem along the stream of behavior. In addition to the boundaries between the behavior units of the behavior stream, there is the boundary where behavior ceases and the nonbehavioral environment begins. According to the record, Brett saw Orin as a friendly companion. Was Orin's friendliness a part of Brett's behavior or was it part of the nonbehavioral channel of his behavior? What about the size and the unmanageableness of the bat? What about the pavement on which the boys played, the schoolmaster's house behind them, and the headmaster within it? Was the coolness of the spring air a component of Brett's behavior, of his environment, or was it totally irrelevant to the phenomena reported in the record. Where did Brett's behavior cease and his nonbehavioral, but relevant environment begin? Wherever the locus of

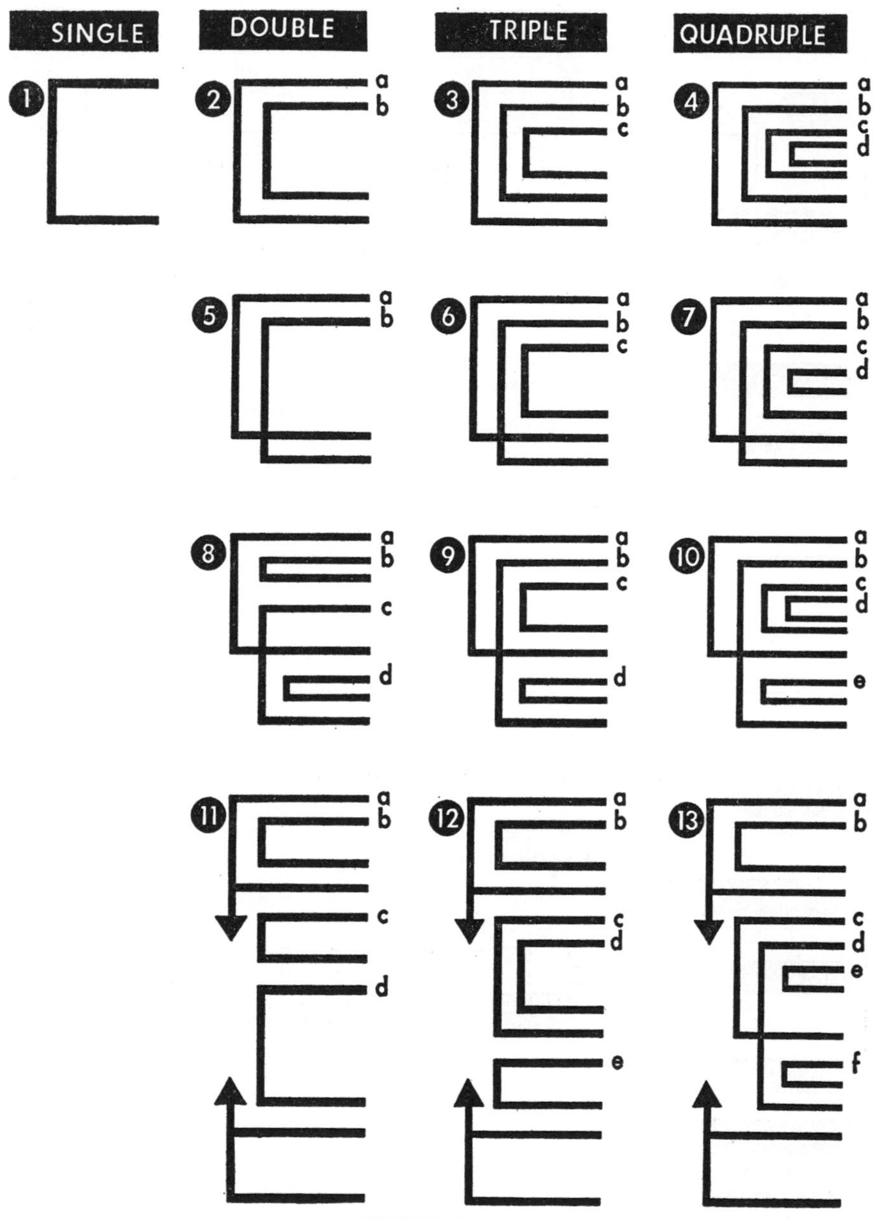

FIGURE 1.3

Relationships Between Behavior Currents within the Stream of Behavior (Reprinted with permission from Barker & Wright, 1955, p. 286)

DOUGLAS CRAWFORD, 8 YEARS OLD

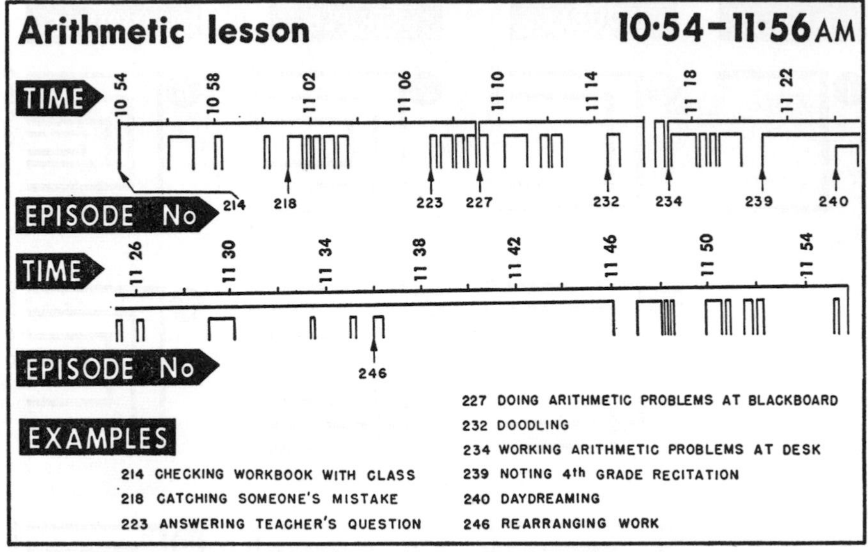

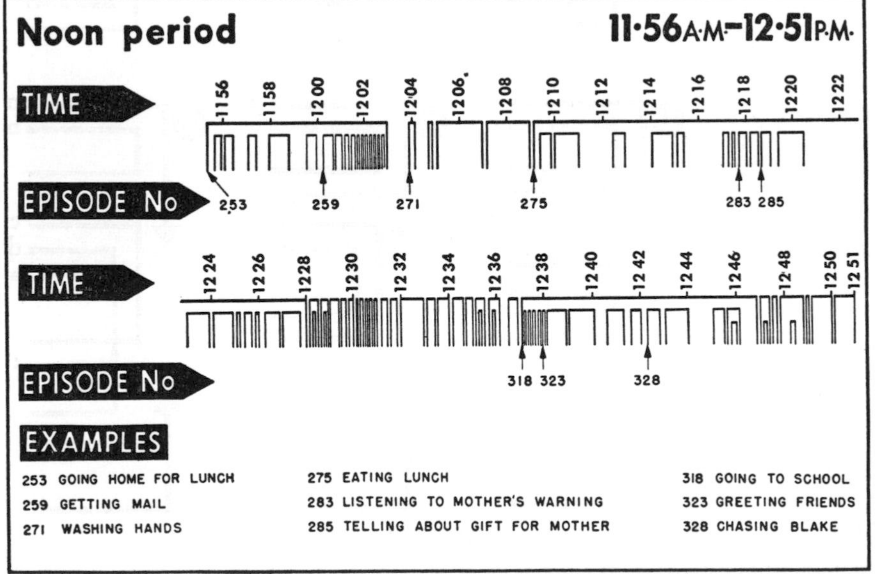

FIGURE 1.4

Behavior Episodes in Three Periods of Douglas Crawford's Day (See Appendix 1.1)

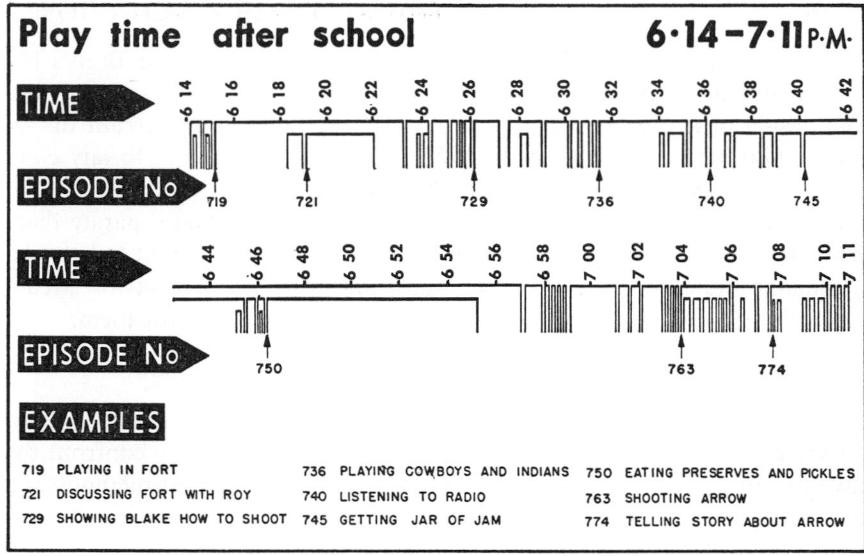

FIGURE 1.4 (*continued*)

MARGARET REID, 4 YEARS OLD

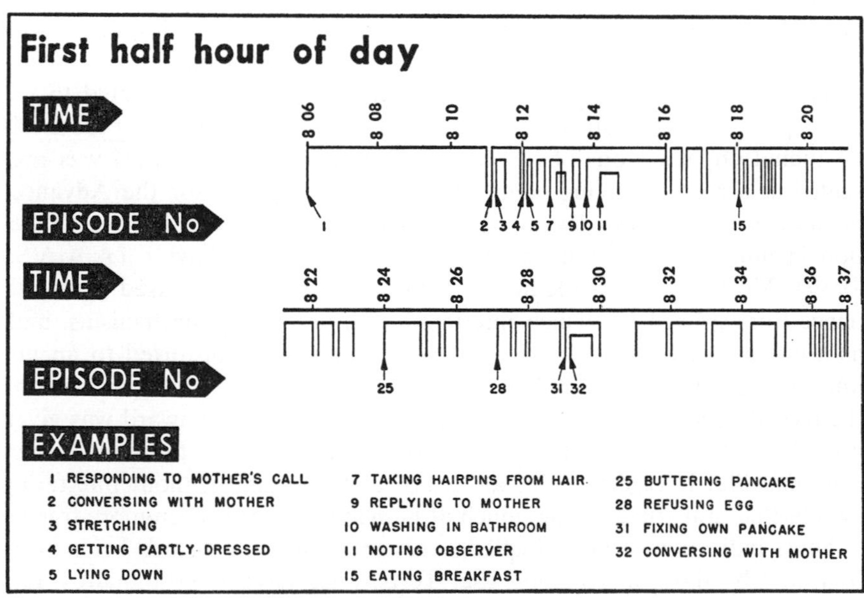

FIGURE 1.5

Behavior Episodes in First Half-Hour of Margaret Reid's Day (See Appendix 1.1)

this point, the nature of the influences across it, e.g., between Brett's behavior and its relevant but nonbehavior context, is crucial and difficult. Here, indeed, is the heart of the ecological problem of the stream of behavior (Barker, 1960; Brunswik, 1955; Lewin, 1951, ch. 8). In any case, it is an empirical fact that across the boundaries that separate the behavior units of the behavior stream, on the one hand, and those that separate them from their nonbehavioral contexts on the other, there are couplings between incommensurate systems. It is a fundamental problem of behavior stream research to investigate these couplings, and to try to account for them.

Discovery, Design, and Research Methodology

Behavior units are discovered and behavior tesserae are designed. Discovery and design require different research methods and they confront the investigator with different kinds of difficulties. These different methods and difficulties have undoubtedly influenced the amount and the nature of research upon the behavior stream; here are some of them.

The Problem of Interference. Much of the behavior stream is so sensitive to external conditions that special arrangements and precautions are required to avoid distorting it by the means used to observe and record it. Behavior units are revealed by gentle, open-minded, receptive methods directed at exposing behavior without altering it. Such methods are in many respects more difficult to devise and apply than the controls which behavior tesserae demand. This is true in many sciences. The search for methods of observing and testing phenomena without distorting them is an old and continuing one in the physical and biological sciences.

There is a society of physical and engineering scientists devoted to the development of nondestructive methods of examining and testing materials (National Organizations of the United States, 1961). An award was presented at a recent meeting of the American Association for the Advancement of Science for the development of techniques of recording heart function in animals without interfering with the heart's behavior (A.A.A.S., 1959). Most theories of the heart's action were previously based upon evidence from procedures which interfered with its control mechanisms, and, as a consequence, the data on cardiac functions were distorted to an unknown degree by the anaesthetics, restraints, and the traumas imposed by the recording techniques. The developments for which the award was given provide continuous records of the heart's operation while the animal lives a normal life. If cardiac behavior is not easy to study without interfering with its "natural" functioning, much of human behavior is even more fragile.

Some indication of how frequently research methods disturb behavior is indicated by those in common use. Tests, interviews, questionnaires, and experiments are designed precisely to destroy the naturally occurring conditions of the subject's life and to substitute for them the new, especially arranged situations that will elicit the behavior tesserae in which the investigator is interested. When these methods are removed from the armamentarium of psychologists, there are not a great number left.

Wright's (1960) survey of noninterfering methods of studying children has already been mentioned; Heyns and Lippett (1954) have made a similar survey, and Barker and Wright (1955) have described in detail methods of preparing specimen records, the type of record which has provided the data for a number of the studies in this volume.

The Problem of Verification. Science in its aim to discover truth continually searches for independent evidence of the adequacy of its methods and proof of its discoveries. In the case of tesserae, external checks and criteria are available at many points in the investigative process. The basic technical problem is to select from or introduce into the behavior stream the tesserae required to answer the questions the investigator brings to behavior. This requires firm, tough-minded, affirmative methods. Control and selection are the passwords: control of the investigator's feedback to the behavior stream and selective sensitivity to the input from the behavior stream. If the problems the investigator brings to behavior are adequately formulated, this includes the operations required to select or create the necessary tesserae. An important part of the work upon research design and experimental methods in psychology deals with general principles of establishing adequate tesserae. Some of these are formal and theoretical, such as those concerned with sampling; others are empirical, such as methods for pretesting interview questions, for validating test items, and for establishing maze reliability. All of them provide some independent evidence of the adequacy of the behavior tesserae used by the investigator, through reference to theories or criteria external to the tesserae, themselves.

There are no similar, external criteria available for research upon behavior units; the behavior stream, itself, decrees the boundaries and the properties of its own parts. The only evidence that reported behavior units actually exist, and are, in fact, self-generated, inherent divisions of the behavior stream, and not products of the methods used by the investigator can be obtained by replicating the observations and analyses. It is only when enough knowledge of the structure and dynamics of the behavior stream has been achieved by patient search, and research, that it may be possible to invoke known properties of the behavior continuum to "prove" some observations of its characteristics.

Problems of Analysis. Behavior tesserae have greater harmony with the theoretical and mathematical zeitgeist of present-day science than behavior units. It has been a triumph of modern psychology to devise behavior tesserae which fit so well the conceptual and methodological canons of modern science which deal so much more adequately with quantitative than with qualitative variation in phenomena (Lerner, 1961).

But here, for example, are the behavior episodes of eight-year-old Mary Ennis on the morning of May 12, 1949, between 7:58 and 8:12 (Barker, Schoggen & Barker, 1955):

Looked for sweater
Talked to mother about beads
Brushed hair
Played with baby brother
Showed off skirt
Talked to mother about some money
Searched for a new half-dollar
Joked with mother about a key
Helped mother fold diapers
Talked baby-talk to mother
Talked to mother about baby brother's bath

One of the facts about Mary's stream of behavior is the rich, qualitative variety of its discrete parts. How does one conceptualize and measure such phenomena? Can one do more than verbally describe them in ever greater detail? Is there a pattern, or is the seeming disorganized complexity beyond the reach of quantitative and theoretical science? These queries can challenge one's scientific endeavor, or they can encourage one to turn away from Mary's ongoing behavior stream to behavior tesserae which fit the assumptions of the available analytical tools.

To an important degree, stream of behavior research, including that reported in this volume, has been limited by the domination of psychology by methods of analysis which require independence of the behavioral items entering the analysis (see, for example, Festinger, 1951, p. 718). This condition is usually met by behavior tesserae obtained from different individuals. Such tesserae can be named, ordered, or measured on one or a number of dimensions (of which some aspect of time is an important one) and then dealt with in terms of frequency distributions and their parameters. The central assumption of these methods, namely, independence of the events which enter the distributions is, of course, strictly false so far as units of the behavior stream are concerned, and manipulation of behavior stream data as these methods require, destroys one of their essential features, namely, that they form a structured system. This distinction occurs whether the items of the distributions be behavior tesserae or behavior units. A dismantled behavior stream is, perhaps, only a little less dismantled because natural units rather than tesserae have been sorted into separate piles.

The Problem of Representativeness. The stream of behavior and its environmental channel is never a single-variable phenomenon, and seldom a simple two-variable interaction. It usually involves the simultaneous occurrence of multiple units with multiple attributes, i.e., of vectors, on both the stream and the channel side of the total process (Ashby, 1956). To include only a few of the units and attributes in a record of analysis, can, in effect, be as destructive of naturally occurring behavior and its conditions as to actively intervene and impose tesserae, or to dismantle the units in the process of analysis. Established research standards are very clear about the disturbing effects of biased sampling of subjects, and Brunswik (1955) has warned that situational representativeness is essential for the correct portrayal of nature. It is clear, too, that behavior stream representativeness is also necessary. To the degree that the behavior stream is a compound entity made up of structured behavior and channel units, the isolation of a single behavior unit, kind of unit, or unit attribute from the whole pattern can, in effect, distort the reality of behavior as surely as direct interference with the behavior stream. The enclosing-enclosed structural arrangements of many behavior units is especially pertinent in this connection. It has been pointed out that the significance of a behavior unit, its "meaning," is to some degree determined by its component and in some degree by its encompassing units. Such a behavior unit, in isolation, does not have a univocal significance.

It is surely not true, however, that every behavior stream unit is without stable meaning when detached from its behavior stream context. It is here that methodological research is needed to discover how to analyze and at the same time preserve the integrity of the stream of behavior phenomena.

Other so-called noninterfering observational and analytical methods have already been mentioned which, in effect, dismantle the behavior stream. This is true of methods which divide the behavior continuum into arbitrary time intervals and number-of-occurrence segments. The destructive effect of these methods is automatic when they involve bits of the behavior stream that are shorter than the units of the behavior phenomenon with which one is concerned. And longer, arbitrary divisions are equally destructive when they are treated as homogeneous segments, i.e., as units.

From these general considerations, some more concrete methodological guides emerge. One of them is that the test of the adequacy of a stream of behavior record is found in the "size" of the units with which the problem is concerned. It is obvious that a specimen record of the kind which reports Brett Butley's behavior stream (p. 8) is not adequate for either very much smaller or very much larger units than the episodes in terms of which it is analyzed. The record does not report the smallest molar units (the phases) in sufficient detail for analysis, and the record is undoubtedly more detailed and confusing than is optimal for larger, and in particular for personality-anchored units. Nonetheless, the subepisodic and the supraepisodic information in the record is valuable, indeed essential, for the task of identifying and analyzing the episodes. This issue has been presented in some detail in Barker and Wright (1955); a great amount of research is needed upon it. It is very likely that the most adequate record for any designated behavior unit level is one that provides a detailed account of the units on the designated level, and also supplementary accounts of the units upon the next lower and next higher levels.

Length of behavior stream records is important, too. A long record reduces the danger of biased selection of behavior units; a record covering 100 units rather than 50 is equivalent to using a larger rather than a smaller population sample. The danger of incorrect unitization and false interpretation of the meaning of behavior units is reduced when they are placed in a context of behavior long enough to make the inclusive-included relations clear.

A verbal narrative has great technical advantages as a recording system for stream of behavior phenomena on the level of molar behavior units. Some of these advantages derive from the narrative's own properties as behavior. A written narrative is continuous, as behavior is continuous: the narrative is isomorphic in this respect with the behavior stream. Furthermore, language has readymade symbol systems for directed actions, for representing single and multiple channels of action, and for describing circumjacent-interjacent structures. The vast number of temporal, relational, and linking terms, and the vaster number of terms describing behavior attributes make language invaluable for recording the behavior stream. Literary language has been suspect as a tool of science, and the effort to achieve greater precision via formulae, graphs, numbers, meter readings, photographs, etc. continues. However, rich, descriptive language is at the present time the recording medium par excellence of the stream of behavior and it appears that it is likely to remain so.

The Behavior Stream: A Tractable Problem

Some other behavior sciences and some of the arts have not found the behavior stream so formidable as psychology has found it. The empirical study of behavior units and their temporal arrangement is a central issue in history, in linguistics, in music, in the literary arts, and in the dance. Laymen, too, find the structure of the behavior stream to be a manageable phenomenon, and they have much practical knowledge of it.

In the ordinary course of life, the beginning and the end of actions are of utmost importance, for awareness of the arrangement of a person's own and his associates' behavior streams is the basis of effective social behavior. Men must be careful not to interrupt each other. To interrupt an associate in the middle of a behavior unit means, in the canons of social etiquette, that an urgency exists which justifies the destruction of another person's behavior, or it means malicious motivation or social insensitivity on the part of the interrupter. Children are admonished "wait until I have finished." A modern etiquette book says, "He [a child] must learn not to interrupt . . . , unless for an important reason, and then he should ask permission first." (Shaw, 1957) Just as one does not step on another person's toes, eat another person's food or wreck another person's toys, one does not destroy another person's behavior-in-progress, and laymen are able to identify such units with considerable precision. Furthermore, detailed written records of behavior are among the most important documents of civilized life. Transcripts of court and legislative proceedings, and minutes of meetings are, in effect, specimen records of individual and group behavior. They have been found to be of utmost importance for reaching crucial decisions regarding both individuals and groups, and exact forms and standards have been developed to make them adequate for the purposes they are intended to serve.

Laymen, linguists, musicologists, historians, poets, novelists, choreographers, judges, legislators, and those few psychologists who have studied it, find that the stream of behavior is not a formidable datum, that it occurs in bursts, pauses, and pieces of many sorts which can be described and evaluated for both scientific and practical purposes. It is with these phenomena that the studies of this volume deal.

The Evidence at Hand

The chapters of this book report the methods and results of some empirical studies of the stream of behavior; they tell of efforts to cope with the problems we have outlined, and of the successes and failures of these efforts.

In one respect the studies tell the same story: they find the behavior stream to consist of discrete, qualitatively different, replicated behavior units. The picture of the behavior stream that emerges from these studies is not quite the confused and confusing, infinitely varying phenomenon it has sometimes been asserted to be.

The reports agree on another important matter which points in the direction of simplicity and order rather than complexity and disorder along the stream of behavior. All of the investigators approached the behavior stream with minimal guidance from prevailing theories; the data and the methods were, in the beginning, atheoretical. However, at many points in the investigations, both in connection with methods and results, theory intruded; both the operations and the data, themselves, announced relationships and pointed to prototheories. The data of the studies have turned out to be sources of ordering generalizations as well as of facts.

On the level of facts, the investigations provide new information about the frequency of behavioral and of environmental occurrences in different cultures, in different situations, and with different people, and they also provide encouraging indications that confirmation of findings can eventually be expected from different approaches to the behavior stream.

Not all the hopes and intentions of the investigators have been realized. The studies were undertaken within an ecological framework, with the intention of using noninterfering methods of observing and analyzing the behavior stream. Although the ecological characteristics of science can be precisely defined, there is, in fact, a continuum of science from pure ecology, with no feedback from the investigator, to highly precise experimentation with both input and feedback carefully controlled. And while the present studies cluster about the ecological end of the continuum, there are "failures" due not to intention but to the undeveloped state of ecological methods in psychology and to the inherent difficulties they present. For the same reasons, important characteristics of the behavior stream have been dealt with only partially. A beginning, but only a beginning, has been made with the primary attribute of the behavior stream: its arrangement in time. The units which have been identified do not violate the natural divisions of the behavior stream, and they all include some of its continuity; they are ready, when the methods and concepts can be developed, to be studied within the larger assemblies, sequences, serials, and personality-anchored themas in which they occur. Similarly, only a beginning has been made in dealing with the total variety of behavior stream attributes on both its behavior and its channel side. The studies range from almost complete concern with the behavior sequence, itself, to almost complete concern with the channel sequence, with some efforts to interrelate these parts of the total complex.

Six of the eleven investigations (Chapters 3, 4, 5, 6, 9 and 11) use as their primary data two or more of the eighteen day-long specimen records which are now available. These records are identified, and sources of further information about them, are given in Appendix 1.1. Two studies (Chapters 7 and 8) use behavior setting specimen records as their primary data. These records have been published (Barker, Wright, Barker & Schoggen, 1961) and two of them are reproduced in Appendix 1.2 where the following behavior units have been marked upon them for illustrative purposes: behavior episodes (as used in Chapters 8, 9 and 10); social contacts (as used in Chapter 5), environmental force units (as used in Chapters 3 and 4), and social actions (as used in Chapter 7).

The studies provide, then, evidence of the usefulness of two kinds of primary data (specimen records and recordings of talk) and of a number of analytical approaches. The studies reveal the richness of these records of behavior for many problems and they demonstrate that they have the value of true scientific specimens.

CHAPTER 2

The Perception of Behavioral Units

HAROLD R. DICKMAN

IS THE STREAM OF BEHAVIOR seen as a continuum or as a sequence of discrete units? If the latter, do different people see the same units? People behave toward others, and they speak and write about their own and other's behavior as if they perceive behavior in units; and the degree of harmony with which interacting individuals guide their behavior suggests considerable agreement regarding the beginning and end-points of the behavior units they discern. The research reported in this chapter provides the first precise and systematic information about these important matters. In addition to his empirical findings, Dr. Dickman presents his thinking about the grounds people use in dividing the behavior stream and about the sources of their agreements and disagreements.

Harold R. Dickman is Chief Psychologist at the Veterans Administration Hospital, Roseburg, Oregon; he received the Ph.D. degree from the University of Kansas.

Introduction

THIS CHAPTER is concerned with the question: to what extent does the human "stream of behavior" attain structure and orderliness in the eyes of other human beings? Inherent in this question is the further one: to what extent is there communality of agreement among independent observers relative to the units of behavior contained in a given sequence?

One might argue that these questions are only esoteric ones and that a satisfactory solution may be found by simply resorting to reflection on everyday experience. The fact that we see people doing many different *things* in the course of an hour or day would seem to support the argument. In fact, we see units of behavior and readily label them in such terms as "eating breakfast," "driving to work," "reading mail." Hence, the fact that we see behavior in terms of organized units is established, and the fact that we can communicate our observations to others or gear our own behavior to approximately fit what we see, indicates significant communality of agreement must exist. However, very little scientific attention has been devoted to this most common of everyday phenomena. We do not know why we see behavior in terms of units, nor what is the nature of the units, nor how general is this manner of perceiving. If we see units we also see continuity. What cues provide recognition of a transition from one unit to the next? Reflective experience is of little help in answering this question. Experience shows that we can just as easily conceive of a unit as small as "sticking one's foot in the door," or as large as "being a successful salesman." With such a discrepancy why should we assume communality of perception at all?

In the study we are presenting, we do not answer all the questions which we have raised, but we focus on the basic phenomenon of perceiving units of human action and ask how uniformly they are seen and what characteristics they possess.

Answers to these questions are desirable from a practical as well as a purely scientific standpoint. Discerning suitable units is a necessary task of any science. In psychology, and particularly social psychology, such a task may be the most difficult one encountered in studying social phenomena. In analyzing naturally occurring, ongoing behavior, the choice of units is particularly difficult. If it can be demonstrated that untrained observers agree significantly in dividing such a continuum, their criteria for unit selection can be adapted to selecting units for scientific study with increased assurance that such units have psychological validity.

Some evidence exists for this assumption. Lyons (1956) found that in comparison with schizophrenic subjects, normal subjects tend more often to structure behavior in larger units. Barker and Wright (1955) found that persons could be trained to divide the behavior continuum into units or episodes with a high level of agreement. The training consisted primarily in learning a conceptual framework, which utilized principles of movement toward and within a goal region as criteria for units. However, a systematic evaluation of agreement in unit selection among persons untrained in the task remains to be done. This chapter is directed toward that task.

The findings reported in this study are admittedly post hoc. The experiment was originally designed and conducted to determine *individual characteristics* in categorizing behavior. Two experimental conditions were presented: (1) grouping of a set of inanimate objects, and (2) breaking into units a sequence of ongoing behavior. The expectation was that individual styles of categorizing would emerge and be apparent in these disparate tasks. Though completed and analyzed from this frame of reference, what emerged from this study was striking evidence that the data on perception of behavior could also be profitably viewed from an entirely different perspective; namely, comparison of extent and nature of over-all agreement among individuals. Cronbach (1957) has amply argued the point that this is a separate kind of approach and one that is legitimate in its own right. Though no a priori hypotheses were made about these findings, they appear to be of general interest and we hope of value.

Method

The procedure aimed at presenting a sequence of behavior to the subject which he could view and divide into units. To achieve this aim, subjects were shown individually an 8-minute 16 mm. sound movie entitled, *A Gift from Dad.* This movie was adapted from a commercial film entitled *Our Vines Have Tender Grapes,* and was chosen for its presentation of a relatively continuous and unbroken sequence of behavior. The plot of the portion used, centered around a little girl, Selma, who accidentally killed a squirrel and subsequently received a baby calf as a gift from her father to alleviate the remorse and guilt that she felt.

Prior to the showing of the movie the subject was told, "I am going to show you a short movie about a little girl named Selma, her cousin Arnold, and her father and mother. All you have to do is to watch the movie as you would any movie you might see at a theatre."

Upon completion of the movie, the subject's attention was directed to a table containing one hundred forty-four 3″ x 5″ cards, through which the sequence of the movie was described. The unit of behavior represented on each card corresponded to a minimal molar unit or *phase.* The methodological concept of the phase has been developed by Barker and Wright (1955, p. 252) and is defined as having as its chief characteristics the following: "A phase is the smallest behavior segment in an action hierarchy. As such it is a minimal unit of action in the sense that descriptive subdivision of it would break it into actones." Actones are used here in the sense that they constitute muscular movements or adjustments which would not necessarily imply behavior of a goal directed type. The cards were numbered and arranged so that the sequence of the cards corresponded to the sequence of the movie. They were laid out in a manner allowing perusal of the entire sequence without having to move any card. This provided a systematically segmented, written description of the behavior observed in the movie. (Appendix 2.1 contains a description of this movie as it appeared on the cards.)

The subject was given the following instructions:

Now I have some cards here which have the behavior in the movie written on them. The cards are numbered to correspond with the sequence of the film and as you see, each card has only a very small part of the behavior of the movie described on it. However, if you went through all the cards in sequence, you would get the story of the movie. Now what I want you to do is to divide these cards into groups so that each group represents a happening in the movie. There is no "right" answer to this test, you may have as many or as few groups as you like as long as each group represents a happening in the movie. I just want you to do this in the way that seems most natural to you. There is no time limit on this test, you may go at your own pace. Please use all the cards. Now do you have any questions about what you are to do?

During the sorting the experimenter made notes on the qualitative features of the subject's performance such as changes in grouping, questions, and comments. Following the grouping of the cards, the experimenter asked for and recorded the subject's description of the happening which each group represented. The experimenter also recorded the numbers of the cards which were included in each group. If the subjects designated only one card as representing a given happening, it was counted as one group, equivalent to those containing several cards.

The subjects for this study were 38 students enrolled in a beginning course in psychology. The group consisted of 12 men and 26 women. The subjects were procured on a voluntary basis, so that the sample was not a random one. No evaluation of intelligence or personality characteristics was attempted, though it seems reasonable to assume that, since all subjects were of at least second-year college standing, they were of at least normal intelligence and probably most were of the bright normal to superior range.

Approximately three weeks after the completion of the initial test, and without prior announcement, the last 20 subjects to participate were asked to return so that the experimenter could gain additional information. Seventeen of these responded and were given a test similar to the first one. The purpose of this test was to check the consistency of the results with a replication of the procedure. The movie used was another 8-minute sequence from the same larger movie from which the first sequence was chosen. The behavior in this movie was also divided into phases and typed on one hundred six 3″ x 5″ cards. The subjects were given the same instructions as on the first test except these were prefaced by the following statement: "First of all I want you to know that I am not asking you to come back because you did anything wrong on the first test. I have discovered I will need some additional information so I have asked you to help me again. The instructions are the same as they were before."

The experimenter then repeated the instructions. The procedure for noting the qualitative aspects of the performance and for quantitative scoring was the same as that described for the first test.

At the completion of this test, the subjects were asked if they had thought of the number of groups they were making, or if they had tried to make their performance comparable in any way to the first test. All subjects stated they did not consider their first performance while grouping the behavior of the second test. (Appendix 2.2 contains a description of the behavior in this second movie.)

Results

FIRST BEHAVIOR GROUPING TEST

The relative ease with which most of the subjects understood and completed the task set for them indicates that the concept of behavior occurring in units was a familiar one to them. Only four of the subjects had any difficulty understanding the instructions. However, with one repetition, they also readily grasped the nature of the task and proceeded readily with it. The number of units discriminated by individual subjects ranged from 3 to 35 with a median of 14. A break in the continuum could have been made between any of the 144 phases. Hence there were 143 possible division points. Of these, the subject group selected 91 at least once as an actual division point. Fifty-two possible division points were never selected as actual division points.

Figure 2.1 presents in graphic form each subject's division of the behavior continuum. Each vertical line represents one subject's division of the continuum. Interruption of the line indicates the ending of one unit and the beginning of another.

Inspection of Figure 2.1 immediately reveals several points along the continuum at which several subjects agreed that one unit ended and another began. These points occur at phases 20 ± 1, 35 ± 1, 51 ± 1, 62 ± 1, 74 ± 1, 99 ± 1, 107 ± 1, and 118 ± 1. At least 75 per cent of the subjects designated division points in each of the above areas. For convenience we have designated those areas as "modal division areas" and the behavior sequence between them as "modal units." Further analysis of these modal units is contained in Appendix 2.3 and their significance discussed in the final section of the chapter.

In order to further elucidate the extent of agreement, each transition from one phase to another may be examined to determine how frequently this transition was seen as either a division point between two units or a continuation of a single unit. Figure 2.2 illustrates the frequency of such agreement at each of the transition points between phases. The longer the bar, the more subjects who designated the between-phase transition as the ending of one unit and the beginning of another. Thus agreement is illustrated in two directions in Figure 2.2; long bars indicate frequent agreement on division, and absence of any bar indicates unanimous agreement that the phase transition did not constitute the ending or beginning of a new unit. The latter indicates agreement on continuity.

In order to test the chance or nonchance nature in the perception of patterns, no single statistical approach is entirely satisfactory. Therefore, we have analyzed agreement at three different levels: (1) over-all patterning of agreement on decision of *break* or *no-break,* (2) level of agreement at each choice point, and (3) agreement on designation of identical total units.

FIGURE 2.1

Units of Behavior Identified by Each Subject on First Behavior Grouping Test. Phases of the Behavior Continuum Are Numbered in Consecutive Order

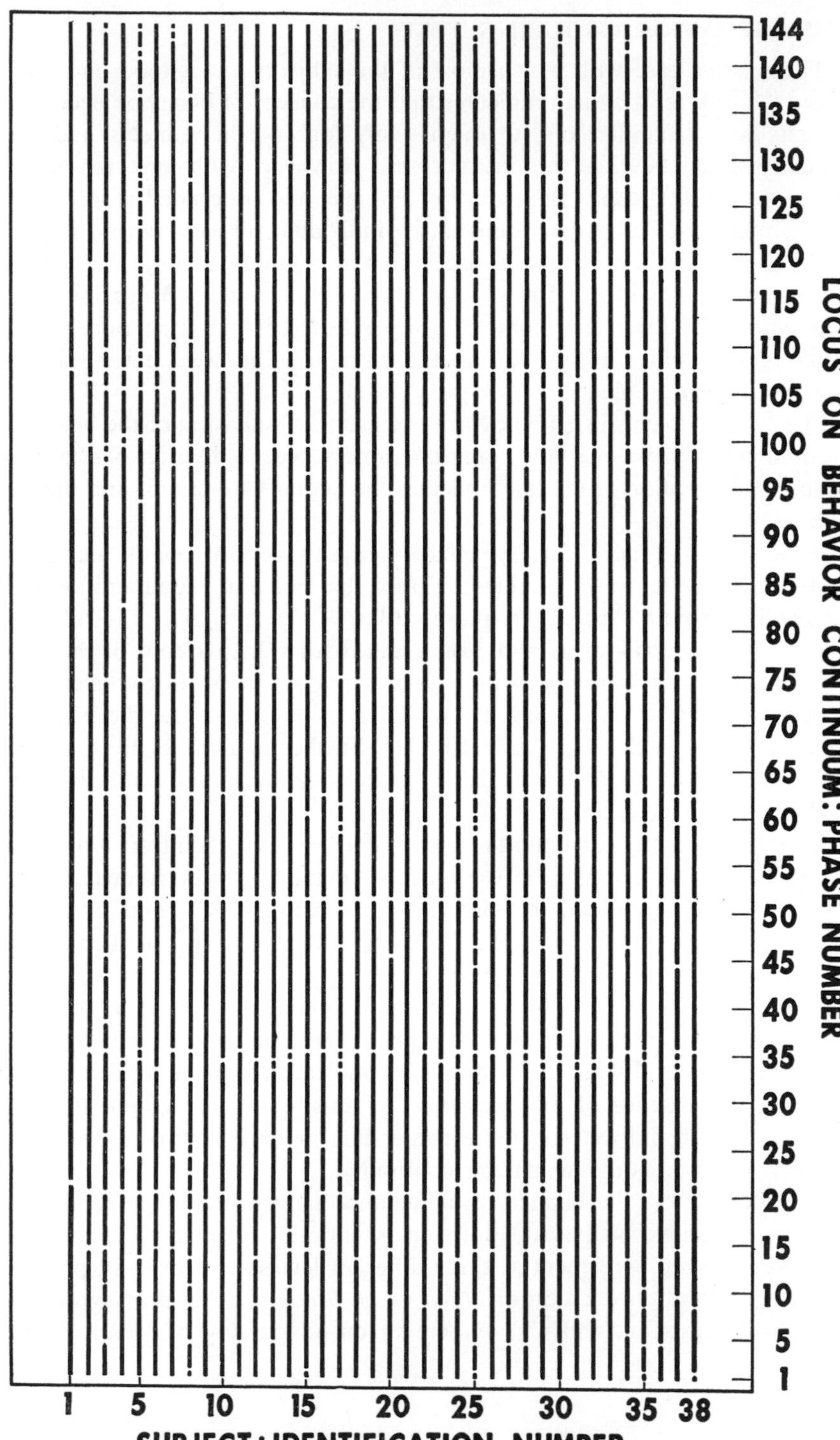

FIGURE 2.2

Frequency with Which Each Consecutive Phase of the Behavior Continuum Is Designated as the Terminus of a Behavior Unit on First Behavior Grouping Text

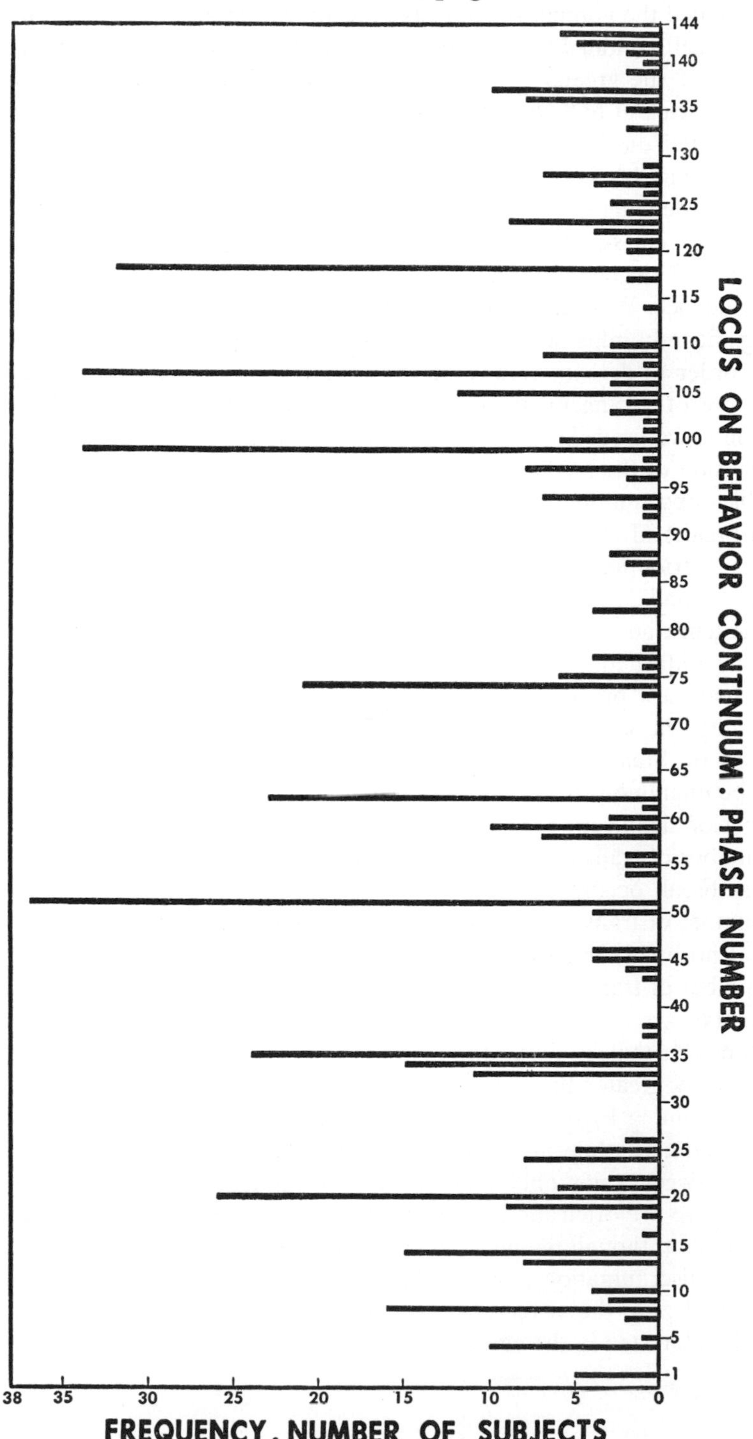

1. Over-all agreement was measured by use of chi square. The chi square consisted of two cells for each possible division point. One of these cells contained the number of subjects indicating a break at that point and the other cell contained the number indicating no-break or continuity. Because of the greater preponderance of designated continuity, expected frequencies in half the cells were less than 5, the chi square value was computed on the basis of only those cells with expected frequency of more than 10. By using total number of degrees of freedom, we were simply denying ourselves benefit of contribution of half the cells to the value of chi square. The chi square thus obtained was 192.65 which, with 142 degrees of freedom, is significant at beyond the .01 level of confidence. We may thus conclude that over-all patterning of choice is significantly influenced by other than chance factors.
2. In order to demonstrate statistically the extent of chance or nonchance nature of arrangement of breaks and continuity at each of the choice points, we used the simple procedure of the expansion of the binomial. Division of the median number of breaks (14) into the number of possible opportunities for breaking the continuum 143 yields a p (probability of break) of .1, and a q (probability of continuity) of .9. Even though this distribution is skewed from the normal, we are justified in applying the binomial expansion. Wilks (1948) states that only if p is less than one-tenth and the n is large, is a substitute method (Poisson Distribution) indicated.

We can now proceed to set confidence limits for agreement on break or continuity. In so doing we discover that agreement among eight or more subjects on break is significant at the .05 level. Agreement on continuity must be unanimous to be significant at the .05 level. If we now examine the number of significant agreements, we find the following:

a. Number of transitions at which there is significant agreement that break occurs 19 13%
b. Number of transitions at which there is significant agreement that no-break or continuity occurs 52 36%
c. Number of transitions at which no significant agreement occurs 72 51%

We conclude that in about one-half (71) of the transition points there was significantly greater than chance agreement among the 38 subjects.

In examining Figure 2.2, we note that there is a phasic character to the spikes. That is, they are distributed throughout the sequence with some space between each one. Note also that immediately adjacent to these spikes there are often moderately high levels of agreement on break which suggests that, though the general area is seen as a changing point, the actual point of discrimination may overlap two or three possible division points.

3. In analyzing the perceived structure of ongoing behavior, we are not only interested in the agreement on beginning and ending points of units.

To get a complete picture we must also consider coincidence, not only of breaking points, but of entire units of behavior. We might ask, "How frequently did subjects agree in seeing a unit begin at a given point and continue on to a given end point?" Though related to agreement on break or continuity at a single transition point, agreement on units is clearly not identical with agreement on separate choice points.

Significance of such agreement is difficult to test statistically. However, one can arrive at an approximation of it logically in the following way, though the results will, for several reasons, underestimate true significance. The joint probability that event B will follow A is the product of the probabilities of their separate occurrence. In our example, events are: (1) agreement that a unit begins at a given point; and (2) simultaneous agreement on its ending point. We are thus ignoring probability of agreement on continuity, which is implied. By examining the table of area under the normal curve, we find that events one standard deviation from the mean have a joint probability of .05 of successive occurrence.

Returning to our data, which by means of the binomial, we find contains a mean of 3.80 (σ of 1.85), we find that if 5.65 or six of the 38 subjects agree on both the beginning and end point of a given unit we may assume significant agreement on that unit. In examining the data we find that a total of 23 episodes or units were seen by six or more subjects as having identical beginning and ending points. On the other hand, there were 73 units agreed upon by more than one but fewer than six subjects, and 497 instances in which an exact unit was designated by only one subject. (Appendix 2.4 contains the phase numbers of units discriminated and the number of subjects who agreed on total coincidence of the unit.)

In short, our results indicate that there is more than chance agreement among the subjects on (1) the general patterning of points of division and continuity, and (2) the designation of "break" or "continue" at one-half of the individual choice points. However, there appears to be surprisingly little agreement among the subjects on the common occurrence of units as such.

Inspection of Figures 2.1 and 2.2 indicates clear evidence of some uniformities in dividing the behavior stream and Figure 2.2 particularly suggests that the organization of the behavior may be even more pronounced than one can demonstrate on a purely statistical basis. Data in Appendix 2.4 even more clearly indicate that we have stringently estimated the amount of agreement on general structure and composition of units as such. For example, phases 1–8 were seen as one unit by nine subjects, phases 1–9 by three subjects. In our statistical analysis, the latter constitute disagreement though it seems clear that the 1–8 and 1–9 phase units were nearly identical in structure and theme. Nevertheless, absolute agreement on designation of units in their entirety appears to be strikingly low.

TABLE 2.1
Relationship Between Performance on First and Second Behavior Grouping Tests

SUBJECT	FIRST TEST *Number of Groups*	SECOND TEST *Number of Groups*
1	3	4
21	5	7
10	7	8
31	8	8
11	9	5
33	9	7
36	9	8
22	11	8
6	11	9
26	11	10
12	12	10
4	13	7
23	14	12
15	18	13
29	21	19
34	24	14
8	29	39
N = 17	r = .86	p < .01 Significant

SECOND BEHAVIOR GROUPING TEST

The study was replicated, using 17 of the original 38 subjects. After a time lapse of one month these subjects were shown a different movie, though the task presented was the same as before. Instead of the previous 144 there were 106 phases differentiated in the second movie. The first question which this procedure allowed us to answer was whether or not subjects showed any consistency in the manner in which they, as individuals, divided the behavior stream into units. Since the two movies were not identical, it was only possible to compare the absolute number of units discriminated by the subjects in the two situations. As can be seen in Table 2.1 there was a significant degree of uniformity between the subjects' performance on the two tasks. This finding is important because it indicates a high level of stability over a short period of time in the individual's responses to dividing a continuum of behavior. From questioning of subjects, it was apparent that this stability was not based on any logical, explicit hypothesis, but occurred unwittingly and automatically insofar as the subjects themselves were concerned.

In examining the level of agreement among the 17 subjects who participated in the replication experiment, we proceeded in the same manner as we did in the initial study. That is, agreement is evaluated from three points of reference: (1) over-all patterning of agreement on decision of break or no-break, (2) agreement at each choice point, and (3) agreement on designation of identical total units.

1. Figure 2.3 is comparable to Figure 2.1 and illustrates the manner in which the continuum was divided in the second film. In evaluating over-all agreement, chi square was not appropriate because utilization of only one-half of chi square table did not give definitive results and expected frequencies in the other half were below 5. For these reasons, over-all agreement was approximated by use of the sign test. A plus was assigned to those choice points at which significant agreement occurred and a minus was assigned to the remaining ones. We thereby obtain an h of 33 which, with an n of 105, is significant at beyond the .01 level. We may thus infer the occurrence of significant over-all agreement, by virtue of fact that the number of individual choice points significantly agreed upon is greater than would be expected by chance.
2. In examining the level of agreement on break or continuity at each of the choice points between phases, our probabilities of break or continuity are again .1 and .9 respectively. Using the binomial, agreement by 5 or more subjects on break, constitutes agreement at the .01 level of significance. Our data on agreement are as follows:

a. Number of transitions at which there is a significant agreement that break occurs 11 10%

b. Number of transitions at which there is significant agreement that no-break or continuity occurs 60 57%

c. Number of transitions at which no significant agreement occurs 34 33%

3. In assessing agreement on identity of units discriminated, by again using the joint probabilities of occurrence of events A and B, we note that if three of the 17 subjects designate identical beginning and end points of a unit, such agreement constitutes significance at the .05 level of confidence. We find 15 units agreed upon by three or more subjects and 13 units agreed upon by only two subjects. There were 93 instances of units designated by only one subject. Appendix 2.5 contains phase numbers of units and number of subjects evidencing identical agreement in designation of the unit.

COMPARISON OF FINDINGS IN TWO TESTS

A comparison of the results obtained from the two studies is presented in Table 2.2.

Inspection of Table 2.2 indicates that the results of the two studies are quite comparable. The greatest discrepancy between them occurs in relation to the percentage of choice points at which subjects unanimously agreed that continuity between adjacent phases occurred. The fact that there were a greater percentage of such points on the second study may be explained by the simple fact that unanimity was the criterion for significance on both

FIGURE 2.3

Units of Behavior Identified by Each Subject on Second Behavior Grouping Test. Phases of the Behavior Continuum Are Numbered in Consecutive Order

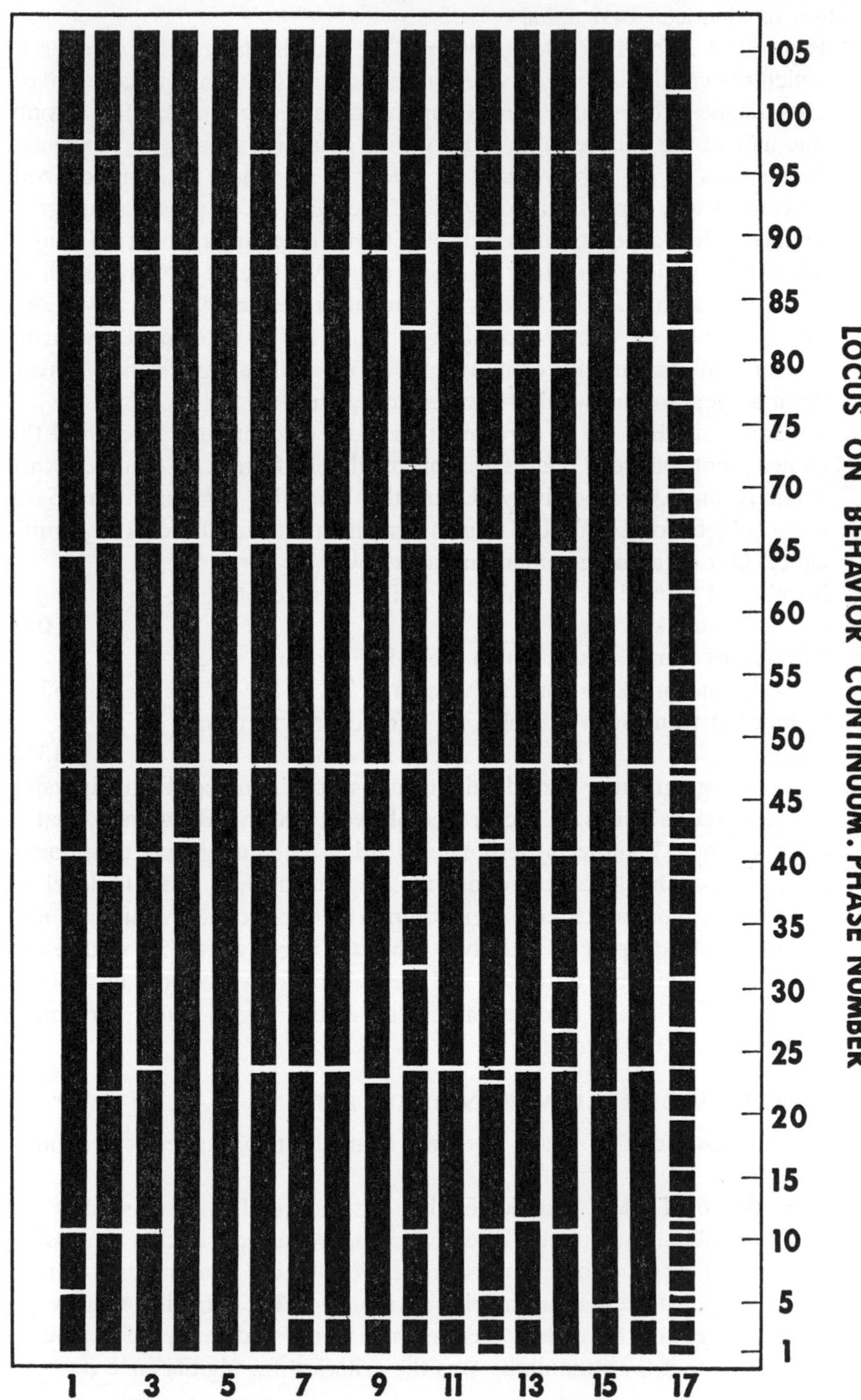

FIGURE 2.4

Frequency with Which Each Consecutive Phase of the Behavior Continuum Is Designated as the Terminus of a Behavior Unit on Second Behavior Grouping Test

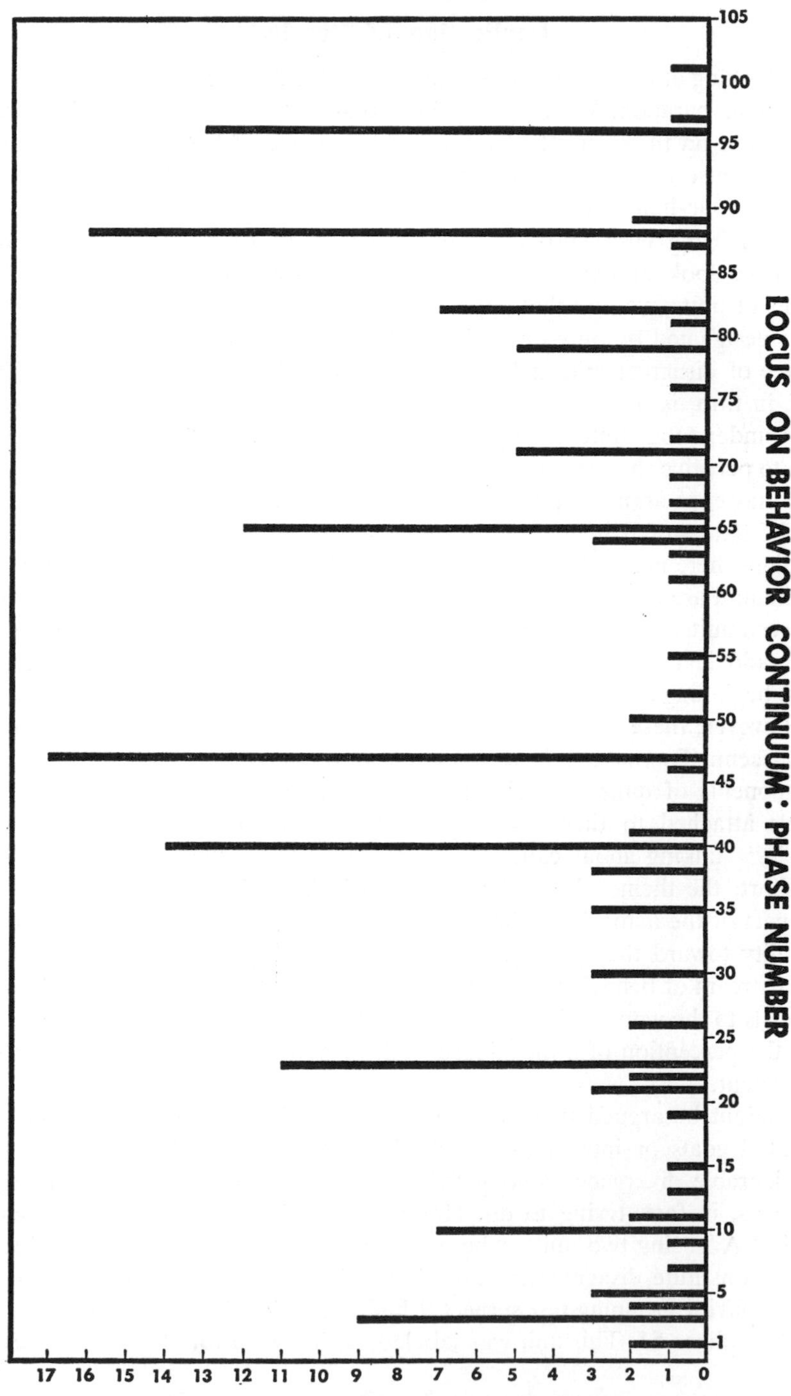

studies, and unanimity was more easily achieved with 17 than with 38 subjects.

Implication of Results

In looking at the results as presented in Table 2.2, we are confronted with a peculiar paradox. We may conclude that statistically there is significant agreement on the over-all patterning or sequence of break and continuity. We may also conclude, though with somewhat less certainty, that a large number (one-half of the possible division points) were significantly agreed upon as being either points of break or points of continuity. However, when we look at the agreement on simultaneous beginning and ending points of units, we find that approximately three-fourths to four-fifths were units designated by only one subject. This latter fact would suggest a high degree of disagreement, at least in the designation of identical units. This fact, in turn, is in distinct contrast to qualitative observation that all subjects understood quite clearly what was going on in the movie and were able to perceive the general course of events and meaning which it conveyed. One may even argue that the data are contradictory and hence, meaningless.

The data would seem to indicate that there is significant agreement regarding where new units begin or end. That is, certain points in the behavior continuum are recognized as part of a continuing unit or as a division point between units. Figures 2.2 and 2.4 graphically support this conclusion. What is paradoxical is that people agree so poorly on the identification of a unit from beginning to end.

However, these apparent contradictions are not as irreconcilable as they may seem. To make this reconciliation we must look first at the basic components of units as such. If we look at the units designated and the labels attached to them, we repeatedly encounter units titled "washing hands," "talking about calf," "ringing dinner bell," "killing squirrel," etc. In short, the theme always implies a goal-directed action or behavior on the part of the actor. The phases comprising a given unit all involve directionality toward the "goal theme" of the unit. Our subjects then, in viewing a stream of behavior, agreed at least to the extent of imputing purposes or goals to the actor. It is our contention that imputation of goal or purpose and the perception of a meaningful unit of behavior are functionally interdependent.

It might be argued that even though all subjects used this concept and imputed goals or intents to the chief actor in the movie, there was still considerable divergence among them as to what they concluded this subject was, in fact, trying to do. However, this is not necessarily the case. Subject A, seeing two units, where subject B sees one unit, does not necessarily constitute disagreement on what is happening. For example, on the first behavior grouping test subject 9 had one unit extending from phase 21 through phase 51. This unit was labeled "doing what told by mother." Sub-

TABLE 2.2

Results of Two Behavior Grouping Tests

	OVER-ALL PATTERNING	*Choice Points*	No.	%	*Identical Units*	No.	%
TEST I	$Chi^2 = 192.65$	Significant agreement Break =	19	13	Significant agreement =	23	04
	df = 143	Significant agreement Continuity =	52	36	More than one designated unit, but less than significant number =	73	12
	$p < .01$	No significant agreement =	72	51	Units discriminated by one subject only =	497	84
			143	100		593	100
TEST II	Sign Test	Significant agreement Break =	11	10	Significant agreement =	15	12
	h = 33, N = 105	Significant agreement Continuity =	60	57	More than one designated unit, but less than significant number =	13	11
	$p < .01$	No significant agreement =	34	33	Units discriminated by one subject only =	93	77
			105	100		121	100

ject 11 used two units to cover the same behavior, phases 21 to 25 and phases 26 to 51. These were labeled "ringing dinner bell" and "washing up." These responses are by no means incompatible and, in fact, are very similar but for one feature. This one feature is how inclusive or delimiting is the definition of the goal. This dimension of imputing broad or delimited goals to the behavior observed has been termed "behavior perspective" by Barker and Wright (1955). It is the chief point on which differences between subjects' ratings hinge.

We can demonstrate that such differences in behavior perspective occur by tabulating the variability of subdivisions within modal units among subjects who agree basically on division at modal areas. Appendix 2.3 contains such a tabulation. Inspection of Appendix 2.3 indicates that within every modal unit there were varying amounts of fractioning of that unit. In every instance some subjects saw the unit as a single complete one; others saw it as having one, two or even six parts. Yet these same subjects agreed on division at modal areas representing the beginning and ending of the unit. This fact would seem to argue strongly for differences in behavior perspective among the subjects.

If one narrows the behavior perspective, the units included may retain the same content and meaning but constitute a somewhat different order of abstraction. In the samples provided in these experiments two absolute extremes were conceivably possible. A subject could have lumped all phases into one unit and entitled it something like "a day at home." On the other hand, the subject could have designated each phase as a separate unit of its own. Actually, no subject approached either extreme. Though divergent, our subjects all utilized a range of behavior perspective similar enough so that meaning was retained. One might expect logically that as extremes are approached, perceived meaning of behavior may also change. Lyon's (1956) study with schizophrenic patients suggests that, for them, behavior perspective is greatly reduced and that units reported are largely lacking in imputation of goals or intent.

However, with differing levels of behavior perspective, significant agreement of division at choice points between phases may still occur because: subject A may begin a unit at point "d" and continue to point "g," begin another unit at point "h" and continue to point "m." Subject B may begin a unit at point "d" and end it at point "m." The two then agree on division points at "d" and "m" and disagree on division at point "g."

We have evidence that, taken as an individual characteristic, behavior perspective remains quite stable over at least a few weeks time. (See Table 2.1) The correlation between the number of units discriminated by the same subjects on Test 1 and Test 2 was .86. One might raise the question that if behavior perspective is a fairly stable characteristic of individuals, in terms of their viewing of other people's behavior, what implications does it have for such factors as ease and accuracy of social perception and communication? One might also raise the question whether these characteristics are related to other personality variables and may perhaps constitute meaningful dimensions in the description of personality. Answers to these questions are as yet quite speculative. Lyon's (1956) findings, mentioned above, suggest that with schizophrenics, whose deficiencies in interpersonal contacts are well documented, relative narrowness of behavior perspective is characteristic. In the collection of data for the present study, systematic questioning of the subjects was carried out after the task was completed. This questioning indicated that those subjects who used a comparatively broad behavior perspective found the task of dividing the behavior-continuum into units much easier than did those subjects who used a more narrow behavior perspective. Whether or not this implies greater ease in social perceptiveness generally, remains to be studied.

Even though we accept the premise that imputing motives or goals to other people is a functional part of seeing their behavior in terms of meaningful units, some questions still remain. We may even accept the explanation that behavior perspective determined the amount of agreement or disagreement on points at which units begin and end, but still legitimately ask, "Why should certain points in the continuum be more frequently chosen as beginning and ending points of a unit?" To put it another way, "What characteristics of behavior clarify or obscure the imputing of the beginning of a new goal?" Characteristics of the stimulus itself may determine the clarity by which the goal is designated and the consistency with which it is pursued. These are stimulus cues that aid the observer and account somewhat for agreement or lack of agreement, particularly at choice points. Barker and Wright (1955), in their discussion of the cues used by trained episoders to mark the beginning and end points of episodes, noted the following:

1. Change in the "sphere" of the behavior from verbal to physical to social to intellectual, or from any one of these to any other.
2. Change in the part of the body predominately involved in the physical action as from hands to mouth to feet.
3. Change in the physical direction of the behavior. Now a child is walking north to the sandpile; next, he is going up a tree; later he climbs down the tree.
4. Change in behavior object "commerced with," as from a knife to a watch to a dog to a person.
5. Change in the present behavior setting. A storm comes up, a fire whistle blows, teacher says, "Pass," and the child goes from one action to another.
6. Change in the tempo of activity, as when a child shifts from walking leisurely to running toward a friend. (p. 236)

In examining our data, items 3, 4, and 5 above appear to be the ones that are most predominately present as potential cues for the ending of one unit or the beginning of the next. These factors may operate singly, or in combination.

Specifically, in considering the eight modal division areas, the stimuli seemingly involved at the division points are the following:

Modal Division Area	*"Stimulus Characteristic" Item Involved*
20	1, 5, 6
35	3, 5
51	3, 4
62	4
74	3, 5
99	3, 5
107	5
118	4

Here again, however, in attempting to understand why some subjects perceive a given change as constituting beginning of a new episode while others do not, one must invoke the concept of behavior perspective. The broader the behavior perspective, the more compatible will be the two kinds of behaviors indicated in the change. For example, if on the first behavior grouping test, the phases from 100 on are described in terms of the unit entitled "eating dinner," then subsequent discussion that ensues during the meal is easily assimilated under the subhead of "eating dinner." However, if one narrows the behavior perspective and discriminates units relative to the discussion that takes place during the dinner, then it becomes quite clear that discussion about the size of the bites Arnold is taking clearly ends, and a new unit begins when the discussion centers on the feeding of the new calf. In short, units of behavior may be seen in somewhat the same manner as the nest of boxes small children use for playthings, each of which fits inside another slightly larger one. If one chooses the largest of these boxes it is quite clear that any of the rest chosen will fit inside. If, however, one chooses the smallest box, then any subsequent box chosen must stand by itself. Similarly, the inclusiveness of the goal around which a unit hinges influences whether stimulus changes in the situation can or cannot be subsumed under this goal.

Hence it would be incorrect to say that the stimulus characteristics of the behavior do not play their part. However, the more critical factor appears to be the inclusiveness of the goal which is imputed to the behavior at the outset.

In answer to the questions posed at the beginning of this chapter, we may summarize our conclusions by saying that the "stream of behavior" attains orderliness in the eyes of other humans to the extent that goals and motives are imputed to the behavior. Independent observers of such a behavior continuum demonstrated significant agreement on general patterning and specifically on the points at which units began or ended. They agreed very poorly on identical incidence of units, yet they were able to agree on the general meaning of the sequence. The latter paradox is understood in terms of the differences in the inclusiveness of the goal or behavior perspective.

CHAPTER 3

Environmental Forces in the Everyday Lives of Children

PHIL SCHOGGEN

THE NATURALLY OCCURRING ENVIRONMENT has entered most studies of environment-behavior relationships as a distal variable with general, pervasive attributes; this is true, for example, of most comparative studies of cultures, classrooms, and homes. It is obvious, however, that the environment is not an undifferentiated medium in which people are immersed; it clearly involves a variety of active processes which selectively spur, guide, and restrain behavior. Dr. Schoggen has studied the varied, dynamic processes within the behavior-stream environment, and his findings have led him to treat the social environment as motivated, i.e., as directed with respect to the child. The success of this approach has wide implications for both theory and practice.

Phil Schoggen is Associate Professor of Psychology at the University of Oregon, he was awarded the Ph.D. degree by the University of Kansas.

THIS STUDY FOCUSES upon the active efforts made by the child's social environment to penetrate his psychological world and to modify his behavior. Other studies have sought to elucidate the structure, dynamics, and content of the child's behavior stream as recorded in specimen records. Central to these efforts has been the directedness of the child's behavior with respect to the behavior objects, persons, and behavior settings of his environment. This study, on the contrary, is concerned with the structure, dynamics, and content of the child's social environment which occurs *pari passu* with his behavior. Central to this problem is the directedness with respect to the child of the behavior of the objects, persons, and settings which make up his social environment. The previous studies have provided some important methodological and conceptual guides for the present undertaking.

The Environmental Force Unit (EFU)

The methods of this study may be described in two main parts. The first is concerned with the identification of basic units of analysis and the second deals with the descriptive ratings of these basic units. Each of these parts will be discussed in turn in this section.

Previously developed procedures for the identification of the child's behavior episodes were adapted to the task of unitizing environmental action with respect to the child. A method for unitizing environmental action was devised which is analogous to the behavior episode methodology and the resulting units are called environmental force units (EFU). Each unit is labeled with a brief descriptive title, the first word of which identifies the environmental agent, usually a person, who is the source of the action. A reading of the consecutive EFU titles from a record gives an impression of the kinds of action which the child's environment took with reference to him during the period covered. Here, for example, are the titles of the first few environmental force units in the record of a four-year-old girl:

1. *Mother:* Getting *S* to Bible School on time (8:00 a.m.)
2. *Mother:* Questioning *S* about cold
3. *Mother:* Getting *S* dressed
4. *Mother:* Chatting with *S* about hair curls
5. *Mother:* Teasing *S* affectionately
6. *Observer:* Commenting on *S*'s hair curls
7. *Mother:* Answering *S*'s questions about observer
8. *Mother:* Feeding *S* breakfast
9. *Mother:* Cautioning *S* to sneeze courteously
10. *Mother:* Asking *S* to turn down radio
11. *Observer:* Responding to *S*'s comment
12. *Mother:* Asking *S* to cover mouth when coughing (8:25 a.m.)

The identification of EFU poses two problems: (1) isolating the environmental phenomena involved in EFU from the total environmental complex, and (2) dividing these phenomena into units of analysis. We shall consider these problems separately.

An environmental force unit is defined as an action by an environmental agent which: (1) occurs vis-à-vis the child, and (2) is directed by the agent toward a recognizable end-state with respect to the child, and (3) is recognized as such by the child.

From this definition it is clear that this study is concerned only with units of environmental action. We include only the observable and successful attempts made by the agents of the environment to penetrate the child's psychological world. Inactive parts of the environment and environmental action which is not directed to the child as well as unsuccessful attempts to "contact" the child are not included.

Not all actions of agents which are directed toward the child occur vis-à-vis the child. Often an agent will do something for the child, something directed to the child, but not in the child's immediate presence, e.g., a mother bakes cookies for the child to have when he comes in after school. On the basis of both practical and theoretical considerations, we elected to eliminate all such action from the present study and to focus upon only those actions which occurred vis-à-vis the subject.

It is obvious that a great deal of what goes on around the subject, much of the environmental action reported in the record, is not directed toward the subject. Such action is not included in the present study. Unless the agent is trying at least to communicate with the child, either individually or as one of a group, we are not here concerned with his action. Thus, for example, a conversation between two parents would not be marked as an environmental force unit provided that neither parent directs action to the child.

The third part of the definition of an environmental force unit cited above states that the action of the agent which is directed toward the child must also be recognized as such by the child. Unless the agent is successful in penetrating the child's psychological world—getting his attention at least long enough to communicate his intention—his action is not included as an environmental force unit. No matter how vigorous the attempt by the agent, it is not marked as a unit unless there is some evidence that it registers upon the child. We did not wish to include influence attempts of which the child was not aware. Rather, we have hoped to focus our analytical efforts upon and to include *all* of the active environmental forces in the immediate situation of the child which are directed toward the child and which are successful at least to the extent of being recognized by the child.

In addition to this basic definition of environmental force units, we have found it helpful to adapt the three primary criteria for identifying behavior episodes (Barker & Wright, 1955, pp. 236–252; Chapter 1, this book) to the task of unitizing the child's active social-psychological environment.

The first of these is concerned with the directedness of the agent's action. It provides that an environmental force unit shall correspond to a single, identifiable goal or end-state with respect to the child. So long as the direction of the agent's behavior with reference to the child is constant, the unit continues. When this direction changes, the unit terminates.

The second criterion has to do with the size of the behavior unit to be considered. It calls for the inclusion of only those actions of environmental agents which fall within the normal behavior perspective of the child. This means essentially that the size of unit studied here falls within the range of behavior units which are commonly perceived by people in general in the course of ordinary living, without special effort or special techniques of observation. This criterion excludes from the study both those actions of the agents which are too small, too molecular, to have significance for the child and those actions corresponding to broad, long-range aims with respect to the child which are beyond the level of the child's normal comprehension.

Finally the third criterion requires relatively constant potency throughout the entire unit of the agent's behavior. When a segment of such a unit appears to equal or exceed the whole unit in potency or importance to the child, the part is itself marked as a separate environmental force unit by virtue of its high potency.

In addition to these principles which provided the major conceptual basis for the identification of EFU, a number of secondary principles were developed in response to particular problems encountered during the process of marking EFU on the specimen records. The more important ones will now be mentioned.

1. *Internalized Environmental Forces.* This study is concerned only with those environmental forces which appear active and external to the child at the time. The concern here, for example, is with the overt attempts by the environment to get the child to play fairly, not with the occasions on which the child behaves with reference to his own internalized notion of fair play. Thus one prerequisite for marking an EFU is the occurrence of overt action by an agent. Lacking this, the action of the child is assumed to be spontaneous.

2. *Unit Initiation and Termination.* Experience showed that, in addition to the basic principles of unit discrimination, some rather specific guides were needed for determining the exact beginning and ending points of the EFU. For unit initiation, the policy adopted states that the EFU begins when either (1) an agent first directs an action to the child if the action is recognized then or subsequently by the child or (2) when the child first directs an action toward the agent if the action is recognized then or subsequently by the agent. Judging the point of unit termination is sometimes rather difficult. As working rules, a unit is judged to continue so long as either (1) the child and the agent continue interacting with regard to the end-state which defines the unit, or (2) the child continues to behave with reference to the goal or end-state under the influence of the agent, even though the agent may not be physically present throughout the entire unit. Thus if an activity which was begun under pressure from an agent somehow captures the child's interest so that he continues in it long after the agent's pressure is removed, the EFU termination is marked at the point where this shift is judged to have occurred.

3. *Discontinuity of EFU.* Sometimes an appreciable period of time will elapse after the initial attempt by an agent to influence the child in a given direction before either the child complies or the agent repeats his effort, perhaps more insistently. Such an occurrence presents the possibility of two interpretations: (1) If the analyst judges that the pressure brought to bear by the agent is felt by the child during the interval—that the child is resisting, procrastinating or whatever—the section is marked as a continuous unit; (2) If, however, the child is so absorbed in something else that the agent's pressure, though initially recognized, has virtually no potency for the child for a time and then later regains potency with or without some further action by the agent, a discontinuous EFU is marked.

The question of continuous *vs.* discontinuous units arises only with instances in which a specific, accomplishable objective is set for the child by the agent, e.g., "Hang up your coat," "Get busy on your homework," "Put away your toys." Repeated admonitions relating to normative standards of, for example, cleanliness, neatness, fairness, politeness, are considered as separate, complete EFU whenever they occur.

4. *Multiple Agents.* EFU commonly result from the action of a single agent. There are cases, however, where two or more agents act simultaneously or sequentially to get the child to do some one thing. Because the EFU is defined in terms of the objectives set for the child by the environment, such cases are marked as single EFU with multiple agents rather than as multiple EFU, one corresponding to each different agent.

5. *Minimal Action Required of Agent.* Many EFU are initiated by the child-subject of the specimen record. A seriously distorted picture can occur if the agent's response to every idle comment of a gregarious, outgoing child is tallied as an EFU. To guard against this, the policy was established to not mark an EFU unless either (1) the agent definitely takes overt action with respect to the child, a smile or a word of acknowledgement, or (2) the action of the child is such that a response of some kind is clearly required, even though the agent chooses to ignore the child.

6. *Inclusiveness Rule.* In cases of doubt as to whether a particular section of the record should be divided into two EFU or only one, the latter choice was preferred because it seems safer to err on the side of combining things that should be separate than to split up natural wholes.

7. *Predominance of the Child's Point of View.* In general, it is assumed that there is high congruence between the agent's and the child's perceptions of the agent's behavior. In the event of a discrepancy, however, as when the child misunderstands the agent's objective, the analyst marks the EFU consistent with the child's interpretation of the agent's behavior.

The EFU constitute only a part of the ecological environment which Barker (1960) has defined as those parts of the regions outside a person with which his behavior is coupled by laws that operate on different levels from those which govern his behavior. Within this total environment, EFU include: (1) *all* actions by other persons (environmental agents) with (2) contemporaneous linkages with *S*'s behavior (3) that are within *S*'s and *A*'s phenomenal world, and (4) behavior perspective, and that are (5) directed (purposive) with respect to the *S,* i.e., have a goal in which the *S* is implicated.

We report below that 663 EFU occurred in the day of Mary C. This means that Mary's associates engaged in 663 actions (no more and no less, within observational accuracy) to direct, control, modify, support, assist, or otherwise cope with Mary's behavior during the course of the day.

It should be emphasized that a single EFU may involve many social interactions. The basic property of an EFU, as of a behavior episode, is persistence in one direction.

The reader may wish to refer at this point to an illustration of EFU shown in Appendix 1.2 as we turn to the mechanics of marking EFU on specimen records. Again the previous work with behavior episode marking (Barker & Wright, 1955, pp. 226–229) served as a model for the present study. A bracket was drawn on the left margin of the manuscript record to mark the points of initiation and termination. A title was written along the vertical line to identify the agent and the action, e.g., Mother: *Asks Maud to pick up toys.* When more than one EFU occurred at a time, the bracket of the later starting unit was made smaller so that there was room to enter its title.

A discontinuous unit was marked with a downward pointing arrow at the point of "interruption" and an upward pointing arrow when the unit was resumed. After the unit identification for an entire record was completed, the EFU were numbered consecutively. Discontinuous units received but one number even though the segments were sometimes separated by several pages.

Three workers shared the task of identifying all EFU in the eighteen specimen day records on file at the Field Station. Fourteen sections of 25 pages each were selected as material for agreement checks from twelve different records representing the full age range (two to ten), both sexes, and both disabled and nondisabled children. Each unit marker was paired with both of the other two so that agreement data are available for any two workers. The two workers assigned to each section marked EFU on identical copies of the record, working independently. Later, their markings were compared and all agreements and disagreements were tabulated. An agreement was credited whenever a unit marked by one analyst was essentially the same in location and content as one marked by the other analyst. For each section an *estimate of accuracy* was computed in the manner described by Barker & Wright (1955, p. 271) for measuring agreement in marking behavior episodes.

Over the fourteen sections used in the study, the values for estimate of accuracy range from 81 to 96 with a median of 85. These values compare favorably with those obtained in the identification of behavior episodes.

The second phase of the analysis involved rating each of the marked EFU on a number of descriptive variables. This process amounted essentially to asking and answering in a standardized way a set of carefully formulated questions about each EFU, e.g., How long did the EFU last? Who was the primary agent? Was the EFU initiated by the child or by the agent? What kind of influence did the agent bring to bear upon the child (helping, pushing, restraining)? What methods did the agent use?

Over a period of several months of preliminary work with the records, a number of such questions were tried out. Finally, several of these were selected for use in the study, careful definitions were developed and written out, and examples of each of the alternative answers were identified in the records and cited as part of the rater's guide. After the raters had become familiar with the several variables, tests of agreement between independent raters were carried out. The results of these agreement checks are reported below along with the results of the ratings.

Specimen day records of twelve Midwest children and four disabled children, and two records of Wally O'Neill were analyzed by the methods which have been presented. The children, and the circumstances of the observations are described elsewhere in this volume (Appendix 1.1), and in *Midwest and Its Children* (Barker & Wright, 1955). The results selected for inclusion in this report describe only a few of the many features of the active social-psychological environments of the children on the days represented by the specimen records, but they bear upon important methodological and substantive issues of psychological ecology.

Number of Environmental Force Units

The over-all results on the frequency of EFU as they are recorded in the specimen records are given in Table 3.1. The second column shows that in this table, and in all other tables, data on the twelve Midwest children are presented for convenience in order of increasing age; data on the four disabled children and from the two records on Wally O'Neill are grouped separately at the bottom of the tables.

The actual number of EFU identified in each record ranged from 259 to 671 with a median of 482. In order to make valid comparisons between children, however, it is necessary to adjust these figures for differences between children in length of day which, in one case, amounts to over three hours. This adjustment was accomplished by reducing all records to the temporal base of the shortest record, i.e., 11 hours, 8 minutes, using the following formula:

$$\begin{matrix}\text{Adjusted N of}\\ \text{EFU in Record X}\end{matrix} = \frac{\text{Duration of Shortest Record}}{\text{Duration of Record X}}\left(\begin{matrix}\text{Actual Number of}\\ \text{EFU in Record X}\end{matrix}\right)$$

The results of these adjustments are shown in the fourth column of Table 3.1 where the values range from 201 to 657 with a median of 386.5. These data from the Midwest children show a weak negative correlation with age which does not meet the usual criteria of statistical significance.

To a person who has read the specimen records, it would come as no surprise that the frequency of EFU in Maud's record is so high—one new EFU beginning every minute. This reflects the responsive, socially rich life situation which Maud enjoyed and her own lively, gregarious behavior. Nor is the low frequency of EFU in Claire's record unexpected in view of this child's characteristically reserved approach to life and the greater maturity of most of her associates.

A comparison of the data on rate of occurrence of EFU shown in the last column with analogous data on the rate of occurrence of behavior episodes reveals the fact that episodes occur with a frequency approximately

TABLE 3.1
Number of EFU and Rate of Occurrence

CHILD	AGE	*Actual No. EFU*	*Adjusted No. EFU*	*Rate Min/EFU*
Mary C.	1–10	663	627	1.06
Jimmy	1–11	364	364	1.83
Lewis	2–11	613	613	1.09
Dutton	3–10	537	469	1.42
Margaret	4–6	618	519	1.28
Maud	5–0	671	657	1.02
Roy	6–2	377	313	2.13
Ben	7–4	388	346	1.93
Ray	7–4	483	398	1.68
Mary E.	8–7	476	368	1.81
Douglas	9–2	480	375	1.78
Claire	10–9	259	201	3.32
Range		259–671	201–657	1.02–3.32
Median		482	386.5	1.73
Wally W.	4–3	466	459	1.45
Sue	7–1	410	351	1.90
Bobby	7–4	542	465	1.43
Verne	7–5	623	484	1.38
Wally O. (Camp)	9–4	584	475	1.40
Wally O. (Home)	9–4	561	457	1.46

twice that for EFU, the median (Midwest children only) being one episode every 0.78 minutes. In general, the EFU rate across the different children varies proportionately with the variation in episode rate (rank correlation, tau, of .71, $p < .01$). This relation would have been even stronger except for Jimmy's record in which environmental action was mediated almost exclusively by his parents and in which he showed a remarkable capacity for long periods of independent, solitary play.

The data from the two Wally O. records suggest that the camp and home days differed little in over-all frequency of EFU. This similarity attests to a vigorous level of social activity in the home situation rather than to a meager social environment at camp. Comparing Wally's totals with that of Douglas, whose age is similar, supports this contention. It will be clear from data to be presented below that this similarity of the two Wally O. records (or any others for that matter) in gross quantitative terms carries no necessary implication for some important qualitative characteristics of the social-psychological environment.

The data discussed so far are based upon all of the EFU identified in the analysis of the records. Data in Table 3.2 and all subsequent tables, however, are based on a study of approximately one-half of the EFU selected at random by including only alternate units. This was done as an economy measure.

The data in Table 3.2 and subsequent tables (except Tables 3.3 and 3.4) differ also in that they are based upon ratings which require the exercise of judgment on the part of the analyst where previously reported results involved mere tabulation. Wherever the analyst was called upon to exercise judgment in rating the units, tests of agreement between independent workers were carried out. In most cases, these tests involved eleven blocks of 50 units each distributed over several different specimen records. Altogther, five different persons participated in the analysis and separate agreement per cents are available for each pair of workers. Average agreement per cents ranged from 81 to 92 on all the variables described below except one which is discussed separately.

Duration of Environmental Force Units

The analysts attempted to estimate the actual length of the EFU on the basis of the time notations and other cues in the records. The results are given in Table 3.2. These estimates are necessarily rough because the time notations in the records and other cues are not precise. The results of the agreement tests show, however, that independent workers agreed fairly well in assigning EFU to the categories shown in the table.

The data in Table 3.2 show that short EFU are much more numerous than long ones. In a way, it is perhaps misleading to report the results in this form because it may exaggerate the importance of the short units. Actually, one of the larger units may carry greater significance than many of the short units combined. On the other hand it is possible to exert strong influence by means of a very brief action, e.g., Douglas' father glowered in disapproval at his antics at the supper table. Caution is called for in the interpretation of these data.

The apparent relation of length and age is supported by rank correlation (tau) of —.43 ($p < .05$) between age and percentage of EFU of one-fourth minute or less in length. A stronger relation is shown in the rank correlation of .588 between age and per cent of EFU lasting one minute or longer ($p < .01$). It may be recalled that a similar relationship between length of behavior episode and age has been reported (Barker & Wright, 1955). It seems reasonable to suppose that these two relationships are not independent.

The data in Table 3.2 show no systematic difference between disabled and nondisabled children. The two records on Wally O'Neill yield virtually the same results.

Age and Role of Environmental Agents

Information about the age and role of the primary agent involved in the EFU is provided in Tables 3.3 and 3.4. (In the case of units with multiple

TABLE 3.2
Per Cent of EFU of Stated Length

CHILD	AGE	*N*	$\frac{1}{4}m$	$\frac{1}{2}m$	*1–2m*	*3–5m*	*6 or more m*
Mary C.	1–10	332	71	15	8	4	2
Jimmy	1–11	181	70	14	10	4	2
Lewis	2–11	307	75	17	7	1	
Dutton	3–10	268	72	17	7	3	1
Margaret	4–6	309	71	15	8	4	2
Maud	5–0	336	61	24	9	2	3
Roy	6–2	190	50	27	16	3	4
Ben	7–4	195	68	17	9	3	3
Ray	7–4	242	62	21	12	2	3
Mary E.	8–7	239	67	16	11	3	3
Douglas	9–2	240	70	13	10	3	4
Claire	10–9	130	55	18	16	3	8
Range			50–75				
Median			69				
Wally W.	4–3	234	64	14	14	5	4
Sue	7–1	206	70	14	10	2	2
Bobby	7–4	270	65	21	8	1	3
Verne	7–5	312	64	18	10	4	5
Wally O. (Camp)	9–4	292	75	12	9	2	2
Wally O. (Home)	9–4	282	72	13	9	2	3

agents, one of them was selected as the primary agent.) In Table 3.3, the age-group to which each subject belongs is indicated by the box drawn around the entries in the appropriate column.

Perhaps the clearest finding with respect to age (Table 3.3) is the apparent negative relation between age of child and per cent of EFU involving an adult as the primary environmental agent. The rank correlation coefficient (tau) for this is —.57, $p < .01$. A related result is shown in Table 3.4 in the entries under the "mother" role. Here, also, the correlation with age is negative (—.76, $p < .001$) and the differences are great between younger and older children. While the "teacher" units make up for some of the decrease in the "mother" and "father" columns, the shift toward a higher per cent of all EFU with peers and siblings with increasing age is pronounced. Here we see evidence that, with increasing age, adults play a less prominent role while peers play an increasingly important role in the socialization process.

In view of the often reported impression that fathers play a minor role in modern child training, it is interesting to note that the per cent of EFU with the father is small in most cases—it just exceeds 10 per cent in only four records and is as high as one-third of the total number of EFU in only

TABLE 3.3
Per Cent of EFU with Environmental Agent of Stated Age

CHILD	*N*	*Infant & Preschool*	*Young School*	*Older School*	*Adol.*	*Adult*	*Aged*	*Cannot Judge*
Mary C.	332	9[a]	0	0	0	90	0	0
Jimmy	181	0	6	0	0	94	0	0
Lewis	307	5	5	6	0	82	0	2
Dutton	268	0	0	0	6	93	0	1
Margaret	309	11	1	8	0	78	0	1
Maud	336	17	0	0	0	76	6	0
Roy	190	5	32	2	8	50	0	3
Ben	195	3	18	19	1	55	0	6
Ray	242	3	20	12	0	60	1	4
Mary E.	239	4	17	6	8	57	0	7
Douglas	240	4	13	0	10	70	0	2
Claire	130	7	2	31	3	55	0	3
Wally W.	234	40	16	1	1	40	0	2
Sue	206	0	5	25	0	70	0	0
Bobby	270	9	1	5	1	51	31	0
Verne	312	6	27	4	0	62	0	0
Wally O. (Camp)	292	0	14	44	2	39	0	1
Wally O. (Home)	282	19	33	16	0	29	0	3

[a] Blocks indicate the age group to which the child-subject belongs.

one case. This is the record on Jimmy, an only child with a very close relationship with his father who spent more time at home than most fathers do. The mother was the highest single contributor of EFU in the records on all preschool-age children and either highest or second highest in the records on children in school. Where the mother was second highest as EFU source, the school teacher was highest.

There is no significant difference between disabled and nondisabled children on per cent of EFU contributed by the mother.

Initiation of EFU

The results of grouping the EFU on the basis of whether the subject or the agent made the initial move are given in Table 3.5. The per cents of subject initiated units range from 28 to 62 with a median of 47. There is no systematic age relation here. The individual personalities and unique situations of the children appear to be reflected in the data shown in the table. The outgoing spontaneity of Lewis and Maud is apparent in their high frequencies of self-initiated EFU (61 per cent and 62 per cent respectively), while the more reserved and reticent approach of Ben, Ray,

TABLE 3.4
Per Cent of EFU with Agents of Stated Role[a]

CHILD	*N*	*Mother*	*Father*	*Sibling or Other Family*	*Teacher*	*Peer*	*Observer*	*CNJ*
Mary C.	332	66	11	9	—	1	12	0
Jimmy	181	48	35	1	—	7	10	0
Lewis	307	50	11	14	—	3	21	2
Dutton	268	45	12	17	—	6	13	7
Margaret	309	50	3	7	6	19	13	1
Maud	336	38	4	13	—	15	30	1
Roy	190	16	3	7	15	42	12	5
Ben	195	29	7	14	11	26	8	6
Ray	242	15	10	—	20	37	12	6
Mary E.	239	18	3	0	13	37	22	7
Douglas	240	13	5	4	15	31	32	2
Claire	130	15	—	23	23	20	15	3
Wally W.	234	27	3	58	—	1	8	3
Sue	206	—	—	—	53	32	15	0
Bobby	270	23	2	45	—	2	27	0
Verne	312	14	9	6	16	34	21	1
Wally O. (Camp)	292	—	—	—	31	60	8	1
Wally O. (Home)	282	16	4	39	—	30	8	2

[a] Where no person of a given role was available in the child's situation on the day of the record, a dash appears in the table.

and Claire is consistent with percentages of self-initiated units of 28, 36, and 37 respectively. This is supported also by the finding of a statistically significant positive rank correlation (tau = .725) between per cent of self-initiated EFU and per cent of self-initiated behavior episodes (Barker & Wright, 1955, p. 296). The data from the records of the disabled children, and of Wally O. are similar to the other data.

Subjects as Single Targets of Environmental Action

Table 3.6 presents data on the degree to which environmental agents single out the subject of the specimen record as the sole target for their actions. It should be noted that the table includes data on only those EFU which were rated as having been initiated by the environmental agent.

The data shown here attest to the impact of group participation by the older subjects. Nine out of ten EFU were directed specifically to the individual child until school age (Mary C. through Maud) then the ratio drops to seven or even six out of ten. Although participation in school groups probably accounts for the major share of this difference, the characteristics of the home situation are also important; e.g., Wally O. shared

TABLE 3.5
Per Cent of EFU Initiated by Subject and Agent

CHILD	*N*	*Subject*	*Agent*	*Cannot Judge*
Mary C.	332	49	51	0
Jimmy	181	49	50	1
Lewis	307	61	38	1
Dutton	268	46	54	0
Margaret	309	42	57	0
Maud	336	62	37	1
Roy	190	40	53	7
Ben	195	28	62	11
Ray	242	36	60	3
Mary E.	239	48	49	3
Douglas	240	51	48	1
Claire	130	37	53	10
Range		28–62	37–62	
Median		47	53	
Wally W.	234	42	55	3
Sue	206	53	47	0
Bobby	270	42	56	1
Verne	312	50	48	3
Wally O. (Camp)	292	43	55	2
Wally O. (Home)	282	40	56	4

with one or two others the directed action of environmental agents more frequently at home than at camp, which probably reflects the presence in the home of four ubiquitous siblings, and the densely populated suburban district in which his home was located.

Conflict between Subject and Environmental Agent

Data on the congruence between the goal set by the agent for the child and the child's own goal are presented in Table 3.7. First, the EFU are grouped according to whether they were judged to involve conflict between the child and the agent. An EFU was counted as a *conflict* unit if there appeared to be any discrepancy between the goal set for the child by the agent and that which the child held for himself in the EFU. Any show of resistance or of negative feeling on the part of either participant toward the proposal of the other was accepted as sufficient evidence of discrepancy to place the EFU in the conflict category. In a test of agreement between independent EFU raters on this distinction, agreement was found on 85 per cent of 550 units.

These results give an overview of the degree of harmony between the

TABLE 3.6
Per Cent of Agent Initiated EFU with Stated Degree of Target Specificity

CHILD	*N*	*To Subject Alone*	*To S. and 1 or 2*	*To S. and Group*	*Cannot Judge*
Mary C.	171	96	4	0	0
Jimmy	93	98	0	0	1
Lewis	121	94	3	1	1
Dutton	144	99	1	0	0
Margaret	177	84	8	7	+
Maud	126	90	9	0	1
Roy	102	68	14	18	1
Ben	133	63	11	17	7
Ray	154	72	6	18	3
Mary E.	120	65	12	20	2
Douglas	116	67	11	20	2
Claire	81	47	14	23	16
Wally W.	134	87	8	0	4
Sue	97	82	5	11	1
Bobby	115	87	9	2	2
Verne	158	80	9	6	6
Wally O. (Camp)	169	66	8	22	4
Wally O. (Home)	170	75	12	6	7

children and their environmental agents on the days of the records. In general, the nonconflict units outnumber the conflict units about two to one. In other words, for every directed action of the environment vis-à-vis a child which met some resistance from the child, there were, on the average, two other significant transactions where resistance did not occur, i.e., where the environmental agent was helpful or supportive. This appears to be an important finding. A number of investigations have been concerned with "influence techniques," "control attempts," and "methods of discipline," all of which presumably would be encompassed by the present definition of conflict EFU. However reports of studies which include data on the frequency of positive or supportive action by agents of the socialization process are rare. The present findings point to the need for interpreting influence techniques as only part of the mosaic comprising the socialization process. An influence attempt may mean one thing when it is thought of as occurring in isolation and something quite different against a background of attempts which are helpful, supportive, or at least neutral.

The wide range of differences among the several records in per cent of conflict EFUs is another major finding shown clearly in Table 3.7. For three children, Margaret, Wally W., and Wally O. (Home), the conflict units

TABLE 3.7

Per Cent of EFU with Stated Congruence Between Goals of Agent and Subject[a]

CHILD		NOT CONFLICT				CONFLICT			
	N	*Casual Ex-change*	*Agent Co-operates*	*Agent Leads*	*Total Not Conf.*	*Agent Pushes*	*Agent Re-strains*	*Agent Resists*	*Total Conflict*
Mary C.	332	27	24	13	64	15	12	8	35
Jimmy	181	29	24	19	72	7	17	5	29
Lewis	307	41	21	10	72	11	8	8	27
Dutton	268	32	17	10	59	13	13	13	39
Marg.	309	28	14	11	53	19	14	12	45
Maud	336	32	22	9	63	14	10	12	36
Roy	190	28	22	13	63	22	5	8	35
Ben	195	34	15	18	67	19	9	2	30
Ray	242	38	19	16	73	17	5	4	26
Mary E.	239	33	23	12	68	19	4	8	31
Douglas	240	28	29	11	68	22	5	4	31
Claire	130	35	19	20	74	15	3	4	22
Wally	234	24	19	15	58	21	9	12	42
Sue	206	42	20	11	73	12	3	11	26
Bobby	270	40	23	21	84	7	5	4	16
Verne	312	30	24	11	65	21	4	8	33
Wally O. (Camp)	292	38	14	17	69	14	3	11	28
Wally O. (Home)	282	32	10	13	55	20	7	15	42

[a] Rows do not always total 100 per cent owing to the omission from the table of CNJ units and to rounding errors.

comprise more than 40 per cent of the total while, at the other extreme, the record on Bobby yielded only 16 per cent conflict units and Claire only 22 per cent. These are, indeed, dramatic differences which perhaps reflect radical differences in the general social-psychological situations of these children. It seems clear also that these differences in our data are not dependent in any simple and direct way upon nonpsychological characteristics of the child's situation such as age, sex, ordinal position in family, or physical disability. Rather, one suspects that such differences can be accounted for only in terms of more subtle, qualitative aspects of the interpersonal relations between the child and the environmental agents.

Next we will consider the three subheadings under each of the two main headings shown in Table 3.7.

Casual Exchange includes those EFUs in which the agent brings little pressure to bear upon the child. These units are mainly brief exchanges of comments, greetings or social amenities in which the agent is peripheral to the child's main interest at the moment.

Agent Co-operates is used to classify those units in which the environmental agent is helpful or co-operative in that he assists the child in making progress toward a goal of the child's own choosing. This category also includes units in which the child and the agent work or play together for mutual benefit.

Agent Leads identifies a group of EFU in which the agent takes the initiative in setting a goal for the child which is clearly attractive to the child. Here the child welcomes the agent's suggestion and accepts it with no resistance. Yet it involves an activity in which the child would not otherwise have engaged.

Agent Pushes is used to identify those units in which the agent takes the lead in setting a goal for the child which is clearly *not* attractive to the child. Any evidence of resistence by the child to either the goal itself or to the agent's approach is sufficient. Included here also are units in which the agent effectively changes the child's position, against the child's wishes, before he can do anything about it. For example, when Ben's sister exclaimed with disgust, "You dope!" and left the room, this unit was placed under the present heading. In general, the two key notions here are (1) the agent puts active pressure on the child to go in some direction, and (2) the child does not (or did not) want to go.

Agent Restrains refers to EFU in which the agent tries to stop the child or to prevent him from doing something he has started or planned. In these cases, the child's activity does not naturally involve the agent—the child is not making a demand on the agent. Rather, the agent interposes himself between the child and his goal as an obstruction to the child's progress. Often the agent thinks he is interfering out of concern for the child's own best interest but the unit is placed under the present heading if, as the child sees it, the agent is getting in his way.

Agent Resists is a heading under which are placed units in which the agent refuses or resists the demands made on him by the child. In these cases, the agent *is* implicated in what the child is trying to do and the agent is more interested in avoiding involvement himself than in preventing the child from doing something. In brief, the agent does not want to do what the child tries to get him to do.

Although Table 3.7 shows results for all six of these subheadings, the data have to be offered on a qualified basis because exact agreement between raters was not high—60 per cent of 550 units. This means that we cannot place great confidence in the rating of particular units. However, if the errors are random, as there is reason to believe they are, the percentages within each subcategory may be accepted as meaningful values.

There is evidence that agreement is somewhat better within the three subcategories of conflict EFU. The per cent of agreement rises to 80 when the total number of subheadings is reduced to four by lumping the three subheadings under *non*conflict into a single group.

A substantial per cent of all units was rated as Casual Exchange, the range being from 24 to 42 per cent. For one thing, this shows that the analytical comb is a fine one; it suggests that few important environmental actions could escape analytical procedures which identify so many EFU of minor significance. Further, these high figures for Casual Exchange again remind us that the environment reaches out for the child in many ways which have significance in other ways than being directive, coercive, and restraining.

In most cases, the per cent of units marked Agent Co-operates exceeds that of units in the Agent Leads category. Thus the agent helps the child more often by assisting him in reaching his own goal than by introducing some new goal of the agent's choosing. When we lump these two subcategories together, we find that the totaled per cents range from 23 to 44 across the entire group of records. Thus it appears that at least one (and usually more) in every four environmental actions with respect to these children was seen by the child as clearly positive, helpful, or consistent with the child's own wishes. This is strong evidence that constructive as well as restrictive and coercive efforts by the environment in relation to the child deserve the careful attention of students of the socialization process.

Among the three subheadings of conflict EFU, Agent Pushes tends to occur more frequently than either of the other two but the differences are not impressively large with the children of preschool age. However, the per cents of units in the Restrains and Resists categories are much smaller for school-age children (Roy–Claire). The median per cent of EFU in these two categories combined is ten for school-age children as compared to 21 for the six children below school age (Mary C.–Maud). A more refined analysis of these findings is called for but these gross data suggest that one of the rewards of attaining school age may be a substantial reduction in the frequency with which the environment seeks to restrict the child's activities through direct, overt influence attempts. It seems likely that such regulation and limitation may be built into the behavior settings which the child becomes involved in for the first time when he goes to school. This possibility is supported by the rather sharp break in the data at the dividing line between the oldest preschool child (Maud) and the youngest school-age child (Roy). Such a clear break also argues against the interpretation that the reduction in external restraints is a gradual change that comes more or less naturally with age. The data of Table 3.7 provide no support for this latter notion.

In view of the fact that mothers in every case were found to be either the highest or second highest contributor of EFU, it is of interest to find that there is no significant difference between mothers of disabled and nondisabled children on per cent of conflict EFU. Nor is there a difference on the subcategories of conflict. This suggests that one important feature of the social-psychological environment of children may be relatively uninfluenced by physical disability of the child.

Techniques of Environmental Agents

We were especially interested in studying the specific techniques used by the agents in those instances in which there was some discrepancy between the goal of the child and the aim of the agent, i.e., in all conflict EFU. We wanted to know in specific, concrete terms how the agent sought to bring about change in the behavior of the child. What particular methods were used by the environment in its active attempts to coerce, restrain, resist or otherwise modify the child's behavior?

Our procedure in trying to answer this question was to examine each one of the conflict EFU individually and to write out a brief, concrete description of the methods used by the agent in each unit. In this stage of the analysis, the analyst merely abstracted the observer's description of the methods in the record. Summarizing or categorizing was kept to a minimum in this first step. Rather, the aim at this point was to maintain intact as much as possible the observer's original report. The task of the analyst was to examine the EFU as a whole and then to write out in a sentence or two a brief description of the main methods used by the agent in the unit. At the same time, the analyst identified the agent's specific goal with respect to the child and also recorded a brief description of it. For example, EFU #87 in Jimmy's record is described as follows:

Methods: (1) Father says playfully, "Hey!"
(2) Father grabs envelope
Goal: Jimmy to let father's envelope alone

A second example is from the Mary C. record, EFU #188:

Methods: (1) Mother says pleadingly, "No, no, Mary. You don't want to break your mother's door, do you?"
(2) (When Mary continues) "Don't do that, Mary."
(3) (When Mary continues) Diverts Mary's attention by pointing out "doggies" seen outside through window.
Goal: Mary to not slam oven door.

But many EFU do not involve such persistent effort by the agent. A fairly typical EFU would be this one, #456, from Douglas' record:

Method: (1) Mother says sharply
Goal: Doug to stop stomping on floor.

Or, #468 from the same record a little later:

Method: (1) Mother says matter-of-factly
Goal: Doug to hurry and get ready for bed.

Finally, an example of a common type of EFU, #46 from the same record.

Method: (1) Charlotte J. ignores Doug
Goal: Doug to let her alone.

This process yielded long lists of brief descriptions of methods and goals recorded unit by unit for each of the conflict units in all the records. While this process inevitably loses much of the richness of the full record, it does provide a somewhat more efficient way of looking at environmental attempts to modify the child's stream of behavior. It may be instructive to reproduce here a part of the list of methods and goals as actually recorded from the record on Margaret.

The section begins just after noon as Margaret, age 4, begins eating lunch with her mother, father, and small brother Bradley.

EFU#	*Methods*	*Goal*
164	(1) Mother suggests that Bradley will be finished first. (2) M. suggests that Margaret can eat faster if she uses a spoon rather than fork. (3) M. says sternly, "Now you go ahead and eat." (4) M. tells Marg. to use whatever utensil is fastest. (5) M. tells Marg. to talk later and eat now.	Margaret to eat her lunch.
165	Mother says with mild scorn, "Well, don't take it that way."	Margaret not to drink lemonade and milk together.
168	Father says sternly, "You know how to eat. Now you eat."	Marg. to eat without playing.
169	Mother exclaims in surprise, "Use your handkerchief!"	Marg. to use handkerchief, i.e., not sniffle.
171	Mother chides, "Oh honey!"	Marg. to restrain from chanting.
173	Father mildly flips her on face.	Marg. to return to eating.
176	(1) Mother reprimands, "No!" (2) Mother explains, "It isn't cocoa." (3) Mother explains, "You don't need to dunk that."	Marg. to stop dunking cookie in fruit cocktail.
177	Mother says, "Don't talk with your mouth full; wait 'til it isn't full."	Marg. not to talk with mouth full.
179	Mother says in annoyance, "Quit whispering."	Marg. to stop whispering.
180	(1) Mother says, "Put it (Kleenex) down in your lap." (2) M. says more firmly, "Put it in your lap, not on the table."	Marg. to put Kleenex in lap.
181	(1) Mother says sternly, "Now listen." (2) M. answers with embarrassment, "No."	Marg. not to talk of such things (food in stomach).

EFU#	*Methods*	*Goal*
182	(1) Mother says sternly, "You better straighten up." (2) M. says, "Now Margaret, eat. You eat that or else." (3) M. says, "Now you can eat faster than that." (4) M. reprimands, "Marg., let's not do that." (5) M. suggests that Marg. hurry. (6) M. coaxes, "Take a drink of milk."	Marg. to eat fruit cocktail.
184	(1) Father whacks Marg. on back of hand. (2) F. threatens, "I'm gonna. . . ."	Marg. to stop teasing and eat.
185	Mother says angrily, "Down on the chair."	Marg. to remove Kleenex from table.
187	Father tells her impatiently to go wash.	Marg. to wash hands.
188	Father ignores Marg's. request for damp washcloth.	Marg. to go to bathroom to wash hands.

This list includes all conflict EFU which occurred during the lunch period, a span of about 25 minutes. While such a listing leaves out a great amount of significant material, it does preserve some of the important qualitative features of the environment's attempts to modify the child's behavior. At the same time, it provides a basis for further quantitative analyses and tabulations.

These lists were made in the form shown above by the EFU analyst at the time that he completed the other ratings of each unit. After such lists had been constructed for all the records, the lists were studied and an attempt was made to group these more detailed descriptions of methods into empirically determined categories of similar techniques. Our aim here was to let the data guide us in establishing meaningfully distinct groupings rather than to impose some arbitrary system of classification on the data. We feel that the resulting classification system is useful, and that it, and the data it has provided, will serve as the basis for more general and theoretical classification schemes.

All together, 27 different categories of methods were identified. Tests of agreement showed that, after training, independent judges agreed well in assigning the specific method descriptions to the 27 categories. These method-classes are presented below by code number and short title:

10 Makes suggestion; positive feeling by *A*
11 Makes matter-of-fact suggestion or request
12 Gives instruction, direction, appeal; slight negative feeling by *A*

13 Gives vigorous instruction, direction, order; strong negative feeling by *A*
20 Ignores *S*'s request
21 Gives minimal response to *S*
22 Refuses *S* matter-of-factly
23 Refuses firmly or vigorously
24 Avoids or leaves *S*
30 Appeals to *S*'s reason by giving explanation
31 Uses physical proximity as implied threat
32 Uses light physical contact or gesture (a nudge or a pat)
33 Uses gross physical contact or gesture (a shove or a slap)
34 Threatens to deprive *S* of something valued
35 Threatens to inflict a negative punishment
36 Promises some reward
37 Points out an exemplary other person
38 Encourages, reassures, gives help, explains
39 Demonstrates how to do something
40 Distracts *S* from disapproved activity
41 Points out aspects of situation *S* has overlooked
42 Attracts attention of others to *S*'s error or wrongdoing
43 Reminds *S* of previous commitment
44 Offers substitute for proscribed object or activity
45 (could not judge)
46 Uses parable or story to illustrate point
47 Threatens to report *S* to authority
48 Challenges *S* to demonstrate skill or ability

In constructing the original lists, the analysts sought to make a separate entry for the occurrence of each identifiable attempt by the agent to implement the goal of the EFU. As noted in the examples given earlier, it was possible in some cases to identify the use of five or six different methods in a single unit but more often only one or two methods were found. Repetitions of the same method within a given unit were recorded whenever an intervening time period gave the repeated use of the method some unity of its own.

In the later phase of the analysis in which the specific descriptions were grouped into the 27 categories listed above, practical limitations of the data handling system required that the number of method-classes tabulated for any one EFU be limited to three. The attempt of the analyst at this point was to identify the methods which were most important in the implementation of the EFU. They were recorded in order of importance within the unit or, if equal, in order of temporal sequence within the unit. Thus, for each EFU, the tabulation showed first, the most important or earliest method used in the unit, followed by a second and third method used in the unit if these occurred in the particular case. But in no case was it possible for more than three methods to be tabulated within a single EFU. We will speak of a *method transaction* (MT) to refer to the occurrence of a particular method one time within one EFU. This special term is needed because the system permitted the tabulation of up to three method transactions in each EFU. In a later section it will be convenient to refer to EFU in which certain kinds of method transactions occur and to the total frequency of occurrence of certain kinds of method transactions irrespective of the particular EFU in which they occur.

Table 3.8 shows some basic data on the occurrence of method transactions in the records. The column showing the ratio of method transactions to conflict EFU indicates that there is some variation among the several records but that on the average, about one and one-half method transactions were tabulated for each conflict EFU. This figure is artificially reduced, however, by the technical restriction mentioned above which permitted the recording of only three method-transactions for any one EFU even though as many as five or six could be discerned in some cases.

The next three columns of the table give more detailed information on tions in the records. Column four showing the ratio of method transactions which occurred as first, second and third within each unit as described earlier. While the range is substantial, somewhat less than two-thirds of the method transactions on the average are accounted for by those listed first within the unit. It is of interest to note that only one (Claire) of the oldest six Midwest children falls below the group median and, conversely, only one (Dutton) of the youngest six children falls above this point. This same relation yields a positive rank correlation coefficient significant at the .05 level. Apparently persistent and repetitive action by the environment decreases with increasing age.

A summary of the main findings on the frequency with which different methods were used by all agents in the 18 records is shown in Table 3.9. Here the ten methods which had the highest frequency of occurrence among all method transactions in the records are shown. For each of these high-frequency methods, the table shows (1) the number of day records in which each method attained one of the top ten ranks when all methods were ranked within each record on frequency of total number of method transactions; (2) the range, and (3) the median number of method transactions across all 18 records. For example, the table shows that method #12, "Gives instruction, slight negative feeling" had a total number of method transactions sufficient to give it the highest rank of all the 27 methods in six of the 18 records; that it ranked second in eight records, third in two records and fifth in the remaining two records. The lowest actual frequency of method transactions with the method was three, the highest was 58, and the median of all 18 records was 22. (It should be remembered here that these data are based on a 50 per cent sample of all EFU, thus the actual frequencies for the entire day would be about twice those shown in Table 3.9.)

This table provides some useful evidence on how the environment went

TABLE 3.8

Per Cent of All Method Transactions Occurring as First, Second, and Third within Each EFU for Each Record

CHILD	*N* *Conflict* *EFU*	*N* *Method* *Transactions*	*Ratio* *MT/EFU:* *Cf.*	*First* (*% MT*)	*Second* (*% MT*)	*Third* (*% MT*)
Mary C.	117	233	1.99	51	33	17
Jimmy	50	88	1.76	58	31	12
Lewis	84	152	1.81	55	31	14
Dutton	107	163	1.52	66	25	9
Marg.	139	225	1.62	62	29	9
Maud	119	193	1.62	62	28	10
Roy	67	85	1.27	79	18	3
Ben	58	74	1.27	78	20	1
Ray	64	96	1.50	67	24	10
Mary E.	74	109	1.47	71	24	5
Douglas	75	102	1.36	74	18	9
Claire	28	45	1.60	62	27	11
Wally W.	97	180	1.85	54	32	14
Sue	54	93	1.72	58	33	9
Bobby	42	74	1.76	56	31	12
Verne	104	211	2.03	49	35	16
Wally O. (Camp)	79	138	1.75	57	30	13
Wally O. (Home)	120	222	1.85	54	34	12

about the task of trying to effect changes in the behavior of these children. It should be realized that all the method transactions reported here occurred when there was some discrepancy between the agent's goal for the child and the child's own goal. With this in mind, it is all but dramatic to find that the method most commonly used by agents in these circumstances was such a mild one as #11, "Makes matter-of-fact suggestion." This method ranked first in twelve records and second in the other six. As one reads down the list of all the high-frequency methods, the same trend is evident—the methods which rank high in frequency of use tend to be rather mild or moderate. Negative feeling by the agent is explicitly recognized in only two of the ten methods listed in Table 3.9. Perhaps the most severe method shown, #13, "Gives vigorous instruction, strong negative feeling," is listed in ninth place, it never had a rank higher than fifth in any record, and it did not place among the top ten methods in ten of the 18 records.

Similarly, it is interesting to note which of the 27 methods listed on page 62 did *not* occur with sufficient frequency to place them among the top ten. Conspicuous by their absence, for example, are threats of punish-

TABLE 3.9

Frequency among All 18 Records with Which Different Methods Attained High Rank within Each Record Based on Total Number of Method Transactions

METHOD CLASS NAME	*Rank by Frequency in Record*										*Range*	*Median*
	1	*2*	*3*	*4*	*5*	*6*	*7*	*8*	*9*	*10*	*Freq.*	*Freq.*
11 Makes matter-of-fact suggestion	12	6									13–61	31.5
12 Gives instruction; slight negative feeling	6	8	2	0	2						3–58	22
20 Ignores S's request	0	2	5	3	2	1	4	1			1–25	9.5
10 Gives gentle suggestion	0	2	3	4	3	0	1	3	1		0–18	9.5
30 Appeals to reason, gives explanation	0	0	6	2	1	5	0	3	0	1	2–26	8
32 Uses light physical contact or gesture	0	0	1	3	3	1	4	3	1		1–16	8.5
22 Refuses S matter-of-factly	0	0	0	5	1	2	1	3	2		0–17	6
38 Encourages, reassures, helps, explains	0	0	1	0	1	2	1	2	4		0–20	5
13 Gives vigorous instruction; strong negative feeling	0	0	0	0	1	3	1	0	1	2	0–13	2
21 Gives minimal response to S	0	0	0	0	1	0	1	0	2	4	0–8	1.5

ment, or deprivation and promises of reward. Neither was gross physical contact a frequently used method, despite the fact that the data of Table 3.9 include EFU with *all* agents, including the children's peers with whom gross physical contact as in roughhousing was not uncommon.

These findings suggest once more that the environment took, in general, a very temperate approach in attempting to modify the child's behavior. Arbitrary coercion and strong pressure counter to the child's will indeed appear to be rare. Again the data here presented emphasize the importance of interpreting such stronger pressures, when they do occur, against a background of a large number of more moderate attempts to influence the child as well as a still larger background of clearly positive and supporting behavior with reference to the child.

Methods used by mothers of disabled and nondisabled children were compared. Method #11, "Makes matter-of-fact suggestion" and #12, "Gives instruction, slight negative feeling" rank first and second, respectively, with both groups of mothers. All methods used by mothers of disabled and nondisabled children correlated .644 (tau). Here again we fail to find much difference in the environmental conditions of the disabled children.

Goals of Environmental Agents

Another general question which we wanted our data to answer concerns the kinds of goals which the environment seeks to set for the child. Specifically, around what kinds of issues does conflict arise between the child and the environmental agents? When discrepancy does occur between the child's goal and the goal of the environment for the child, what kinds of things does the environment demand of the child?

As shown on pages 59–61, the data analyst wrote a brief description of the agent's goal for the child in each of the conflict EFU at the same time he listed the methods used by the agent. Examples of such specific goals of the agent with respect to the child are included in that earlier discussion. It should be noted that only one goal is identified for each EFU, thus the number of goals equals the number of EFU in each record.

The goals were grouped into empirically determined categories on the basis of similarity following a procedure analogous to the one used in grouping methods, described earlier. This grouping produced the 29 different goal-classes which are listed below by code number and title:

(*S* = Subject, *A* = Agent)
10 *S* to do something for *A*
11 *S* to cease his demands of *A*
12 *A* teases *S* for fun
13 *A* scolds or hurts *S* for own satisfaction
14 *A* protects own property
15 *A* hurts *S* as part of a game or activity
17 *S* to not delay activity with digressions
18 *S* to restore status quo after *S*'s misdeed
19 *S* to let *A* join in activity in progress
20 *S* to follow school routine
21 *S* to follow domestic routine
22 *S* to mind manners
23 *S* to play fair, not quarrel
24 *S* to be careful (personal safety)
25 *S* to keep self or clothes clean
26 *S* to conform to mores regarding clothes
27 *A* points out *S*'s responsibility for trouble
28 *A* tries to tell or show *S* something
29 *S* to follow orders or instructions
30 *S* to assist or help in joint activity
31 *S* to improve quality of performance

40 *S* to not waste or damage material things
41 *S* to respect property of others (not-*A*'s property)
42 *S* to not mistreat animals
43 *A* tries to correct *S*'s error of fact
44 Other, unclassified
46 *A* unintentionally hurts *S*
47 *A* defends other person from *S*'s attacks
48 *S* to wait for proper time

In the case of this listing of classes of goals, just as in the earlier case of the listing of classes of methods, we feel the need, finally, for a more systematic and conceptually adequate analysis of goals. However, the goals listed were the ones described in the original records. Our aim at this stage is to avoid imposing a preconceived conceptualization upon the data, but to let the data determine the groupings.

Table 3.10 shows some gross findings on the frequency with which different categories of agent goals for the subject occurred in the several records. In this table, the ten most frequently occurring goal classes are listed with data on how often each attained one of the six highest ranks in a record and the range and median frequency with which each of the ten goal-classes actually occurred in all of the records. (Again the reader is reminded that these data are based on a one-half sample of all units in the day. Actual frequencies approximate twice the values shown in the table.)

The prominence of goal class #11, "*S* to cease his demands on *A*," in these records is quite marked. It ranked either first or second in all records save one where it ranked fifth in frequency of occurrence. This is a surprising result. Even when one takes into account that this goal-class includes a variety of related aims, e.g., *S* to quit bothering *A*, to not question *A* further, to let *A* alone, to not press his suggestion or request, to not attack *A*, one still is hardly prepared for the finding that such agent goals as these occurred more frequently than any other type. Apparently, one feature of the social-psychological worlds of most of these children was relatively frequent resistance by their associates to the children's demands.

The second most frequent class of agents' goals for the child in EFU is #10, "*S* to do something for *A*," which includes a variety of things having in common service of the needs or desires of the agent, e.g., handing something to *A*, giving *A* assistance or information, getting *S* to watch what *A* is doing, to recognize *A*'s achievement or characteristic. Thus we see that both of the two classes of goals occurring with greatest frequency related to the personal wishes of the agent, either for peace, comfort, convenience, or notice. The EFU in these cases is directed toward a benefit to the agent.

In third and fourth ranks are goal-classes which are concerned with maintaining the daily routines of home and school. Here we find actions by the agents intended to get the subject to do what is required by the daily

TABLE 3.10

Frequency among All 18 Records with Which Different Goal Classes Attained High Rank on Frequency of Occurrence within Each Record

GOAL CLASS NAME	*Rank by Frequency in Record* 1	2	3	4	5	6	*Range Freq.*	*Median Freq.*
11 S to cease his demands on A	12	5	0	0	1		3–37	21
10 S to do something for A	0	6	4	3	3	1	1–27	9
21 S to follow domestic routine	0	1	5	4	3		1–11	7
20 S to follow school routine	3	2	2	0	1	0	1–24*	10*
24 S to be careful (personal safety and health)	1	3	0	3	0	5	1–25	5
22 S to mind manners	1	0	2	3	1	2	1–17	4.5
13 A scolds S or hurts S for own satisfaction	0	0	3	1	2	1	1–10	2
40 S to not waste or damage material things	0	0	2	1	1	1	0–11	3
47 A defends another against S	0	1	0	1	0	0	0–11	1
12 A teases S for fun	0	0	0	2	1	0	0–9	1

* Median and range of only nine records because S did not enter a school setting in other records.

schedule of getting up, getting dressed, having meals, getting to school, doing assigned work, passing to the next class or activity and the like. The routine of daily living had a very prominent place in the social-psychological worlds of these children.

Other kinds of goals set by environmental agents for these children with relatively high frequency include attempts to get the child to act in accordance with principles of physical health and safety (#24), to be mannerly, to not be wasteful of material or destructive to objects, and to avoid injuring another person. Finally, in a fair number of cases, the agent was judged to be hurting, scolding, or teasing the child for the agent's own satisfaction or pleasure.

A comparison of the goal classes occurring with high frequency in EFU with mothers of disabled and nondisabled children showed that the same two goals were involved but that the rank order was reversed; for mothers of nondisabled children, goal class #21, "*S* to follow domestic routine" was most frequent whereas for mothers of disabled children, #11, "*S* to cease his demands on *A*" occurred most frequently. This is consistent with an earlier finding that disabled children make more frequent appeals to adults for assistance than do nondisabled children (p. 440, Barker & Wright, 1955). But still, the similarity seems more impressive than the difference.

Summary

This is a study of the active, directed attempts of the environment to modify the child's stream of behavior as recorded in the day-long specimen records. A system for unitizing and analyzing purposive environmental action with respect to the particular child-subject of the record was devised using as a model the system developed earlier at the Field Station for unitizing and analyzing the purposive behavior of the child. The resulting basic unit of analysis is called the Environmental Force Unit (EFU) which is formally defined as an action by an environmental agent (social behavior object) which (1) occurs vis-à-vis the child, and (2) is directed toward a recognizable end-state with respect to the child, and (3) is recognized as such by the child. Using this definition and some supplementary principles, EFU were identified in the 18 specimen records in the Field Station library. Independent unitizers were able to agree acceptably in unit identification.

Once the unitizing was complete, the next phase of the study involved asking and answering on rating scales a series of carefully formulated questions about each EFU. Again tests of interrater agreement were carried out and the results are reported.

Substantive findings from these ratings are presented and discussed. In part, these findings indicate that:

—EFU occurred at the rate of about three every five minutes
—half to three-quarters of all EFU were of very brief (one-fourth minute) duration
—mothers and schoolteachers were the most frequent sources of EFU; fathers usually had few EFU
—the several records differed widely in per cent of EFU initiated by the child and by the agent
—most frequently EFU were directed to the child-subject alone, especially among children below school age
—EFU in which no conflict was involved outnumbered conflict units about two to one
—among conflict EFU, the methods used by the agent to modify the child's behavior were usually gentle and mild; offers of reward and threats of punishment were rare
—the most frequently occurring goal-class was that in which the agent tried mainly to get the subject to cease his demands of the agent
—the data did not reveal any significant differences between the records of disabled and nondisabled children on the variables studied.

Perhaps the one most significant result of this study lies in the demonstration that the social environment of the child, as recorded in specimen records, displays readily recognizable properties of directedness with regard to the child, i.e, the social environment appears to have intentions with respect to the child which are easily discernible as units which can be used for descriptive and analytical studies of environmental forces acting upon children in ordinary, everyday life.

CHAPTER 4

Mothers and Fathers as Sources of Environmental Pressure on Children

HELEN SIMMONS & PHIL SCHOGGEN

THE METHODS OF DESCRIBING the environment of a child reported in the preceding chapter are used here to answer some particular questions: To what degree are fathers and mothers sources of environmental influences? What techniques of control do parents use? How effective are various control techniques?

Phil Schoggen is identified in the introduction of Chapter 3. Helen Simmons is Research Assistant at the University of Oregon; she earned the M.A. degree at the University of British Columbia.

THE PURPOSE OF THIS PAPER is to report upon the occurrence of conflict between parents and children under the natural conditions of everyday life. The Environmental Force Unit provided the basic data of the study (see Chapter 3).

The earlier literature in child development, as well as Dyck's and Schoggen's studies reported in this volume, clearly supports the common observation that, on the average, mothers spend more time per day with their children than do fathers (Radke, 1946; Hoffman, 1960; Barker & Wright, 1955). But the evidence concerning the qualitative aspects of the parent's relationship with the child is less substantial. A number of important questions remain unanswered. Is there a difference between mothers and fathers in the proportion of conflict in their relationships with the child? If so, what methods of control or influence are used by the "high-conflict" parent in contrast to those used by the "low-conflict" parent? Specifically, is there more frequent occurrence of the use of arbitrary authority by either parent? Does the child respond *more* readily to the parent who is more controlling and severe? To what extent is the child compliant or rebellious in the face of the more arbitrary and the more permissive methods? The present study offers some evidence relevant to these questions.

The basic unit of study was the "conflict EFU" as this is defined in Chapter 3. Briefly, such EFU are those in which some degree of discrepancy was judged to exist between the goal of the child and the goal held for the child by the environmental agent. Thus the present study focuses upon those conflict EFU in which either the mother or the father was the environmental agent. All of the day records on the Midwest children were used in the study except the Claire Graves record which was omitted because the father was absent from the home on the day of the record. The study, therefore, included eleven families of child-subjects ranging in age from two through nine years. There were seven boys and four girls.

It will be recalled that the previous analysis of EFU included a description of the method or methods used by the agent in each conflict EFU. A total of 27 different method-classes were distinguished and results were presented on the frequency with which each method occurred in the records. When it was possible to identify the occurrence of different methods in a single EFU, or repeated occurrence of one of the methods, the analyst was able to record a total of three method transactions (MT). (See Chapter 3, pp. 61–63.)

The 27 methods distinguished in the basic analysis include a wide range of qualitatively different approaches to the problem of influencing the child's behavior. We have selected eight methods from the larger group for separate study because they all involve the use of rather arbitrary authority by the agent. Here the parent's behavior seems to say, "Do what I want you to because I say so." No attempt is made to justify, qualify or explain his demand. The parent's action reflects his assumption of a superior power role in relation to the child. The eight classes of methods included in this group are as follows:

12 Gives instruction, direction, appeal; slight negative feeling
13 Gives vigorous instruction, direction, order; strong negative feeling
23 Refuses subject firmly, vigorously
32 Uses light physical contact or gesture
33 Uses gross physical contact or gesture
34 Threatens to deprive subject of something valued
35 Threatens to inflict a negative punishment
47 Threatens to report subject to authority

For convenience we may refer to methods in the eight categories as *arbitrary methods* (MArb).

We were interested not only in the parents' behavior, but also in the responses of the child when his parent's goal for him and his own goal were incompatible. For this purpose, we utilized ratings of the outcome of conflict EFU. These ratings were completed as a part of the general EFU study reported in the preceding chapter but space limitations prevented inclusion of the results there. The original ratings on outcome utilized four subcategories corresponding to different degrees of promptness, shown by the child in complying with the agent's demand, ranging from immediate compliance to complete noncompliance. Because exact item interrater agreement was not high (.66), we combined two of the subcategories. The resulting three-way distinction is sufficiently clear to permit use of these data for the purposes of this report, but we cannot place high confidence in the ratings of particular units.

Conflict with Mothers and Fathers

The data for mothers and fathers on the number of EFU, the number of conflict EFU (EFU:Cf) and the per cent of total units which involved conflict (EFU:Cf/EFU $\times$ 100) are shown in Table 4.1. In every case, the mother was the source of more EFU than the father, (median = 4.4 times as many). The father's contribution tended to be only roughly proportionate to that of the mother. There was wide variation across the different children in actual number of EFU (mothers range from 51–441 and fathers from 9–118).

The first section of Table 4.1 shows the ratio of EFU with the mother to EFU with the father, which ranges from 1.5 for Jimmy to 13.1 for Margaret. To the previously reported finding that mothers have a predominant role in the socialization process, our data suggest the additional generalization that there are very marked differences in the social-psychological situations of individual children in this respect.

The second section of Table 4.1 shows a somewhat similar picture with regard to conflict EFU, i.e., wide variation across the several children and many more conflict EFU with mothers than with fathers. The actual number of conflict EFU with fathers was small in all cases (range 6–27). Note that these figures refer to the entire day, e.g., Margaret's father tried to modify her behavior in a way which produced some resistance by Margaret only ten times throughout the entire day. Her mother, on the other hand, took such a position with reference to Margaret 172 times that same day—a ratio of 17 for the mother to one for the father.

For mothers, the total number of EFU correlates with the number of conflict EFU very highly ($\tau = .891$, $p < .001$) but the correlation between mothers and fathers on number of conflict EFU is low. A comparison of the two sets of mother-father ratios shown in the table indicates that mothers as compared to fathers were even more clearly predominant in the case of conflict EFU than in the case of EFU more generally. The M/F ratio for conflict EFU is higher than for total EFU in 8 of the 11 mother-father pairs. Earlier we noted that the fathers apparently played a relatively minor role vis-à-vis the children in ordinary, everyday life. These data suggest that fathers also were less inclined than mothers to be involved in conflict with the children.

To test this possibility more specifically, we computed the per cent of all EFU which are conflict units for the mother and father of each child (shown in the third section of Table 4.1) and compared the per cents for mothers and fathers using the Wilcoxon matched-pairs signed-ranks test. The difference turned out to be not significant (at the .05 level) when all eleven pairs of parents were included. Because the total number of EFU with the father

TABLE 4.1
Number of EFU and Conflict EFU; Per Cent of EFU Which Are Conflict EFU

SUBJECT	AGE	*Total EFU* *Number* *Mother*	*Father*	*Ratio* *M/F*	*Conflict EFU* *Number* *Mother*	*Father*	*Ratio* *M/F*	*Per Cent* *EFU:Cf/EFU × 100* *Mother*	*Father*
Mary C.	1–10	441	72	6.1	166	22	7.5	38	31
Jimmy	1–11	174	118	1.5	55	27	2.0	32	23
Lewis	2–11	292	67	4.4	120	13	9.2	41	19
Dutton	3–10	223	69	3.2	94	21	4.5	42	30
Margaret	4–6	302	23	13.1	172	10	17.2	57	43
Maud	5–0	267	32	8.3	134	11	12.2	50	34
Roy	6–2	69	12	5.8	34	6	5.7	49	50
Ben	7–4	106	34	3.1	43	16	2.7	41	47
Ray	7–4	72	46	1.6	23	13	1.8	32	28
Mary E.	8–7	87	9	9.7	30	7	4.3	34	78
Douglas	9–2	51	19	2.7	26	9	2.9	51	47
Range		51–441	9–118	1.5–13.1	23–172	6–27	1.8–17.2	32–57	19–78
Median		174	34	4.4	55	13	4.5	41	34

TABLE 4.2
Total Number of Method Transactions (MT); Number of Arbitrary Method Transactions (MT:Arb); Per Cent of MT Which Are MT:Arb.

SUBJECT	AGE	*Method Transactions (MT)* *Number* *Mother*	*Father*	*Ratio* *M/F*	*Arbitrary Method Transactions (MT:Arb)* *Number* *Mother*	*Father*	*Ratio* *M/F*	*Per Cent of MT which are MT:Arb (MT:Arb/MT × 100)* *Mother*	*Father*
Mary C.	1–10	350	44	8.0	105	13	8.1	30	30
Jimmy	1–11	85	50	1.7	39	18	2.2	46	36
Lewis	2–11	227	19	11.9	63	12	5.3	28	63
Dutton	3–10	139	29	4.8	50	8	6.2	36	28
Margaret	4–6	282	16	17.6	90	8	11.3	32	50
Maud	5–0	248	17	14.6	96	9	10.7	39	53
Roy	6–2	48	8	6.0	11	5	2.2	23	63
Ben	7–4	57	20	2.8	17	16	1.1	30	80
Ray	7–4	38	21	1.8	6	0	—	16	0
Mary E.	8–7	53	8	6.6	12	5	2.4	22	63
Douglas	9–2	33	16	2.1	18	10	1.8	55	63
Range		33–350	8–50	1.7–17.6	6–105	0–18	0–11.3	16–55	0–80
Median		85	19	6.0	39	9	2.4	30	53

was extremely small in some cases, making the resulting per cents rather undependable, we recomputed the Wilcoxon test without including the data from the three records having the smallest total number of EFU with the father (Mary E., N = 9; Roy, N = 12; Doug, N = 19). With data from these three records excluded, the difference between mothers and fathers in per cent of conflict EFU was significant at the .05 level in favor of the mothers, i.e., the mothers tended to have a higher per cent of conflict EFU. It should be stressed that this measure concerns only the relative *number* of conflict EFU and says nothing about qualitative variations among them. It is possible, for example, that mothers were involved in a conflict with the child relatively more frequently than fathers and yet—or even because—they were less severe in their demands on the child.

The next question which we asked of our data, therefore, concerned the relative frequency with which mothers and fathers resorted to the use of arbitrary or authoritarian methods in their attempts to induce compliance by the child in the conflict EFU. Table 4.2 shows data relevant to this question. In the second section of this table are the total numbers of method transactions using the eight method-classes identified above as arbitrary methods within conflict EFU. Here again the range across subjects is wide, especially for the mothers; the value for the mother with the largest number of arbitrary method transactions was more than 17 times the comparable value for the mother with the smallest number, 105 and 6 respectively.

We noted earlier (Table 4.1) that the M/F ratio for conflict EFU was greater than the M/F ratio for all EFU in eight of the eleven cases, suggesting that fathers were relatively less likely to engage in conflict with their children than were mothers, even taking into account the large difference between mothers and fathers in absolute number of EFU. With this in mind, it is especially noteworthy that an opposite trend is apparent when we compare the M/F ratios on total number of method transactions and number of arbitrary method transactions. In this case, the M/F ratio for number of arbitrary method transactions was *smaller* than that for number of method transactions in eight out of the eleven cases. This suggests that even though fathers tended to have a smaller proportion of conflict EFU than did mothers, they were more likely than mothers to use arbitrary methods to achieve their objectives within the conflict units.

The third section of Table 4.2 describes this same relation in terms of per cent of all method transactions which involved the use of arbitrary methods; data are given separately for mothers and fathers. Here again, however, the low actual frequencies upon which some of the per cents are based require us to interpret the data very cautiously. These figures show the same general trend noted above, i.e., in most cases the per cent of method transactions involving arbitrary methods was higher for fathers than for mothers. A Wilcoxon matched-pairs signed-ranks test showed a significant difference at the .05 level.

Taken together, the trends reported in Table 4.1 and Table 4.2 provide suggestive leads for further research with better samples and controls. These data suggest that mothers proportionately more frequently than fathers set goals for their children which were in some degree at variance with the goals preferred by the children themselves, and that fathers, significantly more than mothers, were disposed to the use of arbitrary methods in dealing with such situations even though they occurred less frequently with fathers than with mothers.

In considering these trends in the data, it occurred to us that the proportion of conflict EFU involving the use of arbitrary methods might be related to the actual number of EFU with the particular parent, i.e., that the high proportion of arbitrary method transactions by fathers may be a function of the small total number of EFU. If fathers had had more EFU, perhaps the proportion of arbitrary method transactions would not have been so high. Our data cannot answer this question fully but we did check the correlation between total number of EFU and per cent arbitrary method transactions. A nonsignificant negative trend (tau = —.345) was found for fathers, and no relationship was found for mothers. Apparently there is no simple relation between number of EFU and tendency to use arbitrary methods in conflict EFU.

Finally, we turn to the data on the response of the child to the parent's attempt to control his behavior. Table 4.3 shows the results of categorizing the child's response according to his readiness to comply with the parent's demand. The first section shows for mothers and fathers respectively the number of conflict EFU. These figures provided the base for the per cents in the other columns. It should be noted that the number of conflict EFU was sometimes so small that per cents based upon them are hardly meaningful. This is particularly true for the fathers for whom the range was from six to 27 EFU:Cf. With such small numbers, it is questionable even to report per cents based on them but we have done so in the interest of completeness. We will limit our discussion largely to the data for mothers where the *N*'s are more adequate.

In general, the mothers tended to elicit compliance from their children in two-thirds or more of the conflict EFU. In 65 per cent of these cases, on the average, compliance was immediate. As in the results reported earlier, there were marked differences across the several records in the data on compliance; immediate compliance ranges from 26 to 55 per cent of conflict EFU; delayed compliance ranges from 17 to 39 per cent of conflict EFU; noncompliance ranges from 9 to 34 per cent of conflict EFU.

We were interested in the relation between the use of arbitrary methods and compliance by the child. For mothers in the conflict situation the tau rank correlation coefficient between per cent of method transactions involving one of the eight arbitrary methods and per cent of conflict EFU in which the child showed immediate compliance is .236 which is not significant;

TABLE 4.3
Per Cent of all Conflict EFU in which the Child Showed Immediate Compliance, Delayed Compliance, and Noncompliance[a]

SUBJECT	AGE	*Number of Conflict EFU* *Mother*	*Father*	*Per Cent Immediate Compliance* *Mother*	*Father*	*Per Cent Delayed Compliance* *Mother*	*Father*	*Per Cent Noncompliance* *Mother*	*Father*
Mary C.	1–10	166	22	37	27	24	27	33	23
Jimmy	1–11	55	27	55	67	20	15	16	11
Lewis	2–11	120	13	31	46	38	15	22	15
Dutton	3–10	94	21	39	57	31	14	21	19
Margaret	4–6	172	10	33	30	24	20	34	20
Maud	5–0	134	11	26	18	25	9	31	55
Roy	6–2	34	6	50	50	26	33	15	0
Ben	7–4	43	16	42	38	21	13	12	19
Ray	7–4	23	13	26	31	39	23	9	23
Mary E.	8–7	30	7	47	43	17	43	17	14
Douglas	9–2	26	9	54	11	19	44	15	0
Range		23–172	6–27	26–55	11–67	17–39	9–44	9–34	0–55
Median		55	13	39	38	24	20	17	19

[a] Per cents do not always total 100 owing to omission from the table of EFU which could not be judged on compliance.

and there is a nonsignificant negative relation (tau = —.327) with delayed compliance. These findings suggest a trend toward more prompt compliance when the mother uses an arbitrary method. The picture is further blurred, however, by the additional finding of a weak positive relation between per cent of method transactions involving an arbitrary method and per cent of EFU in which the child showed noncompliance. The tau here is .218 which is not significant at the .05 level. One might suppose that when compliance occurred, the use of arbitrary methods by the mother was associated with a tendency to comply without delay, but that the tendency to comply or not comply *per se* was not influenced by the mother's use of arbitrary methods.

We think it is not an insignificant finding in itself to establish that the number of conflict EFU with fathers during the course of an ordinary day was generally so small that meaningful comparisons could not be made in terms of the child's relative readiness to comply to the father vs. the mother.

We tested the relation between compliance and age by means of the data of Table 4.3. The tau coefficients for these data (mothers only) are .109, —.218, and —.400 for immediate compliance, delayed compliance, and noncompliance, respectively, none of which is statistically significant. There is a trend which suggests that the older children were *less* likely than the younger children to delay complying with their mother's bidding and even less likely to refuse to comply at all. One might say that the older children, by complying more promptly than younger children and refusing to comply less often, showed a greater degree of socialization than the younger children who more often complied less promptly or refused to comply at all.

Summary

Our findings support the idea that mothers play a predominant role in the socialization process and suggest moreover that there are very marked differences in the social-psychological situations of individual children in this respect. Mothers were involved in approximately four times as many EFU with their children as were fathers but wide variation across children in absolute number of EFU was clear.

Similarly the analysis of conflict EFU revealed a larger number of conflict units with mothers than with fathers and a wide variation in this respect across children. Among mothers, those having a large number of EFU also had a large number of units in which conflict occurred.

Fathers, in addition to playing a relatively minor role vis-à-vis their children, were found to be less often in conflict with them. Although this does not mean necessarily that fathers are less important in the socialization process, it led us to a closer examination of our data on the specific methods used by the parent and on the readiness of the child to comply with parental demands.

We found that despite the fathers' less frequent involvement in conflict they were significantly more frequently disposed than mothers to use arbitrary methods in an attempt to gain compliance from the child. In comparing total number of EFU with use of arbitrary methods, fathers with low EFU tended to use proportionately more arbitrary methods than did fathers with higher total number EFU, whereas mothers' use of arbitrary methods was not significantly correlated with number of EFU.

With regard to the success of parents in their attempts to elicit compliance from their children we found that mothers elicited compliance in two-thirds of the conflict units and that marked differences obtained across children on the compliance variable. Where compliance was the response of the child, he may have complied immediately or after some delay. Our results showed the use of arbitrary methods to be associated with a tendency to comply without delay, but that the tendency to comply or not comply was not significantly associated with the use of arbitrary methods.

It is a significant finding that the number of conflict EFU for fathers in an ordinary day was so small as not to afford a meaningful analysis of the breakdown into compliance due to the small frequencies falling in the subcategories.

Finally, our findings relating compliance by the child in conflict with parents to age of the child suggested that older children exhibit a greater degree of socialization than younger children in that the former are less likely to delay complying with their mothers' bidding and even less likely to refuse to comply at all.

CHAPTER 5

The Social Contacts of Some Midwest Children with Their Parents and Teachers

ARTHUR J. DYCK

THIS INVESTIGATION identifies a unit of social interaction, termed a social contact; it investigates with great thoroughness the structural and dynamic properties of this unit; and, in terms of the social contact, the study explores the frequency and some of the attributes of children's social behavior vis-à-vis their parents and teachers. This research is a good example of the profitable wedding of theory and technique in the earliest stages of the investigation of the stream of behavior, and it demonstrates how even small molar behavior units can have a complex structure which, when known, contributes greatly to the richness of the information the unit provides about the behavior stream.

Arthur J. Dyck holds the M.A. degree in both Psychology and Philosophy from The University of Kansas. At the present time he is studying Philosophy at Harvard University.

THIS STUDY was primarily concerned with the social interaction of children and their parents, and secondarily with teacher-pupil interaction. The inquiry had three main purposes: (1) to identify a unit of social interaction within the behavior stream, (2) to investigate, by means of this unit, certain aspects of the relationships between children and their mothers, fathers, and teachers, and thus (3) to explore some of the scientific uses of ecological data as they occur in the specimen record.

A Preview of Method

The primary data were day-long specimen records of twelve Midwest children; six preschool children, and six school-age children. In addition, shorter specimen records from the school days of fifteen other Midwest children provided data about teacher-child interactions for comparison with the main body of parent-child data. The subjects of the study are described elsewhere in this volume (Appendix 1.1).

A specimen record describes the stream of ongoing behavior in which a child is engaged during the course of his waking hours. Since this study was focused upon the child's interaction with other persons, it was necessary first of all that we identify *units* of interaction with other persons and, in this way, separate such social interaction from the rest of the behavior in the specimen record. Our task, however, was not finished at this point. We were interested in specifying the extent to which the child interacted with specific persons such as his mother, his father, his teacher, and his friends. This meant that we had to be able to state exactly where one interaction began and ended. In other words, we required that a unit of social interaction have specific criteria. We called the unit of social interaction which we identified the *social contact* and, by means of it, we were able to obtain measures of the amount of social interaction taking place between children and various associates. Here, in outline, are the problems we investigated by means of the social contact unit, arranged according to three sets of variables:

A. *Variables Associated with Persons*

1. Frequency of mothers' and fathers' social contact with children.
   a. Frequency over the whole day. The relative frequency of contacts of mothers and fathers with their children provided evidence regarding the common notion, expressed by Mead (1930) and Baldwin (1955), among others, that mothers have the major responsibility in child-rearing.
   b. Frequency of social contact when both the mother and father were present. Comparing the relative frequency of the mother's and the father's contacts when both were at home, roughly equalized the opportunity the parents had for interaction with the child. The data bear upon the view expressed by Mead (1930) that American fathers are not interested in matters of child-rearing.
2. Frequency of parents' contacts with children of different ages. Data presented by Barker and Wright (1955) suggest that certain differences in the behavior of parents vis-à-vis their children are related to the ages of the children, and Baldwin (1955) states that the behavior of parents must change with the age of the child if it is to continue to meet the cultural prescription of the parents' role. A subordinate, related issue was the frequency of parents' contacts with preschool and school children.
3. Frequency of parents' contacts with boys and girls.
4. Frequency of teachers' and parents' contacts with children.

B. *Variables Associated with Behavior Occurring within the Social Contact Unit*

1. The originator of the contact. The relative frequency with which the children and the parents originated social contacts provides information about such important issues as parents' awareness and concern

for the needs, wants and activities of the child (their "child-centeredness"), and about the children's needs and their freedom to interact with their parents.

2. The *raison d'être* of the contact. As part of the criteria for judging the beginning point of a social contact unit we specified 12 different originating grounds or *raisons d'être* for social interaction. These *raisons d'être* provided data concerning important qualitative differences between social contact units.

C. *Variables Associated with Situations*

Five situations that are common to Midwest and the larger American culture, were identified and a rating of the "ritual-relatedness" of the social contacts occurring within them was developed. By means of this measure, we were able to study the extent to which parents carried out the "demands" of these culturally important situations. The resulting data bear upon the common view, expressed, for example, by Brim (1957), that the parent-child system performs a function for society at large, and by Baldwin (1955) that parent behavior may be seen as an adjustment of the adult personality to cultural demands.

The questions investigated and the social contact unit by means of which this was done, have carried out the third major purpose of our present study, namely, to explore some of the uses of ecological data.

The Social Contact

The social contact serves to differentiate social interaction into units having determinate durations; it is therefore a useful tool for analyzing records of a person's stream of ongoing behavior. By means of the social contact unit it is possible to make statements about the amount of social interaction in a behavioral record, and to make quantitative comparisons of varieties of social interaction.

Our definitions of social interaction and of the social contact unit constitute an attempt to describe the structure of naturally occurring social behavior as it is revealed in a specimen record. The detailed instructions for identifying social contact units within specimen records are given in Appendix 5.1. Here we shall discuss these definitions and criteria, and give a rationale for our belief that the social contact is experienced as a unit.

Social interaction occurs when an action by one person is in some way responded to by another person, when each person is aware of the other and of the action in question; and when the action responded to is directed to or is about the person who is responding.

Social interaction is not limited to the direct attempts of a person to induce some kind of response from another person or group of persons. In instances where one person talks about another person, and the person being talked about responds in some way (listens, watches, etc.), social interaction is taking place provided, of course, that the person who is talking about another person is aware that the person being talked about is present, i.e., within communication distance and so can hear what is being said. It is sometimes difficult to judge whether all the conditions for social interaction are fulfilled by certain actions described within a record of ongoing behavior, and, where such a behavioral record does not give sufficient evidence that the conditions for social interaction have been fulfilled, we have excluded the behavior from consideration as social interaction.

By so defining social interaction, we are able, as analysts of specimen records, to differentiate social interaction from all other forms of behavior. However, social interaction comprises quite a large portion of most children's behavior. It is not uncommon for a child to engage in social interaction over fairly long periods of time, interspersed by momentary diversions from it; although, on occasion, there are also long interims between one period of social interaction and another. Even the social interaction which persists more or less continuously through a given period of time is not necessarily, as far as we are concerned, homogeneous and all of one piece. The social interaction of a given child is not only interrupted by behavior that is not classifiable as social interaction, but it also varies with respect to the persons with whom the child is interacting, the originating grounds of the interaction, and, the topics of the conversation or other social exchange carried on by those who are socially interacting. When the social interaction of a given person changes in any of the three ways just enumerated, we are willing to assume that social interaction has changed in a way that is of psychological significance to the interacting persons. Our criteria for marking a social contact and counting it as one social interaction are based upon these very changes in the personnel, the originating grounds, and topics during the course of ongoing social interaction.

The following is a very brief excerpt of social interaction taken from *One Boy's Day* (Barker & Wright, 1951a, p. 32) which is more or less continuous in time and yet, on the basis of our criteria, comprises three units of social interaction: It is such units we call social contacts. In our sample excerpt, the boy being observed is seven-year-old Raymond Birch who is out in the yard of his home watching his father cast with a fishing rod equipped with a reel and line.

The units of social interaction, the social contacts, marked off by the brackets to the left of the quoted material, possess a certain kind of psychological unity which we shall now define.

The social contact is a unit of social interaction which contains within its boundaries (1) one subject, (2) one agent, (3) one *raison d'être,* and (4) one continuous topic. The subject is the person whose behavior is recorded and whose social interaction is being studied. An agent is a person with whom the subject is interacting; an agent is sometimes called the environmental person. One *raison d'être* means one originating ground for social interaction; twelve different grounds have been specified for use in

Raymond said, "Hey, daddy, what's under this?" He pointed to a slanting embankment next to the house.

His father said, "Well, I guess the drain comes out under there."

7:48 As Mr. Birch cast again, the plug came off. He said, "Well, I lost the plug," and added, "we'll have to find it."

Raymond immediately ran down toward the barn looking for the plug.

His father walked toward the barn to search for it.

7:49 Raymond picked up a big rusty spike and said, "Here's a weight, daddy." This was offered as a joke.

Mr. Birch answered mildly, "That would be just a little heavy." Just then he found the plug.

discriminating and describing the social contact. One continuous topic refers to a topic which one person (the agent or subject) presents as a unit and to which the other person (the agent or subject) reacts as a unit.

The psychological unity of a social contact within a person's behavior stream consists in there being only one agent, one *raison d'être,* and one topic within its boundaries. A change in an agent or a *raison d'être* or a topic is assumed to be a psychologically significant change in the ongoing flow of social interaction and any one of these changes is sufficient to mark the beginning of a social contact. The unity of the social contact is defined by the unity of the agent, the *raison d'être,* and the topic included within its boundaries; these characteristics are the major criteria used by anyone who marks the social contacts which occur in a behavioral record. The criteria for marking the social contact, are further clarified and elaborated in Appendix 5.1.

An assumption made by psychologists and also by laymen is that one's social interaction with some person "X" differs in important ways from one's social interaction with some other person "Y." Mothers, fathers, teachers, children, and so forth, vary, both as to the role they play and, of course, as to their psychological characteristics. It seems highly appropriate, therefore, to divide social interaction into units which contain the subject being studied and *one agent.* By so doing, we preserve one feature of the psychological unity of a social contact, and we also obtain the frequency of social contacts associated with each of the agents who engage the subject of our investigation in social interaction.

Social interaction may originate from the wishes, needs, plans, intentions, aspirations, and so forth of the agent or it may originate from those of the subject. Certainly, psychologists and laymen would agree that the originating sources of social interaction are important factors in determining how social interaction is experienced. Educators, for example, have made a major issue out of the contrast between approaching the child with a lesson completely prepared in advance, especially one that ignores the special needs or wants of the child, and approaching the child with questions to elicit his needs or wants, and building the lesson around these. Our second criterion therefore, for judging where one social contact ends and another begins during the course of social interaction, is concerned with its various originating grounds: We have specified twelve such originating grounds for social interaction which we call *raisons d'être.*

The *raisons d'être* describe the overt, molar behavior of agents. They indicate (A) whether the agents are seen as coming to the child on grounds of their own choosing, independently of what the child is doing, wishing, asking, demanding, or (B) whether the agents are responding to the child's immediate deeds, wishes, questions, demands, and so forth. Further, the *raisons d'être* identify five kinds of behavior, A, i.e., reasons why agents originate social interaction with the subject, and they identify seven kinds of behavior, B, i.e., responses of agents to grounds which reside in what the child is saying or doing or in the way the child appears, at the moment, to the agent. These twelve *raisons d'être* describe different psychological relationships which may obtain between a given subject and the agent with whom he is interacting. Or, to put it in another way, the *raisons d'être* depict twelve distinguishable perceptions which the subject may have of the agent, five of them associated with the agent when he originates social interaction, seven of them associated with the agent when he reacts to the subject who is in the agent's immediate presence.

When the agent is the originating source of social interaction (behavior A), the subject with whom he is interacting, may perceive him in the five ways listed below: a detailed description of each *raison d'être* is provided in Appendix 5.1.

The subject sees the agent:

IA 1 As someone who wants, or otherwise seeks, an activity from me (i.e., the subject).

IA 2 As someone who wants, or otherwise seeks an action with me (i.e., the subject).

IA 3 As someone who wants, or otherwise seeks to present himself, or something in unit with himself, to me (i.e., the subject). See Heider (1958) for an exposition of the concept "in unit with."

IA 4 As someone who wants, or otherwise tries to induce me (i.e., the subject) to present myself, or something in unit with me, to him.

IA 5 As someone who presents me (i.e., the subject) or something in unit with me, to someone else.

When the subject is the originating source of social interaction (behavior B), the agent may be perceived by the subject in the following seven ways:

IB 1 As someone who responds to my (i.e., the subject's) expressed desire that he act for me.

IB 2 As someone who responds to my (i.e., the subject's) expressed desire that he act with me.

IB 3 As someone who responds to me (i.e., the subject) presenting myself, or something in unit with me, to him.

IB 4 As someone who responds to me (i.e., the subject), or something in unit with me, prior to, or without any explicit request from me so to respond.

IB 5 As someone who responds to what I (i.e., the subject) am doing, about to do, or requesting to do.

IB 6 As someone who responds to my (i.e., the subject's) expressed desire that he present information to me.

IB 7 As someone who responds to my (i.e., the subject's) expressed desires, of whatever sort, by discernibly ignoring them.

All social interaction, as we have defined it, takes place within the immediate presence of the participants and hence, these *raisons d'être* occur only under such circumstances. For example, if the subject, a child, were accidentally locked into an upstairs room, and its mother, washing in the cellar, could not hear the child's cries for her help, this would not constitute social interaction and, therefore, the mother would not be judged to be ignoring the child, as defined in the IB 7 category, even though the child's private perception of the mother may very well be that she is someone who is "ignoring my expressed desires that she act on my behalf." We judge that an agent is perceived as ignoring or behaving in the other ways described by the *raisons d'être,* when it is possible for an analyst of a behavioral record to judge that ignoring, or one of the other eleven sorts of behavior attributed to agents, is actually occurring. Our *raisons d'être* are intended to provide the basis for reliable judgments of what the agent is doing in coming to or responding to the subject.

We believe that the twelve classes of agent behavior represented by the *raisons d'être* comprise twelve psychologically distinguishable points of origin for social interaction. Let us exemplify some of the sorts of things the *raison d'être* categories separate from one another by reference to the sequence of social interaction between Raymond Birch and his father, cited above (see p. 82). There is only one agent, Mr. Birch, in this segment of social interaction so it is one unit in this respect. When we look, however, for the grounds for the social interaction between the boy and his father within the confines of our excerpt, we find three such grounds or *raisons d'être.* The first *raison d'être* constitutes a "Responding to a request for information" (IB 6), for Raymond asks his father about a certain embankment next to the house and the father responds to his question. Immediately subsequent to this social contact, Mr. Birch loses the plug with which he is casting and he approaches Raymond with the proposition of hunting it together. A new social contact has begun since Mr. Birch provides a new ground for social interaction, namely, that of "Seeking an activity with the subject" (IA 2), the second *raison d'être* in this particular interaction sequence. Just before the social interaction of "looking for the plug together" has ended, Raymond introduces a third ground for social interaction, the third *raison d'être,* when he picks up a rusty spike and "jokes" with his father by suggesting that he use it as a weight; here the father is "Responding to the overt expression of the subject" (IB 3). By means of our *raison d'être* categories, we have divided this more or less temporally continuous social interaction into three units (social contacts).

These three units correspond roughly to three experiences which Raymond had while interacting with his father, experiences he would describe in a diary, a letter, or in a conversation by saying: "I learned from my dad what that embankment is next to our house; I also helped dad look for his "plug" when he lost it; and, do you know, while we looked for it, I pulled a good joke on him—I told him to use a big, rusty spike, that I found, for a weight and he said it was too heavy." In effect, we are trying to divide social interaction into the "units of experience" so that a subject has as many social contacts as he has "things happening to him" in the course of all his social interaction. He may forget many of the things that happen to him, and many of these events may be of minor importance to him, but, nonetheless, they are of the sort that he can report when he remembers some single event or incident of social interaction. We say *can report* because we know that anyone may well lump all his social interaction together into chunks of various sizes as when someone says, "I heard nothing but good things today," or "all my contacts with my teachers have been pleasant." The purpose of all the criteria for the social contact, including those for the *raisons d'être,* is to differentiate social interaction into the smallest possible units that have any psychological significance for the participants.

Up to this point in our discussion, we have mentioned our reasons for having one agent and one *raison d'être* per contact. These same reasons apply to the criteria we use for judging a change in the topic of social interaction. Usually we do not have to make any judgment about changes in topics once we have made our judgments about changes in agents and *raisons d'être,* but when we do, we are trying to discriminate between things that would be distinguished by the participants in a sequence of social interaction. Returning once more to our sample excerpt from the Raymond Birch record (see p. 82 above), we note such "topics" as the "embankment" the "plug," and the "rusty spike." Perhaps the "rusty spike" is included under the topic of the "plug" but this is one of those instances in which we do not have to make this judgment; the *raisons d'être* have already divided the social interaction into three units, and we have judged that there are no further divisions possible on the basis of any of our criteria. The topic is, essentially, the thing or event around which the social interaction revolves and, since it is what we can recall about a conversation, it apparently forms a unit of some kind in our memory. We may remember, for example, that we talked to our friend about the weather and about hydrogen bombs. Topics fairly often persist through changes in social contacts based upon changes in *raisons d'être* or agents. This is why we seldom have to judge a shift in the topic of social interaction. Nevertheless, the judgment must be made sometimes in order to have each social contact singular with respect to its topic. As with agents and *raisons d'être,* we are assuming the psychological significance of differentiating them in a way that closely approximates what we normally experience.

Social contacts have been marked on the sample specimen record in Appendix 1.2 for further exemplification.

The Ritual-relatedness Rating

Once social contacts have been identified within a record of behavior, they can be described by any number of further ratings to answer various questions about social interaction. The ritual-relatedness rating is one such rating; it is independent of the marking of contacts. Instructions for making the ritual-relatedness ratings are given in Appendix 5.2.

By means of this rating, it is possible to answer a number of questions about the extent to which social contacts reflect the necessity to carry out the ritual associated with situations (behavior settings) which are an integral part of a given culture. In this particular study, we examined mothers and fathers with respect to their presence in five "cultural situations," and with respect to the ritual-relatedness of their social contacts with their children within these situations. This gives us a picture of the extent to which mothers and fathers are bearers of the culture and how they compare with one another in this regard. We asked these same questions about teachers in the classroom situation and compared them with mothers and fathers.

We selected these five cultural situations as being common to all Midwest homes and as having certain ritual connected with them: (1) Getting up and ready for the day; (2) breakfast or the morning meal; (3) lunch or the noon meal; (4) supper or the evening meal; and (5) getting ready for and going to bed. The contacts that occurred within the boundaries of these situations were judged as to whether or not they were related to the ritual, the ritual being any activity perceived as appropriate, necessary, and fitting to the situation in question. Contacts were considered to be ritual-related if they included ritual behavior *per se* or if they referred to the ritual that was part of the situation within which such contacts took place. The criteria used to delimit the boundaries of cultural situations and to judge whether contacts within them were ritual-related appear in Appendix 5.2 in full detail.

We chose these five cultural situations, and no others, because they have discernible and rather well-known ritual connected with them. Furthermore these situations existed for all Midwest children used in our study, and they exist for practically every American child. Though the actual ritual carried out in these situations or behavior settings varies somewhat, the rating is designed simply to designate whether or not a given social contact is concerned with the ritual, whatever it may be.

The Accuracy of Social Contact Identifications and Ratings

Two analysts identified and categorized the social contacts reported in the 12 specimen records. The accuracy with which this was done was checked by a third independent worker; he worked with at least 5 per cent of each of the records in sections selected at random. The independent analyst received no training or practice in the task, and he did not discuss the criteria with anyone, as it was the intention to discover the adequacy with which the system of identifying and categorizing social contacts was communicated by the written description alone. The work of the independent analyst checked not only the accuracy with which the criteria could be applied, but also unreliability due to carelessness, fatigue, and satiation at all periods during the extensive task of analyzing some 4,712 typewritten pages of records.

Agreement checks were made of four judgments. First, the contacts were identified, and if there was disagreement at this point the other ratings were not investigated. However, if there was agreement on identification, the degree of agreement regarding the originator of the contact was checked. If there was disagreement concerning the originator of the contact, the work of checking rater agreement stopped at this point. But if there was agreement on social contact origination, the *raison d'être* and ritual-relatedness ratings were checked for agreement. A substantial number of all the contacts were investigated in this way: 374 or 8 per cent for identification of the social contact unit, 307 or 7 per cent for origination of the unit, 279 or 6 per cent for *raison d'être* ratings, and 300 or 6 per cent for ritual-relatedness.

The "per cent accuracy" with which social contacts were identified was estimated for each record by the special method used by Barker and Wright (1955, p. 271). To measure the accuracy of the other three judgments, the per cent of agreed upon judgments was calculated. The resulting ranges and means for the twelve records are as follows:

JUDGMENT	PER CENT ACCURACY	
	Range	*Mean*
Identification of social contact	75–95	85
Originator of social contact	85–100	92
Raison d'être of social contact	65–93	78
Ritual-relatedness of social contact	82–100	93

The details concerning the methods and results of the agreement checks are to be found in Dyck (1958).

Since this is not a theory-oriented study with specific predictions, all the probabilities reported in what follows are two-tailed.

The Frequency of Social Contacts

The number of social contacts each child had with both parents, and with the mother and with the father separately, are presented in Table 5.1. In this table, the children are listed in order of age. These data show that the twelve children engaged in a total of 4,723 social contacts with their parents during the course of the 12 days. The number of contacts per child ranged from 883 from Mary C. to 56 for Claire (whose father was not present during the day the specimen record was made). Mary C., the youngest child, had a contact with her mother or her father once every minute, on the average; Douglas, the oldest child whose parents were both present during the day, had a social contact with one of his parents every nine minutes, on the average.

The data of Table 5.1 reveal also that the contacts with mothers exceeded those with fathers for each of the eleven subjects whose parents were both present. This difference is significant beyond the .01 level (Wilcoxon matched-pairs, signed-ranks test). The total number of contacts with fathers was 23 per cent of the number of contacts with mothers; for individual children, fathers' contacts ranged from 77 per cent of the mothers' for Jimmy to 6 per cent for Margaret.

Data on the number of contacts with parents when both were present with the child are given in Table 5.2. When both parents were at home and equally accessible to the child, there were, in all but one of the cases (Mary C.), more contacts with mothers than with fathers ($p < .01$). The total number of contacts with fathers under these conditions was 61 per cent of the number of contacts with mothers, ranging from 172 per cent for Mary C. to 14 per cent for Roy.

The number of contacts with the parents singly and together decreased as the age of the children increased; the rho correlations between the age of the child and the number of contacts with the mothers was —.82, with the fathers —.87, and with both parents —.85 (in all cases $p < .01$). Negative correlations were obtained, as well when both parents were accessible to the child; the rho correlation with the mothers was —.59 ($p < .05$), with the fathers —.79 ($p < .01$), and with both parents —.85 ($p < .01$).

The ratio of the mothers' social contacts to those of the fathers was not related to the age of the child. This was true for all contacts, and for those contacts occurring when both parents were accessible to the child.

There were striking differences in the number of social contacts of preschool and school-age children with their parents. No school-age child had as many contacts with both parents or with the mother alone as any pre-

TABLE 5.1
Number of Social Contacts with Parents

	SUBJECT	SEX	AGE	Length of Record Hrs. Min.	NUMBER OF CONTACTS Both Parents	Mother	Father
Preschool Children	Mary C.	F	1–10	14:45	883	747	136
	Jimmy	M	1–11	12:50	560	317	243
	Lewis	M	2–11	14:15	641	523	118
	Dutton	M	3–10	14:10	486	389	97
	Margaret	F	4–6	14:17	653	615	38
	Maud	F	5–0	11:18	669	599	70
School-age Children	Roy	M	6–2	13:31	108	95	13
	Ray	M	7–4	13:33	206	119	87
	Ben	M	7–4	12:27	187	152	35
	Mary E.	F	8–7	14:25	179	168	11
	Douglas	M	9–2	14:17	95	65	30
	Claire	F	10–9	14:20	56	56	*Not present*
	Totals				4723	3845	878

TABLE 5.2
Number of Social Contacts with Parents During Periods When Both Parents Were With the Child

	SUBJECT	NUMBER OF CONTACTS Both Parents	Mother	Father
Preschool Children	Mary C.	215	79	136
	Jimmy	429	232	197
	Lewis	229	123	106
	Dutton	279	220	59
	Margaret	194	156	38
	Maud	214	147	67
School-age Children	Roy	40	35	5
	Ray	186	99	87
	Ben	149	114	35
	Mary E.	26	15	11
	Douglas	66	36	30
	Claire	*Father Not Present*		
	Totals	2027	1256	771

school child; by the Mann-Whitney test the difference is highly significant in both cases ($p < .002$). There was some overlap in the number of contacts with fathers by preschool and school children, but nevertheless, the contacts of fathers with preschool children were more numerous ($p < .018$).

No sex differences in the number of social contacts with parents were found. A Mann-Whitney test applied to the difference in the total parent contacts of the seven boys and five girls yielded a nonsignificant difference.

The Origination of Social Contacts

The number of social contacts originated by each child, and by his mother and his father are recorded in Table 5.3. This table does not include the 38 contacts with the mothers and the 27 contacts with the fathers, the origination of which it was impossible to judge. We note that every child except Claire originated more contacts with his parents than the parents originated with the child; the differences are highly significant for all parent-child comparisons ($p < .002$, using the Sign test). Children originated 66 per cent of all parent-child contacts; for individual children this ranged from 50 per cent for Claire's contacts with her mother to 84 per cent of Maud's contacts with her father.

Mothers originated a much greater number of contacts than fathers, 1,240 as compared with 308. But mothers did not originate a greater proportion of their social contacts than fathers, mothers originating 33 per cent of all mother-child contacts, and fathers originating 36 per cent of all father-child contacts.

Parents differed greatly from teachers in the extent to which they originated social contacts with children. Whereas parents originated an average of 36 per cent of their contacts with the six school-age subjects, teachers originated an average of 73 per cent of their contacts with the 15 Midwest children in our sample. This difference is highly significant ($p < .002$ using the Mann-Whitney test).

THE ORIGINATING GROUND OF SOCIAL CONTACTS

Table 5.4 records the various *raisons d'être,* in the order of their relative frequency among the social contacts of the parents with their children. Responding to the activity of the subject (IB 5) was the *raison d'être* occurring most frequently, accounting for about one in four of all parent-child social contacts. Seeking an activity on the part of the subject (IA 1) was the next most frequent originating ground for social interaction, comprising about one in six of all contacts. Responding to the overt expression of the subject (IB 3) constituted about one in seven of all contacts. Over 50 per cent of all parent-child contacts fell within these three *raison d'être* categories.

Since mothers had a greater number of contacts with children than fathers, we would expect them to exceed fathers in the frequency of con-

TABLE 5.3
Origination of Social Contacts with Parents

	SUBJECT	CONTACTS WITH MOTHER *Originated by* *Mother*	*Child*	CONTACTS WITH FATHER *Originated by* *Father*	*Child*
Preschool Children	Mary C.	268	476	53	82
	Jimmy	99	206	107	127
	Lewis	157	349	28	86
	Dutton	150	236	35	52
	Margaret	197	415	15	23
	Maud	168	431	11	59
School-age Children	Roy	25	70	5	8
	Ray	52	67	33	54
	Ben	54	98	6	28
	Mary E.	50	117	5	6
	Douglas	20	45	10	19
	Claire	28	28	*Father not present*	
	Totals	1268	2538	308	544

TABLE 5.4
Parents' Social Contacts in *Raison d'Être* Categories
The Frequency of Social Contacts Occurring in Each Category

RAISON D'ÊTRE CATEGORY	*Category Number*	*Frequency of Contacts*
Responding to the activity of the subject	IB5	1151
Seeking an activity on the part of the subject	IA1	739
Responding to the overt expression of the subject	IB3	637
Responding to the subject's request for information	IB6	409
Responding to subject's request for activity on the part of the agent	IB1	404
Seeking an expression on the part of the subject	IA4	327
Seeking to express oneself to the subject	IA3	258
Responding to the state of the subject	IB4	206
Failing to respond	IB7	181
Seeking an activity with the subject	IA2	130
Expressing oneself about the subject to someone other than the subject	IA5	122
Responding to the subject's request for activity with the subject	IB2	96
Cannot judge		63
Total		4723

tacts within the different *raison d'être* categories. Using the Wilcoxon matched-pairs signed-ranks test, we discovered that mothers' contacts exceed fathers' contacts significantly ($p < .01$) in 9 of the 12 *raisons d'être.* The three exceptions were (1) seeking an activity with the subject (IA 2), (2) seeking to express oneself to the subject (IA 3) (3) responding to a request of the subject for activity with the agent (IB 2); mothers and fathers did not differ significantly with respect to these three *raisons d'être.*

When, however, we consider percentage of contacts, mothers and fathers did not differ significantly on 11 of the 12 *raisons d'être.* The Wilcoxon matched-pairs signed-ranks test showed that mothers and fathers differ significantly only with respect to category IA 3, seeking to express oneself to the subject, for a greater per cent of the fathers' contacts were of this type ($p < .02$).

Teachers differed from parents in the way their social contacts with children were distributed among the various *raisons d'être.* The parent-child contacts of the sample of 6 school-age children and the teacher-child contacts of the separate sample of 15 school-age children were compared on the several *raison d'être* categories. The differences found with the Mann-Whitney test, based on an n_1 of six and an n_2 of 15, were as follows:

1. Teacher (Te) exceeded parent (Pa) in the per cent of their contacts:
   a. in which they seek an activity on the part of the child (IA 1).
      Pa = 20.75, Te = 55.86; $p < .002$
2. Parents exceeded teachers in the per cent of their contacts:
   a. in which they seek an activity with the child (IA 2).
      Pa = 0.80, Te = 0.18; $p < .02$
   b. in which they express themselves about the child (IA 5).
      Pa = 2.80, Te = 1.76; $p < .05$
   c. in which they respond to a request of the child for activity on their part (IB 1).
      Pa = 5.00, Te = 1.55; $p < .02$
   d. in which they respond to a request of the child for activity with them (IB 2).
      Pa = 2.25, Te = 0.00; $p < .02$
   e. in which they respond to the overt expression of the child (IB 3).
      Pa = 16.38, Te = 4.62; $p < .002$
   f. in which they respond to the state of the child (IB 4).
      Pa = 4.61, Te = 0.15; $p < .002$
   g. in which they respond to the activity of the child (IB 5).
      Pa = 28.61, Te = 16.40; $p < .05$
   h. in which they fail to respond to the child (IB 7).
      Pa = 1.64, Te = 0.15; $p < .02$
3. Parents and teachers did not differ with respect to the per cent of their contacts:
   a. in which they seek to express themselves to the child (IA 3).
      Pa = 5.36, Te = 8.15; $p > .05$

b. in which they seek an expression on the part of the child (IA 4).
Pa = 5.85, Te = 5.97; $p > .05$

c. in which they respond to a request for information (IB 6).
Pa = 5.57, Te = 4.31; $p > .05$

The Ritual-relatedness of Social Contacts

Getting up and getting ready for the day, having breakfast, having lunch, having supper, and going to bed were the five cultural situations common to all Midwest homes in which ritual-related behavior was studied. The contacts that occurred within the boundaries of these situations were judged as to whether or not they were "appropriate, necessary and fitting" to the cultural situation, and, those that were, are called ritual-related contacts.

Thirty-eight per cent (1,800) of the parent-child contacts during the days of the 12 subjects occurred in the five cultural situations, and 51 per cent (919) of these contacts were ritual-related.

Fathers were present in 67 per cent and mothers in 93 per cent of the cultural situations. A father was alone with his child only once in a cultural situation and mothers were alone with their children in cultural situations on 15 occasions. Within the cultural situations, mothers had more contacts with children than fathers, but mothers and fathers did not differ in the proportion of their contacts which were ritual-related: 51 per cent of the mother-child contacts and 52 per cent of the father-child contacts were related to the ritual of the five cultural situations.

The cultural situation in which both parents were simultaneously present most frequently was the supper situation, both parents being present in ten of the twelve supper situations. In each of these, mothers exceeded fathers in the number of ritual-related contacts ($p < .01$). In fact, 73 per cent of all ritual-related supper contacts were mother-child contacts.

Ritual-related contacts were investigated further to discover who originated them. For all 12 subjects studied, mothers originated more of their ritual-related than of their nonritual-related contacts with the children. On the average, mothers originated 46 per cent of their ritual-related contacts and 31 per cent of their nonritual-related contacts ($p < .002$). However, fathers did not significantly differ in the extent to which they originated their ritual-related and their nonritual-related contacts.

Teachers' ritual-related contacts are those contacts within the school classroom which carry on, or in some way refer to, the business of the classroom. Using once again the data for the 15 Midwest school-age children and the data for the 6 school-age children in our present study, we discovered that, on the average, 93 per cent of the teachers' contacts, and 46 per cent of the parents' contacts were ritual-related ($p < .002$). Within culture-related situations, teachers devote themselves more exclusively to the immediate demands of the situation than do parents.

A Discussion of the Results

We turn now to a discussion of the results as they relate to some of the existing generalizations about parent behavior.

There exists, first of all, the very widely-held notion that mothers have the major responsibility in rearing children. Mead (1930) and Baldwin (1955), among others, have expressed this view. Our data, in general, substantiated this generalization. We found that the mother always exceeded the father in the number of contacts with the child throughout the day, and when both parents were present with the child, the mother still had more contacts than the father in 10 out of the 11 cases analyzed.

The mothers' greater share of responsibility for child-rearing was exhibited in still another way in that mothers were almost always present for what we have called cultural situations. We found what is generally reported and believed to be true, namely, that mothers very largely see to it that the children get dressed and ready for the day, eat the "right" food in the "proper" manner, get to sleep at the "appropriate" time after carefully washing, and so forth. Although the per cent of ritual-related contacts within cultural situations did not differ significantly for mothers and fathers, the mothers have a significantly greater number of ritual-related contacts. This was true not only because mothers were more often the only parent present in the cultural situations, but also because, when both parents were present, as in the supper situation, mothers had more ritual-related contacts than fathers.

There is a further measure of the greater concern of the mother that the child meet cultural demands. Mothers originated a greater number of their ritual-related contacts than of their nonritual-related contacts. This was not true for the fathers. Here we have some indication that mothers are less content than fathers to let ritual-related behavior take its course, for they try, more than they do with nonritual-related behavior, to elicit and prevent, in advance of their occurrence, certain actions on the part of the child. Once more, therefore, we are led to the general conclusion that the mother plays a more leading role than the father in the upbringing of children, in this instance, in the process of transmitting culture.

Our data showed that fathers were away from home to a considerable extent, but that, even during the time when both parents were at home, only one out of eleven fathers had more contacts with the child than the mother. In contrasting the American boy's relation to his father with that of the New Guinea boy, Mead (1930) tells us that the American boy is not permitted the more intimate contact with his father which would enable him to grasp his father as an individual, rather than as a member of a sex group. The New Guinea boy is said to have considerably more contact with his father than the American boy. One reason Mead offers for this is that Americans regard bringing up children as women's work. Our findings suggest that this view is too drastic. Half of the contacts of fathers in the five cultural situations were ritual-related; fathers helped in bathing the children, correcting their table manners, and so forth. This certainly shows that the fathers were "interested" in some of the cultural necessities of child-rearing, but were less involved than mothers. As long as fathers are away from home as much as they were in our present sample, they will have a secondary role in raising their children. Of course, our data represent typical week days, and it may be that fathers "take over" on the weekends. However, even though there may be instances of this, it is more likely that mothers and fathers share the duties of child-rearing on weekends, with mothers doing the major part of it. But such a conjecture needs to be tested.

A common, more recent view of American fathers is opposed to the one expressed by Mead in 1930. An article in *Life* magazine (Dec. 24, 1957) laments the trend on the part of fathers in the American culture to take over increasingly more of the functions and duties of child care that were once traditionally reserved for mothers. As a matter of fact, Margaret Mead herself was quoted by newspapers in 1958 as saying that America is unprecedented as a society in the extent to which fathers take care of young children! To test Mead's more recent contention we would require data of the sort that we have on Midwest parents from cultures where fathers are thought to have much to do with the care of young children. Possibly the American father's leisure time is more taken up with child care than the leisure time of fathers in other societies, but this remains to be investigated.

It is not surprising that mothers, who exceeded fathers so much in the frequency with which they interacted with children, also exceeded fathers on 9 out of 12 of the *raison d'être* categories. We are interested in the three exceptions. Two of these were concerned with *activity with* the child, seeking it and responding to requests for it (IA 2 and IB 2). Despite the fact, then, that fathers had so much less contact with their children than mothers, their *activity with* the child was no less frequent. In Hurlock (1956), we find the claim that mothers play more with their children than fathers; our data seem to be different in this respect. We should look at these "activity with" contacts, of course, to see how many of these involve "play" in order to test Hurlock's assertion directly. Nevertheless, *activity with* the child, as we have defined it, is important to the child, and these contacts deserve further study and analysis.

The *raison d'être* category "seeking to express oneself to the subject" (IA 3) was the one category with respect to which fathers' social contacts exceeded mothers' in the per cent of occurrence. Perhaps this reflects, at least in part, the father's greater concern to share his activities, his thoughts, and his feelings with the child. The father, aware of his frequent absences, may feel that the child does not have much opportunity to know his world. Mothers' days are quite manifest to their children, especially to preschool children. But fathers, if they are to make themselves well acquainted with their children, must use more of their available time for this purpose. For whatever reasons, Midwest fathers were doing just this. These matters certainly are worth investigating.

A finding of considerable importance is that the children generally exceeded their parents in originating social interaction. For the most part, parents reacted to what the child said or did in their presence and did not plan or determine in advance the kind of behavior they wished from their children. The picture is strikingly different for teacher-child social contacts, to which we shall now turn.

Teachers within the classroom greatly exceeded children in the origination of social interaction and in this respect they differed a great deal from parents in the home. This difference between teachers and parents, we believe, is largely a difference between the demands of quite different situations. Teachers, by necessity, have a curriculum to follow and, in conjunction with it, lesson plans to make. Should a mother take on the job of a teacher in the classroom, we have every reason to expect that her behavior, even toward her own child, would change accordingly. She would have expectations of her child independent of the child's wishes, wants, or immediate activity; she would not wait to see what her child was doing before deciding whether she would break in upon the child's ongoing stream of behavior. As we have seen, the mother's ritual-related contacts were more often originated by her than were her nonritual-related contacts. These ritual-related contacts occurred within situations which, like the classroom, reflect some definite demands made upon behavior by the larger culture of which the home and school are a part. The cultural situations which we specified in this study force parents, especially mothers, who are more active in child-rearing, to *require* certain behavior from their children.

Studies of the parent-child relation must include "situation" determinants of behavior. Barker and Wright (1955) and Barker (1960) have hypothecated how one type of situation, the behavior setting, "coerces" behavior. And Henle has called attention to the need to study field forces as well as ego forces (1957), field forces, in this instance, referring to forces that arise outside the self, such as the experienced requirements of a situation. This study has made a bare beginning in using contacts and cultural situations in an effort to describe how the situation plays a role in coercing behavior. There are other situations comparable to the five used in this study and the classroom is a case in point.

Other data than those on the origination of teacher-child contacts reflected the coercive power of the classroom situations. The *raison d'être* analysis revealed that the majority of teacher contacts in the academic classroom were dedicated to "seeking an activity" (IA 1) as a ground for social interaction with the child. The difference between parents and teachers, in this respect, was very great.

For the children of this study, home was, much less than the school, a place where activity was sought from them. Parents exceeded teachers on all except one of the *raison d'être* categories which describe the agent as *responding to* the child. The one exception to this, "responding to a request for information" (IB 6), showed no significance difference between parents and teachers. Teachers give out most of their information without being asked, but there are occasions when the child needs to request information. An interesting study could be made of the frequency and origination of information-giving and information-receiving by means of social interaction at home and at school. Also consistent with these differences between teachers and parents is the finding that teachers' social contacts in the classroom were more ritual-related than parents' social contacts in the five cultural situations. The classroom is much more businesslike, much more demanding so that its agents and its subjects get on with the requirements of the setting. This is something most of us more or less take for granted. In Midwest homes, even in situations which made definite demands upon parental behavior and, in turn, upon children, there was time to permit social interaction about matters unrelated to the ongoing ritual and mechanics of the settings. Home, in Midwest at least, did not have any settings that were as inflexible in prodding the child's behavior as the academic classroom.

We have found that ecological data of the kind used in this study can provide us with information about parent-child behavior and about certain variables pertinent to parent-child interaction. The present study is a small sample of the wealth of factual material contained within the specimen records used, as a number of the other studies reported in this volume testify. The study has demonstrated that the flow of social behavior can be reliably marked into social contact units. It is important, we believe, that the reliability figures reported were achieved without training the independent rater, and without discussing with him how the units were to be discriminated. The aim of the investigator was to achieve a definition and a set of criteria for the social contact which others could use reliably by reading what was written about it. Repeatability is, after all, one of the primary requisites of a scientific study.

One of the important results of identifying the social contact unit, is that, by means of it, we are able to make quantitative statements about naturally occurring social phenomena. Much of the data on parent-child interaction, based as they are upon the questionnaire or the interview, depend upon reports from memory of those who have done the interacting. Under these conditions, answers to questions, or other units invented by the investigator prior to the examination of the data are often the units of analysis. The social contact unit draws upon the actual structure of social interaction for its defining properties, and although social interaction may indeed be divided in other ways, we believe the social contact corresponds fairly well to one of the units around which our experience of social interaction is organized. We have attempted to use the social contact unit in order to count "what happens to us" through social interaction. Having identified such a unit, the description of it serves to provide further quantitative measures of the psychological properties of human interaction in the natural habitat.

The use of cultural situations and the specification of contacts as ritual or nonritual-related should prove valuable in studying certain cultural changes over time, as well as in comparing cultures. When we are told that there is a trend for fathers to participate more in the routine care of children, we are not provided with quantitative data which tell us to what extent this happened, say, ten years ago, and to what extent this occurs now. In this study, a step has been taken in the direction of providing a quantitative measure of the degree to which the interactions of parents are concerned with some of the culturally prescribed ways of caring for children.

CHAPTER 6

Disturbances Experienced by Children in Their Natural Habitats

CLIFFORD L. FAWL

IT WAS POINTED OUT in Chapter 1 that natural units of the behavior stream can be identified by either their structural-dynamic or the material-content properties. Disturbances are of the latter type. Dr. Fawl explores the incidence, the intensity, and the duration of unpleasant disruptions in the everyday lives of children. But he goes much beyond a mere census of the unhappy experiences of children; he investigates their social and psychological origins in a way that demonstrates impressively how an atheoretical approach can lead to theory with wide implications.

Clifford L. Fawl is Associate Professor of Psychology at Nebraska Wesleyan University; he was awarded the Ph.D. degree by the University of Kansas.

THIS IS A STUDY of incidents experienced as disturbing by children in their natural habitats. We have aimed to discover how common, how intense, and how long these disturbing incidents are. Since some disturbances obviously are socially evoked, we have attempted to evaluate the role of other people as causal factors in the disturbance of children, distinguishing between adult and child associates, and in some analyses, between mothers and fathers. In addition we have hoped to gain at least a rudimentary notion of the various psychological determinants of disturbance.

The background for the present investigation was a study of the frustrations occurring in the natural habitat of children. "Goal blockage" was employed as the working definition of frustration. The results of the study were surprising in two respects. First, even with a liberal interpretation of blockage, fewer blocked goals were detected than we expected (mean, 16.5 per child for an entire waking day). Second, frustration defined as goal blockage usually failed to produce an apparent state of disturbance on the part of the child. Meaningful relationships could not be found between blockage, analyzed in several respects, and consequent behaviors such as aggression, regression, sublimation, disturbance and other theoretically relevant behavioral manifestations. The data indicated, moreover, that many incidents that were experientially disturbing had been omitted by the goal-blockage approach. Therefore, since blockage evidently was neither a sufficient nor necessary condition for producing a state of disturbance, we decided to restructure our orientation to focus upon experientially disturbing incidents *per se*.

The Concept of Disturbance

In keeping with the reorientation of the research, disturbance was conceptualized as

> *an unpleasant disruption*
> in the *ongoing feeling tone of immediate awareness,*
> *evoked by,* and *in reference to,*
> a *discernible event or situation.*

Following is an incident taken from one of the records employed in this investigation which illustrates disturbance as here defined:

> As Roy was standing in line at the drinking fountain, Geoffrey came up from behind him, and with considerable vigor swatted Roy on the back with the palm of his hand.
>
> Roy turned around, faced his assailant.
> He looked somewhat hurt and angry.
> Certainly Roy had done nothing to Geoffrey.
>
> As soon as Geoffrey saw Roy's expression, he dashed into the toilet room.
>
> Roy gave immediate chase.

Our concept of disturbance, although independently arrived at, has points in common with an earlier formulation by Angyal regarding emotions in general (1941, pp. 71–72): "We consider the feeling tone of emotions as the *experience of the state and of the situation of the person under the aspect of value.*"

Both conceptualizations make explicit the notion of feeling tone, i.e., both are addressed to the experiential aspect of emotion. This facet of emotion has been investigated surprisingly little by present day psychologists. Lindsley points out in his review of emotions in the *Handbook of Experimental Psychology* (1951, p. 473) that, ". . . such basic data as there are on emotion have come largely through the study of its expressive aspects [e.g., facial expressions in photographs] and objectively recorded bodily activities [e.g., gastrointestinal motility]."

Angyal's and our own conceptions are similar, too, in emphasizing a referent; Angyal writes of the "experience of the state *and of the situation* . . . ," and our own definition includes, "evoked by, and *in reference to, an occurrence. . . .*" This means not only that there is a stimulus which evokes the experience but that the referent is an integral part of the experience.

The main sources of data for this study were the twelve day-long specimen records of Midwest children, the four records of children with marked physical disabilities, and the record of Wally O. at home. Wally O., who resided in a large metropolitan community, was the only child for whom there was prior clinical evidence of maladjustment (p. 170).

In this report a detailed analysis is presented of disturbances experienced by the Midwest subjects, who represent a fairly homogeneous group in ways other than age, and a brief survey is made of the analyses in which non-Midwest subjects differed significantly from the Midwest subjects.

Instructions for identifying disturbances were designed to present in molar, atheoretical terms the type of descriptive evidence which raters were to consider as indicative and as not indicative of disturbance. We emphasized in these instructions that disturbance was to be regarded as a *behaviorally inferred* construct of experiencing. Criteria were provided for distinguishing more than one incident of disturbance, and for treating borderline cases. These instructions, with minor changes which are mainly grammatical, will be found in Appendix 6.1.

Following the development of the instructions for identifying disturbances, but prior to the final marking of disturbances on the records, an agreement check was performed between an independent analyst and the author. This analyst was requested to identify, without opportunity for practice, the units of disturbance in a sample of 150 pages from the records of four children, which amounted to slightly over five hours of behavior. Since the independent analyst was unfamiliar with the study, the instructions and 10 sample disturbance units served as his sole criteria for identifying disturbances. The author identified independently the units of disturbance in the same material.

There was good agreement as to the total number of disturbances identified: 48 by the independent analyst and 44 by the author. This is an important finding since most of the analyses of this report are based on the total number of disturbances for each child. Good agreement as to totals does not indicate, however, that the analysts included the same incidents. Theoretically, analysts could agree perfectly as to totals yet include completely different incidents as disturbance units. Our results show that 32 incidents were identified as disturbance units by both analysts, 16 disturbances were identified by the independent analyst and not by the author, and 12 were identified by the author and not by the independent analyst.

Where a given incident was included by one analyst but not the other, it usually was judged to be mild by the analyst who did include it, or it was unitized as one large unit of disturbance by one analyst and broken into two separate units by the other. In the latter case, then, this did not actually represent disagreement regarding the existence of a disturbance but, rather, disagreement as to whether the incident should be differentiated into more than one disturbance unit. Of the 16 disturbances marked by the independent analyst but not by the author, four (25 per cent) were incidents that had been differentiated into more than one unit by the independent analyst and rated as one undifferentiated unit by the author, and 10 (62.5 per cent) were judged to be no stronger than mild by the independent analyst. Thus, only two (16.5 per cent) were really major disagreements. Of the 12 incidents identified as separate units of disturbance by the author but not by the independent analyst, 2 (16.7 per cent) had been identified as a single disturbance by the analyst, 9 (75 per cent) were judged to be no stronger than mild by the analyst, and 1 was a major difference in judgment. Of the total number of 28 disagreements, then, 3 (10.7 per cent) were incidents judged to be disturbances of moderate or strong intensity by one of the analysts, yet were not identified as disturbances by the other analyst.

From the foregoing analysis we concluded that agreement between independent analysts left much to be desired, but that there was evidence that our criteria for demarking units of disturbance were not private; another person even without the benefit of training or discussion could identify disturbance units much as the author intended. The next step was to identify the disturbance units in the 17 behavior records under investigation. Thirteen of the records were unitized by the author, the other 4 (Raymond, Maud, Bobby, Claire) were done under the supervision of the author by an associate who was fully familiar with the study and the disturbance criteria.

To assess the consistency with which the final markings were done, an agreement check between the associate analyst and the author was performed on a total of 290 pages taken from ten behavior records representing nine and a half hours of behavior. This check was made after the task of identifying the disturbances was completed. Eight of the records had been analyzed solely by the author and two by the associate. Here again excellent agreement was found in the total number of disturbances: 104 by the associate analyst and 100 by the author. Eighty-three incidents were identified as disturbance units by both analysts independently. Of the 21 disturbance units marked by the associate but not by the author, 15 (71.4 per cent) were judged to be mild in intensity by the associate and 5 (23.8 per cent) were due to disagreement regarding the number of units within disturbance incidents. Of the 17 disturbance units marked by the author but not the associate analyst, 11 (64.7 per cent) were judged to be mild by the author and 5 others (29.5 per cent) involved disagreement as to number of units in incidents. Only 2 of the total 38 disagreements (5.3 per cent) involved clear-cut disturbances. Our conclusion is that the disturbance units were marked with a satisfactory degree of consistency.

For further discussion and analyses pertaining to agreement checks, in-

TABLE 6.1

Frequency of Disturbances Occurring in the Days of Midwest Children

Subjects Are Arranged in Order of Increasing Age

SUBJECTS	*Total Number of Disturbances in Day*	*Average Number of Disturbances per Hour*
Preschool subjects		
Mary C.	143	11.39
Jimmy	30	2.68
Lewis	119	10.60
Dutton	94	7.32
Margaret	86	5.97
Maud	90	7.52
Preschool mean	93.67	7.58
School-age subjects		
Roy	75	5.58
Ray	58	4.28
Ben	32	2.56
Mary E.	57	3.94
Douglas	27	1.90
Claire	18	1.26
School mean	44.50	3.25
Midwest mean	69.08	5.42

cluding the theoretical problems involved, the reader is referred to Fawl (1959, pp. 44–50)

Frequency of Disturbance

As indicated earlier, one of our principal aims was to gain some perspective as to how commonly disturbance occurs in the everyday lives of children. Children can be expected to differ considerably in this respect as a function of both situational and personality variables, and the seventeen subjects of this investigation cannot be considered representative of the universe of children. But to know the number of disturbances experienced by even a few children represents a step forward from the almost total ignorance now existing.

The data for the Midwest children are presented in Table 6.1 and Figure 6.1.[1] They show that these children experienced a daily average of 69 disturbances, at the rate of 5.4 disturbances per hour. The data show, too, that

[1] Disturbances for which the observer was primarily responsible have not been included in the frequencies. Seventy-nine disturbances, or 6 per cent of the grand total of 1,330 were excluded on this basis.

There were sections missing from several of the behavior records, varying from 10 to 60 minutes, approximately; it was necessary, therefore, to compensate for these

the children varied considerably in number of disturbances. The range of daily totals was from 18 to 143, and the standard deviation of the individual totals was 39.2.

Much of the variability among subjects in Midwest was related to the age of the child. Preschool children had an average of 93.67 disturbances compared to 44.50 for the school children. The nonparametric Mann-Whitney statistic for independent samples indicates that this difference between age groups is statistically significant at the .026 level of probability.[2] Expressed in terms of a rank-order correlation coefficient (Spearman's rho), the age of the child was correlated —.73 with the number of disturbances occurring during the day ($p = .01$). Age and frequency per hour of disturbance were correlated approximately the same: rho = —.76.

One explanation for the drop in frequency of disturbance with age is that only the older subjects were within the protective and restrictive setting of the formal classroom a large proportion of the day. Two findings indicate that something other than the classroom setting must be operative, however. In the first place, if we analyze for disturbance only those portions of the day in which each child was at home, we still find a negative correlation between age and frequency of disturbance; rho = —.70. Secondly, as Figure 6.1 suggests, there was a tendency for the frequency of disturbance to fall with age when comparing subjects within each age group as well as between age groups.

Frequency of disturbance was not related to the sex of subject, to the number of siblings present on the day of the observation, or to the social class of the child's family. This fact is apparent from inspection of Figure 6.1 where each subject is identified with respect to the variables mentioned.

Intensity of Disturbance

Each incident of disturbance was judged as either mild, moderate, or strong in intensity. The instructions for rating intensity are given in Appendix 6.1. Whereas a six-point scale is outlined there, in the analysis it was collapsed to three points for the sake of greater reliability.

In a spot check of 68 randomly selected disturbances taken from 10 rec-

---

minor omissions by adjusting the total number of disturbances (Fawl, 1959, pp. 69–72). This adjustment was based upon the subject's own rate of disturbance for the time of day at which the omission occurred. Only 29 disturbances were added by this procedure to all 17 records combined; this represents less than 3 per cent of the unadjusted grand total of 1,251 disturbances actually detected. Some variation among subjects in number of disturbances was due to differences in length of waking day; this ranged from 11 hours and 45 minutes for Maud to 14 hours and 25 minutes for Mary E. The total number of disturbances reported in Table 6.1 and Figure 6.1 are adjusted for omissions in the records, but not for differences in length of day. To deal with the latter problem, the frequency rate, i.e., number of disturbances per hour was computed and is reported in Table 6.1.

[2] Since this is not a theory-oriented study with specific predictions, two-sided statistical tests have been employed throughout.

FIGURE 6.1

Frequency of Disturbance in Days of Midwest Children with Respect to Age, Sex, Social Class of Family, and Number of Siblings

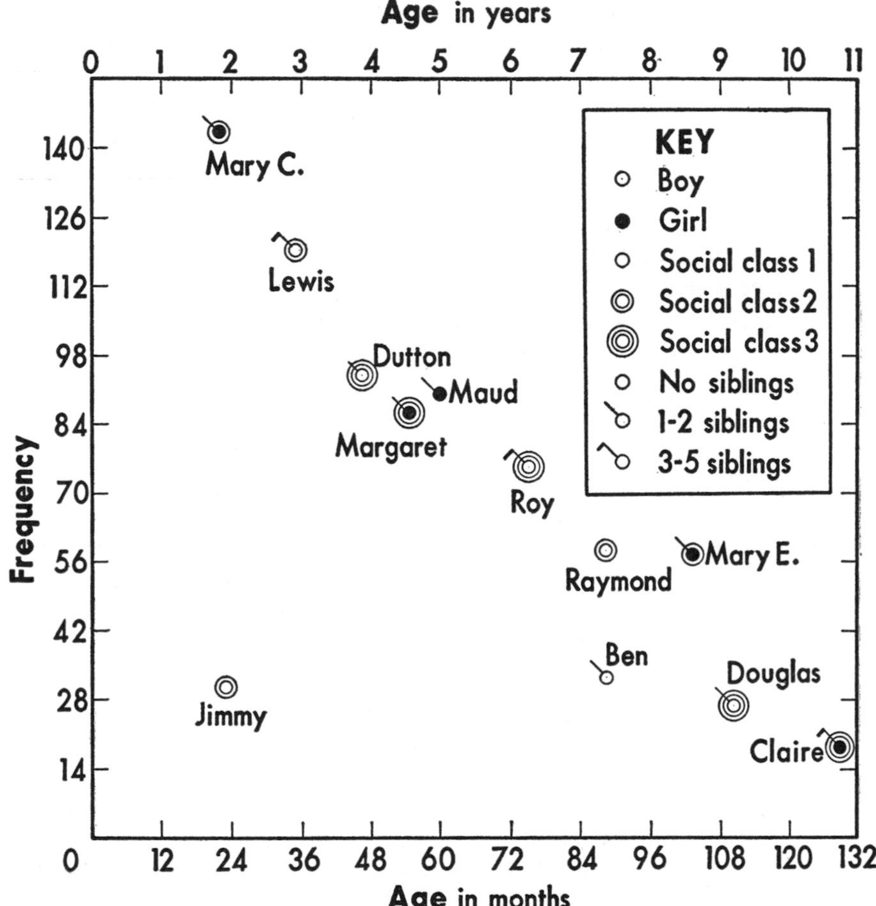

ords, the author and an independent analyst rated identically 87 per cent of the incidents. In no case was there disagreement of more than one point on the three-point scale. No discussion regarding the rating criteria took place between the judges prior to the agreement check, hence it is concluded that intensity of disturbance can be rated satisfactorily on the basis of instructions alone.

For some analyses, disturbances judged to be mild in intensity were assigned a weight of 1; moderate disturbances, 2; and strong disturbances, 3. The average intensity rating per disturbance could then be determined for each subject. Thus if a child had 30 mild, 15 moderate, and 5 strong disturbances, the average disturbance rating for intensity would be 1.5.

TABLE 6.2
Rate of Occurrence of Disturbances of Different Degrees of Intensity Mean Number of Disturbances per Hour for Midwest Children

SUBJECTS	*Intensity rating* *Mild*	*Moderate*	*Strong*
Preschool subjects	4.50	2.82	0.26
School-age subjects	2.15	1.01	0.10
All Midwest subjects	3.32	1.91	0.18

By and large the disturbances experienced by Midwest subjects were mild in intensity. Of all 829 Midwest disturbances, 61.7 per cent were rated mild, 35.1 per cent moderate, and only 3.2 per cent strong. The mean of the average intensity rating for the Midwest children was 1.37.

The mean frequency rates of disturbances of each degree of intensity are presented in Table 6.2. The rate of occurrence was lower for the older subjects at each intensity level. The difference between age groups in the rate of mild disturbances was significant at the .02 level of confidence; in terms of rank-order correlation, the hourly rate of mild disturbances was inversely related to age: rho = —.74 (p = .01). The frequency rate of disturbances of moderate intensity was less definitely higher for the preschool subjects than for school-age subjects (p = .064); the correlation with age was —.57 (.576 required for significance at the .05 level of confidence).

There were few disturbances of strong intensity, and their frequency was not clearly related to age of subject. If we combine as one figure those disturbances that were greater than mild in intensity, the correlation with age was —.57.

The average disturbance intensity per child was not related to his age; the means were 1.38 for the preschool children and 1.35 for the school-age group. The rank-order correlation between age and mean intensity rating was —.37; this falls well short of statistical significance.

Duration of Disturbance

Duration judgments were trichotomized as brief (less than 1 minute), medium (1–3 minutes), and long (greater than 3 minutes). The duration refers to the span of time over which the subject was judged to be actually disturbed; it does not refer to the duration of his concern regarding the evoking referent of disturbance.

Of 77 randomly selected disturbances from 17 records, the author and an independent judge agreed exactly on 94 per cent of them. In no case was the disagreement more than one point on the three-point scale.

Weights of 1, 2, and 3 were assigned to disturbances which were brief,

TABLE 6.3
Rate of Occurrence of Disturbances of Different Durations
Mean Number of Disturbances per Hour for Midwest Children

SUBJECTS	Less than One Minute	Duration Rating 1–3 Minutes	Longer than Three Minutes
Preschool subjects	6.85	0.68	0.07
School-age subjects	2.75	0.48	0.04
All Midwest subjects	4.80	0.58	0.05

medium, and long, respectively, and the average weighted duration of the disturbances was determined for each subject.

The vast majority of Midwest children's disturbances (88.1 per cent) were less than 1 minute in duration. A few (10.9 per cent) were between 1 and 3 minutes, and very few (1.0 per cent) were longer. The mean duration rating per disturbance per child was 1.14.

The data of Table 6.3 show that the frequency of each range of duration was greater for preschool than for the older subjects. Only with respect to the brief disturbances, however, was the difference statistically significant ($p = .016$). The rank-order correlation between age and frequency rate of brief disturbances was —.76 ($p = .01$). When the frequencies of all disturbances greater than one minute in duration are combined, we find that age and the frequency rate of these longer disturbances were correlated —.52; this is slightly short of the .576 required for significance at the .05 level of confidence.

Social Determinants of Disturbance

Here we turn to those disturbances in whose evocation another person clearly had a role, was the "causal source," if you will. In these cases another person was the referent of the child's disturbance or was in some way identified with the referent. An example of a disturbance of the latter type would be a boring, unpleasant lesson which was required by the teacher. Excluded from this section are disturbances in which we judged that the referent of the disturbance was the child himself, a physical object or physical conditions (e.g., the prospect of rain when a picnic was being planned), or an animal.

No agreement checks were obtained since the required judgments were thought to be fairly straightforward.

Obviously the frequency of socially evoked disturbances for a particular child is in part a function of the frequency of his social interaction: the more often the child is in contact with other people the more opportunity there is for socially evoked disturbances. To take this factor into account we have employed a rather rough measure we call the "D/EFU index." Following Schoggen, who studied the same children (Chapter 3), we have used the frequency of environmental force units (EFU) as a measure of the child's degree of social interaction. The D/EFU index is the ratio of the frequency of disturbances to the frequency of environmental force units. This index does *not* represent the proportion of EFU in which there was disturbance, since it is possible for more than one disturbance to occur in a given EFU and for more than one EFU to occur in a given disturbance unit. One can think of the index as the *number of disturbances per social interaction.* The index is employed to reflect in one figure the relation between disturbance frequency and social interaction frequency for a subject. It can refer to interaction with other people in general or to a given class of associates, e.g., to adults.

Most disturbances were evoked by another person; for 72.4 per cent of all disturbances another person was the referent or was closely implicated with the referent. Socially evoked disturbances outnumbered nonsocially evoked disturbances in the case of every Midwest subject. This unanimity far exceeds chance expectation ($p < .01$, by sign test). The proportion of a child's disturbances which were socially evoked was independent of his age, but the mean rate per hour was related to age; the older the child, the lower the rate of socially evoked disturbances, rho $= -.72$ ($p < .01$). Schoggen's discovery that the number of EFU decreases with the age of the Midwest subjects suggests a declining opportunity for socially evoked disturbances to take place. Nevertheless, when we take the interaction frequency into consideration by means of the D/EFU index we find that, the older the child, the lower the frequency of disturbances per social interaction, rho $= -.578$ ($p < .05$). This amplifies the earlier findings that the age of the child was negatively related to the frequency of his disturbances (p. 104).

Social disturbances were more intense than nonsocial disturbances, the means of the average intensity ratings were 1.39 for social disturbances and 1.29 for the nonsocial disturbances. This difference, although not great, is significant at the 5 per cent level of confidence as determined by Wilcoxon's sign-ranks matched-pairs test. Social disturbances were more intense for 5 of the 6 preschool children and for 3 of the 6 school children.

The average duration of social disturbances was greater than the duration of nonsocial disturbances for 9 of the 12 subjects, but the differences tended to be very small. Wilcoxon's test does not reveal a significant difference.

Adult and child associates of our subjects differed in the roles they played as evokers of disturbances. The data of Table 6.4 show that adults evoked a far greater per cent of the disturbances of preschool children than did child associates, but that by school age, adult and child associates were essentially equivalent in the extent to which each was the source of disturbance. Per cent frequency of adult-evoked disturbances declined with age,

TABLE 6.4
Per Cent of Disturbances Evoked by Adults, by Children, and by Both Adults and Children. Midwest Children

SUBJECTS	EVOKERS OF DISTURBANCE *Adults*	*Children*	*Adults and Children*
Preschool subjects	55.2	18.3	73.5
School-age subjects	32.8	37.4	70.2
All Midwest subjects	47.8	24.6	72.4

TABLE 6.5
Rate of Occurrence of Disturbances Evoked by Adults and by Children Mean Number of Disturbances per Hour for Midwest Children

SUBJECTS	EVOKERS OF DISTURBANCE *Adults*	*Children*	*Adults and Children*
Preschool subjects	4.10	1.37	5.53
School-age subjects	1.04	1.21	2.25
All Midwest subjects	2.57	1.29	3.89

TABLE 6.6
Number of Disturbances per Social Interaction (D/EFU Index) with Child Associates and with Adult Associates. Midwest Children

SUBJECTS	EVOKERS OF DISTURBANCE *Adults*	*Children*	*Adults and Children*
Preschool subjects	.123	.184	.135
School-age subjects	.085	.099	.093
All Midwest subjects	.104	.142	.114

rho = −.77 ($p < .01$), and per cent of child-evoked disturbances increased with age, rho = +.77 ($p < .01$). The data of Table 6.5 show that the findings with respect to hourly rate of disturbance differ from the results just given in only one respect: the rate of child-evoked disturbances did not increase with age of child. That the per cent of child-evoked disturbances was higher for school-age subjects than for preschool subjects, even though the absolute number of child-evoked disturbances was lower is, of course, due to the fact that the number of disturbances in general for school-age children was very low.

The fact that adult-evoked disturbances were especially common among preschool subjects is related to the fact that the preschool children had more social interactions with adults than with other children. Schoggen's EFU analysis (1957) revealed that 73 per cent of the EFU of the preschool children were with adults and only 23 per cent with children. For the school-age children, 50 per cent of the EFU were with adults and 50 per cent with children. When we use the D/EFU index, the resulting picture as given in Table 6.6 is revealing: the D/EFU index was significantly higher for EFU involving child associates than for EFU involving adult associates ($p < .05$). In other words, the Midwest children had more disturbances per social interaction with children than with adults. This was especially true at the preschool level; in this case the D/EFU index was higher for all six of the children. With both child and adult associates the D/EFU index tended to drop with the age of the child, although only for child associates was the correlation significant, rho = −.62 ($p < .05$). Thus, the older the subject, the fewer were the disturbances per interaction with other children.

Disturbances evoked by children differed little in intensity from those evoked by adults, and with neither associate was intensity of disturbance related to the age of the subject.

Disturbances evoked by adults tended to be slightly longer than those evoked by children; the mean duration ratings were 1.18 and 1.07, respectively. This difference barely misses significance at the .05 level of confidence. There was some tendency for adult-evoked disturbances to be longer for the school-age children than for preschool children; the difference in the mean ratings was 1.24 and 1.12 ($p < .08$). The correlation between mean duration of adult-evoked disturbances and age of child +.66 ($p = .02$). No age relationship was found for duration of child-evoked disturbances.

The mother evoked more disturbances than the father in every case where both parents were present on the day the record was made; this difference is significant beyond the .01 level of confidence by Wilcoxon's matched-pairs signed-ranks test. Mothers evoked, on the average, 3.37 disturbances per hour of preschool children and 0.54 per hour of school children; the mean hourly rate of father-evoked disturbances was 0.43 for preschool children, and 0.15 for school children. However, the D/EFU index revealed no significant difference between mothers and fathers in disturbances per unit of social interaction, and none of the analyses contrasting the D/EFU index for parents of the same sex with parents of the opposite sex produced significant differences.

Father-evoked disturbances were more intense than those evoked by the mothers for 10 of the 11 subjects whose parents were both present ($p < .01$); however, the intensity differences were not great, the mean ratings being 1.65 and 1.33 for father- and mother-evoked disturbances, respectively. On the other hand, the duration of disturbances evoked by mothers and fathers did not differ, and there were no differences in the frequency, intensity, or duration of disturbances evoked by parents of the same sex in contrast with those evoked by parents of the opposite sex.

Psychological Determinants of Disturbance

One of the purposes of the study was to determine the causes of disturbance, the "causal types" as they will be called. Causal types of disturbance occur at different levels of explanation, and we have attempted to deal with a single level, namely with the *contemporaneous* causes of disturbance on a *psychological* level.

Goodenough (1931) recognized the importance, and also the difficulty, of specifying the "immediate causes" of anger outbursts in young children. We would consider her classification of immediate causes to be "nonpsychological." For instance, one of her classes was "Routine Physical Habits," which included "Going to toilet," "Washing face, bathing, combing hair, brushing teeth, dressing," and "Objection to specific kinds of foods." Inselberg (1957) on the other hand mixed nonpsychological with psychological or quasipsychological categories: for example, "Medical and dental care" along with "Conflict with children." The different orientation of our effort to type causes of disturbance should be evident in the presentation below.

Various causal types of disturbance were empirically identified before they were given conceptual formulation. The conceptualizations of Lewin and of Heider influenced these formulations, although the types were not derived from them. From Lewin, emphasis on goal-directed behavior, and the concept of force in particular, were found to be useful. Force, being a key concept in the formulation of several causal types, requires formal definition. Leeper (1943, p. 208) has succinctly summarized Lewin's concept of force as "a hypothesized variable, or construct, conceived as the immediate determinant of the locomotions [actions] of a person." Every force has a direction, which is an important consideration in the present analysis. A force serves to move the subject toward or away from something specific. Force also has magnitude and point of application. In our classification we have spoken of force only when the point of application was the child or something pertinent to the child's specific goal (the path to the goal and the goal itself in Lewin's life-space analysis).

The technique for symbolically describing a subject's perception of a situation is borrowed from Heider (1958). Application of Heider's concise statements often enables one more easily to get at the essentials of a description. The notations used and their meanings are:

ch . . .	child
C . . .	causes
not C . . .	does not cause
W . . .	wants
WC . . .	wants to cause
TrC . . .	tries to cause
S . . .	suffers, experiences, undergoes
x,y . . .	specific entities, things, situations
(+) (−) . . .	positive (pleasant) negative (unpleasant)

A colon (:) is to be translated as the conjunction "that." See Heider (1958, pp. 299–300) for further clarification.

Imposition is another key term we have employed which requires comment. By imposition we have reference to something that is thrust upon the child or which confronts the child not by choice of the child. This something can be an act of another person or simply physical conditions not produced by the child. Baldwin (1955, p. 142) defines impositions as those events which are "the results of the actions of someone else or of natural processes." Functionally, we have used the term when the child has attributed the cause of his disturbance to foreign factors.

Seven causal types of disturbance were identified in the records. These were: Interference, Failure, Imposed Driving Force, Choice Conflict, Offending Imposition, Own Act, and Psychological Loss. The types are presented below in the form employed in the analysis of each of the 1,251 disturbances of the 17 subjects.

Interference. Either (a) an imposed force operates in a direction diametrically opposed to the one in which the subject is striving; or (b) an imposed incident or situation, not necessarily operating as a force, serves to impede, or hinder, the subject's ongoing goal-directed behavior. Neither the absolute magnitude of the interference, its magnitude relative to the subject's own force, nor its duration enter into the determination of this type.

Symbolically: ch WC x, but
imposition C: ch not C x.[3]

Examples: (a) Margaret wanted to enter the house, but the door was locked. (b) Verne had to wait until the girls had left the bathroom before

[3] This statement may be read: the child wants to cause something or do something, but some foreign factor (person or thing) causes that the child *not* do or cause the desired act.

he could enter. (c) Dutton wanted to continue playing with his sister, but she wanted to stop. (d) A conversation taking place in the classroom interfered with Roy's recitation.

Failure. Failure to attain or maintain to the subject's satisfaction a goal accepted by the subject is attributed by him to his own inadequacies. The failure need not be complete or permanent.

Symbolically: ch WC x, but
ch C: ch not C x.

Examples: (a) Wally O. wanted to climb a certain tree, but he failed to reach the first branch even though his little brother had been successful. (b) Douglas shot an arrow which fell short of the mark. (c) Claire had great difficulty getting the correct answer to an arithmetic problem.

Imposed Driving Force. A force is applied to move the subject *toward* a specific region (activity) by someone or something other than the subject himself. Whether or not the subject yields to the force is of no consequence. Also, it is of no consequence for the identification of this disturbance type whether the disturbance is in reaction to the application of the force, or to the anticipated negative valence of the region toward which the child is being forced.[4]

Symbolically: imposition C: ch C x, or
imposition TrC: ch C x.

Examples: (a) Maud was told to pick up her toys. (b) Douglas was assigned a lesson that was very boring to him. (c) Mary E. was having a good time playing outside and did not want to stop when her mother called her to supper.

Choice Conflict. Mutually exclusive forces acting on the subject present a situation in which a movement in any direction has negative consequences, either directly by leading the subject toward an activity of negative valence, or indirectly by leading the subject away from an activity of positive valence.

Symbolically: ch WC x, but also
ch not WC x; or

ch WC x, but also
ch WC y; or

ch not WC x, but also
ch not WC y (forced choice).

[4] When an imposed force *toward* a specific region also operated as a restraining force opposing the subject's own force, the Imposed Driving Force rating took precedence (see example "c"). In one sense, if we assume continuous purposivism, *all* Imposed Driving Forces are Interferences, that is, every Imposed Driving Force interferes with something already going on, yet we consider it to be important to distinguish between those incidents where the foreign agent is perceived as driving subject *toward* or *away* from a region.

In each of the above cases, "x" and "y" are assumed to have different directions in the Lewinian sense of direction.

Example: (a) Douglas was momentarily confused when he started in the direction of the boy's rest room and remembered that the observer was a woman. (b) Mary C. became disorganized when she could not decide what to play.

Offending Imposition. This refers to actions or conditions or situations impinging upon the subject, or upon a personal belonging, which are not determined by the subject, and which are disturbing in their own right rather than as a result of the effect that they might have on the subject's ongoing goal-directed behavior. The marking of this causal type is not dependent on the hostile intention of the offender, or on the subject being the intended target of the offending action (see example "d" below).

Symbolically: imposition C: ch S −x.

Examples: (a) Roy was annoyed by a slap on the back he received while standing in line at the drinking fountain. (b) Wally W. was chagrined by his cousin's criticism of a remark Wally made. (c) Lewis was both disgusted and embarrassed by the presence of cow dung in the adjoining field. (d) Raymond was disturbed by the way another boy treated a dog.

Own Act. The subject performs an act which he himself negatively evaluates; or the subject attributes the cause of his disturbance to an impact with the environment brought about as a consequence of his own, not necessarily intended, act. The impact is disturbing in its own right rather than as it relates to the subject's ongoing goal-directed behavior. If there is evidence that the subject places the blame on the environment, then the incident is judged as Offending Imposition rather than Own Act.

Symbolically: ch C −x, or
ch C: ch S −x.

Examples: (a) Margaret regretted that she had been hostile toward her little brother. (b) Lewis rolled off the davenport and hurt himself slightly. (c) Jimmy accidentally stuck himself with a pin.

Psychological Loss. Something valued by the subject no longer exists, or if it still exists there has been a sharp drop in its value. Emphasis is on the lost or damaged object itself rather than on who or what might be responsible.

Symbolically: +x followed by
no +x

Examples: (a) Lewis entered the room to find that his toy gun had fallen apart. (b) Roy had hoped to listen to his favorite radio program, but it was already over when he arrived home. (c) Maud was quite anxious when she thought that her mother was going to leave the house.

TABLE 6.7
Distribution of the Disturbances of Midwest Children among Causal Types of Disturbance

SUBJECTS	CAUSAL TYPES *Interference*	*Failure*	*Imposed Driving Force*	*Choice Conflict*	*Offending Imposition*	*Own Act*	*Psychological Loss*	*Cannot Judge*
	Number of Disturbances							
All subjects	281	64	153	2	191	57	39	22
	Per Cent of Judged Disturbances							
Preschool subjects	41.3	5.7	19.8	0.2	18.5	8.4	6.1	
School-age subjects	24.4	13.0	18.7	0.4	35.9	4.9	2.7	
All subjects	35.7	8.1	19.4	0.3	24.3	7.2	5.0	

Prior to the final judging of the disturbances as to causal type, the investigator and an assistant independently analyzed a randomly selected sample of 70 disturbances. Each analyst listed a preferred and an alternative judgment of the causal type. In 80 per cent of the 70 disturbances the analysts agreed on their preferred judgment. In 92 per cent of disturbances, the analysts agreed with respect to either their preferred or their alternative judgments. Consequently there was evidence prior to the use of the types that independent analysts could agree in judging the causal type of most disturbances and that radical disagreements were rare.

After the disturbances had been judged, an agreement check was performed on a different sample of 70 randomly selected disturbances. This check was designed to test the consistency with which the disturbances had been judged over the entire time span of judging. Seventy-seven per cent of the causal types judged by the author were judged identically by the independent analyst, and an additional 16 per cent were the same as the latter's alternate judgment. Consequently either the preferred or alternate judgment of the independent analyst was the same as the author's analysis of the causal type in 93 per cent of the cases sampled. See Fawl (1959) for additional data regarding the agreement checks.

The number and per cent of each type of disturbance are given for Midwest children in Table 6.7; data are given for all children and for the younger and the older children separately. These data show that there were a substantial number of each causal type except Choice Conflict. We were unable to analyze, for a variety of reasons, about 3 per cent of the disturbance units.

Three causal types predominate: Interference, Offending Imposition, and Imposed Driving Force. Together they account for roughly three-quarters of all disturbances. A greater per cent of the older than of the younger children's disturbances were Offending Imposition and Failure types (the rho

TABLE 6.8
Rates of Occurrence of Causal Types of Disturbance
Mean Number of Disturbance Per Hour for Midwest Children

SUBJECTS	*Interference*	*Failure*	*Imposed Driving Force*	*Choice Conflict*	*Offending Imposition*	*Own Act*	*Psychological Loss*
Preschool subjects	3.01	0.42	1.47	0.01	1.36	0.62	0.45
School-age subjects	0.79	0.41	0.59	0.01	1.15	0.16	0.09
All subjects	1.90	0.42	1.03	0.01	1.26	0.39	0.27

correlations with age are +.68 and +.65, respectively); the reverse was true of Interference, Psychological Loss and Own Act (the rho correlations with age are —.82, —.78, —.70, respectively). Imposed Driving Force was unrelated to age.

Table 6.8 provides data regarding the mean hourly rate of each causal type for all subjects, and for the two age levels. The rates for Interference, Offending Imposition, and Imposed Driving Force were higher than for the other types, and are therefore in accord with the data of Table 6.7. Furthermore, the mean hourly rate of occurrence of Interference, Psychological Loss, and Own Act declined significantly with age (rho correlations with age are —.77, and —.80, and —.80, respectively). The rate of Imposed Driving Force decreased also, but not significantly; whereas Failure, Choice Conflict, and Offending Imposition showed virtually no tendency to decrease in rate with age.

The intensity and duration of Interference, Failure, Imposed Driving Force, and Offending Imposition were analyzed for all subjects. The other disturbance types did not occur with sufficient frequency for an over-all analysis. A Friedman two-way analysis of variance of ranks revealed that neither intensity nor duration varied significantly among the four types. And no sizeable differences in intensity or duration were found between the two age groups with respect to the four causal types.

Social and Psychological Determinants Related

Our problem here is twofold: (1) to determine for each causal type of disturbance that proportion which was socially evoked, and (2) to determine among all socially-evoked disturbances those proportions which were classified as falling into each causal type. Clearly these are related but not identical issues; a high proportion of a given causal type might be social in origin and yet the causal type itself might be socially evoked less often than another type. For example, 9 out of 10 disturbances (90 per cent) in one type might be socially evoked, and 20 out of 40 (50 per cent) of another

TABLE 6.9

Per Cent of Each Causal Type of Disturbance Which Was Evoked by Adults (Ad), by Children (Ch), and by Both Adults and Children (Both) for Stated Subjects

MIDWEST SUBJECTS	*Interference* Ad	Ch	Both	*Failure* Ad	Ch	Both	*Imposed Driving Force* Ad	Ch	Both	*Offending Imposition* Ad	Ch	Both	*Psychological Loss* Ad	Ch	Both
Preschool subjects	66[a]	20	86	14	0	14	92	8	100	35	39	74	32	23	55
School-age subjects	33	45	78	13	0	13	65	35	100	28	53	81	17	17	33
All subjects	59	26	84	13	0	13	83	17	100	31	46	77	30	22	51

(Column heading over the causal types: CAUSAL TYPE)

[a] To be read: 66 per cent of all preschool children's Interference-type disturbances were adult-evoked.

might be socially evoked, with the result that the first type yields a much lower per cent of the total when all socially-evoked disturbances are considered.

Our analysis has been restricted to five of the seven causal types since Own Act, by definition, was never socially evoked, and Choice Conflict only occurred two times, of which one was socially evoked.

We turn first to the initial question outlined above. Table 6.9 reports the per cent of each causal type that was evoked by adults, that was evoked by children, and that was socially evoked (by adults and children combined). Well over half of the disturbances of each of the three major causal types, Interference, Offending Imposition, and Imposed Driving Force, has a social origin; this was true of about half of Psychological Loss disturbances, and of only 13 per cent of Failure disturbances. The per cent of disturbances that was socially evoked was not significantly related to age of subject in the case of any causal type.

Interference disturbances were evoked in preschool children more frequently by adults than by children; this was true, also, to a lesser degree (which was not quite statistically significant) for subjects in general. The older the subject, the higher was the per cent of Interferences evoked by child associates (rho = .52) and the lower the per cent evoked by adults (rho = —.58).

The few socially evoked Failure disturbances (8 instances) were always evoked by adults.

Imposed Driving Force was mainly an adult-evoked type of disturbance; adults were the source for 83 per cent of all Driving Force disturbances. Even though high for both age groups of subjects, the per cent evoked by adults was especially high for the younger subjects; the correlation with age was negative (rho = —.72). With respect to no other causal type was the role of adults as prominent as with Imposed Driving Force.

TABLE 6.10

Mean Number of Disturbances Per Hour Evoked by Adults (Ad), by Children (Ch), and by Both Adults and Children (Both) for Stated Disturbance Types and Subjects

	CAUSAL TYPE														
MIDWEST SUBJECTS	*Interference*			*Failure*			*Imposed Driving Force*			*Offending Imposition*			*Psychological Loss*		
	Ad	*Ch*	*Both*	*Ad*	*Ch*	*Both*	*Ad*	*Ch*	*Both*	*Ad*	*Ch*	*Both*	*Ad*	*Ch*	*Both*
Preschool subjects	2.0	0.6	2.6	0.1	0.0	0.1	1.3	0.1	1.5	0.5	0.5	1.0	0.1	0.1	0.2
School-age subjects	0.3	0.4	0.6	0.1	0.0	0.1	0.4	0.2	0.6	0.3	0.6	0.9	0.0[a]	0.0[a]	0.0[b]
All subjects	1.1	0.5	1.6	0.1	0.0	0.1	0.9	0.2	1.0	0.4	0.6	1.0	0.1	0.1	0.1

[a] Actually, 0.01
[b] Actually, 0.02

Offending Imposition was the only causal type of disturbance more often evoked by child associates than by adult associates. The difference was not large enough to be statistically significant, however.

Psychological Loss was not evoked differentially by adults and children.

Tables 6.10 and 6.11 provide the data for the second question: the relative occurrence of disturbance types among socially-evoked disturbances. Table 6.10 reports the mean rates and Table 6.11 the per cents of socially-evoked disturbances of each causal type. Each table distinguishes between adult- and child-evoked disturbances and between school and preschool subjects. For example, we find that preschool subjects exhibited a mean of 2.0 adult-evoked Interference disturbances per hour, and that 50 per cent of all adult-evoked disturbances for preschool subjects were classed as Interference.

According to these data socially-evoked disturbances were most frequently of the Interference, Imposed Driving Force, and Offending Imposition types, but the relative frequencies of these three types depended on the age of the subject. The rate and per cent of socially-evoked Interference was greater than the rate and per cent of socially-evoked Offending Imposition in the case of all preschool subjects; the reverse was true in the case of all school-age subjects. The preponderance of Interference disturbances for preschool subjects held whether the source of evocation was adults or children. For school-age subjects, however, the type of disturbance most commonly evoked depended more on the age of the associate. Among school-age subjects, the most common type of child-evoked disturbance was Offending Imposition (51 per cent), but the most common type of adult-evoked disturbance was Imposed Driving Force (39 per cent). Thus we can conclude that the type of disturbance evoked by associates was related both to the age of the subject and to the age of the associate.

TABLE 6.11

Per Cent of All Disturbances Evoked by Adults (Ad), by Children (Ch), and by Both Adults and Children (Both) for Stated Disturbance Types and Subjects

	CAUSAL TYPE														
MIDWEST SUBJECTS	*Interference*			*Failure*			*Imposed Driving Force*			*Offending Imposition*			*Psychological Loss*		
	Ad	*Ch*	*Both*	*Ad*	*Ch*	*Both*	*Ad*	*Ch*	*Both*	*Ad*	*Ch*	*Both*	*Ad*	*Ch*	*Both*
Preschool subjects	50[a]	45	49	1	0	1	33	8	27	12	39	19	4	7	5
School-age subjects	25	30	28	5	0	2	39	18	27	31	51	42	1	1	1
All subjects	45	38	42	2	0	1	34	13	27	16	45	26	3	4	3

[a] To be read: 50 per cent of all preschool disturbances evoked by adults were judged to be Interference disturbances.

Adult associates evoked significantly more Interference and Imposed Driving Force disturbances at the preschool level than did child associates. For subjects in general, adults evoked more Interference, Failure, and Imposed Driving Force disturbances than did children. In none of the causal types did child associates elicit significantly more disturbances than adult associates. In interpreting these results we must bear in mind that our subjects had more social contacts with adults than with children, particularly at the preschool level. When we take into consideration this factor by use of the D/EFU index, the only differences noted above which stand up are those of Failure and Imposed Driving Force for subjects in general. On the other hand, the index was higher for child than for adult associates in regard to Offending Impositions. In other words, adults, as compared with children, evoked more Failure and Imposed Driving Force disturbances per interaction and fewer Offending Impositions.

A significantly higher proportion of adult-evoked disturbances was of the Imposed Driving Force and Failure types than was true of child-evoked disturbances. There was a tendency, not statistically significant, for a higher per cent of child-evoked disturbances, as compared to adult-evoked, to be classed as Offending Imposition. See Table 6.11.

Rate of adult-evoked Interference disturbances declined with age of subject (rho = —.90). This was true, too, of adult-evoked Imposed Driving Force disturbances (rho = —.60). The child-evoked frequency rates of individual causal types were not age related. Disturbances evoked by associates in general decreased in frequency with age in the case of Interference (rho = —.84), Imposed Driving Force (rho = —.53, $p < .10$), and Psychological Loss (rho = .88).

Again it is necessary to bear in mind the differential rate of social contact which adult and child associates had with the subjects. By the D/EFU index, the older the subject the less frequent was the evocation of Interferences per interaction by both adult (rho = —.88) and child (rho = —.51, $p < .10$) associates. This, in keeping with other analyses of Interference, points to the conclusion that Interference was particularly characteristic of the disturbances experienced by the preschool subjects. The D/EFU index for associates in general showed a drop in the number of Psychological Loss disturbances. This, too, is consistent with other data indicating that Psychological Loss was more characteristic of preschool than of school-age disturbances.

On the basis of the analyses, it appears legitimate to draw three major conclusions: (1) Interference and Psychological Loss, especially the former, were characteristic of the disturbances of preschool children, regardless of the source of evocation; (2) Imposed Driving Force was essentially an adult-evoked type of disturbance; and (3) Offending Imposition was the most common type of disturbance evoked by child associates. Clearly, then, these data suggest that child and adult associates played different roles in the evocation of disturbance, and that their roles varied with the psychological type of disturbance and with the age of the subject.

The last question to be raised about causal types of disturbance concerns the place of mothers and fathers in their evocation. Due to the infrequency of father-evoked disturbances, adequate statistical comparisons of mothers and fathers were not possible. However, the frequency and per cent of each type of disturbance evoked by mothers and by fathers was determined. The results are presented in Table 6.12. There was remarkable similarity between mothers and fathers in the types of disturbances they evoked; only in the case of Psychological Loss was there even a suggestion of a difference.

Disturbances of Deviant Children

Only the children of Midwest have thus far been considered in this report. In this section, the data from the non-Midwest subjects will be presented which appear to have most direct relevance to the problems of physical disability and emotional maladjustment. In interpreting these comparative data, it must be kept in mind that physical disability in the cases of Wally W., Sue, Bobby and Verne, and maladjustment in the case of Wally O., were by no means the only variables upon which the children differed.

The physically disabled children had the following numbers of disturbances: Wally W., 116; Sue, 54; Bobby, 68; and Verne, 114. During his day at home Wally O. experienced 99 disturbances. When we place these frequencies on the age-frequency diagram of Figure 6.1, we find that only Verne is in any degree out of line with Midwest children, having an excessive number of disturbances for this age. These deviant children's disturbances fall within the Midwest range with respect to frequency; none of them diverge as much from the general trend as the "normal" Jimmy.

TABLE 6.12

Frequency and Per Cent of Various Causal Types of Disturbance Evoked by Midwest Mothers and Fathers

	SOURCE OF EVOCATION			
	Mother		*Father*	
TYPE	*f*	%	*f*	%
Interference	130	47	19	46
Failure	6	2	0	0
Imposed Driving Force	91	33	13	32
Offending Imposition	44	16	5	12
Psychological Loss	6	2	4	10
Totals	277	100	41	100

The intensity and duration of the disturbances of the non-Midwest children did not differ significantly from those of the Midwest subjects.

The disturbances of the non-Midwest children were somewhat more often socially evoked than those of the Midwest children: the mean per cent of socially-evoked disturbances was 81 per cent for the physically disabled children, and 72 per cent for the Midwest children ($p < .05$). Eighty-three per cent of Wally O.'s disturbances were socially evoked. The higher proportion of socially-evoked disturbances for the non-Midwest subjects is related to the fact that they had more frequent social interactions, especially with other children. The D/EFU index failed to reveal a difference between the two groups of subjects.

More of the disturbances of the non-Midwest than of the Midwest children were child-evoked; the mean hourly rate was 3.10 for the physically disabled children and 1.29 for the Midwest children ($p < .02$); 5.18 per hour of Wally O.'s disturbances were evoked by children. The mean per cent of all disturbances that were child-evoked was 47 for the disabled children, and 27 for the Midwest subjects ($p = .002$); 43 per cent of Wally O.'s disturbances were child-evoked. However, when the number of social interactions with children was equated via the D/EFU index, the greater frequency of child-evoked disturbances among the disabled children disappeared.

The fathers of the disabled children evoked a higher mean number of disturbances per social interaction than the Midwest fathers (.20 vs. .10), though the difference was significant at only the .11 level of confidence. Wally O.'s father evoked about the same number as the average Midwest father.

For each non-Midwest subject except Sue, both of the child's parents were present on the day of the observation. In each of the 4 cases the mean intensity of the disturbances caused by the father was greater than that caused by the mother. This is in keeping with the Midwest findings.

The causal types of disturbance were similar in frequency of occurrence for Midwest and non-Midwest children. However, Offending Imposition, rather than Interference, was the most common type for the disabled children; it occurred at a mean rate of 2.41 per hour for the disabled children and 1.26 per hour for Midwest children ($p < .10$). Offending Imposition was high for Wally O., also, occurring at the rate of 3.38 occurrences per hour.

Complete details of the Midwest–non-Midwest comparisons are given elsewhere (Fawl, 1959). The picture that emerges, as was true of Barker and Wright's (1955) study, is one of similarity rather than difference in the frequency, the types, and the evokers of disturbance. The differences that do appear are suggestive for the directions further research could profitably take.

Discussion

It was the purpose of this research to explore the emotional disturbances of children in their natural habitats. In Table 6.13 we have attempted to summarize some important findings for the Midwest sample of children. Many analyses revealed differences between subjects on the basis of age; we have, therefore, juxtaposed the findings for the preschool and the school-age children.

The most characteristic disturbance of Midwest preschool children was mild in intensity, lasting only a few seconds; it resulted from an Interference by the mother. For the school-age children, the most characteristic disturbance was an Offending Imposition imposed by a child associate; it was mild in intensity and of less than a minute in duration. Although the sample of disabled children was very small, we consider it significant that they fell within the Midwest range in almost every major analysis. The age of the child has turned out to be more relevant to the occurrence of disturbance than his physical capability.

It is of some significance, we think, that a substantial number of disturbances was not connected in any way with ongoing, goal-directed behavior. Offending Imposition was the most prominent of these. All subjects considered, it was the second most common causal type, and for school-age children, it was the most common type. In identifying this particular type, we have done nothing more than indicate that certain events or situations can be intrinsically disturbing. We have not spelled out the perceptual conditions under which the event or situation is found disturbing. However, our findings indicate that the occurrence of nongoal-related disturbances is sufficiently common to justify intensive investigation of their conditions. Since so many of this type of disturbance involve other people, Heider's analysis of common-sense interpersonal perception appears to be useful (Heider, 1958, p. 17). Undoubtedly the perception of intentionality, for example, is important. If someone steps on your foot, your reaction, and especially the likelihood that you will be disturbed, is influenced by whether

TABLE 6.13

Characteristics of the Disturbances Experienced by the Children of Midwest

CHARACTERISTIC	AGE LEVEL *Younger* *Preschool*	 *Older* *School-age*
Frequency	Over 90 per day per child	About 45 per day per child
Intensity	Mostly mild	Mostly mild
Duration	Brief; less than one minute	Mostly brief; but some longer disturbances
Source	Mostly social a. Evoked by adults (usually mother): over 50 per cent b. Evoked by children: 20 per cent c. Other evokers: 25–30 per cent	Mostly social a. Evoked by adults: 33 per cent b. Evoked by children: over 33 per cent c. Other evokers: 30 per cent
Common causal types (each accounting for more than one in six of all disturbances; in order of occurrence)	a. Interference (usually by mothers) b. Offending Imposition (unrelated to child's goal, usually social) c. Imposed Driving Force (always social, usually mother)	a. Offending Imposition (unrelated to child's goal, 50 per cent by other children) b. Interference (usually by adults) c. Imposed Driving Force (always social, usually by adults) d. Failure

you perceive that he intended to do so. Informal study of this problem has revealed that intentionality is but one variable among many, however, and that it is neither a sufficient nor necessary condition for a disturbance reaction. Common-sense variables seem to us to be a profitable aid to further inquiry.

Adult associates evoked more disturbances than child associates. Adults in our society, especially mothers, are the responsible environmental agents for directing the behavior of children, and this is a consuming job, especially in the case of preschool children. It is our impression that this role accounts for both the high frequency of interactions with children and the high number of adult-evoked disturbances. However, child associates evoked more disturbances per interaction (EFU). This may mean that child associates provided a more antagonistic social environment than adult associates. We use the word "antagonistic" rather than "hostile," since child-evoked disturbances were not more intense than adult-evoked disturbances. A truly more hostile environment would be the source of more intense disturbances as well as more frequent disturbances per interaction.

By virtue of her much greater contact with the child, the mother was in the position of accounting for more of the child's disturbances than was the father. However, the father, when in interaction with the child, was almost as likely as the mother to evoke a disturbance, and he evoked the same types of disturbances. But there was this difference: when the father was responsible for a disturbance, it tended to be more intense: in fact, in 14 of the 15 cases analyzed. Why this should be is not clear. It did not seem to matter, so far as the evocation of disturbances was concerned, whether the parent was of the same or the opposite sex as the child. All in all, differences between mothers and fathers as they related to the child were not as great as we had anticipated.

That a relationship between age and emotional behavior exists seems fairly certain on the basis of several other observational studies of children as well as this one. Goodenough (1931) and Ricketts (1934) each report that the frequency of anger incidents decreases with age; Blatz et al. (1937) and Inselberg (1958) report a drop with age in the occurrence of "emotional episodes." These findings raise an interesting theoretical question, namely, does the relationship between age and frequency of disturbance represent a developmental change in the psychological characteristics of the child, or does it reflect a change in the role of the environment as the child matures, or both?

Probably all theories of child development allow for changes occurring within the child *and* for changes in the role of the environment impinging upon the child as he grows older. In 1962 it is a truism to state that the child is a component in a social system; and that changes in the child affect changes in the child's social environment, and vice versa. So, when we oppose person-centered and environment-centered explanations of the age-disturbance relationship, we do not imply that one can argue one position to the exclusion of the other. Rather, we wish to point to differences in the emphases of the person-centered and environment-centered orientations. The positions considered represent divergent ones that *can* be taken; they are not necessarily positions that *have* been taken by theoreticians.

From the person-centered point of view, the child becomes less vulnerable to disturbing experiences as he grows older, he becomes less sensitive to, or more tolerant of, negative incidents. Changes occur within the child in a personality sense as well as physically and intellectually. These changes can be thought of as changes in the dynamic structure of the child's personality.

Lewin's (1935) theory of the inner-personal development of the child can be used to illustrate the person-centered orientation, keeping in mind that Lewin also recognized the importance of social factors for psychological understanding. Following Lewin, we can think of the person as a system of needs represented by topological regions. Briefly, development can be characterized in part as involving the following changes within this system: an increasing differentiation of needs (more regions), an increasingly definite demarkation between the self and nonself (a more rigid boundary for the system as a whole), and increasingly greater articulation among needs (boundaries separating regions less permeable, more rigid). These changes are illustrated topologically in Figure 6.2 where the younger and older child are compared.

One of the consequences of the process outlined is the distinction between central and peripheral needs or regions. Impinging stimuli can be thought of as having less access to the central regions of the older child due to the presence of intervening regions and to the lesser permeability of all boundaries. Assuming that an experience of disturbance is directly related to the involvement of the central needs (regions) of the person, it follows that the older child is better buttressed against disturbing stimuli. Not only would disturbances be expected to be less frequent for the older child (as was found), but also less intense (as was detected to only a slight degree). An additional expectation would be that the disturbances of the older child would be longer in duration (as was found), since the greater impermeability of boundaries would make it more difficult for tension to dissipate.

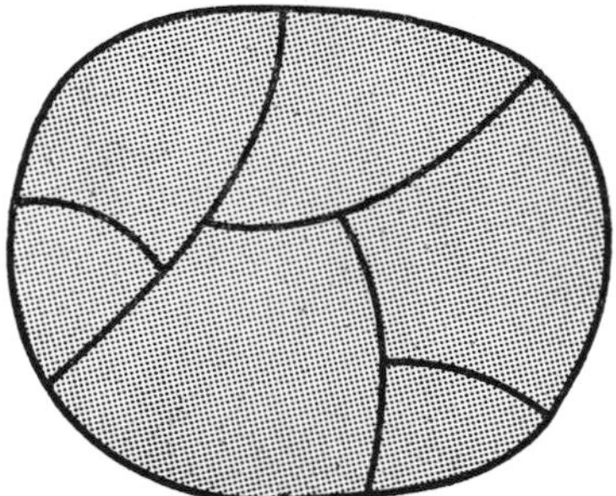

(a) younger child

(b) older child

FIGURE 6.2

A Topological Representation of the Need System of (a) a Younger Child and (b) an Older Child (After Lewin, 1935)

An interesting feature of the disturbance data is the distinction among causal types. Arguing from a person-centered position, it is not clear to us why some types would be age-related (Interference and Imposed Driving Force) and others (Offending Imposition and Failure) would not be.

The fact that so many of the disturbances were evoked by other people urges us to consider the merits of an environment-centered orientation. Here we think in terms of the social psychology of disturbance. It is assumed that the child undergoes change with age from this point of view also. As he matures physically, he requires less guidance from other people. As a creature capable of learning, he comes to realize what is encouraged and what is discouraged by his culture. In short, he becomes socialized. We do not need to assume, following this orientation, that the dynamic structure of the child's personality undergoes change. Rather, the decrease in frequency of disturbance can be seen as a function of the older child being more in tune with his environment: he is disturbed less often because he has fewer conflicts with the environment. Especially appropriate from this point of view is the finding that Interference and Imposed Driving Force disturbances decrease sharply with age, since each implies conflict with the culture. Again, however, not all findings are so clearly in line with the environment-centered contention. The longer duration of disturbance in the case of the older child is not as easily explained here as by the person-centered theory, for instance.

Speculation regarding the relative merits of the two orientations is profitable only up to a point. The data necessary for further consideration of the issue are not available. We need a better basis upon which to calculate the role actually played by the environment in life situations. We need to know, for example, how often children *do* encounter interference by their environment. Knowing this, we would be much closer to answering the important question: Does the older child have fewer Interference disturbances than the younger child because he is *more tolerant of interference,* or because he is *interfered with less often* by his environment? If the older child truly is more tolerant of interference, then we should expect that the percentage of environmental interferences resulting in disturbance would be lower for him than the younger child. If, on the other hand, it is not a question of tolerance level but rather a case of less environmental interference for the older child, then the percentage of interferences resulting in disturbance should not be substantially different for the older and younger child: the one-third as many Interference disturbances which we observed for the school-age child would be based upon one-third as many interferences by the environment.

We have not succeeded in covering all facets of the problem we have outlined. Clearly, though, there seems to be a need for further ecological investigation. An important theoretical issue is at stake, namely, the conceptualization of child development itself. The relationship of ecology to theory has not always been stressed, but it nevertheless exists. Not only is the field situation a fruitful source for the origin of hypotheses, but, as exemplified in the theoretical question raised in the present study, it also is occasionally preferable to the laboratory as the vehicle for evaluating them.

CHAPTER 7

Social Actions in the Behavior Streams of American and English Children

ROGER G. BARKER & LOUISE SHEDD BARKER

DIFFERENCES in the living conditions and behavior of American and English children are explored here by means of methods which introduce some innovations into field studies of human behavior. The methods adapt a standard biological field procedure to behavior phenomena, they use a large behavior unit, they deal simultaneously with a number of behavior stream attributes, and they make use of a wide variety of primary data.

Roger G. Barker, a Stanford Ph.D., is Professor of Psychology at the University of Kansas, where he has been associated since 1947 with the Midwest Psychological Field Station. Louise Shedd Barker holds the M.A. degree in biology from Stanford University; she has engaged in research in psychological ecology at the University of Kansas since 1947.

THE DATA OF THIS INVESTIGATION consist of measures of the occurrence of 118 kinds of social actions within the behavior streams of children in 141 American and 141 English behavior settings. Examples of the kinds of behavior we have investigated are:

Adult dominates child.
Child resists child.
Adult enjoys child.
Child dominates adult.
Adult is friendly with child.
Child is polite to adult.
Child plays with child.

The verb of each sentence designates the variety of the action, and the subject and object of the sentence gives its social context.

The general method of the study is one that is widely used in biological ecology. It consists, there, of recording the presence and absence of species within sample areas of the region studied, without regard for their frequency within the areas. The basic results are expressed in terms of the numbers of areas in which species are present. Thus Beals and Cottam (1960) reported that *Quercus borealis* occurred in 27 of 75 stands of forest on the Apostle Islands of Lake Superior; while *Pinus strobus* was present in 14 of the same stands. These "presence values" indicate that *Quercus borealis* was encountered in more Apostle Island Forest stands than *Pinus strobus,* but they provide no information on the relative density or dominance of the species in the stands where they occurred. The presence ratios, $^{27}/_{75}$ and $^{14}/_{75}$, express the chances that the species would be encountered when stands were inspected at random.

The adequacy of this method depends (1) upon the degree to which the primary sampling units (e.g., forest stands) represent the total region they are intended to represent, and (2) upon the adequacy with which the primary units are inspected for the presence and absence of the designated species. The latter procedure usually requires two steps, namely, (1) systematically sampling the primary units via secondary units, e.g., points and quadrats, and (2) making complete inventories of the designated species within the secondary sampling units or, again, sampling them via tertiary units.

In this research, we have followed with fidelity the main lines of standard ecological technique. We have tabulated below the corresponding phases of the methodology of the present study and of Beals and Cottam's (1960) investigation of forest vegetation. The English field methods are methodologically identical to those listed for the United States.

	FOREST STUDY	PRESENT STUDY
Region studied	Apostle Islands	United States
Primary sampling units	75 forest stands	141 behavior settings
Secondary sampling units	Points and quadrats located at equal intervals along compass lines through the forest stands	A particular child's behavior stream within each behavior setting
Tertiary sampling units	(a) The nearest tree to each point (b) an inventory of all herbs, shrubs and saplings within each quadrat	Inventory of social actions in the behavior stream of the child

The general parallel between the methods is clear enough; however, some particular points deserve discussion.

The primary and secondary sampling units are less adequate in the present investigation than in the forest study. One hundred and forty-one behavior settings and a few hundred persons cannot represent the United States or England as adequately as 75 stands and several hundred points and quadrats can represent the forests of 22 small islands of Lake Superior. However, limited resources made it impossible to obtain more representative samples; so we have proceeded in two ways. (1) Within the two cultures we have sampled the social behavior of limited, but well-defined and equivalent ranges of children and situations. We have done this by working in a single American and a single English town selected for equivalence on cultural dimensions. Within the towns, we have sampled the social behavior occurring in pairs of analogous American and English behavior settings, and within the settings we have sampled the social behavior of American and English children equated for age, sex, and social class. (2) In addition, we have sampled the social behavior of a wider range of behavior settings and persons in the two cultures. To accomplish this, we have used descriptions of the social behavior of American and English behavior settings and children as these appear in the writings of representative writers of fiction. We have, in effect, asked the authors of the selected works to choose behavior settings and children, and to describe the social behavior for us.

By the first method, we have taken the behavior streams of equivalent children in equivalent settings of equivalent towns of America and England as the "compass lines" along which to inspect the behavior with which we are concerned. In this way, we have allowed American and English behavior to vary within sharply restricted, precisely defined ecological limits. By the second method, the sample of behavior is less restricted, and the universe it represents with greater or less adequacy is much less well known. However, the sample is not biased by the investigators; it is "biased" by independent authors. A comparison of these two different views of American and English social behavior provides a useful check upon the adequacy of each of them.

We shall end this introduction by emphasizing that this is a study of the stream of behavior. It is concerned with the social actions which occur within, and circumjacent to, the behavior streams of the selected children. The unit of the study is the *behavior setting unit*. This is a macro-unit extending from the moment the child enters a behavior setting until he leaves it. The behavior setting unit is a natural unit; the child's behavior and situation determine its beginning and end points.

In practice, some behavior setting units are too long to be analyzed in their entirety; in these cases a sample of the whole unit must be used.

Behavior Settings, Specimen Records, and Subjects

Behavior settings, which provide the larger circumstances, and the initial and terminal bounds of the behavior setting units of the stream of behavior, are self-bounded parts of a community. They are extraindividual behavior

TABLE 7.1
Variety, Number, and Time of Behavior Setting Units in Midwest (M) and Yoredale (Y)

VARIETY OF BEHAVIOR SETTING UNIT NUMBER	NAME	*No. of Pairs of Matched Units*	*Total Duration of Units in Minutes*		*Per Cent of Total Time*[a]	
			M	*Y*	*M*	*Y*
1	School, Academic Classes	24	706	640	35.14	41.08
2	School, Music Classes	5	85	103	2.10	3.24
3	School, Phys. Ed. Classes	4	62	53	.72	1.05
4	School, Girl's Room	1	4	2	2.78	1.04
5	School, Lunch Room	1	22	30	4.90	3.15
6	Open Spaces (School Playground & Home, Outdoors)	12	155	160	11.13	7.45
7	Athletic Contests, Outdoors	1	5	18	1.78	3.71
8	Religious Services and Classes	1	13	27	4.01	3.85
9	Meetings, Social Cultural	1	6	21	1.45	.75
10	Home, Indoors	1	21	28		
	Total	51	1079	1082	64.01	65.32

[a] Total time school children spent in each variety of behavior setting expressed as a per cent of the total time they spent in all community behavior settings, i.e., in behavior settings outside of their homes.

entities with easily identified internal features and external relationships. These characteristics of settings make it possible to identify community parts of Midwest and Yoredale that are equivalent in known respects. Behavior settings have been described in detail in other publications (Barker, 1960; Barker & Wright, 1955) and can perhaps be adequately denoted for the present purpose by listing the varieties of settings within which units were studied in Midwest and Yoredale. This list, with the number of settings, and the total duration of the behavior setting units in each variety is given in Table 7.1; further details will be found with the published records (Barker, Wright, Barker, & Schoggen, 1961).

Although the behavior settings within which the specimen records were made were not adequate samples of the varieties of settings of the two towns, they represented rather well the particular community settings which school children of the towns inhabited. Of all the time children 6 to 12 years of age spent in community settings, Midwest children spent 64.0 per cent of this time in the varieties sampled and Yoredale children spent 65.3

TABLE 7.2

Sex, Age, and Social Class of Matched Pairs of Midwest and Yoredale Subjects, and Behavior Setting Variety in Which Behavior Setting Unit Occurred

UNIT NUMBER	B.S. VARIETY[a]	SEX	SUBJECT NUMBER *M*	SUBJECT NUMBER *Y*	AGE *M*	AGE *Y*	SOCIAL CLASS *M*	SOCIAL CLASS *Y*
1	1	F	1	1	6:4	6:4	2	2
2	1	F	2	2	6:4	6:3	2	2
3	1	M	3	3	6:2	6:2	3	3
5	1	F	4	5	7:2	6:9	1	2
6	1	M	5	6	7:5	7:11	1	2
7	1	M	6	7	7:4	7:9	2	2
8	1	F	7	8	7:4	7:8	3	3
9	1	F	8	9	7:10	7:11	3	3
10	1	F	9	10	7:4	7:7	2	3
11	1	M	5	11	7:5	7:2	1	2
12	1	M	10	12	9:10	9:5	1	2
13	1	M	6	13	9:0	8:6	2	2
14	1	M	11	14	10:0	9:3	2	1
15	1	M	12	15	9:11	9:7	3	3
16	1	F	7	16	9:4	9:0	3	2
17	1	F	13	17	8:7	8:6	2	3
18	1	M	14	18	9:3	8:11	2	3
19	1	F	15	19	10:0	10:1	2	2
20	1	F	16	20	10:11	10:1	3	3
21	1	M	17	21	11:1	11:5	2	2
22	1	M	18	22	10:7	11:4	3	3
23	1	F	19	23	10:6	10:9	2	2
24	1	F	20	24	11:3	11:5	2	2
25	1	M	21	25	11:8	12:2	1	3
26	2	M	6	7	7:4	7:9	2	2
27	2	M	22	26	8:10	9:2	1	1
28	2	F	13	27	8:7	8:9	2	2
29	2	M	14	26	9:3	9:2	2	1
30	2	F	23	28	11:10	11:9	3	3
31	3	F	24	1	5:11	6:4	3	2
32	3	F	25	29	8:2	7:6	3	3
33	3	F	26	27	8:10	8:9	2	2
34	3	F	27	24	11:6	11:5	2	2
35	7	M	28	12	9:6	9:5	2	2
36	6	F	29	1	6:6	6:4	2	2
38	6	M	5	11	7:5	7:2	1	2
39	6	F	13	31	8:7	9:0	2	2
40	6	M	30	12	8:11	9:5	3	2
41	6	M	14	26	9:3	9:2	2	1
42	6	M	31	32	10:7	10:6	2	2
43	6	F	32	33	11:2	10:11	3	2
44	6	F	13	34	8:7	9:6	2	3
45	6	F	13	20	8:7	10:1	2	3
46	4	F	33	1	7:0	6:4	3	2
47	5	F	34	35	8:10	9:4	3	3
49	8	M	35	37	6:6	6:9	2	3
50	9	F	36	38	8:4	8:8	1	1
52	6	M	14	14	9:3	9:3	2	1
53	6	M	37	40	8:2	8:9	2	2
54	6	M	14	18	9:3	8:11	2	3
56	10	M	14	14	9:3	9:3	2	1

[a] See Table 7.1 for Variety names.

per cent of this time in the varieties sampled. Furthermore, the distribution of children's time among the different behavior setting varieties of our sample was very similar to the distribution of children's time among these varieties as they lived in the towns.

The equating of American and English behavior setting units was carried one step further in the analysis. The matched pairs of settings did not necessarily provide the same social action contexts; if there was no adult present in the Midwest setting of a pair, for example, this prevented the occurrence of adult-child and child-adult social actions in Midwest. In the analysis, therefore, social actions whose contexts occurred in only one setting of a matched pair were omitted from the count.

Within each setting, the stream of behavior of the selected, target child was recorded by means of a specimen record (see Ch. 1; also Barker & Wright, 1955). These specimen records provide descriptions of the behavior setting units; they constitute the permanent field data.

Data were collected in Midwest prior to their collection in Yoredale, and included both sexes, and the age, and social-class ranges of primary school children. Each Yoredale child was selected to match a Midwest child with respect to age, sex, social class. Details of the matched pairs of subjects are given in Table 7.2. Thirty-seven different Midwest subjects and 40 different Yoredale subjects participated in the fifty-one behavior setting units.

In addition to the subjects there were other children present as associates in every setting. The associates ranged in age from year-old infants to 15-year-old adolescents. Adult participants, other than the observer, were present in 43 of the Midwest settings and in 46 of the Yoredale settings. The social actions of the associate children and adults vis-à-vis the subjects, and also vis-à-vis each other were also inventoried.

The specimen records which provide primary data for this study have been published, and with them are further details about the subjects and behavior settings (Barker et al., 1961).

Narratives of child behavior, and descriptions of the behavior settings in which they live, written by selected novelists, constitute one source of the data of this study. It is important, therefore, to state clearly how the books and the settings within them were selected.

The following guides were used in selecting the books:

1. Books of fiction written by American authors, about American children, for American children (primarily), made up the American list; books written by English authors, about English children, for English children made up the English list.
2. Only stories about "real life" situations and experiences were selected; fairy stories, science fiction, animal stories, were eliminated.
3. The lists included only recently written stories about contemporary times in America and England; historical books and books about chil-

dren of other lands were excluded. The year 1930 was selected as the earliest publishing date to be included.

4. Stories written for particular, didactic purposes were eliminated; religious and political tracts, and books about vocations and limited social problems were rejected.
5. Only books whose "authenticity" had been demonstrated by a fair degree of popularity among children were included.
6. Books whose main characters ranged in age from 7 to 16 years were retained.
7. In order to avoid the biases of the investigators, nominations of books suitable for our purposes were secured from American and English library associations.

From the lists submitted to us by the librarians we eliminated a number by applying the selection principles more uniformly and stringently than they were able to apply them; others were eliminated in order to secure roughly similar age distributions of the main characters. After these eliminations we had 18 American and 18 English books. The titles, authors, publishers, and publication dates of books are reported in Appendix 7.1.

Behavior settings within the books were selected for analysis as follows: The total number of pages (X) in a book was divided into 6 equal parts. At the X/6th page, we began reading until the principal character, or characters, entered a new behavior setting; this was marked as the origin of a behavior setting unit. The place in the text where the locus of the behavior changed to another setting was marked as the termination of the unit. The same procedure was repeated beginning with the 2X/6th page of the book, and it was continued, similarly, at the 3X/6th, 4X/6th, 5X/6th pages. Five behavior settings were thus selected from every book, making 90 American and 90 English behavior setting units.

For some of the analyses, we selected from the behavior setting units of the books a special group of paired American and English units that were equivalent with respect to the variety of the setting and age-range of the children involved. These matched settings were so selected that a behavior setting of variety *Z* containing children of ages *a* to *e* in the American books was matched with a behavior setting of variety *Z* with child occupants of ages *a* to *e* in the English books. The maximum number of pairings was made within the 90 settings from the American and English books; 56 matched pairs of behavior settings were obtained.

The text of the story within each selected setting provided the "specimen record" that was inventoried for the 118 social actions. Data regarding the persons appearing in the behavior settings of the books are given in Table 7.3.

TABLE 7.3
Number, Age, and Sex of Persons in the Behavior Setting Units of the Books

	American	*English*
TOTAL NUMBER OF CHILDREN	82	100
Number of children per book (range)	1–7	3–12
Average number of children per book	4.6	5.6
Number of settings with more than one child	62	80
Number of settings in which an adult was present	76	75
AGE DISTRIBUTION OF CHILDREN		
Infants (under 2 years)	1	1
Preschool (2–5:11)	7	5
Younger school (6–8:11)	10	10
Older school (9–11:11)	31	33
Younger adolescent (12–14:11)	17	41
Older adolescent (15–17:11)	16	10
Median age	10.9	12.1

Varieties and Contexts of Social Actions

The research dealt with 118 kinds of social action distributed among 40 varieties. These varieties of social action are described and illustrated in detail in Appendixes 7.2 and 1.2. The descriptions constitute definitions of the social behavior we have studied; the reader should, therefore, be familiar with them. The names of the social action varieties and summary definitions of them are listed below. In these, X stands for the actor (child or adult), and Y for the social referent of the action (child or adult). The actor and the referent, together, make up the social context of the action.

1. X dominates Y. X applies maximal personal pressure on Y.
2. X manages Y. X applies medium personal pressure on Y.
3. X influences Y. X applies routine personal pressure to Y.
4. X provides opportunity for Y. X increases positive valence or removes obstacle for Y.
5. X asks favor of Y. X makes own need explicit to Y.
6. X punishes Y. X determines Y's behavior by his authority plus actual punishment.
7. X disciplines Y. X determines Y's behavior by his authority plus threat of worse to come.
8. X accepts Y's control. X willingly accepts Y's influence.
9. X complies with Y. X accepts Y's authority realistically.
10. X surrenders to Y. X complies under Y's duress.
11. X resists Y. X does not comply with Y's efforts at domination.
12. X disagrees with Y. X engages in verbal opposition to Y.

13. X exploits Y. X uses his power over Y to benefit himself.
14. X gratifies Y. X gives to Y without request or effort on Y's part.
15. X helps Y. X adds his power to Y's efforts.
16. X co-operates with Y. X joins with Y in common task.
17. X accommodates his behavior to Y. X adjusts his behavior, including his thinking, to Y.
18. X comforts Y. X consoles Y when Y is sad or hurt.
19. X defends Y. X is protective of Y.
20. X forgives Y. X overlooks faults or misdemeanors of Y.
21. X deprives Y. X withholds or withdraws something of value from Y.
22. X hinders Y. X tries to prevent Y from reaching Y's goal.
23. X competes with Y. X tries to win over Y.
24. X is antagonistic to Y. X tries to inflict maximal injury of which he is capable on Y (not as punishment).
25. X is impatient with Y. X inflicts medium injury on Y.
26. X teases Y. X inflicts minimum injury on Y.
27. X is affectionate to Y. X shows by explicit behavior that he loves Y.
28. X is friendly with Y. X shows medium affection for Y.
29. X enjoys Y. X shows by specific expressive action that he is pleased to interact with Y.
30. X values Y. X makes specific positive evaluation of Y.
31. X hates Y. X expresses maximal negative emotion toward Y.
32. X is unfriendly to Y. X expresses medium negative emotion toward Y.
33. X is grieved by Y. X expresses distress at Y's behavior.
34. X devalues Y. X makes specific negative evaluation of Y.
35. X understands Y. X expresses insight into reasons for Y's behavior.
36. X is baffled by Y. X does not show insight into Y's behavior.
37. X plays with Y. X enters into game with Y, not as a supervisor or official, but as a player.
38. X works with Y. X engages in serious activity.
39. X is distant from Y. X appears indifferent to Y.
40. X is polite to Y. X shows proper forms of conduct with Y.

These varieties of social action were chosen as the focus of the study before the field work was begun, and do not represent the total range of social action varieties occurring. They represent our own preoccupations which are based upon theories of American-English culture differences.

Thirty-eight of the varieties of social action were studied in three actor-referent contexts: adult-child, child-adult, and child-child; two varieties, #39, *distant with* and #40 *polite to* were studied in two actor-referent contexts, namely, adult-child and child-adult. Each variety-of-social-action-in-context, i.e., each kind of social action, describes a directed, social relationship. These relationships carry no logical implications regarding the nature of the reciprocal relations between actors and referents. For example, nothing can be logically derived from the social action *adult dominates child* regarding the simultaneously occurring child-adult social action; a number of social actions occur in association with *adult dominates child:* child may submit to adult, resist adult, avoid adult, etc. Implicit in this method of enumerating kinds of social action is the asumption that a variety of social action in one context (e.g., *child is friendly with child*) is a different social phenomenon from the same variety in other social contexts (e.g., *adult is friendly with child* or *child is friendly with adult*). The discovery of the interrelations between kinds of social action is a problem of empirical and theoretical psychology.

An inventory was made of the 118 kinds of social action in each of the 102 specimen records of Midwest and Yoredale, and in each of the 180 narratives of the books. If a social action occurred one or more times in a behavior setting unit it was marked present; if it did not occur, it was marked absent. To check upon the accuracy with which the social actions were identified, two workers independently inventoried 43 records and narratives. For each record and narrative there were 118 decisions to be made with respect to presence and absence of social actions. The workers agreed on every decision in the case of three records and they agreed on 82 per cent of the the decisions in the case of the record where their ratings were most discrepant; the mean agreement was 95 per cent.

Measures of Social Actions

The basic measure of a social action is its presence or absence in a behavior setting. Upon this datum, we have based other quantitative assessments of social actions, as follows.

Presence value (PV) is a property of a social action; it is the number of behavior settings in which the action is present. PV is a measure of the distribution of the social action among the behavior settings inventoried. It may be expressed, also, as a per cent of the number of behavior settings inventoried; in this case, we speak of the presence index (PI) of a social action. The social action *adult values child,* for example, occurred in 23 of the 46 Yoredale behavior setting units in which adults were associates of children, and in 13 of the 43 comparable Midwest units. PI for *adult values child* was, therefore, 50 in Yoredale and 30 in Midwest; i.e., it was more widely distributed among the behavior settings of Yoredale than of Midwest.

PV can be determined for both varieties (PV:V) and kinds (PV:K) of social action; it is important to understand the relation between the two values (and indexes) in the two cases. For illustration we shall take the social action variety *X is friendly with Y* in Midwest. The presence index of friendly as a variety of social action (PV:V) was 86; it was present in some context, i.e., between adult and child, child and adult, or child and child within 86 per cent of Midwest's 51 behavior settings. As a kind of social action (PV:K), friendly was present in 28 per cent of Midwest's adult-child contexts, in 14 per cent of Midwest's child-adult contexts, and in 78 per cent of Midwest's child-child contexts. It will be noted that the sum of the presence indexes of friendly in the three contexts of Midwest is greater than the presence value of friendly as a single variety of social action: PV:K = 120; PV:V = 86. This occurs because the same variety of social action can be present in more than one context in the same behavior setting. If the social actions *adult is friendly with child* and *child is friendly with adult* are both present in a behavior setting, they constitute one variety, but two kinds, of social action.

It will be clear from this discussion that PV is an indicator of the breadth of the distribution of a social action among behavior settings.

Social action *heterogeneity* is a property of one or more behavior settings; it is the number of kinds of social action with a presence value of one or more in the settings inventoried. Within Midwest's 51 behavior settings, 63 kinds of social action had a presence value of one; this was also true within Yoredale's 51 settings; the heterogeneity with respect to social actions of the behavior settings sampled in Midwest and Yoredale was the same.

Heterogeneity can be determined for a single behavior setting unit or for a number of settings. There were, for example, 10 kinds of social action present in the adult-child context of Yoredale behavior setting unit #1, listed in Table 7.2; in setting unit #2 there were eight kinds of social action present. Two social actions that were present in the second setting were not present in the first setting. Using these data, here are the various measures of the social action heterogeneity of Yoredale behavior setting units #1 and #2:

Heterogeneity of behavior setting unit #1	10
Heterogeneity of behavior setting unit #2	8
Heterogeneity of behavior setting units #1 and #2	12
Average heterogeneity of units #1 and #2	9

It should be noted that the heterogeneity of a class of behavior settings, the heterogeneity of individual settings within the class, and the average heterogeneity of the settings of the class will usually differ. All of these measures of behavior setting heterogeneity are reported in this paper. They provide measures of the multiformity of social behavior.

The *commonality* of behavior settings with respect to social actions is a property of two or more behavior settings, or classes of settings; it is a measure of the extent to which the settings overlap with respect to social actions. The measure of social action commonality we have used is the number of kinds of social action present in all the settings, or classes of settings, investigated. There were, for example, 77 kinds of social action present in the 102 behavior settings of Midwest and Yoredale, and of these, 50 occurred in the settings of both towns. Fifty, then, is a statement of the commonality of the social actions we inventoried in Midwest and Yoredale. For some purposes, a more meaningful statement is the number of common kinds of social action expressed as a per cent of the total number of social actions present in the behavior settings compared. For the settings of Midwest and Yoredale, the commonality index is $^{50}/_{77}$ x 100, or 65 per cent. For the behavior setting units #1 and #2 of Table 7.2 (mentioned above) the commonality index is $^{6}/_{12}$, or 50 per cent. The average index of commonality of a number of pairs of settings can also be determined.

The presence value, heterogeneity, and commonality of social actions refer to their distribution among behavior settings as separate social events. Social actions can also be ordered into series according to the degree in which they display common attributes. We have ordered social actions upon five attribute dimensions.

The *harmony-disharmony dimension* of social actions is grounded upon Heider's (1958) conception of interpersonal balance. The 40 varieties of social action have been ordered upon a scale from those with the greatest tendency to increase the momentary, interpersonal harmony of the persons involved in an action, to those with the greatest tendency to increase interpersonal disharmony. In placing the social action varieties in order from those that are harmony-increasing to those that are disharmony-increasing, we have followed the guides of naive psychology. On the harmony end of the scale we have placed social actions which promote the closeness and interpersonal stability of the persons involved in an action, and on the disharmony end we have placed actions which increase stress, interpersonal instability, and distance between the parties to an action. We have not attempted to define this interpersonal variable with precision, and we have not tested the validity or the reliability of our ordering of social actions upon it. We have given weight to the ease and subjective certainty with which the ranking can be done.

In the list below, social action varieties are placed in order from those we considered to be most harmony-increasing to those we judged to be most disharmony-increasing. The identification number of each social action is given in the parentheses.

1. Gratifies (14)
2. Affectionate (27)
3. Comforts (18)
4. Defends (19)
5. Friendly (28)
6. Enjoys (29)
7. Helps (15)
8. Values (30)
9. Co-operates (16)
10. Plays (37)

11. Works (38)
12. Accepts control (8)
13. Accommodates (17)
14. Provides opportunity (4)
15. Forgives (20)
16. Understands (35)
17. Polite (40)
18. Influences (3)
19. Complies (9)
20. Asks favor (5)
21. Manages (2)
22. Exploits (13)
23. Baffled (36)
24. Surrenders (10)
25. Distant (39)
26. Competes (23)
27. Disagrees (12)
28. Deprives (21)
29. Hinders (22)
30. Devalues (34)
31. Distressed (33)
32. Dominates (1)
33. Resists (11)
34. Teases (26)
35. Impatient (25)
36. Unfriendly (32)
37. Disciplines (7)
38. Punishes (6)
39. Antagonistic (24)
40. Hates (31)

The particular circumstances under which a social action occurs contribute to its behavioral significance. For example, help that is rejected does not increase interpersonal harmony, and in this circumstance help should have a lower position in the scale than that assigned to it. Punishment that is accepted as deserved by the recipient may promote interpersonal harmony. Three points are relevant in this connection: (1) Each social action in the books and in the specimen records was identified in terms of the apparent intentions and cognitions of the actor and of the recipient. An action which was superficially helpful, but which was clearly intended to be a teasing action, and was so seen by the recipient, was identified as the social action variety *teases,* not as the variety *helps.* In other words, the perceived motives and cognitions of the parties to the action guided the identification of the action. (2) The momentary situation in which the action occurred was considered in making the inventories. This removed some of the uncertainty about the placement of social actions on the harmony-disharmony scale. It is doubtful, for example, that punishment, even when given with righteousness and accepted as just, increases or is intended to increase the momentary harmony of the relationship between the persons involved. (3) Furthermore, the harmony-disharmony scale refers to the direction of change in interpersonal relations, and not to persisting relationships. Being polite is often a symptom of interpersonal stress, yet at the moment of its occurrence, a polite action will usually reduce the existing disharmony. In fact, it appears that an important function of polite actions is to reduce momentary tension.

When social actions are ordered on the harmony-disharmony scale their presence values become a frequency distribution of the number of behavior settings in which social actions of different degrees of harmony occur. On the basis of this distribution, the median social action on the harmony dimension can be computed for the behavior settings being considered. The harmony scale rank order numbers can also be used to score the social actions occurring in particular behavior setting units.

These techniques of analysis were used in connection with the other scales to be described.

Some varieties of social action can be ordered on a *scale of social power,* ranging from those which attempt to control the behavior of others without the application of power, to those which rely heavily upon social or physical force. The following varieties of social action form an interpersonal power scale from *X asks favor of Y,* where weakness is used as a social control technique, to *X punishes Y,* based upon physical power.

1. Asks favor (5)
2. Provides opportunity (4)
3. Influences (3)
4. Manages (2)
5. Dominates (1)
6. Disciplines (7)
7. Punishes (6)

The definitions of these varieties of social action provide a description of the social power dimension.

A scale of *reaction to social power* ranging from the ready acceptance of others' control efforts to resistance to the social controls imposed by others is as follows:

1. Gratifies (14)
2. Helps (15)
3. Co-operates (16)
4. Comforts (18)
5. Defends (19)
6. Forgives (20)
7. Deprives (21)
8. Hinders (22)
9. Competes (23)
10. Teases (26)
11. Impatient (25)
12. Antagonistic (24)

Six varieties of social action are concerned almost entirely with the expression of feelings vis-à-vis an associate. These social actions have been ordered on a *scale from positive to negative emotional expressions,* as follows:

1. Accepts control (8)
2. Complies (9)
3. Surrenders (10)
4. Disagrees (12)
5. Resists (11)

The social action varieties listed below form a *benefit-harm scale* that ranges from social actions which benefit other persons to those which harm them.

1. Affectionate (27)
2. Friendly (28)
3. Enjoys (29)
4. Distressed (33)
5. Unfriendly (32)
6. Hates (31)

Statistical Problems and Terminology

The statistics used in the standard ecological investigation assume that the sampling units are, indeed, unitary with respect to the phenomena studied, e.g., that the likelihood of discovering *Quercus borealis* in a forest stand is the same wherever the compass lines are laid within the stand, and that the likelihood of discovering *Quercus borealis* in one stand is unrelated to its occurrence in any other forest stand (Greig-Smith, 1957).

We have not examined the internal arrangements of behavior setting units of the behavior stream with respect to the distribution of social actions. In view of the constancy of persons and situations within each unit, however, the possibility that a new "compass line," i.e., a replication of the specimen record on the same subject in the same behavior setting, would produce different findings seemed so remote as to not justify the work involved. It is pertinent to note, here, that behavior settings are in this respect more adequate units than quadrats or behavior stream tesserae. Behavior settings are complete, integrated, natural units of extraindividual behavior; they are organized and bounded units. Quadrats and tesserae, on the other hand, are fragments, and they have arbitrary boundaries unrelated to their inner content and arrangements. Behavior settings are units in the way that molecules, cells, and persons are units (Barker & Barker, 1961), and specimen records within them partake in some degree of their unitary nature.

The degree of independence of the behavior setting units we have studied is indeterminate. Behavior settings within each town have, to varying degrees, the same persons as occupants: the same teachers and classmates enter a number of different settings as associates of the subjects, and some subjects appear in more than one behavior setting unit. These facts suggest that the behavior settings we have inventoried are to some degree interlinked with respect to the social behavior that occurs within them by way of common elements.

The independence of social actions within behavior settings is also indeterminate, although the few social actions we have studied provide no evidence of an appreciable association. Thus, we have found that PV of the social action *adult helps child* in a setting is not correlated with PV of the social action *adult friendly with child*. However, we have not made a thorough study of the contingent occurrence of social actions within settings.

There is reason for suspecting lack of independence between the five settings of each of the 38 books. We have tested the hypothesis that behavior settings within the same books are not independent with respect to the occurrence and nonoccurrence of particular kinds of social actions. The technique of making the test is shown in the following example:

Source of data: 18 English books.

Social action: Child values child.

Behavior settings investigated: first and third setting of each book.

The obtained frequencies are as follows:

In this case there is no evidence that the occurrence of the social action *child values child* in the first settings of the English books is significantly associated with an increased or a decreased likelihood of occurrence in the third settings of the same books; deviations from the expected cell frequencies (on the basis of the marginal frequencies) as great or greater than those obtained can be expected to occur by chance in 38 cases in 100. We have tested 96 such distributions, selected at random from the 2400 the data provide, and in 95 of them p > .01 that the obtained deviations would occur by chance.

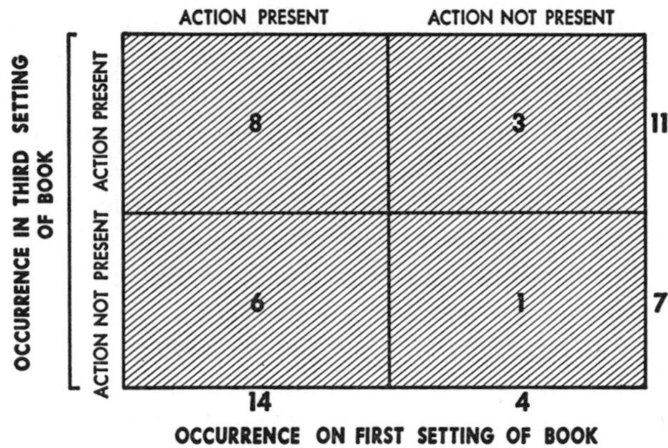

Comparative studies with the measures of social action which we have devised require that subjects, social actions, behavior settings, and sample sizes be equivalent. Otherwise, errors will be introduced similar to those occurring if a biologist were to count different species, to note different characteristics of species, to use different sampling units, or to use different numbers of sampling units in the regions being compared. It seems certain that the subjects of the study are equivalent phenomena in the United States and England, and we have presented arguments and evidence elsewhere (Barker & Barker, 1961) that this is true too, of behavior setting units. We have carefully judged social actions by the same criteria in both cultures; however, this does not assure that social actions which are identical within the rating contexts have the same significance within the culture contexts. Finally, we have inventoried equal numbers of behavior setting units in the two countries; this is essential, as the number of social actions and their presence values vary with the number of units examined (Greig-Smith, 1957).

Data are presented separately for the behavior settings of the books and the towns, and within the towns for three categories of settings: academic (category #1, Table 7.1), nonacademic (categories #3–#10, Table 7.1), and music (category #2, Table 7.1).

In evaluating the data presented, the uncertainty regarding the independence of behavior settings must be kept in mind. It is this that has led us to depend more upon the degree of agreement between the data of the books and of the towns, and upon the consistency of the total picture of culture differences, than upon the usual statistical tests. This line of study presents so many new technical issues that it is necessary to choose whether to postpone substantive research until all technical issues are solved, or to investigate ecological problems despite unfinished technological business. We have made the latter choice.

The special terms used in this report have been defined. However, to avoid confusions that may easily arise, some points should be clarified.

The term "kind of social action" when used in the singular refers to one of the 118 behavior-varieties-in-context, irrespective of the number of settings in which it is present. For example, if the social action *child helps adult* occurs in one setting and again in another setting, these constitute one kind of social action with a presence value of two. If *child helps adult* is present in one behavior setting, and *child enjoys child* is present in another setting, these are two kinds of social actions, each with a presence value of one. "Kinds of social actions" (plural) always refers to more than one of the 118 kinds of social action, never to the presence of a single kind of social action in more than one setting, or to more than one occurrence of a kind of action in a single setting. To avoid repetition, it is sometimes convenient to omit "kind," and refer simply to social action, but this is always elliptical for "kind of social action."

The terms behavior setting unit, behavior setting, and setting are used interchangeably in the exposition; they all refer to a behavior setting unit of a behavior stream.

Heterogeneity of Social Actions

All of the 40 varieties of social action and 117 of the 118 kinds of social action were present in the combined sample of 282 American and English behavior setting units. Within individual behavior settings, the number of social actions ranged from 0 to 35, forming a near-normal frequency distribution with mean of 14.48, and a standard deviation of 6.15.

All varieties of social action were present in both the American and the English behavior settings. Data regarding kinds of social action within the behavior setting sample of each culture are reported in Table 7.4. According to these data, the total number of social actions within the American behavior settings did not differ from the number within the English behavior settings; the small culture differences within subordinate categories of settings are not consistent. However, the data of Table 7.4 provide evidence

TABLE 7.4
Heterogeneity of Social Actions in Behavior Setting Units of American and English Books and Towns[a]

CATEGORY OF BEHAVIOR SETTING UNITS	KINDS OF SOCIAL ACTION: *Total Number within Setting Category* *American*	*English*	*Average Number within Setting Category* *American*	*English*	
All units	114 (141)	112 (141)	13.9 (107)	15.0 (107)	
Units of books	112 (90)	111 (90)	16.5 (56)	16.7 (56)	$p = .8$
Units of towns	63 (51)	64 (51)	11.0 (51)	13.2 (51)	$p < .001$
Academic units	48 (24)	49 (24)	11.2 (24)	13.6 (24)	$p < .04$
Nonacademic units	46 (22)	52 (22)	10.4 (22)	12.5 (22)	$p < .016$
Music units	34 (5)	38 (5)	12.8 (5)	15.0 (5)	

[a] The number of behavior settings inventoried is given in the parentheses; for total number within the category, this is the number of behavior settings in the category; for average number within the category, this is the number of matched, equivalent settings in the category.

that the *average* number of social actions within English settings was greater than the average number within American settings. The greater heterogeneity within English settings occurred in both the books and the towns, and within the towns, in the academic, nonacademic and music settings. The greater average English heterogeneity was not large, particularly in the case of the books.

Data regarding the heterogeneity of the social actions within the adult-child social context are given in Table 7.5. These data indicate that English adults engaged in more kinds of social actions with children than did American adults, and that the average number of adult-child social actions per setting was greater within the English than within the American settings. The greater heterogeneity of social actions within the total English sample of behavior settings and the average heterogeneity within the settings themselves was true for both the books and the towns. The American deficit was not great, it ranged from 2 to 5 social actions (95 per cent to 72 per cent of the English social actions) in the various categories of settings, and from 0.7 to 2.2 social actions (91 per cent to 61 per cent of the average heterogeneity of English social actions) within the settings.

The data on heterogeneity of social actions in child-adult contexts of American and English behavior settings are presented in Table 7.6. These data show that American children engaged in more kinds of social actions vis-à-vis adults than English children, but that the average heterogeneity within the settings tended to be less. However the differences are so slight that conclusions regarding the trends are not warranted.

No consistent cultural differences in the heterogeneity of social actions of child to child appear in the data, which are given in Table 7.7. This is true for the total number of social actions, and for the average heterogeneity within the settings. It is noteworthy, however, that the only category of behavior settings in which the average number of social actions was lower in

TABLE 7.5

Heterogeneity of Social Actions in the Adult-Child Context of American and English Behavior Setting Units[a]

CATEGORY OF BEHAVIOR SETTING UNITS	KINDS OF SOCIAL ACTION				
	Total Number within Setting Category		*Average Number within Setting Category*		
	American	*English*	*American*	*English*	
All units	38 (119)	40 (121)	5.7 (89)	6.9 (89)	
Units of books	37 (76)	39 (75)	7.5 (47)	8.2 (49)	p = .3
Units of towns	21 (43)	24 (46)	3.7 (42)	5.4 (42)	p < .002
Academic units	16 (24)	18 (24)	4.5 (24)	5.9 (24)	p < .008
Nonacademic units	13 (14)	18 (17)	2.4 (13)	4.3 (13)	p < .04
Music units	10 (5)	13 (5)	3.4 (5)	5.6 (5)	

[a] See note, Table 7.4.

TABLE 7.6

Heterogeneity of Social Actions in the Child-Adult Context of American and English Behavior Settings Units[a]

CATEGORY OF BEHAVIOR SETTING UNITS	KINDS OF SOCIAL ACTION				
	Total Number within Setting Category		*Average Number within Setting Category*		
	American	*English*	*American*	*English*	
All units	39 (119)	35 (121)	4.2 (89)	4.6 (89)	
Units of books	38 (76)	35 (75)	5.5 (47)	6.1 (47)	p = .3
Units of towns	15 (43)	11 (46)	2.9 (42)	3.0 (42)	p = .5
Academic units	13 (24)	11 (24)	3.1 (24)	3.4 (24)	p = .4
Nonacademic units	8 (14)	7 (17)	1.9 (13)	2.2 (13)	p = .4
Music units	8 (5)	9 (5)	4.2 (5)	3.2 (5)	

[a] See note, Table 7.4.

TABLE 7.7

Heterogeneity of Social Actions in the Child-Child Context of American and English Behavior Setting Units[a]

CATEGORY OF BEHAVIOR SETTING UNITS	KINDS OF SOCIAL ACTION				
	Total Number within Settirg Category		*Average Number within Setting Category*		
	American	*English*	*American*	*English*	
All units	37 (113)	37 (131)	6.7 (89)	6.6 (89)	
Units of books	37 (62)	37 (80)	8.2 (38)	6.9 (38)	p = .2
Units of towns	27 (51)	29 (51)	5.6 (51)	6.3 (51)	p = .2
Academic units	19 (24)	20 (24)	3.7 (24)	4.2 (24)	p = .5
Nonacademic units	25 (22)	27 (22)	7.8 (22)	8.6 (22)	p = .3
Music units	16 (5)	16 (5)	5.2 (5)	6.0 (5)	

[a] See note, Table 7.4.

the English than in the American behavior settings is the child-child context of the books. When we examined this exception, we discovered that the heterogeneity of social actions between children was associated in the books with the presence and absence of adults. The average numbers of child-child social actions in behavior settings where adults were present and where they were not present are as follows:

	Average Heterogeneity of Child-Child Social Actions	
	American Books	*English Books*
Adults not present	11.14	11.80
Adults present	7.37	6.91

Fewer kinds of child-child social action were portrayed in both American and English books when adults were present. However, the inhibition in heterogeneity by adults was somewhat greater in the English than in the American books, with the result that in behavior settings where adults were *not* present, the average child-child heterogeneity of social actions was greater in the English than in the American books; when adults were present the reverse was true.

We were unable to investigate this issue within the settings of the towns, as an adult in addition to the observer was present in 43 of the 51 Midwest settings, and in 46 of the 51 Yoredale settings. It is clear, however, that any adult-induced differential restriction upon heterogeneity within the child-child social action contexts of the towns was not sufficient to lower Yoredale's heterogeneity below that of Midwest.

The heterogeneity of social actions differed in the behavior settings of books and the towns. Forty varieties and 117 kinds of social action were present in the 180 behavior settings of the books; 36 varieties and 78 kinds of social action were present in the 102 settings of the two towns. The average heterogeneity per setting was 16.6 for the books and 12.1 for the towns. These differences were influenced by differences in sample size, so an analysis was made of subsamples of equal numbers of behavior setting units of the towns and the books. This analysis showed that both the total repertory of social actions in the behavior setting samples, and the average heterogeneity within the settings were greater in the behavior settings of the books than of the towns. Here are the data for the 51 pairs of matched settings of the towns and for 51 randomly selected, similarly matched pairs of settings of the books.

	Total Number of Social Actions in Sample		*Average Number of Social Actions per Setting*	
	Towns	*Books*	*Towns*	*Books*
American sample (51 settings)	63	101	11.0	16.0
English sample (51 settings)	64	107	13.2	16.6

The greater number of social actions in the settings of the books is not unexpected. Fiction is concerned with action, and can quickly pass over periods of inaction which must be reported in the specimen records. Furthermore, the time span of the book settings was greater than that of the town settings, and there were more different types of settings in the books than in the towns.

The heterogeneity of social actions in the different contexts is reported in Tables 7.5, 7.6, and 7.7. The average number of child-adult social actions per setting was smaller than the average number of adult-child or child-child social actions. This was true for the American and English settings of both the books and the towns. The heterogeneity of adult-child and of child-child social actions did not differ.

In conclusion we can say with respect to social action heterogeneity that the total repertory of social actions did not differ between the American and English or between the book and town behavior setting samples; however, fewer kinds of social action were displayed by children vis-à-vis adults than by adults vis-à-vis children or by children vis-à-vis children. Within behavior settings, the average number of social actions per setting was greater in the English than in the American behavior settings, and it was greater in the settings of the books than in those of the towns; the average number of social actions per setting was less in the child-adult social context than in either the adult-child or child-child social action context.

Commonality of Social Actions

Of the total repertory of 117 social actions present in the 282 American and English behavior settings, 93 per cent were present in the settings of both cultures; of the 117 social actions present in the 180 settings of the books, 91 per cent were present in both the American and the English books, and of the 77 social actions present in the 102 behavior settings of the towns, 65 per cent were present in both towns. Some of the difference between the books and the towns in this respect is due to the different numbers of behavior settings inventoried, and to the fact that the behavior settings of Midwest and Yoredale were matched for age, sex, and social class of subjects and for variety of behavior settings. To avoid these disturbing factors, we compared the 51 matched pairs of behavior settings of the towns with 51 matched settings of the books (the settings used in connection with the heterogeneity comparison, p. 146). The data are reported in Table 7.8, and they show (1) that the total repertory of the social actions occurring in the matched settings of the American and English books had a greater degree of commonality than the total repertory of social actions in the matched settings of the towns, but (2) when taken pair by pair, the *average* degree of social action commonality of the books was smaller than that of the towns. These findings hold for all social action contexts. We can only speculate about the reasons for this reversal in relative degree of commonality. The data of Table 7.8 show, too, that the degree of social

TABLE 7.8
Commonality of Social Actions in Fifty-One Matched American and English Behavior Setting Units

CONTEXT OF SOCIAL ACTION	*Index of Commonality for All Settings*		*Average Index of Commonality for Pairs of Settings*	
	Towns	*Books*	*Towns*	*Books*
Adult-child context	50	82	27.3	18.8
Child-adult context	53	76	34.7	16.7
Child-child context	87	95	20.0	18.9

action commonality between the American and English behavior settings varied widely among social action contexts with no pattern apparent in this variation.

These data dramatically reveal that inspection of single settings, or single contexts of settings in two cultures, provide a very inadequate picture of the over-all social action commonality which may obtain. The analysis has provided an example of the importance of sample size in making generalizations about commonality: reduction of the sample of book settings from 90 to 51 reduced the obtained commonality of the total repertory of social actions from 91 per cent to 84 per cent. This occurred despite the fact that the settings in the smaller sample were more carefully matched for age, sex, and social class of the principal subjects and for variety of behavior settings than the settings in larger samples.

It is clear that the measurement of cultural commonality is a complicated matter, and that our efforts here have done little more than point to some of these complications.

Presence Values of Social Actions

The greater average number of social actions within the English than within the American behavior settings means that English social actions were present in more behavior settings, on the average, than American social actions. In fact, the average presence values of the social actions of the books were 13.4 for the American books and 15.2 for the English books. Within the towns, the average presence values were 9.0 for the social actions occurring in Midwest, and 10.9 for those occurring in Yoredale. Culture differences in presence values varied greatly among social actions; we turn to this next.

The basic data are presented in Table 7.9 for behavior settings of the towns, and in Table 7.10 for the behavior settings from the books. In these tables, presence indexes are given for the three social action contexts of the American and English behavior settings. The number of behavior settings inventoried in each context is reported at the top of the appropriate column. The number of contexts varied because the populations of the behavior settings varied. For example, if no adult was present in a particular setting, the setting is not included in the adult-child or the child-adult contexts because these contexts did not occur in the setting. Similarly, settings are omitted from the child-child context if only one child was present. In the analysis which follows, therefore, the American and English behavior settings are strictly comparable with respect to social action possibilities.

We shall first consider the presence values of social actions in terms of the scales we have defined; thereafter we shall consider culture differences with respect to particular social actions.

Harmony and Disharmony of American and English Social Actions. The median varieties of social action on the harmony-disharmony scale were computed, using the presence values as frequency distributions (p. 139). Within all contexts, the median varieties were: #14 *provides opportunity* for the American behavior settings, and #19 *complies* for the English behavior settings. The median varieties were the same for both the towns and the books. According to the median test, these are very significant differences ($p < .002$); they indicate that American social actions were displaced relative to English social actions to the more harmonious end of the harmony-disharmony scale. Within the particular social action contexts, American social actions were more harmonious than English social actions in the adult-child and child-adult contexts of the books, in the adult-child context of the towns ($p < .002$ in both cases); the child-child social actions of the books were also somewhat more harmonious in the American than in the English books ($p < .10$). However, the median American and English social actions were the same for the child-adult social actions of the towns and child-child social actions of the books.

The greater presence values of harmonious social actions in the American behavior settings were especially clear within the adult-child contexts; upon this, the books and the towns were in agreement. The median adult-child social action in the American books was #14 *adult provides opportunity for child;* in the English books it was #18 *adult influences child.* The median adult-child social action in the American towns was #18 *adult influences child,* and in the English towns #25 *adult distant with child.* The presence values of adult-child social actions on the harmony-disharmony scale are represented in Figure 7.1.

Power of American and English Social Actions. The median test indicates that social actions of adults vis-a-vis children involved the use of power in more English than American behavior settings. This was true of the behavior settings of both the books and the towns; in both cases $p < .002$. The median American social action was #3 *adult influences child,* and the median English social action was #5 *adult dominates child.* There were no culture differences in the use of social power by children vis-à-vis adults or by children vis-à-vis other children.

Reactions to Social Power in American and English Social Actions. No

TABLE 7.9

Social Actions in Midwest and Yoredale Behavior Setting Units

Per Cent of Behavior Settings in Which Social Actions Were Present

VARIETY OF SOCIAL ACTION	CONTEXT OF SOCIAL ACTION					
	Adult-Child		*Child-Adult*		*Child-Child*	
	Midwest $N = 43$	*Yoredale* $N = 46$	*Midwest* $N = 43$	*Yoredale* $N = 46$	*Midwest* $N = 51$	*Yoredale* $N = 51$
dominates	32.6	93.5	0	0	2.0	13.7
manages	93.0	80.4	0	0	23.5	27.5
influences	51.2	26.1	51.2	32.6	35.3	17.6
provides opportun.	14.0	26.1	7.0	0	72.6	66.7
asks favor	2.3	2.2	16.3	8.7	2.0	3.9
punishes	0	13.0	0	0	0	0
disciplines	7.0	47.8	2.3	0	0	2.0
accepts control	0	0	55.8	50.0	21.6	56.9
complies	0	8.7	90.7	87.0	13.7	29.4
surrenders	0	2.2	0	0	0	0
resists	0	2.2	9.3	21.7	7.8	17.6
disagrees	2.3	0	7.0	0	23.5	9.8
exploits	0	0	0	0	2.0	11.8
gratifies	0	6.5	2.3	0	19.6	5.9
helps	20.9	17.4	2.3	15.2	25.5	35.3
co-operates	2.3	0	2.3	0	29.4	35.3
accommodates	4.7	0	0	0	3.9	7.8
comforts	9.3	8.7	0	0	2.0	0
defends	9.3	2.2	0	0	3.9	2.0
forgives	0	2.2	0	0	0	0
deprives	0	0	0	0	7.8	5.9
hinders	0	0	0	0	0	13.7
competes	0	0	0	0	23.5	29.4
antagonistic	0	0	0	0	0	9.8
impatient	14.0	37.0	0	0	11.8	15.7
teases	0	2.2	0	0	13.7	13.7
affectionate	0	0	0	0	0	0
friendly	27.9	13.0	14.0	10.9	78.4	60.8
enjoys	4.7	4.3	7.0	15.2	68.6	60.8
values	30.2	50.0	0	2.2	15.7	19.6
hates	0	0	0	0	0	0
unfriendly	2.3	0	0	0	3.9	9.8
distressed	0	4.3	0	0	3.9	2.0
devalues	14.0	63.0	0	0	11.8	19.6
understands	16.3	6.5	0	0	0	0
baffled	0	0	0	0	0	0
plays	4.7	0	2.3	0	41.2	31.4
works	0	0	0	0	0	0
distant	0	6.5	0	4.3		
polite	7.0	0	11.6	34.8		

TABLE 7.10

Social Actions in Behavior Setting Units of American and English Books

Per Cent of Behavior Settings in Which Social Actions Were Present

VARIETY OF SOCIAL ACTION	CONTEXT OF SOCIAL ACTION					
	Adult-Child		*Child-Adult*		*Child-Child*	
	American $N = 76$	*English* $N = 75$	*American* $N = 76$	*English* $N = 75$	*American* $N = 62$	*English* $N = 80$
dominates	46.1	69.3	5.3	1.3	11.3	18.8
manages	30.3	20.0	5.3	8.0	24.2	35.0
influences	59.2	32.0	38.2	34.7	43.5	30.0
provides opportun.	52.6	50.7	30.3	25.3	70.8	72.5
asks favor	11.8	8.0	30.3	36.0	19.3	13.8
punishes	1.3	8.0	1.3	0	0	0
disciplines	7.9	40.0	1.3	0	4.8	13.8
accepts control	51.3	37.3	77.6	68.0	85.3	77.5
complies	15.8	10.7	35.3	52.0	20.9	28.8
surrenders	3.9	0	5.3	9.3	1.6	2.5
resists	5.3	6.7	6.6	14.7	11.3	12.5
disagrees	10.5	13.3	29.0	17.3	25.8	37.5
exploits	21.1	16.0	19.7	33.3	22.5	12.5
gratifies	40.8	46.7	9.2	6.7	17.7	12.5
helps	34.2	37.3	21.1	26.7	32.2	21.2
co-operates	18.4	9.3	17.1	9.3	29.0	55.0
accommodates	9.2	6.7	40.8	17.3	4.8	3.8
comforts	23.7	21.3	3.9	0	25.8	17.5
defends	7.9	5.3	1.3	0	9.7	12.5
forgives	0	10.7	2.6	0	9.7	1.2
deprives	7.9	8.0	1.3	1.3	3.2	1.2
hinders	10.5	14.7	1.3	2.7	8.1	10.0
competes	0	4.0	0	4.0	9.7	17.5
antagonistic	1.3	5.3	1.3	9.3	9.7	3.8
impatient	13.2	30.7	6.6	16.0	29.0	27.5
teases	15.8	10.7	3.9	9.3	24.2	15.0
affectionate	30.3	13.3	29.0	9.3	16.1	2.5
friendly	48.7	48.0	39.5	38.7	49.9	47.5
enjoys	18.4	17.3	17.1	18.7	35.4	26.2
values	42.1	36.0	27.6	21.3	49.9	36.2
hates	1.3	2.7	1.3	4.0	3.2	3.8
unfriendly	2.6	8.0	1.3	8.0	6.4	8.8
distressed	9.2	20.0	9.2	14.7	6.4	8.8
devalues	11.8	44.0	5.3	21.3	32.2	38.8
understands	40.8	26.7	14.5	4.0	30.6	7.5
baffled	6.6	25.3	3.9	17.3	1.6	7.5
plays	1.3	4.0	0	4.0	35.4	32.5
works	10.5	4.0	11.8	5.3	8.1	6.2
distant	2.6	28.0	2.6	17.3		
polite	0	8.0	6.6	20.0		

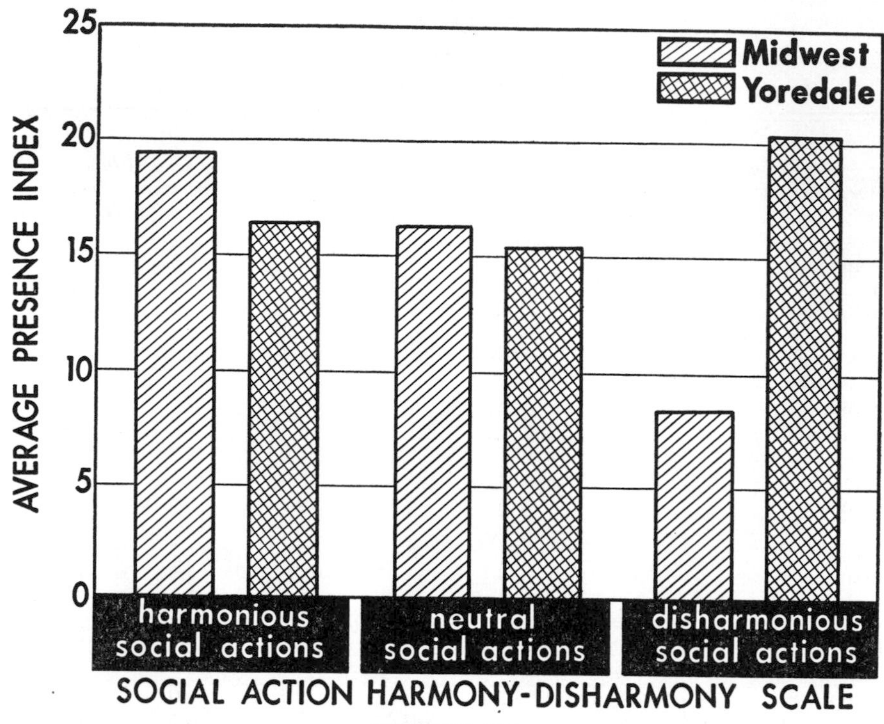

FIGURE 7.1

Average Presence Indexes of Social Actions Occurring in the Harmonious, Neutral, and Disharmonious Thirds of the Social Action Scale

culture differences in the presence values of social actions on this scale were discovered.

Benefit and Harm of American and English Social Actions. No culture differences were found in the distributions of presence values along the benefit-harm scale.

Positive and Negative Emotions in American and English Social Actions. In all contexts of the behavior settings of both the books and the towns positive emotional actions were present in greater numbers of American than English behavior settings, and negative emotional actions were present in fewer American than English settings. However, it was only when the data of the books and the towns were combined, that the median variety of social action on the emotion scale differed as much as one scale point; in this case #2 *friendly* was the median American variety, and #3 *enjoys* was the median English variety.

Individual Social Actions in American and English Behavior Settings. The product-moment correlations between the presence indexes of social actions obtained from the two sources, i.e., the behavior settings of the towns and the behavior settings of the books, are as follows:

	Adult-Child Context	*Child-Adult Context*	*Child-Child Context*
American data	.51	.63	.66
English data	.66	.76	.81

These are all significant correlations ($p < .01$), and their magnitudes suggest that the occurrence of social actions, as measured by the presence index, tended to be similar across the very differently selected samples of behavior settings. The social action presence indexes appear to measure social phenomena that are broadly based within each of the cultures. In view of this evidence of the generality of social actions, we have computed a single American and a single English presence index for each social action. We have done this by treating the settings of the books and the towns as one sample of behavior settings. The resulting *general presence index* gives smaller weight to the data of the towns than to the data of the books, inasmuch as the towns contribute 36 per cent of the general sample of settings and the books contribute 64 per cent of the sample.

Social actions are listed in Table 7.11 in order of the magnitudes of their general presence indexes. These lists provide the most broadly based evidence the data afford of the degree of dispersion of social actions among the American and English behavior settings. Social actions which were present in 5 per cent or less of the behavior settings, i.e., with presence indexes between 0 and 5 are omitted from Table 7.11.

The lists in Table 7.11 are, in effect, summaries of the absolute and relative extensity of occurrence of kinds of social actions in the behavior settings sampled in America and England. Read downward, the columns inform one of social actions of decreasing prevalence within cultural and social action contexts; read across, the pairs of neighboring columns reveal the culture differences in the occurrence of social actions, and scanned across the two sets of three alternating columns the data of Table 7.11 tell us of social context differences within the two cultures.

The rank correlations (rho) between the general presence indexes of American and English social actions in the three contexts are:

adult-child $= +.75$ ($p < .001$)
child-adult $= +.78$ ($p < .001$)
child-child $= +.88$ ($p < .001$)

These are all significant correlations and they indicate that the relative breadth of dispersion of social actions across the American and English settings was, in general, similar. The correlations show that the intercultural similarity was greatest for the social actions of child vis-à-vis child and that it was least for the social actions of adult vis-à-vis child.

We turn, next, to differences in the breadth of distribution of individual social actions among American and English behavior settings. This is denoted by the difference between the American and the English general presence indexes of social action. In Table 7.12, social actions are distributed by the magnitude of this difference: American general presence index minus English general presence index. For example, the social action *child polite to adult* occurs in this table in the interval —13 to —17, indicating that its presence index in the English behavior settings exceeded its presence index in American behavior settings by an amount ranging between 13 to 17 points, i.e., per cent. Because of their small importance, social actions that were present in fewer than 5 per cent of the behavior settings of both the American and the English settings are omitted from Table 7.12. The social actions of the different contexts are placed in separate rows of the table to facilitate the study of American-English differences within and between contexts. An asterisk marks the social actions whose presence values in the two cultures differed, according to X^2 tests, with a $p < .05$.

The data of Table 7.12 provide the most general picture of culture differences in the occurrence of particular social actions which this investigation provides. The data show, first, that American-English differences were greatest in the case of the social actions of adults vis-à-vis children. The most distinctively American social action (*adult influences child*) and the four most distinctively English social actions (*adult devalues child, adult dominates child, adult disciplines child, adult is impatient with child*) occurred within the adult-child context. "Most distinctively American" (or English) designates the social action, or actions, whose breadth of distribution among American (or English) behavior settings most exceeded its distribution among English (or American) behavior settings.

The data of Table 7.12 show, also, that within every context, the greatest differences are negative differences. This means that in every context some English social action was more widely distributed among the English behavior settings than any social action was distributed among the American settings. (This was true of the social actions *child polite to adult* and *child accommodates to adult* although both actions fall within the same interval of Table 7.12.) However, these differences must not be overemphasized. Only three social actions had a wider distribution among English behavior settings than any social action had among American settings; and while there were 22 English social actions with presence indexes that exceeded their American counterparts by eight or more, there were 16 American social actions with presence indexes that exceeded their English counterparts by eight or more. These data do indicate, however, that if one were to visit the behavior settings of Midwest and Yoredale, and to read the fictional account of the American and English settings, one would find more kinds of social action in the English than in the American settings, and a few of the English social actions would be more commonly encountered than any of the American social actions.

TABLE 7.11

General Presence Indexes of Social Actions in Three Contexts of American and English Behavior Settings

ADULT-CHILD CONTEXT		CHILD-ADULT CONTEXT		CHILD-CHILD CONTEXT	
American Settings	*English Settings*	*American Settings*	*English Settings*	*American Settings*	*English Settings*
Influences 56	Dominates 79	Accepts Con. 70	Complies 66	Provides Opp. 71	Provides Opp. 70
Manages 53	Devalues 51	Complies 55	Accepts Con. 61	Friendly 62	Accepts Con. 69
Friendly 41	Manages 43	Influences 43	Influences 34	Accepts Con. 56	Friendly 52
Dominates 41	Disciplines 43	Friendly 30	Friendly 28	Enjoys 50	Co-operates 47
Provides Opp. 39	Provides Opp. 41	Accommodates 26	Asks Favor 26	Influences 40	Enjoys 39
Values 38	Values 41	Asks Favor 25	Polite 26	Plays 38	Plays 32
Accepts Con. 33	Friendly 35	Provides Opp. 22	Helps 22	Values 34	Manages 32
Understands 32	Impatient 33	Disagrees 21	Exploits 21	Helps 29	Devalues 31
Helps 29	Gratifies 31	Affect. 19	Enjoys 17	Co-operates 29	Values 30
Gratifies 26	Influences 30	Values 18	Resists 17	Disagrees 25	Complies 29
Affect. 19	Helps 30	Helps 14	Provides Opp. 16	Manages 24	Helps 27
Comforts 18	Accepts Con. 23	Enjoys 13	Values 14	Devalues 23	Disagrees 27
Exploits 13	Distant 20	Exploits 12	Devalues 13	Impatient 21	Influences 25
Enjoys 13	Understands 19	Co-operates 12	Distant 12	Teases 19	Impatient 23
Impatient 13	Comforts 17	Understands 9	Disagrees 11	Gratifies 18	Competes 22
Co-operates 13	Baffled 16	Polite 8	Accommodates 11	Complies 18	Dominates 17
Devalues 13	Distressed 14	Resists 8	Baffled 11	Understands 17	Resists 14
Complies 10	Enjoys 12	Works 8	Impatient 10	Competes 16	Teases 14
Teases 10	Punishes 10	Gratifies 7	Distressed 9	Comforts 15	Exploits 12
Asks Favor 8	Complies 10	Distressed 6	Co-operates 6	Exploits 13	Hinders 11
Defends 8	Exploits 10		Antag. 6	Asks Favor 11	Comforts 11
Disciplines 8	Hinders 9		Teases 6	Affect. 11	Asks Favor 10
Accommodates 8	Affect. 8		Affect. 6	Resists 9	Gratifies 10
Disagrees 8	Disagrees 8		Surrenders 6	Dominates 7	Disciplines 9
Hinders 7	Teases 7			Defends 7	Unfriendly 9
Works 7	Forgives 7				Defends 8
Distressed 6	Asks Favor 6				Distressed 8
	Co-operates 6				Antag. 6
					Accommodates 5

TABLE

Differences Between American and

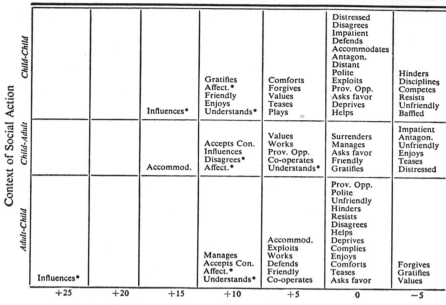

Context of Social Action	+25	+20	+15	+10	+5	0	−5
Child-Child			Influences*	Gratifies Affect.* Friendly Enjoys Understands*	Comforts Forgives Values Teases Plays	Distressed Disagrees Impatient Defends Accommodates Antagon. Distant Polite Exploits Prov. Opp. Asks favor Deprives Helps	Hinders Disciplines Competes Resists Unfriendly Baffled
Child-Adult			Accommod.	Accepts Con. Influences Disagrees* Affect.*	Values Works Prov. Opp. Co-operates Understands*	Surrenders Manages Asks favor Friendly Gratifies	Impatient Antagon. Unfriendly Enjoys Teases Distressed
Adult-Child	Influences*			Manages Accepts Con. Affect.* Understands*	Accommod. Exploits Works Defends Friendly Co-operates	Prov. Opp. Polite Unfriendly Hinders Resists Disagrees Helps Deprives Complies Enjoys Comforts Teases Asks favor	Forgives Gratifies Values

American Presence Index Minus English Presence Index

We shall attempt to characterize for each social action context the culture differences revealed by the data from which Table 7.12 has been constructed. (Note that these data can be reconstituted from the data of Tables 7.9 and 7.10 by converting the presence indexes to presence values, adding the presence values for the book and town settings, and transforming to the general presence index.) The social action definitions and presence values provide a basis for describing the most distinctively American and the most distinctively English social actions. In the analysis that follows we include only those social actions whose presence indexes were five or greater in either the American or the English sample of behavior settings, i.e., the social actions reported in Table 7.12.

Adult-Child Social Context: Social Actions of Adults vis-à-vis Children. Five social actions occurred in fewer than five per cent of both the American and the English behavior settings, leaving the 35 presence index differences reported in Table 7.12. These differences form a distribution ranging from +26.4 to —38.9 with a mean of —2.94 and a standard deviation of 13.7. The social actions whose American presence indexes exceeded their English presence indexes by eight or more indicate that American adults (1) exercised routine, personal influence over children (made requests, asked advice, gave suggestions) in 188 per cent as many settings as English adults, (2) used the authority that attaches to adult roles and

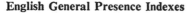

7.12
English General Presence Indexes

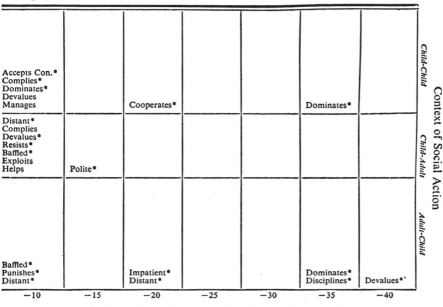

Context of Social Action	−10	−15	−20	−25	−30	−35	−40
Child-Child	Accepts Con.* Complies* Dominates* Devalues Manages		Cooperates*			Dominates*	
Child-Adult	Distant* Complies Devalues* Resists* Baffled* Exploits Helps	Polite*					
Adult-Child	Baffled* Punishes* Distant*		Impatient* Distant*			Dominates* Disciplines*	Devalues*

American Presence Index Minus English Presence Index

* Social actions whose presence values differed with $p < .05$

to the greater competence of the adult (taught, supervised, regulated, led, cautioned, guided) in 120 per cent as many settings as English adults, (3) responded willingly to routine personal influences from children (answered requests, accepted advice, considered suggestions) in 141 per cent as many behavior settings as English adults, (4) attempted to gain insight into the motives and circumstances of children's behavior (analyzed, probed, explained, withheld judgment) in 170 per cent as many settings as English adults, and (5) expressed affection for children in some explicit way (hugged, kissed, stated devotion) in 132 per cent as many settings as the English adults. English adults, on the other hand, (1) used maximal personal power upon children without threat of punishment (bossed, commanded, gave orders, decided issues, made decisions, determined behavior) in 191 per cent as many settings as American adults, (2) made negative evaluations of children (deprecated, disapproved, belittled, compared unfavorably with others) in four times as many settings as American adults, (3) threatened to punish children and displayed "dangerous" emotions (scolded, rebuked, admonished, expressed exasperation) in twelve times as many settings as American adults, (4) expressed impatience with children (annoyance, provocation, anger) in two and a half times as many settings as American adults, (5) were distant with children (unconcerned, indifferent, inattentive, unaware) in over eleven times as many settings as American adults, (6) were baffled by children's behavior (confused, uncomprehending) in over three times as many settings as American adults, and (7) punished children (smacked, shook, sent away, denied privileges) in over twelve times as many settings as American adults. Upon the remaining 23 adult-child social actions, i.e., 66 per cent of all social actions with an appreciable representation among the behavior settings inventoried, American-English differences were small.

Child-Adult Social Context: Social Actions of Children vis-à-vis Adults. Eleven social actions were present in fewer than 5 per cent of both the American and the English behavior settings leaving the 29 presence index differences reported in Table 7.12. These differences form a distribution ranging from 15.2 to —17.3, with a mean of —0.87 and a standard deviation of 8.1. The distinctively American social actions, i.e., those with presence index differences of eight or more, indicate that American children (1) accommodated their behavior to adult standards (adjusted to adults, acted maturely) in two and a half times as many settings as English children, (2) expressed affection for adults (hugged, kissed, voiced devotion) in three times as many settings as English children, and (3) disagreed with adults (disputed, argued, ignored, delayed) in twice as many settings as English children. According to the distinctively English social actions, English children (1) were polite to adults (well-behaved, courteous, used titles of respect, stood with respect) in three times as many settings as American children, (2) complied with adult's supervision without enthusiasm as a fact of life (obeyed, took subordinate roles, followed instructions, carried out directives) in 120 per cent as many settings as American children, (3) were distant with adults (ignored, disregarded, expressed indifference) in seven times as many settings as American children, (4) resisted adults (defied, combated, refused) in over two and a half times as many settings as American children, and (5) made negative evaluations of adults (criticized, deprecated, disapproved, belittled, compared unfavorably with others) in four times as many settings as American children. In the remaining 72 per cent of the social actions reported in Table 7.12, the behavior of American and English children toward adults did not differ greatly.

Child-Child Social Actions: Social Actions of Children vis-à-vis Children. There were 36 child-child social actions with presence indexes of five or more in the American or the English behavior setting sample. The American-English differences in the presence indexes of these social actions reported in Table 7.12 form a distribution ranging from 14.5 to —18.1; the mean of the distribution is —0.20 and the standard deviation is 7.7. The most distinctively American of these social actions can be described as follows: American children (1) exercised routine personal influence over other children (made requests, asked advice, gave suggestions) in 157 per cent as many settings as English children, (2) tried to understand the behavior of other children (analyzed, probed, conjectured, withheld judgment) in two and a half times as many settings as English children, (3) enjoyed other children (laughed, were merry, showed pleasure) in 127 per cent as many settings as English children, (4) were friendly with other children (welcomed, befriended, expressed liking) in 120 per cent as many settings as English children, and (5) were affectionate with other children (hugged, kissed, voiced devotion) in seven times as many settings as English children. In the most distinctively English of these social actions, English children (1) co-operated with other children (planned, participated in joint action, shared responsibilities and rewards) in 162 per cent as many settings as American children, (2) willingly behaved in accordance with the routine personal influence of other children (answered requests, accepted advice, considered suggestions) in 123 per cent as many behavior settings as American children, (3) complied with another child's control without enthusiasm (obeyed, followed instructions, acted as subordinate) in 160 per cent as many settings as American children, and (4) dominated other children (bossed, demanded, gave orders, made decisions) in 238 per cent as many settings as American children. The remaining 75 per cent of the social actions of child to child had similar presence values in the settings of the two cultures.

Listing and describing in this way the social actions that differentiated the cultures omits the important fact that the impact of each culture's distinctive social actions was undoubtedly qualified by social actions with opposite or modifying effects. The social action *adult devalues child,* with a presence index of 51.5 in the English behavior settings is balanced by the social action *adult values child* with a presence index of 41.5. What is the experiential significance and behavioral consequence for English children of the 51.5 per cent to 41.5 per cent balance of negative and positive evaluation by adults? And how does this differ from the 12.6 per cent to 37.8 per cent balance of negative and positive evaluation of children by American adults? Furthermore, fully as important as the differences we have discovered is the finding that most of the social actions were common to the behavior streams of the American and English children, and that they did not differ in their breadth of distribution across the American and English settings. The social life of American and English children is, according to our data, basically the same. The differences are differences of emphasis.

This study has explored the usefulness of a macrounit of the stream of behavior, the behavior setting unit, and some technical problems involved in its use. Valuable features of the unit lie in its occurrence in many sorts of behavior records, in its quantifiability, and in its varied attributes. The behavior setting unit has yielded some precise information within the difficult area of cross-cultural behavior studies.

CHAPTER 8

Structure of the Behavior of American and English Children

MAXINE SCHOGGEN, LOUISE S. BARKER & ROGER G. BARKER

STRUCTURAL CHARACTERISTICS of the behavior streams of American and English children are investigated here using the same specimen record data that Barker and Barker used in their study of social actions (Chapter 7).

Maxine Schoggen is Research Associate in the Department of Psychology of the University of Oregon. Louise Shedd Barker and Roger G. Barker are identified in the introduction to Chapter 7.

IN THIS STUDY we have sought to determine if there were structural differences in the behavior streams of the American and English children which Barker and Barker (Chapter 7) investigated and found to differ in social content. Structure has been studied in terms of behavior episodes, the behavior unit about which we know most (Barker & Wright, 1955; Wright, 1960; Schoggen, 1954; and Chapters 9 and 10 of this book).

The same pairs of specimen records used by Barker and Barker provided the data of the investigation, with the exceptions noted below. The records are listed in Appendix 1.1, and described in Chapter 1. For statistical reasons it was necessary to eliminate (1) records in which there were fewer than 10 episodes in either one of the pair of records (records 8, 9, 17, 23, 35, 39, 45, 46, 55, 56) and (2) records in which the target children were identical with those in another pair (records 7, 41, 54).

The 39 remaining specimen records of the Midwest and Yoredale children were divided into two sets for analytical purposes. One set consisted of 19 pairs of Midwest-Yoredale records made in the behavior setting variety School Academic Classes (reading, arithmetic, writing, spelling, geography, current events, and opening ceremonies). The other set of records consisted of 20 pairs of records made in six varieties of behavior settings, as follows: School Music Classes (five pairs of settings), School Physical Education Classes and Outdoor Athletic Contests (five pairs of settings), Open Spaces and Home, Outdoors (seven pairs of settings),

Restaurants and Taverns (one pair of settings), Religious Services (one pair of settings), Social Cultural Meetings (one pair of settings). The ages of the target children of the selected records ranged from six years two months to twelve years two months, and the social classes of their families varied from upper lower to upper middle; there were records for 19 girls and 20 boys in each community. The records varied in length from three to 63 minutes, and the average length was 29 minutes.

Inasmuch as the samples of children were matched so closely (by characteristics of the towns, the behavior settings, and the children), it seemed feasible to use the Wilcoxon matched-pairs signed-ranks test (Siegel, 1956). This test utilizes information about the direction and magnitude of a difference within pairs. Midwest-Yoredale differences are reported by means of this test separately for the 19-pair sample of academic specimen records and for the 39-pair total sample; two-sided tests are reported in all cases.

Behavior Episodes

Behavior episodes are illustrated in the sample record reproduced in Appendix 1.2 of this volume, and all of the episodes that entered the analyses are marked upon the published records (Barker et al., 1961). A behavior episode has three defining characteristics. These will now be presented briefly; however, the research student should study the behavior episode criteria in detail as these are presented in Barker and Wright (1955).

Constancy in the direction of behavior is the basic criterion of a behavior episode; the behavior of an episode continues in one direction from its beginning to its end point. Identifying an episode in the stream of behavior requires, in the first place, diagnosing the end (goal) to which the person is moving. The research of Dickman (Chapter 2) supports the view that it is the apprehension of the ends of behavior-in-progress which gives the behavior stream unity, and that apparently the directionality of behavior, the end to which it is moving, is almost as immediately perceived as the unity of a visual form or of an auditory pattern.

Occurrence within the normal behavior perspective, the second defining feature of an episode, serves to delimit the size of the segment of the behavior stream within which directionality is apprehended. The phenomenon of behavior directedness is a prime example of the inside-outside paradox mentioned in the introduction to this book. The units of the behavior stream which, together, make up a more inclusive unit do not have equal directions themselves, yet the direction of each coincides with the direction of the more inclusive behavior unit; i.e., they exhibit their own unique properties (directions) and, at the same time the common property (direction) of the superordinate unit which they compose. Within an inclusive behavior stream segment, AD, with included units Ab, bc, and cD, direction Ab = direction AD, direction bc = direction AD, and direction cD = direction AD; but direction Ab $\neq$ direction bc $\neq$ direction cD. For example, within the action "Going to School," the direction of each of the included behavior units Finding Coat, Telling Mother Goodbye, and Getting Bicycle, coincides with that of Going to School, yet the direction of Finding Coat is not equal to the direction of Telling Mother Goodbye, or to the direction of Getting Bicycle. Directionality, which determines the beginning and the end points of a behavior episode is dependent, itself, upon the extent of the behavior stream segment within which directionality is determined. To escape from this paradox and achieve univocality of behavior stream direction, and therefore agreement with respect to behavior stream units, it is necessary to define the behavior stream segment within which units are discriminated. This is what the episode criterion of behavior perspective does; it specifies the behavior stream segment within which direction is to be determined. This segment is the length of the behavior stream within which people normally perceive behavior to occur. It eliminates from consideration short units that usually "run off" with no or only vague awareness of the person himself, or of others observing him (e.g., Stepping Down First Step as part of Getting Bicycle), and it eliminates long units that occur outside the limits of ordinary perception (e.g., Getting an Education). The behavior perspective criterion designates, by means of a perceptual co-ordinate, the span of the behavior continuum within which the primary episode criterion of directionality is to be applied.

The third defining characteristic of a behavior episode is that the whole episode has more potency than any of its parts, and conversely, that if any part of a behavior sequence with constant direction exceeds or equals the whole in potency, that part becomes a separate episode. The assumption behind this criterion is that when a part of a behavior stream with constant direction, such as Stepping Down First Step equals or exceeds in potency the whole directed unit (Going to School), the part takes precedence over the whole within the behavior perspective of the person and in the total dynamics of the continuing behavior.

However abstract these criteria may appear, they provide defining characteristics which make it possible for independent analysts to agree not only on those points in the behavior stream where directionality changes, as Dickman has demonstrated for uninstructed subjects, but also to agree upon directional units of the same size and with the same beginning and end points. Reliability studies have shown that agreement in identifying episodes of behavior, as defined by the three criteria, is within the 72 per cent to 87 per cent range. Details of the reliability of episode identification and of various episode ratings are presented in *Midwest and Its Children* (Barker & Wright, 1955).

The task of episoding the specimen records of this study was carried out by a single, experienced analyst who had participated in the original episoding studies. Work on Midwest records was alternated with work on Yoredale records in order to mitigate the effects of possible shifting standards from satiation and other influences.

Length of Episodes

During 853 minutes of observation the Midwest children produced 1,131 behavior episodes, and during 903 minutes of observation, the Yoredale children produced 777 behavior episodes. This amounts to 1.33 episodes per minute for the Midwest children and 0.86 episodes per minute for the Yoredale children. The greater rate of episode production of the Midwest children occurred within all the varieties of behavior settings. The Wilcoxon Test of significance indicates that the difference in rate was significant for both the academic behavior settings ($p < .01$) and for all behavior settings ($p < .001$). The average number of episodes per minute within behavior setting varieties is given in Table 8.1.

TABLE 8.1
Average Number of Episodes per Minute within Specified Behavior Setting Varieties

BEHAVIOR SETTING VARIETY	*Midwest*	*Yoredale*
School, Academic Classes	0.99	0.69
School, Music Classes	1.87	0.92
School, Physical Education Classes	2.38	1.21
Open Spaces and Home, Outdoors	1.75	1.26

Midwest children produced more short episodes and fewer long episodes than the Yoredale children. Episodes that were not more than one minute long constituted 89 per cent of all Midwest episodes and 84 per cent of Yoredale's episodes; while episodes five minutes or greater in length constituted 4.2 per cent of Midwest's and 5.7 per cent of Yoredale's episodes.

Initiation and Termination of Behavior Episodes

All episodes were judged on three categories with respect to their initiation as follows:

1. *Spontaneous episode:* the action of the episode begins in the absence of any observed and reported environmental change; the action is initiated without evident dependence upon active behavior objects.
2. *Instigated episode:* the action is seen to occur in response to some observable event or change in the situation, provided only that the event or change does not constitute pressure, as defined in item #3.
3. *Pressured episode:* the action appears to begin as a result of external influence that is opposed to the child's momentary direction of behavior.

The per cents of all Midwest and Yoredale episodes which received these ratings are given in Table 8.2. These per cents were computed on the basis of all episodes whose initiation could be judged; 2 per cent of both the Midwest and Yoredale episodes could not be judged as to initiation.

TABLE 8.2
Per Cent of Episodes Whose Initiation Was Judged to be Spontaneous, Instigated, and Pressured

TYPE OF INITIATION	ALL EPISODES *Midwest*	*Yoredale*	ACADEMIC EPISODES *Midwest*	*Yoredale*
Spontaneous	55	38	55	34
Instigated	43	55	41	56
Pressured	2	7	3	10
N	1131	777	548	385

In order to test the significance of the greater frequency of spontaneously initiated episodes in the Midwest behavior streams, a spontaneity index (SI) was computed for each specimen record by the following formula:

$$SI = 3\left(\frac{Sp:E}{E}\right) + 2\left(\frac{In:E}{E}\right) + 1\left(\frac{Pr:E}{E}\right)$$

where, E = Number of episodes in specimen record (omitting all episodes whose initiation could not be judged)
Sp:E = Number of spontaneous episodes in specimen record
In:E = Number of instigated episodes in specimen record
Pr:E = Number of pressured episodes in specimen record

The spontaneity index weights the per cent of episodes of a specimen record initiated without apparent environmental involvement of any sort by a factor of three; it weights per cent of episodes initiated *pari passu* with environmental change by a factor of two; it does not weight for spontaneity episodes initiated as a result of pressure from the environment.

Within the total sample of behavior settings, the average spontaneity index was 253 for the Midwest children and 225 for the Yoredale children; $p < .001$. Within the School Academic Classes, the mean spontaneity indexes of Midwest and Yoredale children were 252 and 225, respectively; $p < .01$.

Termination of episodes was judged in the same way as their initiation. The results of the analysis are reported in Table 8.3.

Midwest children produced relatively more behavior episodes with spontaneous endings than Yoredale children, and relatively fewer episodes whose termination was instigated or pressured by the environment. However, the differences were smaller than in the case of episode initiation. Within the total sample, the mean spontaneity index was 282 for Midwest children and 269 for Yoredale children ($p < .001$); within the School

TABLE 8.3

Per Cent of Episodes Whose Termination Was Judged to be Spontaneous, Instigated, and Pressured

TYPE OF TERMINATION	ALL EPISODES *Midwest*	ALL EPISODES *Yoredale*	ACADEMIC EPISODES *Midwest*	ACADEMIC EPISODES *Yoredale*
Spontaneous	83	75	82	77
Instigated	16	20	17	17
Pressured	1	5	1	6
N	1131	777	548	385

Academic settings the mean spontaneity index was 281 for Midwest and 270 for Yoredale ($p < .02$).

Following Jordan (Chapter 10) the episodes of the Midwest and Yoredale children were partitioned into those with spontaneous initiation and spontaneous termination (S/S), those with spontaneous initiation and instigated or pressured termination, i.e., with termination influenced by the environment (S/E), those episodes with environmentally influenced initiation and spontaneous termination (E/S), and episodes with environmentally influenced initiation and termination (E/E). The results, stated in terms of per cents, are given in Table 8.4.

TABLE 8.4

Per Cent of All Episodes with Certain Kinds of Initiation and Termination Combinations for Midwest and Yoredale Children

SUBJECTS	*N*	KINDS OF INITIATION AND TERMINATION *S/S*	*S/E*	*E/S*	*E/E*	*CNJ*
Midwest	1131	48	6	29	14	3
Yoredale	777	34	7	30	27	2

A chi square test indicates that the chance that the two distributions came from the same population with respect to initiation and termination combinations is remote; $p < .001$. The differences between the communities accrues almost entirely from the greater frequency of completely spontaneous episodes (S/S) among the episodes of the Midwest children, and from the greater frequency of completely nonspontaneous episodes (E/E) among those of the Yoredale children.

The data here reported for Midwest children are not directly comparable with those reported for Midwest children by Jordan (Chapter 10). The latter data involved equal numbers of preschool and school-age children, and many were from specimen records within the children's homes. We do not know to what degree these factors are associated with episode initiation and termination; in the present study only school-age children were involved, and there were no behavior settings within homes.

Episodes Discriminated on the Basis of Potency

It will be recalled that the primary criterion of a behavior episode is constancy of direction within the normal behavior perspective, but when a part of an episode attains a potency greater than that of the whole episode, the part with the superior potency is designated as an independent episode. Such episodes are called *contained* episodes. Midwest children displayed a higher per cent of contained episodes than Yoredale children within both the academic behavior settings ($p < .01$) and all behavior settings ($p < .0002$). The data are given in Table 8.5.

TABLE 8.5
Per Cent of All Episodes Discriminated on the Basis of Potency Rather than Direction

	ALL EPISODES		ACADEMIC EPISODES	
	Midwest	*Yoredale*	*Midwest*	*Yoredale*
Range of per cents	0–30	0–18	0–30	0–17
Mean per cent	9.6	3.0	9.8	4.1
N	1131	777	548	385

Other Episode Attributes

The behavior episodes of the Midwest and Yoredale children were analyzed with respect to the following structural-dynamic properties. In all these results there were no significant differences between the Midwest and Yoredale children. The results are therefore given in terms of the entire group.

Total Number of Overlapping Episodes: The number of other episodes which overlapped with each episode throughout its entire course. The number of overlapping episodes ranged from none (isolated episodes) to more than 15.

Maximum Number of Simultaneously Overlapping Episodes: The number of other episodes which overlapped with each episode at any one time. The number of simultaneously overlapping episodes ranged from none to three.

Type of Overlap: Five types were identified. A *coinciding* episode is one such that the whole of it intersects with the whole of another.

An *enclosing* episode is one such that a part of it overlaps with the whole of another. An *enclosed* episode is one such that the whole of it intersects with a part of another. An *interlinking* episode is one such that a part of it overlaps with a part of another. An *interpolated* episode is one which occurs during the interruption of a previously begun and subsequently resumed episode. All types of episode occurred; the most frequent was *enclosed,* comprising almost 60 per cent of all episodes.

Form of Episode Transition: Two forms were identified. In an *abrupt* transition the target episode ceases and is immediately succeeded by a new episode. In a *merging* transition the succeeding episode begins before the target episode is completed. The target episode and its successor overlap during a part of their courses. About two-thirds of all transitions were merging and one-third abrupt.

Continuity of Episode Course: Two forms of continuity were identified. A *continuous* episode continues without interruption by other behavior episodes from its beginning to its end. A *discontinuous* episode is interrupted by other episodes at one or more places during its course and subsequently is resumed. Ninety-nine per cent of all episodes were continuous.

Actone Interference: Five degrees of conflict between the molecular implementation of simultaneous episodes were identified. The reader is referred to Schoggen (1954) for the definitions which are too extensive to be reported here.

Relative Weight of Overlapping Episodes: Three weights were discriminated. A *primary* episode is one that equals or outranks all other overlapping episodes in potency throughout its entire course. A *secondary* episode is one that is outranked in potency by one other overlapping episode. An episode that is *less than secondary* is one that is outranked in potency by two or more overlapping episodes. Approximately 17 per cent of episodes were primary, 57 per cent secondary, and 6 per cent less than secondary. Twenty per cent were isolated episodes.

Episode Issue: Eleven episode endings were identified, six were endings of complete episodes (acquittance, attainment, gratification, success, satiated consummation, other), and five were endings of incomplete episodes (nonattainment, frustration, failure, nonsatiated consummation, other). About 45 per cent of all episodes were acquittance episodes (brief, secondary, unimportant episodes) and 10 per cent attainment (goal reached after child overcomes appreciable resistance). The other forms of issue were less frequent. About 6 per cent of all episodes did not reach their goal, were incomplete; about 78 per cent were complete; and for about 16 per cent episode completeness could not be judged.

When we inspect the episode characteristics that differentiated between the Midwest and Yoredale behavior streams, it appears that three of them indicate that child-determination of behavior episode characteristics was more frequent in the behavior streams of Midwest than of Yoredale children. This is true of spontaneity of episode initiation, spontaneity of episode termination, and episode discrimination on the basis of potency. The other culture-differentiating characteristic, is not opposed to this interpretation of the meaning of the Midwest-Yoredale differences. The number of episodes per minute appears to depend upon the nature of the environmental control. Powerful environmental agents can, presumably, impose short or long episodes upon a child's behavior stream, making episodes flow at a faster or slower rate. In this case we know only that the more frequent intrusion of the Yoredale environment in the initiation and termination of episodes was accompanied by a slower rate of episode production, and that the less frequent intrusion of the Midwest environment was accompanied by a faster rate of episode production.

The episode categories which describe the structural complexity of the behavior stream (degree and form of episode overlap, form of transition from unit to unit, degree of interference of simultaneous episodes) reveal no culture differences in the behavior streams.

The most general suggestion of this study with regard to the structural-dynamic properties of the behavior streams of the American and English children involved is that (1) differences are few; (2) those differences which do appear are related more to the dynamics than to the structure of the stream of behavior, and (3) the locus of episode differences resides relatively more often in the Midwest child and relatively more often in the Yoredale environment.

It is of some relevance to note that both the social-content analysis (Chapter 7) and the present structural-dynamic analysis agree in discovering greater environmental dominance of the child behavior streams in Yoredale than in Midwest.

CHAPTER 9

The Behavior of the Same Child in Different Milieus

PAUL V. GUMP, PHIL SCHOGGEN & FRITZ REDL

IT IS WIDELY BELIEVED that a change of milieu will provide a new life for a child. The research presented here provides evidence bearing upon this common assumption. It reports in detail, by both new and old analytical methods, how a day at camp was similar and different from a day at home for nine-year-old Wally O'Neill. Here is an "experiment in nature" that identifies camp-home differences in living conditions and in their consequences for behavior.

Paul V. Gump is Associate Professor of Psychology at the University of Kansas; he earned the Ph.D. degree at the University of Colorado. Phil Schoggen is identified in the introduction to Chapter 3. Fritz Redl is Distinguished Professor at Wayne State University. The research was carried out when the three authors were on the staff of Wayne State University.

The Problem

THE BASIC RESEARCH from which this study was derived investigated the psychological impact of recreational activities upon children. The aim of that research project was to identify and describe certain psychologically relevant characteristics of common recreational offerings, e.g., crafts, swims, cook-outs, games, and to discover relationships between these characteristics and the behavior of children who participate in the activities. Results of these studies demonstrated that behavior of children is markedly and differentially affected by the activities in which they are placed (Gump, Schoggen & Redl, 1957; Gump & Sutton-Smith, 1955a; Gump & Sutton-Smith, 1955b; Millen, 1958). However, such studies necessarily gave a fragmentary picture. It became of interest to know how a series of activities —a more nearly total activity environment—would affect behavior, and it became a special concern to learn how behavior in a special child-centered milieu would differ from behavior occurring in the more usual home-neighborhood setting. It was decided to study a child-centered environment that is common in our culture, namely, a summer camp. The general problem was: What is the impact of camp upon the behavior of a camper? A detailed record was made of the life of one boy on a typical day at camp, and a similar record was made of a typical day of the camper in his home.

The purposes of the study were the following:

1. To compare, on some important dimensions, camp behavior with behavior at home.
2. To relate these differences in behavior to some known differences in the two living situations.
3. To develop concepts and measures which may be of value in determining the nature and behavioral effects of other special environments for children; e.g., residential treatment homes, detention homes, special living-in schools.

One assumption behind the study has been that many questions about the impact of camp, or of any environment, upon children can be answered most adequately and certainly by a direct approach. This direct approach involves actually observing and recording what is done for and to children and what children do in response.

The Method

SUBJECT

Wally O'Neill, a nine-year-old camper, was the subject chosen for the study. Wally O'Neill was the oldest of five children. His father was a maintenance worker for the County Construction Agency. The family was a stable one in the upper lower-income group. Wally had some emotional problems, as did most of the other boys in camp. He had been a regular client of a publicly supported counseling center for more than a year. His problems did not result in behavior which greatly concerned camp personnel. Although he was sometimes more tentative in his responses than other boys his age, he was looked upon by camp people as better adjusted than many other campers. Wally's case-worker felt that a camping experience might be of value to Wally. The present study is an attempt to determine what the camp milieu, as represented by a one-day slice, actually did to and for Wally as compared to his home environment.

MILIEUS

The first milieu was University Boys' Camp, a camp for boys whose adjustment was such that attendance at a regular camp might not be beneficial. The nature of this camp is described elsewhere (see Appendix 1.1). It is only necessary to report here that, in matters of program and environment, the camp was reasonably typical of camps in general. Exceptions were the absence of competitive activities at University Boys' Camp, and therapeutic handling of adjustment difficulties.

The second milieu was Wally's home and neighborhood which has also been described elsewhere (see Appendix 1.1). Wally lived in a modest, three-bedroom frame house on a busy residential street in the suburb of a large city. There were two public parks within walking distance of home, but shopping centers were usually reached by car.

DATA COLLECTION

Two day-long specimen records of Wally's behavior and situation were made (see Appendix 1.1). One record was made during a typical day at University Boys' Camp, the other was made ten days later at Wally's home. In making these two records, the observing and recording was done according to procedures described by Barker and Wright (1955, Ch. 6). Trained observers, working in half-hour intervals, made continuous and detailed records of what Wally did and said, and what was done and said to him; they sought to describe accurately and completely and in ordinary, nontechnical language the boy's behavior and situation.

It is important to emphasize that these records do not constitute a type of case study. Wally O'Neill's days at camp and home were recorded in order to compare the impact of two environments, not to understand the personality of a particular child. The situations and events in these two days and Wally's response to them served as basic data for measurements of the effects of the camp and home milieus.

DATA ANALYSIS—A PREVIEW

Once a day-record has been made, the problem arises as to what kind of unit to use in its description. The unit employed was the episode, a unit already developed and described in detail (see pp. 161–62 for description and Appendix 1.2 for examples). Briefly, an episode is a unit of behavior which (1) occurs within the normal behavior perspective of the behaving person, and (2) is characterized by constancy of direction, i.e., the behavior is directed toward a single, particular goal. These episodes, over 1,000 in each day, served as basic units. They were described in terms of a variety of characteristics: play form, nature of social interaction, behavior initiation, and emotional tone. Determination of the frequency with which episodes of a given kind occurred made possible a quantitative description of each day. Such quantitative descriptions of each specimen record were then compared, resulting in a quantitative statement of similarities and differences between Wally's day at camp and his day at home.

Such, in brief, was the method of data analysis used for the study; complete definitions of the coding categories and analytical procedures for episode attributes concerned with play, social interaction, type of initiation, and emotionality will be offered as they become relevant in the report.

TABLE 9.1
Log of Prominent Scenes in Wally's Days at Camp and Home

Time	*Camp*	*Home*
7:00 AM	Getting up	Breakfast with the family
	Getting dressed with cabinmates	Playing upstairs
8:00 AM	Flag raising ceremony	Card game with mother and brother
	Breakfast in dining hall	Play and work around the house
		Taking baby brother to park
9:00 AM	"Working" on clean-up of craft shop	Play at park
	Impromptu nature hike with cabinmates	Going home ..... and .....
10:00 AM	Visit with pal to Luke's dispensary	Back to park
11:00 AM	Going swimming	Watching carrom games at park
Noon	Getting ready for cook-out in woods	Pitching horseshoes
	Prelunch play at tree hut	Going home again
1:00 PM	Cook-out	Lunch
	Play at tree hut	Watching T.V. in living room
2:00 PM	Swimming and water games	Cleaning bird cage
		Watching .....
3:00 PM	Fun alone on playground barrel horse	more .....
4:00 PM	Making bracelet in craft shop	T.V. .....
	Return to play at tree hut	in living room
5:00 PM	Flag lowering ceremony	Supper with family
6:00 PM	Supper in dining hall	Fooling around inside and out
		Playing ball with friends
7:00 PM	Playing in front of dining hall	Helping on family tasks
	Attending Indian council fire	Play outside with friends
8:00 PM	Going to bed	Bathing and getting ready ....
9:00 PM	In cabin	for bed

General Pictures of the Camp and Home Days

ACTIVITIES LOG

A complete picture of Wally's days at camp and at home can be gained only by reading the specimen records which describe these two days. The quantitative descriptions cannot give the reader a sense of how the days progressed from one set of specific activities and places to another. The reader may obtain some orientation to this sequence by referring to Table 9.1; here are listed the major scenes as they developed on each day.

BEHAVIOR SETTINGS ENTERED

The preceding activity log offers a sketchy and common-sense description of how Wally spent his two days. Another general but more objective method of description would be to list, in order, the behavior settings Wally entered on the two days.

Since there were over seventy entries into behavior settings on each day, the reader will not be burdened with such a list. However, it is possible to list the varieties of behavior settings in which Wally spent his time on the two days. The concept and measurement of behavior setting variety is fully described by Barker and Wright (1955, pp. 81–83). Briefly, variety refers to "classes" of settings. Two grocery stores represent two separate settings but one variety; a swimming pool and a dining hall, however, are not only separate settings but are of different varieties. The number of behavior setting varieties entered by an individual is a measure of the variety of experience opportunities offered by that individual's environment. This is true because, by definition, behavior settings of different varieties induce or support different perceptions and behaviors. Discrete varieties of settings are likely to have dissimilar locations, behavior objects, persons, and to serve dissimilar functions. Table 9.2 lists the varieties of settings entered by Wally on the two days.

TABLE 9.2

Varieties of Behavior Settings Entered by Wally at Camp and at Home

Camp	*Home*
Cabin M Indoors	Home, Meals
Paths in Camp	Home, Indoors
Camp (Boys') Toilet	Home, Outdoors
Washing Machine & Clothes Line Area	Home, Bathroom
Flag Ceremony	City Streets and Sidewalks
Main Lodge, Meals	Booster Park
Clean-Up of Crafts Shop	Total no. entered—6
Woods	
Luke's Dispensary, Outside	
Luke's Dispensary, Clinic	
Swimming	
Cook-Out in Woods	
Athletic Field	
Crafts in Craft Shop	
Main Lodge, Free Play	
Main Lodge, Outside	
Indian Council Fire	
Total no. entered—17	

The difference in number of behavior setting varieties which Wally entered on the two days gives a rough measure of how varied his experience could be. It is apparent that the potential variety at camp was substantially greater than that at home. It cannot be said at this point that actual experience and behavior at camp were more varied; it would be possible for an individual to penetrate dissimilar settings so minimally and to respond to them so slightly that experience and behavior would not be significantly changed by these shifts in environment. The point made here is that the potential for variety was markedly greater at camp. Just how much, and in what manner, this potential was realized must be determined by the analyses to follow.

Play at Camp and Home

So far, the picture of Wally on the two days has been built around major places and occasions in which he behaved (behavior settings). Another phase of life important to children, that of play, will indicate the nature of the two days. For a variety of reasons, play is also important to adults who wish to understand children. The amount and kind of a child's play indicates his mood and his needs, frustrations and fears; it also indicates the extent to which his environment and his relation to this environment give him pleasure and satisfaction.

A camp is usually established to support and encourage children's play, particularly play of certain types. It was of interest, then, to know whether these special provisions resulted in a different amount and kind of play than the play which occurred in Wally's usual home-neighborhood environment.

DATA ANALYSIS

In order to draw an objective and quantitative account of Wally's play on the two days, each episode was coded. The first coding task was to decide whether or not the behavior recorded in the episode represented play; if play was decided upon, it was necessary to determine what form of play was involved. The following are the definitions of play and nonplay episodes, and of the forms of play which guided the coding.

Play Episodes Versus Nonplay Episodes. Play episodes involved the seeking or obtaining of enjoyment, fascination, pleasure, or thrill; they involved behavior carried out primarily "just for fun." Nonplay episodes involved matters of routine, orientation, necessary locomotion and other "means" actions; self-care and protection; help to and direction of others; chores, and matter-of-fact greetings and goodbyes. Primary evidence for the play *versus* nonplay judgment was found in the subject's voice, facial expression, and general demeanor; kinds of objects and events with which he transacted behavior furnished supplementary evidence. Objects and events with characteristic entertainment or amusement value (comic books, yo-yos, TV programs) tended to support a judgment of play, whereas more serious, workaday behavior supports (shoes, chairs, tableware) suggested a judgment of nonplay. But these were indirect evidences; the behavior and attitude of the subject were the primary considerations.

Forms of Play. The code for play forms was developed empirically.

Some ideas for categories were obtained from previous work (Wright & Barker, 1950b, pp. 219, 220). Direct experience with children, the reading of other records of children's activity, and the present two records also provided suggestions. A code was developed which included the major forms of play with which the authors were familiar and which described most of the cases encountered in Wally's days at camp and home. The code provides only a rough description and, no doubt, better codes can and should be developed. It is offered here because it is believed that it aids in classifying and assessing the effect of two different environments upon a significant aspect of Wally's behavior.

WATCHING

The subject watches or listens because he is entertained by what he observes. There are many episodes in which watching is the major activity but not all of these are playful watching; for example, idle looking at or watching for orientation were neither considered play watching.

Examples: Wally smilingly watches a counselor control an unruly boy. Wally watches a TV program.

SENSUAL ENJOYMENT

The subject is concerned with receiving pleasant sensations. These sensations are usually tactile and kinesthetic and represent a passive, receptive type of orientation to outside stimulations.

Example: Wally pours warm sand over his bare feet, apparently enjoying the warmth and movement of the particles as they touch his skin.

READING

The subject reads for fun and fascination. Sensual Enjoyment and Reading occurred infrequently; they seemed psychologically allied with Watching and were collapsed into the play form, Watching.

Example: Wally reads a comic book.

MANIPULATIVE AMUSEMENT

The subject "fools around" with an object; he "toys" with it. He does nothing constructive with it, nor does he really investigate it.

Examples: Wally picks up a hunk of bark, breaks off small pieces and, one by one, tosses them aside. Wally "fiddles" with a string; he draws it about his throat, then slips it loose, pulls it over his knee, etc.

INVESTIGATION AND EXPLORATION

The subject is curious and wants to "find out," but no utilitarian purpose is involved. The subject doesn't have to learn in order to get a job done, he continues for the fun of it.

Examples: Wally breaks open a rotting log to see what's inside. Wally opens a cupboard at home which he hasn't seen for some time saying, "Hey, let's see what's in here!"

STUNTS

The subject does, or attempts, something tricky or daring. Coder should feel safe in inferring that subject sees his activity as a stunt, not just as pleasant bodily exertion.

Examples: Wally carefully walks a log. Wally tries to jump from a picnic table to catch an overhanging branch.

UNORGANIZED SPORT

The subject seems to enjoy action for action's sake. He romps, skips about, jumps, swings, runs, etc. The bodily action is the main source of pleasure. If any specific goal is involved, it is an "excuse" for the action, not the reason for the action.

Examples: Wally climbs a tree for fun—not as a stunt or as a part of some competition. Wally, just out of exuberance, clambers up one side of a pile of lumber and dashes down the other.

ROUGHHOUSING

The subject and one or more associates tussle in a manifestly friendly, nonserious fashion. There may be aggressive underpinnings but the participants maintain an "it's all in fun" front for their activity.

Example: Wally wrestles with a cabinmate, both boys grinning.

INFORMAL ACTIVE GAME

The subject and one or more associates engage in a simple, usually spontaneous, game. The activity has a simple structure and competitive goals.

Examples: Wally races another boy to the craft shop. Wally and neighborhood children play tag.

FORMAL ACTIVE GAME

The subject and his associates participate in a traditional, relatively complex game which requires physical skill and strength.

Example: Wally plays baseball with other boys on his street.

STATIONARY GAMES

The subject engages in a traditional game of relatively complex structure which does not require vigorous bodily activity. Such games emphasize mental alertness, manipulative skill or luck.

Example: Wally plays card game *War* with mother and brother.

CONSTRUCTION

The subject makes something for the fun of making and having. Construction may be *reproductive,* in which case the subject makes a duplicate of a model which is present or is very clear in his mind; or, construction may be *creative,* when the subject develops and organizes his materials in a relatively inventive or self-expressive manner.

Examples: Reproductive. Wally makes a bracelet, model for which is present, in craft shop.

Creative. Wally builds a system of dams to retain and to guide overflow water from the camp drinking fountain.

VERBAL JOKING

The subject puns, "verbally plays around," often making a word show of nothing.

Example: Wally recites in silly fashion, "Help, murder, police, my mother fell in the grease."

TEASING

The subject is lightly and playfully aggressive, insulting, or provocative; he tries, in a sporting fashion, to make his associate look silly.

Examples: Wally calls to his obese acquaintance, "Patty, the fatty!" Wally pretends to slug his brother, hoping to make him duck unnecessarily.

DRAMATICS

The subject takes on a fantasy role, acting out some event or situation. He pretends to be something or someone he is not; he engages in unreal acts. The subject may do this as sole actor or may be one of the several actors involved in the "play."

Examples: Wally pretends to be an army commander fighting off the enemy. Wally and his brother pretend that some empty storage places are cabins of space ships and they "blast off."

OTHER

If an episode was coded play and yet did not fit any of the forms specified above, it was coded *Other*. An example would be hunting.

A single episode was given only one play form code. On those occasions when more than one play form could be distinguished in an episode, the form which appeared to have the most importance to the subject was used.

Reliability in using the code was as follows:

1. For determining play versus nonplay; agreement of two independent coders on 200 episodes: 85%
2. For determining kind of play once it was decided that play was involved; agreement: 82%
3. For over-all coding agreement: 81%

After each episode had been coded, it became apparent that the *number* of episodes would be a misleading index of the amount of various play forms enjoyed. Some play episodes were very long but happened only once, while play forms of other types were often quite short. For example, Wally spent 27 minutes with the play form Construction when building his system of dams. On the other hand, many of his 60 Watching episodes were less than 30 seconds in duration. If the one episode is given a unit of one, the relation of Creative Construction to Watching at camp would be 1 to 60. This misrepresents the relative importance of the two play forms in his camp day. The number of episodes devoted to a particular play form is an exact measure of the number of occasions play of a certain form was *attempted*. However, total duration of episodes involving a certain play form is a better indication of the amount of that kind of play. Accordingly, in the results that follow, both play episode frequency and total time of play episodes will be used to indicate the relative importance of various play forms.

RESULTS

Wally engaged in 1,054 episodes at camp and in 1,016 at home.[1] Episodes involving a play form equaled 284, or 27 per cent, at camp; 307, or 30 per cent, at home. Total behavior time at camp was 1,165 minutes; at home, 1,132 minutes. Time in play episodes at camp was 497 minutes, or 43 per cent; at home 633 minutes, or 56 per cent. As will become clear later, the extra amount of play at home is due to several hours of TV watching.

The patterns of distribution of play forms are shown in Figures 9.1 and 9.2.

Inspection of Figure 9.1 shows that although certain marked differences occur, there was considerable similarity in number of episodes of various play forms on the two days. It is possible to rank the different play forms on each day in order of frequency and determine the degree of relationship between the two days. This process yields a tau coefficient of .49 ($p < .01$). If frequency is taken as a measure, there is similarity in the occurrence of play forms in the day at camp and in the day at home.

Figure 9.2 reveals that similarity of play forms when total duration of episodes is used as the index no longer exists. The tau coefficient is —.16 ($p > .40$). It seems that Wally attempted a similar pattern of play forms on the two days, but that camp and home differed markedly in the extent to which they provided the supports necessary for extended devotion to particular play forms.

The greater duration of play at home is a result of several hours of TV watching. Watching may be considered a special and rather weak form of play. If active play, play to which Wally manifestly contributes his own action and ideas, is used as a base for play, the amount of play at camp is considerably greater than at home. Active play (all play forms except Watching) at camp amounted to 411 minutes, or 35 per cent, of the total behavior time; such play at home amounted to 206 minutes, or 27 per cent. Wally engaged in an hour and 45 minutes more of active play episodes at camp than at home ($p < .01$).[2]

In terms of duration and frequency of various play forms, the following statements are descriptive of similarities and differences between Wally's play behavior at camp and at home. All comparisons are significant at the .05 level or better.

[1] In order to reduce any differences due to observer effects, episodes in which an observer became a social associate were omitted. Total episodes, including observers, were: 1,184 at camp; 1,090 at home.

[2] Unless stated otherwise, all p values for differences in this study are derived from a critical ratio test of the difference of proportion.

1. Wally, facing two different milieus, attempted a similar play pattern in each; however, time spent in various play forms was markedly dissimilar from one milieu to the other.
2. Camp exceeded home in: duration of active play; frequency and duration of Investigation and Exploration; duration of Drama; duration of Construction.
3. Home exceeded camp in: duration of nonactive play; frequency and duration of Roughhousing; frequency and duration of Verbal Joking; frequency and duration of Manipulative Amusement; duration of Formal and Stationary Games.

DISCUSSION

In general terms, Wally's play at camp was more active, exploratory, construction-oriented, fantasy-tinged, and physically exuberant. In contrast, his play at home was more passive, more dallying, and more formally competitive. Probably some differences in child's play form would result on any two days even in the same milieu. However there were obvious supports and invitations to particular play forms which were inherent in the camp and home milieus; the presence of these supports lends credence to the judgment that the differences obtained here were a result of environmental differences (opposed to differences resulting as from mood or special circumstances). In order to relate the two environments to specific outcomes in Wally's behavior, it is worthwhile to consider a few of the prominent environmental factors (behavior settings, behavior objects, customary routines, etc.) possibly responsible for the behavioral differences.

The preponderance of Watching play time at home was related to the presence of a TV set at home and none at camp. Wally watched a great deal in both situations. Much of the camp watching was directed toward conflicts between other campers or between campers and counselors. At home, Wally enjoyed watching competitive encounters between other children in games and between cowboys or soldiers on TV programs. The Watching time at camp was less than at home, because camp did not have the necessary behavior objects or props to support extended watching. A by-product of the extended TV watching was an increase of Manipulative Amusement at home. Wally engaged in more episodes of Manipulative Amusement while watching TV at home than he did during the entire day at camp. So little physical activity was invited by the nature of this TV activity that Wally apparently had to develop some outlets for his energies. A number of these outlets were simply restless movements but others involved episodes of "dallying" with strings, bits of upholstery, and odd objects.

The increase in Unorganized Sport at camp was related to the behavior settings and props in camp which invited vigorous and pleasurable physical action: the swimming area, the paths through the woods, the trees for climbing, etc. Dramatics also was related to the behavior setting Woods and

FIGURE 9.1
Number of Episodes in Each Play Category

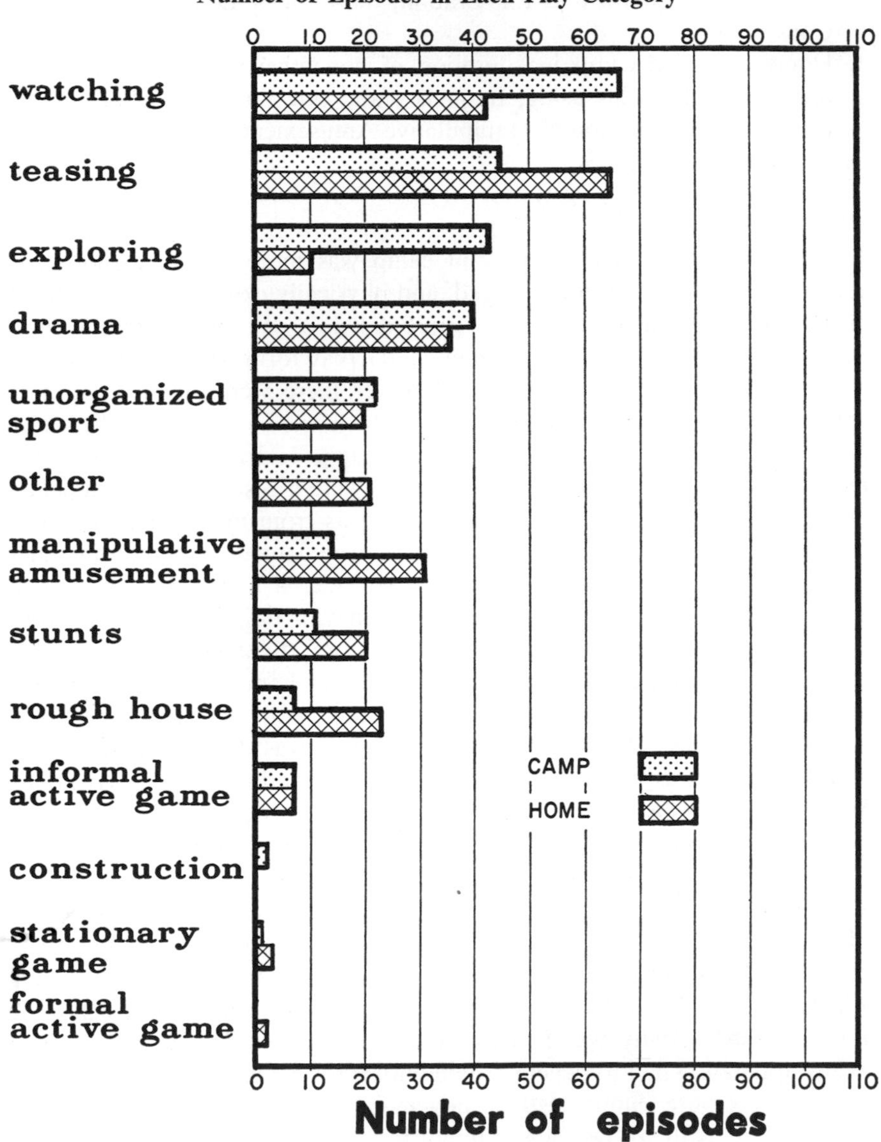

FIGURE 9.2

Total Duration (Minutes) of Episodes in Each Play Category

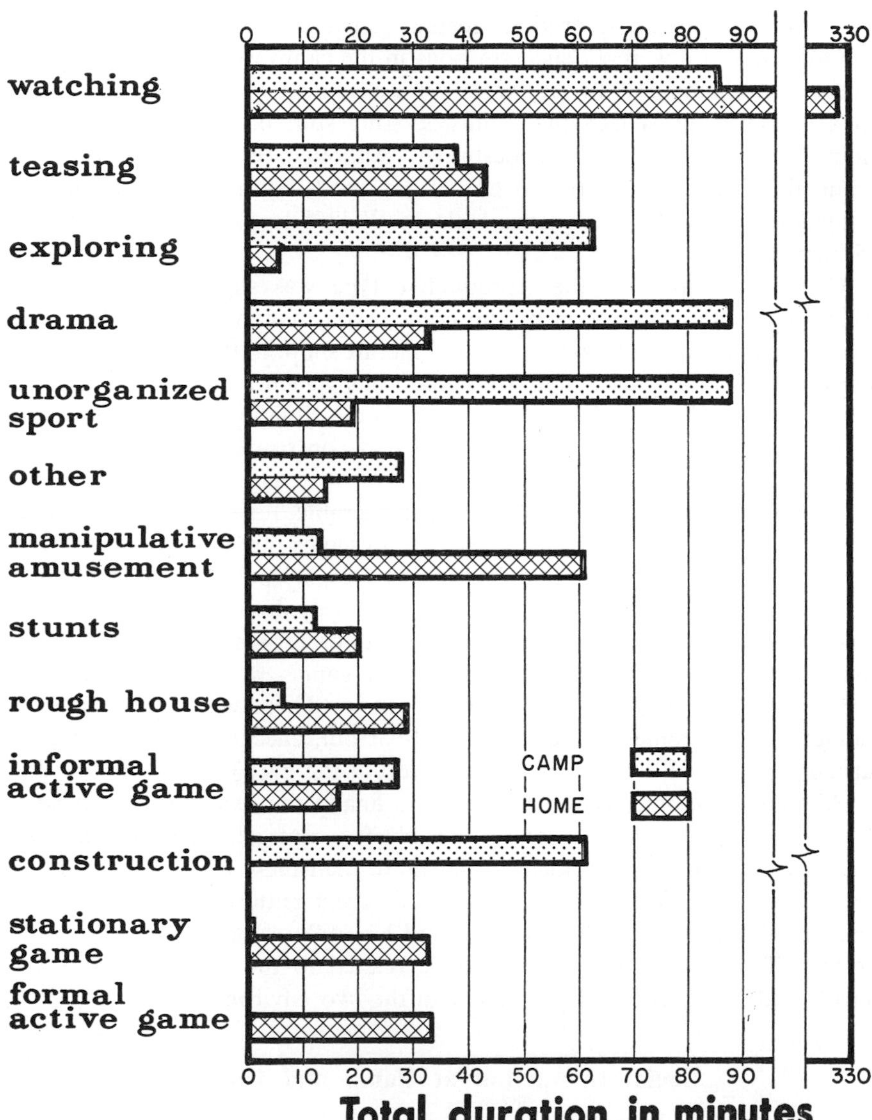

to a tree hut in these woods. In the woods were hidden places for pretenses of ambush, or searching, of danger in the "wilds." The tree hut also lent itself to much dramatic fantasy. Here, Wally and his cabinmates were temporarily above the world and acted out fantasies reflective of their commanding position.

Investigation and Exploration seemed also related to the availability of the woods. There were 27 such episodes in the camp woods alone; only 10 in the entire home day. In the woods were a number of unknowns. What is in a hollow tree? What's that funny looking stuff on the ground? What animals or bugs are in the underbrush? Although the boys had been at camp almost four weeks, the novelty of the woods had not yet worn off; no comparative novelty seemed available in Wally's home-neighborhood environment.

Construction play of the reproductive type was supported more emphatically by the camp than by the home, even though materials for such play were available at home. Camp had a craft shop; in the shop were other boys making things and adults who could help. Such a situation was more invitational to Construction play than the home situation in which one had to employ initiative and be more alone if a construction project were to result.

Finally, the presence at home of considerable Formal and Stationary Game play forms and their absence at camp seems obviously related to the customs of the children and adults, and to the play possibilities in the two environments. University Boys' Camp deliberately de-emphasized competitive activities, at the same time offering many other possibilities for fun. In Wally's neighborhood, however, traditional games were the custom and served as a major play possibility for children. There were card games at home; baseball games in the street; and carrom, checkers, and horseshoes at the park (and little else significant to do at the park).

Although it is impossible to determine finally the extent to which contrasts in the two milieus were responsible for contrasts in play behavior, the foregoing discussion indicates that more than mere chance fluctuations are at issue here. Wally produced quite different patterns of time spent in various play forms on the two days, and less different patterns of play attempts. These differences appear to be related to the specific encouragements and supports for play inherent in the two environments.

Social Interaction at Camp and Home

The personal relationships one enjoys, or suffers, are key aspects of experience. The extent to which one's associates are aggressive or nurturant, distant or sharing, can influence the enjoyment life offers and the picture one develops of himself. On the other hand, the response one makes to these associates may indicate the freedom, the power, the affection one feels and is able to express. This section will describe the social actions taken by associates toward Wally and Wally's action toward his associates. Several indices which deal with both aspects of the interaction will also be employed to assess the degree of mutuality in social activity behavior of Wally and his associates.

ASSOCIATES AT CAMP AND HOME

At camp, Wally's primary living group consisted of two women counselors and his cabin mates, seven boys of his own age. At home, his primary group included his mother and father and two younger brothers and two younger sisters. Thus, age and sex peers dominated the primary social potential at camp but were absent at home. General descriptions of possible associates beyond the primary living groups cannot be stated so precisely. The social potential at camp included forty counselors and 110 other boy campers. At home, this potential included an aunt and uncle living nearby, neighborhood children and their parents, tradesmen who came to the neighborhood, and a playground supervisor. The total number of theoretically possible associates at home was obviously much larger and more varied than at camp. However, the number and kind of reasonably likely associates at home was severely restricted by the style of living in the home community. At camp, certain arrangements of architecture and routine made contact between a boy and persons beyond his primary living group quite likely; similar factors at home tended to restrict contact to only certain persons beyond the primary group. Although Wally could conceivably contact a number of housewives on his block, he was not likely to do so; he was, however, quite likely to contact a number of counselors other than his own. Even without an exact census, it was possible to predict that the number of contacts with different adults would be quite low at home as compared to camp. The reasonably possible social potential at camp *vs.* home may be grossly described as follows: camp presented more possibilities for peer contact and much more variety of adult contact; home presented more variety of child contact (different ages and sexes) and less variety of adult contact.

A summary of the kinds of individuals with whom Wally actually experienced social interaction on the camp and home days is displayed in Table 9.3. Both the number of different individuals and the number of episodes related to each class of individuals are described.

Two related results stand out in Table 9.3. The number of different peer and adult associates was more than twice as great at camp as at home; the number of episodes devoted to adults and peers was twice as great at camp. On the other hand, the number of different nonpeer children, and the number of episodes with them was much greater at home than at camp.

TABLE 9.3
Kinds of Associates at Camp and Home and Number of Episodes Involved

KIND OF ASSOCIATE	NUMBER OF DIFFERENT ASSOCIATES *Camp*	*Home*	NUMBER OF EPISODES *Camp*	*Home*
Peers (Similar Age, Same Sex)	20	8	234	121
Adults	22	5	188	90
Children and Adolescents of Different Age and/or Sex	6	17	142	391
Mixed: (Adults and Children in Same Episode)	1[a]	1[a]	89	18
Totals	49	31	653	620

[a] One person in addition to those already represented in Peer, Adult and Children categories.

Clearly, Wally's camp day was marked by heavy adult and peer contact, his home day by nonpeer contact. It should be mentioned here that the nonpeer contact at home is divided between Wally's younger siblings and neighborhood boys and girls.

KIND OF SOCIAL INTERACTION AT CAMP AND HOME

The primary interaction code applied to the social episodes was the Mode Code employed previously by Barker and Wright (1955). Since a full description of this code is available, a summary account will be offered here. The Mode Code measures the frequency and intensity of occurrence of the following attributes of social action:

Dominance E.g., "Give me that ball, right now!"
Aggression E.g., "You're a bum!" (or blows and threats).
Resistance E.g., "I won't do it."
Submission E.g., "All right, I'll do it."
Nurturance E.g., "Here, I'll help you with that."
Appeal E.g., "Can I play too?"
Avoidance E.g., "I'm leaving—I don't like it here."

In using the code, the judge determined, for each social episode, whether or not dominance was shown by the subject, and if so, the intensity of that dominance (1—mild, 2—moderately pronounced, 3—strong). A similar judgment was made regarding the associates' social activity during the episode. This procedure was continued for the seven modes of social interaction. Reliability in using the code was 78 per cent agreement on the presence or absence of a given mode. It should be emphasized that the Mode Code categories are not mutually exclusive; for example, an episode could contain both dominance and aggression, or both submission and appeal.

Of the 728 social episodes [3] analyzed, 25 per cent were without subject modes and 27 per cent without associate modes. Inspection revealed that most of these "modeless" episodes seemed to deal with a social interaction which might be called *sharing*. The sharing social action is one which describes experience without any attempt to dominate, aggress, give, get help, and so forth. Much of what we ordinarily call conversation is of this type. One person tells another about events or objects of interest, he recounts his plans, or he explains his ideas. Sharing is a kind of nondemanding, nonpressuring social intercourse. Examples include the following comments:

> "Say, this sure is fun!"
> "Look at that boat—it's a beauty!"
> "We have a police dog at home."
> "After camp is over, we gotta go back to school."

It would seem that sharing is most likely to occur when people do not have strong needs to "get something from" or "do something to" one another. We could infer that sharing occurs more frequently among adults than among children and most often between "satisfied," rather than "dissatisfied," individuals. It would seem also that sharing might increase when persons are in a stimulating environment and have a strong similarity of interest regarding that environment.

The interaction Sharing was added to the social interaction ratings. The per cent of agreement on sharing vs. nonsharing was 82 per cent.

RESULTS OF MODE ANALYSIS

The number of social interaction episodes in each day, which showed each of the modes, or sharing, is presented in Table 9.4. Since there were 366 social interaction episodes in the camp day and 362 in the home day, direct comparison of numbers is legitimate.

The patterns of Wally's and associates' social action are also indicated in Figure 9.3. It can be seen that, at home, Wally was more dominant, aggressive, and tended to be more submissive; at camp, he was more nurturant. On the other hand, Wally's associates were more aggressive, resistant, and appealing at home; more nurturant and sharing at camp.

A complexity in the data relating to associate aggression must be reported: while associates were more frequently aggressive at home, sharp aggressions (those coded beyond a minimum of *one* in intensity) were more frequent at camp. Wally's associates aggressed sharply against him in 25 camp episodes and in only 11 home episodes ($p < .01$). Hostility from associates was less frequent at camp, but when it came it was likely to be

[3] Not all episodes involving an associate were necessarily social interaction episodes. Only when the social interaction was "complete," when both subject and associate acted with regard to each other, was the social interaction of an episode coded for mode. This accounts for the fewer number of episodes here than offered in Table 9.1.

TABLE 9.4
Number of Episodes Showing Social Modes Employed by Wally to Associates and by Associates to Wally

SOCIAL MODE	BY WALLY TO ASSOCIATES			BY ASSOCIATES TO WALLY		
	Camp	*Home*	*p*	*Camp*	*Home*	*p*
Dominance	46	66	.04	74	66	—
Aggression	98	127	.02	86	115	.02
Resistance	88	88	—	75	110	.01
Submission	78	98	.07	75	59	—
Nurturance	26	13	.04	40	20	.01
Appeal	63	51	—	52	77	.02
Avoidance	18	17	—	11	13	—
Sharing	71	57	—	73	44	.02

severe. It should be mentioned also that every one of the sharp camp aggressions came from peers. This reversal occurred only in the aggressive mode, associate's side. In all other comparisons, the frequencies in the minimum degrees of a category were positively related to those in the intense degrees.

It was of special interest to tabulate the amount of mutual sharing on the two days. Mutual sharing occurred when both Wally and his associates were sharing. There were 62 (17 per cent) such mutual sharings at camp, 42 (12 per cent) at home ($p < .05$).

The data in Figure 9.3 might be summarized employing the concept of demand. If demand is defined as that quality of social action expressed by dominance, aggression, resistance and appeal, it is clear that Wally was the target of much more demand at home than at camp. And, on his own part, Wally engaged in considerably more forceful demand (dominance and aggression) at home. In contrast, camp was characterized by more nurturance, on both sides, and by more sharing actions by associates.

A description of the over-all interaction is too gross to reveal all the aspects of social action and experience. It is probably true, for example, that the kind of associate who expresses or receives a mode of social action, affects the meaning of the social action. If one is a child facing domination attempts, it probably "feels differently" if the domination is by a child than if it is by an adult.

In order to gain some understanding of why the camp and home days showed the differences they did, it is necessary to know the contribution made by various classes of associates. The classes of associates used in the analysis were adults and children; the children at home were further divided into siblings, all of whom were younger than Wally and of both sexes, and neighborhood children who were both older and younger and of both sexes.

SOCIAL INTERACTION WITH ADULTS

It will be recalled (Table 9.3) that Wally's contacts with adults were twice as frequent at camp as they were at home. Some of these contacts resulted in complete social episodes. When complete social episodes are used as an index of amount of interaction with adults, the much greater frequency of such interaction at camp is again apparent. Wally had an adult as his only associate in 37 per cent of the camp complete social episodes and in 18 per cent of the home episodes ($p < .001$).

Wally's social action and experience on the camp and home day could have been affected by adults in three ways. One, Wally-Adult interactions could have been the same in quality, yet the days could have differed because adult contact was much more extensive on one day than on the other. Two, Wally-Adult interactions could have been different in quality. Three, a different social experience could have resulted from both a heavier concentration of adult contact and a different quality of adult interaction. As will become clear, the third of these operated to produce the over-all social interaction differences.

The qualities of Wally-Adult interactions are shown in Figure 9.4. It is important to recognize the similarity of the Wally-Adult interactions on both days. If one compares the two sides of Figure 9.4, it is clear that, regardless of milieu, adults dominated Wally, he did not dominate them; they were nurturant to Wally, he was not nearly as nurturant to them; Wally appealed to adults much more frequently than they appealed to him.

Despite the over-all similarity of interaction patterns on the two days, certain significant differences did occur. Wally was more submissive to home adults than to camp adults ($p < .02$). For their part, home adults were more likely to be aggressive to Wally ($p < .01$). There was also a tendency for home adults to resist Wally more ($p < .06$). Put in other words, one difference in the "with adults" experience on the two days seems to have been a more adult-over-child relationship at home. When one reads the record, one does not get a picture of home adults who were especially hostile or unyielding. One rather is impressed that the parents were acting like our stereotype of parents: they managed, prevented, cared for, etc.; counselors engaged in much of this same parental activity but they also engaged in more peer-like behavior, responding to Wally's play interests or inviting Wally to share their own interests.

A simple code was devised to describe episodes in which Wally interacted with an adult.

1. *Parent-like Role:* Adult treated Wally as if he were a child and required "parental guidance, manipulation, or help." Or, Wally approached adult as if adult had a parent role: Wally asked help, accepted direction, etc.

FIGURE 9.3

Per Cent of Social Episodes in Which Various Interaction Modes Were Displayed by Wally and by Associates

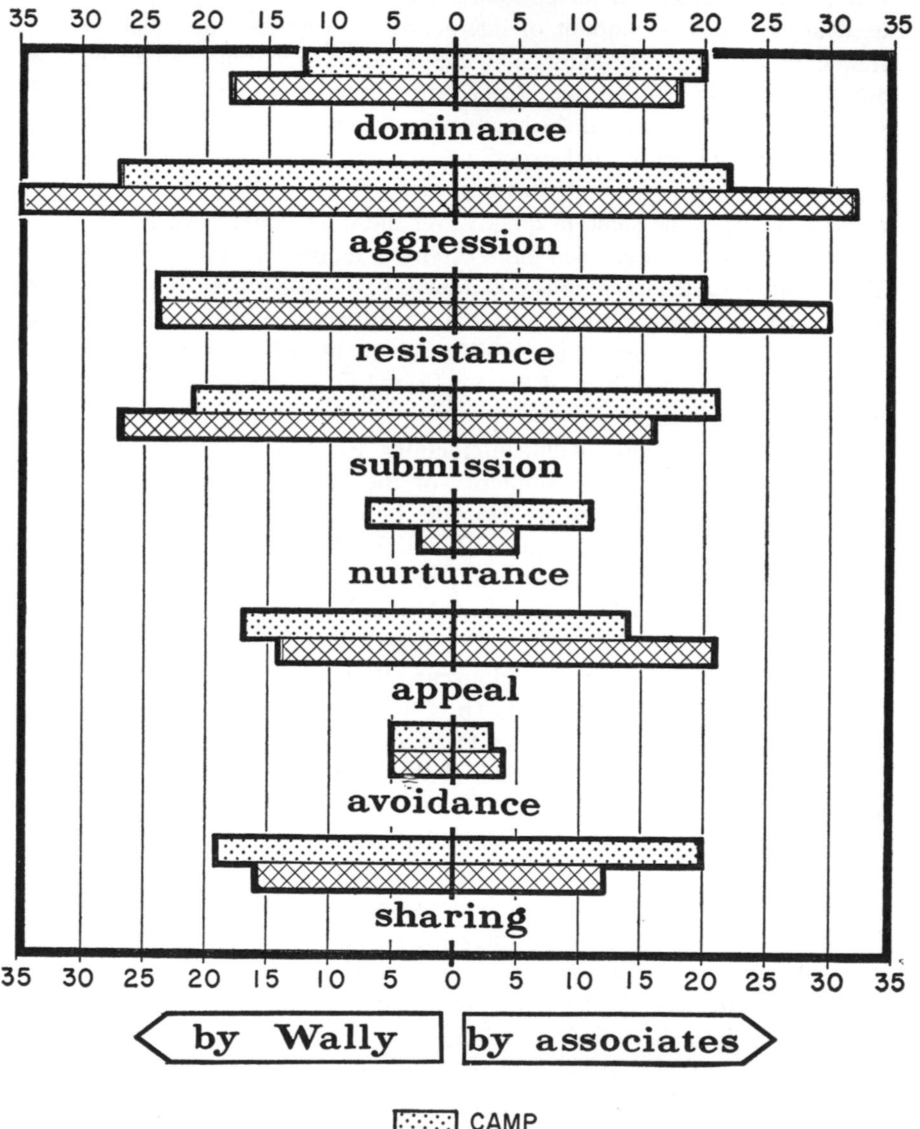

FIGURE 9.4

Per Cent of Social Episodes with Adult Associates in Which Various Interaction Modes Were Displayed by Wally and by Adult Associates

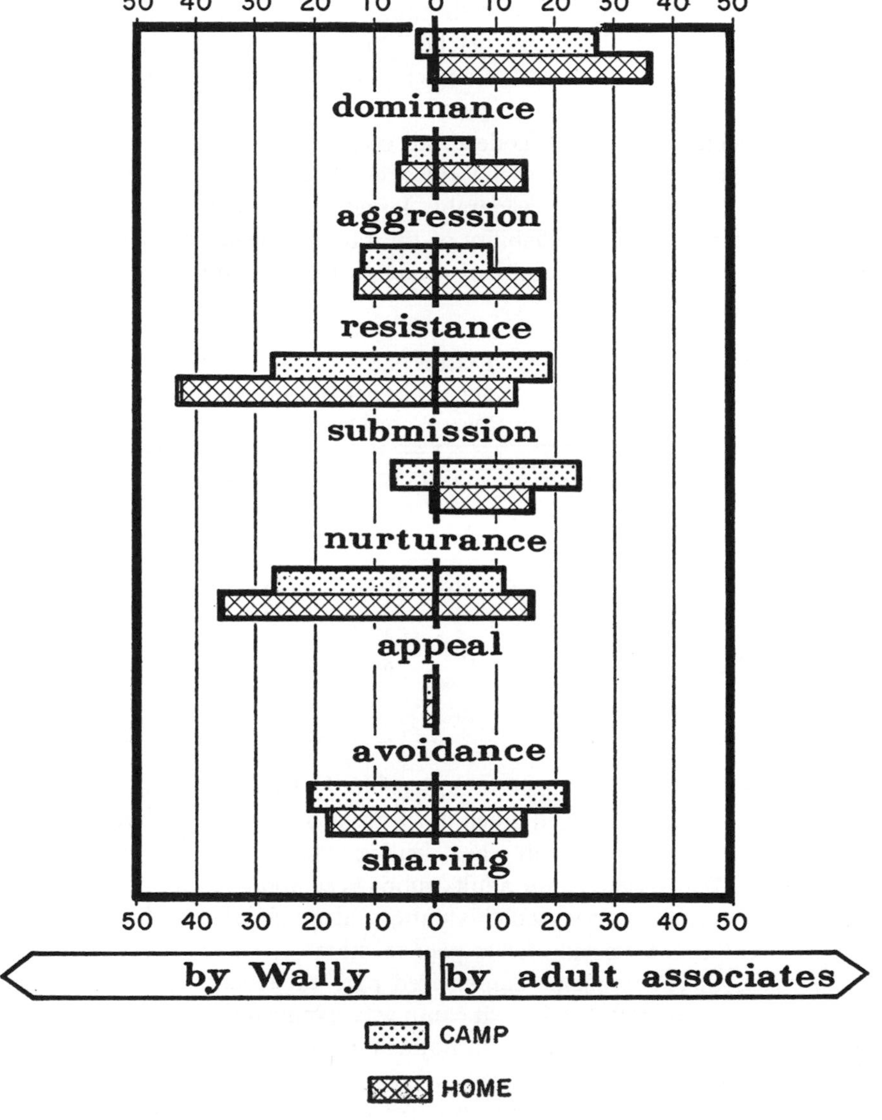

2. *Peer-like Role:* Adult treated Wally as he might treat a peer: asked opinion, played with, told story about self; listened to Wally's adventures (and responded without parental warnings). Or, Wally approached adult as if he were a peer: competed with him, played with him.
3. *Pleasantries and Greetings:* "Hello," "nice day."
4. *Cannot judge:* Contact too short or too ambiguous to be coded.

It was possible to apply this code to all observation episodes involving an adult, not only to complete social episodes. Thus the number of episodes involved in the analysis is considerably larger than in the analyses of mode of adult interaction. The reliability of the raters in using this code was 86 per cent. Table 9.5 gives results of a comparison of camp and home days using this adult-role code.

TABLE 9.5

Social Behavior by Wally and His Adult Associates Described in Terms of Frequency of Episodes in which Certain Roles Were Imputed to or Taken by Adults

	IMPUTED TO ADULTS				TAKEN BY ADULTS			
	Camp		*Home*		*Camp*		*Home*	
ROLE	*N*	%	*N*	%	*N*	%	*N*	%
Parent-like	122	38	70	48	124	55	93	72
Peer-like	147	46	59	40	75	33	30	23
Pleasantry	10	3	5	3	4	2	1	1
Cannot Judge	44	13	12	8	23	10	6	4
Totals	323		146		226		130	

From these data two trends are noticeable. In terms of absolute amount, Wally expressed and received much more of each type of social action when dealing with camp adults than when dealing with home adults. In terms of proportion, Wally gave camp adults more peer approaches and fewer parental approaches; he reversed this pattern at home where adults received more parental reactions and fewer peer reactions ($p < .05$). On their side, adults in both environments emphasized parental reactions. However, the proportion of parental reactions at camp was significantly less than at home; camp adults were more likely than home adults to engage in peer reactions with Wally ($p < .01$).

The more frequent and more peer-like interactions of camp adults may be attributable to their special philosophy as counselors. But another possible source of the difference between camp and home adults may lie in the pressures upon adults generated by their respective milieus. For example,

Wally's mother attempted to have fun with her older boys by playing a card game; she was drawn away at first by a man who came to the door, later by the baby who needed a diaper change. The father took time out to josh with Wally while both were gardening; but he returned to work after a short interplay. The camp milieu relieved counselors from many of the concerns which draw parents away from their children's interests.

The question was raised previously as to how adults at camp and home contributed to the over-all differences in social interaction in the two settings. Analysis of the data shows that Wally's greater nurturance to others at camp was primarily a result of some nurturance toward camp adults and no nurturance toward home adults. Greater nurturance by others to Wally at camp was a result of many more frequent nurturant approaches by camp adults. Adults tended, *in pattern,* to be more nurturant at camp; this, plus an expanded frequency of adult interactions at camp, increased the over-all camp nurturance. The increased sharing by associates at camp is contributed to, but not primarily caused by, a more adult sharing at camp.

In general, the differences in experience with adults at camp were primarily differences of frequency of contacts and, secondarily, differences in quality of these contacts.

SOCIAL INTERACTION WITH CHILDREN

Most of Wally's sociality on both days was with children, not adults; however, child interaction was considerably more frequent at home than at camp. There were 231 social episodes with campers (63 per cent) and 296 with siblings and neighborhood associates (82 per cent). During the home day, interactions with siblings and with acquaintances were roughly equal: 153 and 143 respectively.

The qualities of these with-children interactions are shown in Figure 9.5.

The balance of interaction by Wally and child associates was generally equal. This balance contrasts markedly to the imbalance with adults shown in Figure 9.4. Social interaction on the two days was similar in one important respect: adults at both camp and home tended to dominate and nurture, not be dominated or nurtured; and Wally tended to appeal to them, not they to him. Children at both camp and home dominated but were also dominated; they did not nurture, neither were they nurtured. The general power superiority of adults and the power equality of children operated to a marked degree in both environments.

It is clear from Figure 9.5 that the child interaction patterns in the two milieus are similar. The exceptions are that camp associates shared more ($p < .01$) and tended to appeal less ($p < .06$) than did home associates. On his part, Wally shows no statistically significant differences in modes of response to children at home and camp, although there was a trend for him to submit more frequently at home ($p < .08$).

Since the child populations and the behavior settings at camp and home

FIGURE 9.5

Per Cent of Social Episodes with Child Associates in Which Various Interaction Modes Were Displayed by Wally and by Child Associates

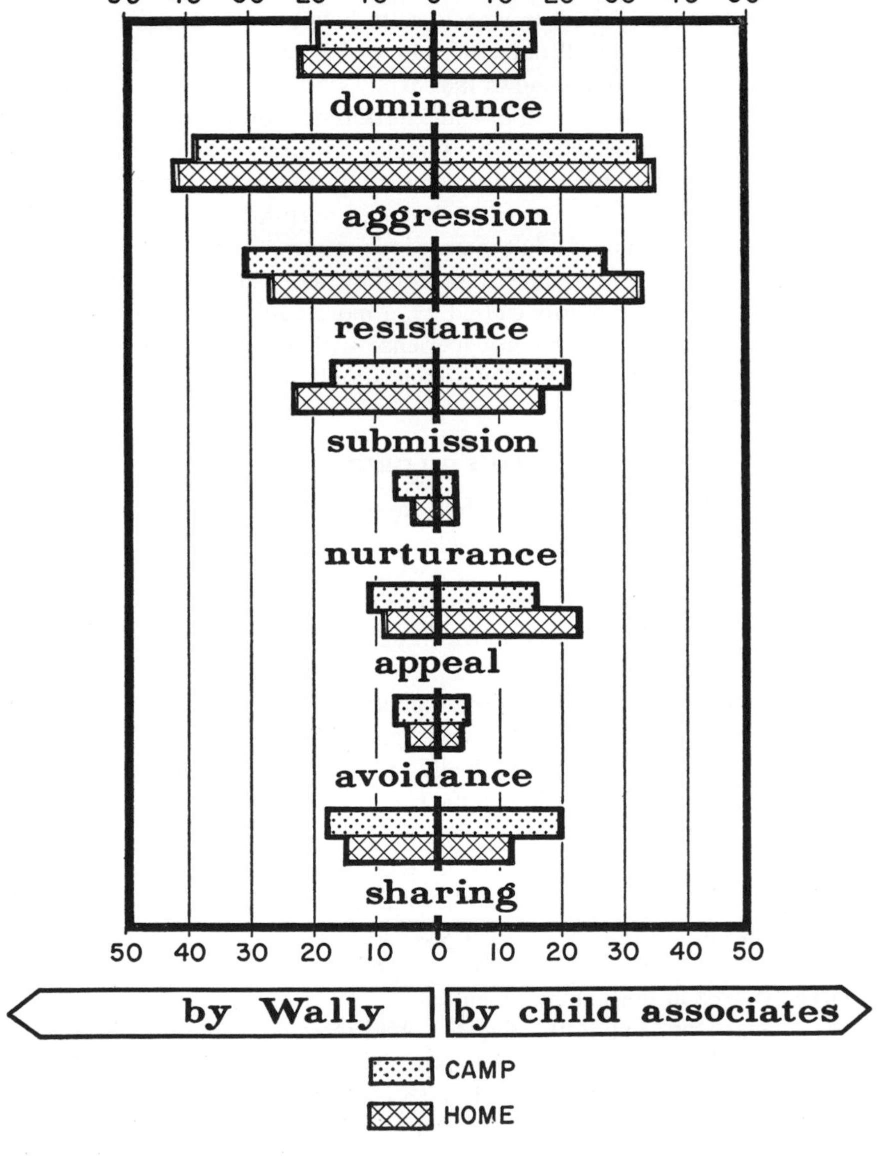

FIGURE 9.6

Per Cent of Social Episodes at Home with Siblings and with Neighborhood Children in Which Various Interaction Modes Were Displayed by Wally and by These Associates

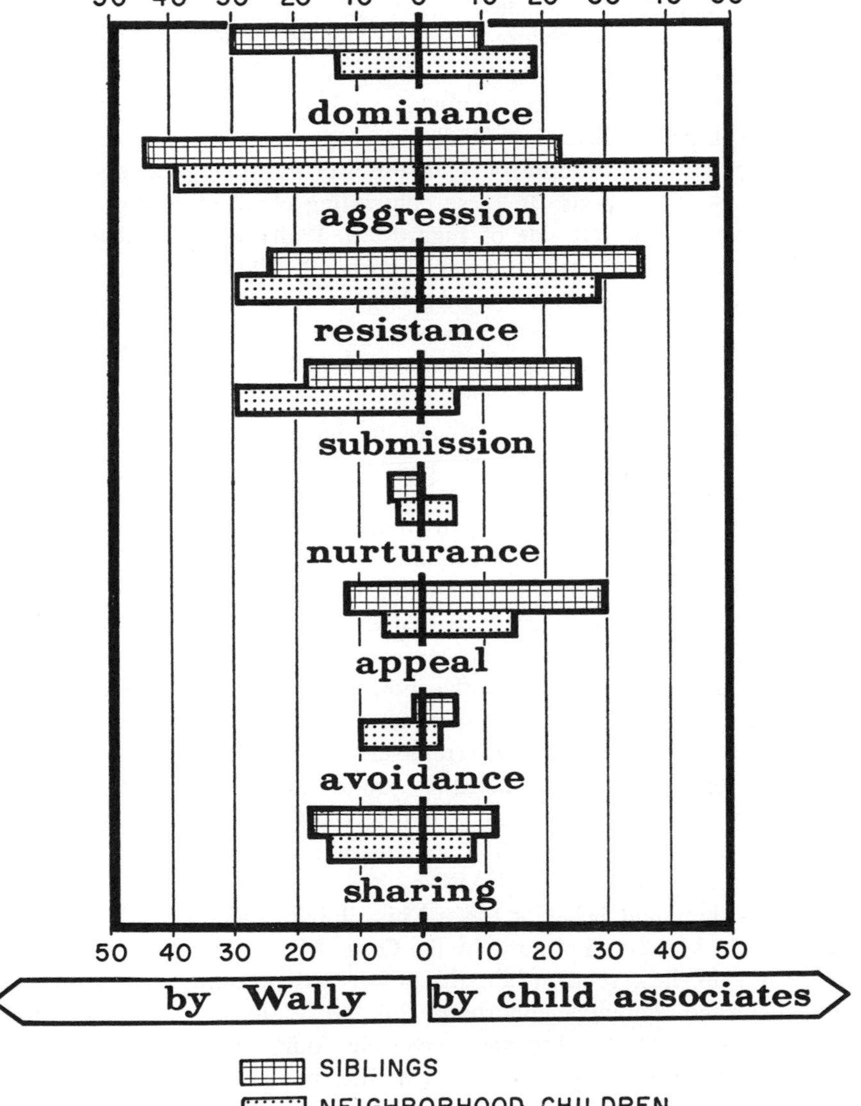

were so sharply discrepant, this finding of so few differences is surprising. It might arise from the fact that Wally had two child-interaction situations at home: in and around the house with younger siblings and out in the neighborhood with acquaintances the same age or older. Interaction patterns in these two situations could differ sharply and cancel each other when summed. In Figure 9.6 the social interaction modes at home are separated for siblings and other associates.

The associate side of Figure 9.6 shows that Wally was treated quite differently by the two associate groups. Siblings showed Wally much more submission and appeal, much less dominance and aggression than neighborhood children (all p's $< .02$). Since Wally's siblings were all younger, these differences make sense in terms of relative power positions of associates.

Wally's social response to these contrasting child-interaction situations can be seen on the left side of Figure 9.6. Wally was significantly more dominant toward siblings than to neighborhood children, and he was more submissive and avoidant to neighborhood children than to siblings (all p's $< .04$). Again Wally's superior power over younger siblings seems reflected here. Wally lived in two different social worlds at home: in and around his house with his siblings, where he was in a superior power position; out in the neighborhood with acquaintances where he was in an inferior power position.

One method of investigating this further is to determine the power relationships established between Wally and his major child associates on the two days. One can, for example, look for power discrepancies in the total social episodes Wally had with each child associate. A power discrepancy is an episode in which one party showed dominance or aggression and the other showed submission and no dominance, aggression or resistance. These are pure cases because they involve power assertions which are accepted without counterefforts. For convenience, an episode which Wally dominated will be labeled Wally Power Discrepancies (WPD), and those which an associate dominated will be labeled Associate Power Discrepancies (APD). An equalitarian climate would be indicated by a general balance in the frequency of WPD's and APD's; a nonequalitarian climate, by an imbalance in the frequency of WPD's and APD's.

Wally's dominant behavior toward his siblings and their submissive reaction toward him are indicated by the Gene, Maud, and Hughie entries on Table 9.6; in these relationships the power was primarily with Wally. On the other hand, among neighborhood children, Wally was no match for Sid who gained uncontested dominance over him fourteen times. Relations with other neighborhood boys were less extreme, but generally Wally was the dominated one.

It can be seen that Wally established dominance over two campers, Dexter and Sammy, the cabin scapegoats, just as he established dominance over siblings at home. In both environments, Wally tended to dominate

TABLE 9.6

Number of Episodes Showing Power Discrepancies Between Wally and Major Child Associates at Camp and Home

CAMP ASSOCIATE	*WPD*	*APD*	*PD Diff.*	HOME ASSOCIATE	*WPD*	*APD*	*PD Diff.*
Earnest (best friend)	7	9	−2	Gene (sib—7 yrs.)	12	4	+8
Lyle	1	2	−1	Maud (sib—5 yrs.)	6	1	+5
Eddie	2	2	0	Hughie (sib—2 yrs.)	9	1	+8
Dexter (fat boy)	6	0	+6	Sid	0	14	−14
Sammy (fat boy)	4	0	+4	Warren	1	3	−2
Ikey	0	1	−1	Barney	0	0	0
Floyd	0	0	0	Randolph	0	3	−3
Tim	0	0	0	Bert	0	1	−1
Lester	0	0	0	Cliff	0	1	−1
Neville	0	1	−1	Roger	1	0	+1

weaker children. However, at camp Wally was less frequently either the master or the servant in his relationships with other children.

Another way of looking at the data on Table 9.6 is to consider the total amount of uncontested power display regardless of direction. In an equalitarian climate one would expect fewer cases in which one party to a relationship tamely accepted the domination attempts of the other. The total number of uncontested dominance episodes at camp was 37; at home, 57. It seems clear, then, that child relationships at camp involved more expressed power equality than those at home; in colloquial terms, camp involved more "give-and-take"; home resulted in more "give-or-take."

The association of relatively equalitarian interpersonal relationships with camp milieu factors is fairly obvious. University Boys' Camp made a concerted effort to group boys so that differences in power and aggressiveness among cabin mates would not be extreme. From the data offered here this attempt appeared moderately successful; exceptions seem to have been Sammy and Dexter. The camp controlled the social environment so that a boy's primary associates would be his power peers. (This control did result in heavy peer contact; see Table 9.1). No such control occurred in the home situation; power differences between Wally and other children were large and were reflected in the power imbalances of the child-interaction patterns.

SUMMARY OF SOCIAL INTERACTION

The major difference between social interaction at camp and home may be characterized as follows:

At camp Wally had more frequent contact with adults and interaction with a wider variety of adults.

At camp Wally enjoyed more peer-like relationships with adults.

At camp Wally associated more with peers rather than with children of different ages and sexes.

At camp associates were less frequently demanding (although when aggressive, they were very aggressive).

At camp associates were more nurturant and sharing.

At camp Wally engaged in more equalitarian or "give-and-take" relationship with children.

At camp Wally showed associates more nurturance and less dominance and aggression.

Certain milieu factors supportive of these differences have been cited.

Behavior Stimulation at Camp and Home

The descriptions of Wally's play and sociality have dealt with kinds of associates and kinds of behavior. It is also possible to investigate the manner in which the behavior episodes were started and the emotional reaction occurring during them. Such an approach ignores specific acts, events, or persons, and deals with the classes of beginnings and types of emotional "backlash."

INITIATION OF EPISODES

Observation of behavior leads to the inference that new activity may start with apparent spontaneity, or may be stimulated from without. Among the episodes of behavior initiated by outside stimulation, it is possible to distinguish between those coerced by the environment and those invited by the environment.

The code describing these various behavior initiations was developed by Barker and Wright (1955, pp. 279–280). An abbreviated explanation of the categories is offered below:

Spontaneous— A subject behaves as if he "just happened to think of it." Wally remarks to a peer: "Let's go back to the tree hut."

Instigated— A subject responds to some change or event in his situation, but not because of coercion. Wally suddenly comes upon a leaf magically swaying in midair. (The leaf is really dangling at the end of an invisible spider thread.) Wally

Pressured— The subject is put under external influence (usually social) begins to explore this mystery.
to behave in contrast to his present wishes. Wally, after his counselor insists, grudgingly apologizes to a cabinmate.

Cannot Judge—Ambiguous, not sufficient information, etc.

Certain effects of situations upon a person can be assessed by comparing the relative proportion of episode initiation types within the situations. A sample of a person's episodes with a large percentage of *pressured* initiations means that he was heavily coerced by the situations in which the episodes occurred; many *spontaneous* episodes indicate that considerable freedom of action obtained; a preponderance of instigated episodes reveals much environmental invitation.

The positive connotations of the term "spontaneous" should not lead to the inference that the more frequently the episodes are spontaneous, the more optimal is the situation. Sparse, unstimulating environments would yield more spontaneous episodes and fewer instigated episodes. Since camp was especially designed to be a stimulating and noncoercive setting for children, it might be expected that camp, as compared to home, would show more episodes coded as Instigated and fewer as Pressured and Spontaneous.

TABLE 9.7

Number of Episodes in Different Initiation Categories at Camp and Home

CATEGORY	CAMP. *N*	CAMP. %	HOME *N*	HOME %	*Diff. in %*
Spontaneous	441	41.8	484	47.6	−5.8
Instigated	530	50.3	448	44.1	+6.2
Pressured	50	4.7	57	5.6	−0.9
Cannot Judge	33	3.1	27	2.7	+1.4

Chi square = 8.71, $p < .02$

It is clear from Table 9.7 that pressured initiations were relatively infrequent on both days and that there was no significant difference between camp and home in this respect. However, the expected high proportion of instigated episodes at camp is confirmed. There were 82 more instigated episodes at camp than at home and 43 more spontaneous episodes at home than at camp. Since more of Wally's behavior units at camp started from changes in the environment, it would appear that this milieu was more stimulating than the home milieu.

EMOTIONAL TONE OF EPISODES

What were Wally's feelings within the episodes that have been identified in his behavior stream? Was he happy or unhappy, calm or excited? Since the camp was established as a place for children to have fun, one might expect to find more excitement and more positive reactions there.

The measure of emotionality employed was the following six-point satisfaction-dissatisfaction scale, plus a category for ambivalance.

EMOTIONAL TONE

Unusually positive—High pleasure, hilarity, full joy.
Strongly positive—Marked satisfaction, considerable pleasure.
Mildly positive—Mild pleasure, muted fun.
Neutral—No clear, consistent signs of emotion.

Mildly negative—Mild dissatisfaction, irritation.
Strongly negative—Marked dissatisfaction, anger, disappointment.
Unusually negative—Severe pain, rage, or sorrow.
Markedly ambivalent—Strong satisfaction *and* dissatisfaction in the same episode.

Coding of emotional tone was based upon manifest cues: smiles, frowns, statements of triumph or discouragement. Doubtless many episodes coded as neutral were experienced by Wally as satisfactory or unsatisfactory. However, in the interests of reliability, coders did not attempt to infer emotionality when overt behavioral signs were missing. Reliability of the code was 87 per cent. Results of the coding are given in Table 9.8.

TABLE 9.8
Distribution of Episodes at Camp and Home by Emotionality Categories

CATEGORY	CAMP	HOME
Unusually Positive	2	0
Strongly Positive	23	15
Mildly Positive	171	160
Neutral	723	723
Mildly Negative	88	91
Strongly Negative	21	14
Unusually Negative	6	0
Markedly Ambivalent	14	7
Cannot Judge	6	6

Chi square = 8 602, $p < .15$

Emotionality shows roughly the same pattern on the two days ($p < .15$); there was a tendency for camp to produce more of the Unusually and Strongly positives and negatives and more of the Ambivalent reactions. Although none of the categories of strong emotionality showed statistically significant differences when taken separately, each comparison tended in the direction of stronger emotionality at camp. There were a total 66 of these strongly emotional episodes at camp and only 36 at home. The percentages were 6.3 vs. 3.5 ($p < .01$).

Singling out the more emotional episodes for comparison may be a questionable procedure. It was decided to check on the trend of increased emotionality at camp by using the episode time as the measure of extent of emotionality. It was found that, at camp, Wally spent 171 minutes in episodes of marked emotionality; at home, 70 minutes ($p < .001$).

The stronger emotionality at camp was related to certain factors in that environment. This assertion is based on an inspection and qualitative analysis of all strongly emotional episodes at camp and at home. Strong negative emotionality occurred in 27 camp episodes and in 14 home episodes. The more numerous episodes at camp came about primarily from difficulty with peers and involved 21 cases of anger and frustration. At home, strong anger and frustrations with children occurred only seven times. It might be hypothesized that competitiveness and combat are more likely among peers than among children of heterogeneous power. Camp provided more peers of relatively equal power, and this resulted in more combativeness, and more angry emotional reactions. In this connection, it should be recalled that intense aggression by others was more frequent at camp (cf. p. 185).

A further difference in Wally's emotional behavior on the two days relates to fear-disgust reactions occurring in the woods at camp. Wally's reaction to bugs, swamps, and decaying bark was usually strong and ambivalent; he showed "horrible fascination." Wally had eight disgust-fear episodes at camp, none at home. Six of the eight disgust-fear episodes related to the woods; such natural supports for disgust and "horrible fascination" simply did not occur frequently in Wally's suburban, cleaned-up neighborhood.

The distinguishing feature of highly positive emotion at camp was the amount of fun related to the exploration, hunting, and war games made possible by the woods and its tree hut. Nine such highly positive and "adventurous" episodes occurred at camp, none at home. On the other hand, home was distinctive for its support of short but gleeful satisfaction in observation of defeats and triumphs of others in competitive games (carrom board games and street baseball); six such episodes occurred at home, none at camp.

Summary

Adults often send a child to camp because they believe that life in this milieu will be different from life in the child's home and neighborhood. Furthermore, these adults presume that some of the differences at camp are positive. The present research recorded a full day's behavior of one boy, Wally O'Neill, at camp and another full day of his behavior at home. By dividing these records into units (episodes) and by classifying and rating the units, it was possible to make a quantitative comparison of the boy's behavior and experience in the two milieus.

FINDINGS AND RELATIONSHIPS

The major results of the investigation can be divided into three areas. First there are the general environmental factors which impinged upon Wally; these included variety of behavior settings and types of associates. A second area, pertinent to social interaction, refers to how other persons behaved toward Wally, i.e., the particular social actions actually received by the subject. A third area is Wally's behavior in the context of the general and specific environmental factors. Rather than listing the differences occurring between home and camp and then discussing the relationships, the findings and their relationships will be considered together.

On the camp day, Wally entered a wide variety of behavior settings, many of which were explicitly child- or play-centered; he behaved in a craft shop, a woods (with its tree hut), a swimming area, a cook-out, and an Indian Council fire. At home, Wally entered a narrow variety of behavior settings few of which were specifically designed for children's play. Wally's response to these differences in general environmental factors was to engage in active, exploratory, constructive, and dramatic play at camp and in passive (several hours of TV watching), dallying and formally competitive play at home.

Differences in the settings were also related to aspects of Wally's emotionality on the two days. More strongly positive and more ambivalent emotionality occurred at camp than at home, mostly as a consequence of the challenges and dangers in the camp-setting woods.

Wally's camp associates included many contactable adults, many peers and few nonpeer children. This difference in types of associate would appear to be related to the second and third areas of results: Wally's treatment by others, and his behavior toward them.

Camp adults, as compared to those at home, extended to Wally more frequent, more interest-centered, less aggressive and less resistent social behaviors. It might be speculated that this difference in adults' treatment of Wally was related to the roles taken by the adults. Camp adults, by training or by reality-defined function, were able to maintain other than parental roles toward campers. Wally's response to this difference in adult social behavior was to deal more frequently with camp adults and to show them less parent-centered and less submissive behavior.

Children at camp treated Wally differently from children at home. The fact that most child associates at camp were peers is probably a source of the finding that more equalitarian social relationships developed at camp. It will be recalled that, at home, younger siblings submitted and appealed to Wally while neighborhood children were much more dominating and aggressive toward him. Wally, in turn was dominating toward siblings but submissive toward neighborhood children. No child campers maintained a consistently dominant relationship toward Wally. Camp associates were occasionally sharply aggressive toward Wally. He responded to their aggression with frustration and anger; these feelings were behind the increase in strong negative emotionality at camp.

To balance the presentation of Wally's behavior and experience on the two days, it is necessary to point out similarities as well as differences. For example, Wally attempted a somewhat similar play pattern on both days: although time spent in various play forms was quite dissimilar at camp and at home, passive watching and dramatic play were frequently attempted on both days. One might speculate that Wally's personal needs and habits determined the attempts, but that ecological supports determined the duration of these attempts.

In certain respects, relationships with adults and children were also similar. At camp and home, adults dominated and nurtured, and Wally submitted or appealed. The over-all interaction patterns with children were similar at camp and home; it was only when the home associates were divided between siblings and neighborhood children that the differences in child interaction were clear. Finally, when he could, Wally dominated weaker youngsters. At home, the environment offered more support to this tendency, but, when the opportunity existed at camp, Wally exploited it, as in Wally's dominance over the fat boys.

To a certain extent behavioral similarities were probably a result of environmental similarities on the two days. For example, adults who take care of children behave with some similarity even in milieus as contrasting as camp and home; and a child responds to such adults in a somewhat similar fashion in both environments. It is also reasonable to suppose that Wally's personality determined some of the similarity in play pattern and in over-all reactions with children. For example, Wally's typical adjustment to his own aggressive impulses and to the anxiety these impulses stimulated can be inferred from the play forms Watching and Dramatic Play, and from his social behavior. Much of Wally's camp watching was directed toward the conflicts between campers; much of home watching was related to competitive encounters between other children in games, or to cowboy and war conflict on television. Watching was often a pleasurable but completely safe way to experience aggressive or competitive issues. More expressive, but still indirect, assertion was managed by the dramatic play. Direct domination of others was reserved for those situations in which Wally had a clear power superiority: for cabin scapegoats at camp and for younger brothers and sisters at home.

PROBLEMS AND PROSPECTS

This investigation has been an attempt to study environmental effects by recording and analyzing naturally occurring behavior in contrasting milieus. Differences in one subject's behavior have been described and related to differences in environmental supports and coercions. It would appear that the differences in Wally's behavior and experience displayed in his play, social interactions, and emotionality reflected differences in milieu. Other environments for children can be similarly assessed by a direct look at the behavior occurring in these milieus. We might expect that the types of behavior settings and associates provided would be particularly coercive in shaping behavior.

It is apparent that the use of full-day studies of many subjects in a variety of milieus will be exceedingly expensive. To expand subject and milieu samples, less taxing inventions are desired. One possibility would be to determine the settings typically entered by a group of subjects and then obtain specimen records which sampled behavior within these settings. The amount of time covered by the records could reflect the usual proportion of time spent in the settings. From such recordings, one could extrapolate a picture of what life was like in this milieu for a typical day. More ambitious investigations could be adapted for a week, or a month's behavior in a milieu.

It is the authors' belief that continued overdependence upon a personality and counseling-centered approach to the problems of helping children is narrow and relatively ineffective. Children live in milieus and in behavior settings. The psychological impacts of these settings should be understood; scientific methods of selecting and designing settings and milieus should be developed.

CHAPTER 10

Some Formal Characteristics of the Behavior of Two Disturbed Boys

NEHEMIAH JORDAN

THIS IS A PIONEER INVESTIGATION of the structure of the behavior of disturbed children, and it provides, too, evidence regarding the consequences of a changed educational regimen for behavior structure.

Nehemiah Jordan is Psychologist at the RAND Corporation; he received the Ph.D. degree from the University of Kansas.

THERE IS A GROWING CONVICTION that psychotherapy should not be restricted to the therapeutic hour, and that in order to study, to understand, and to improve the therapeutic process, research should also be directed to the "other twenty-three hours." The present investigation falls within this current of thought; it is a study of behavior within a part of the general therapeutic milieu provided by a large research hospital.

The subjects of the study were two eleven-year-old boys, C and D, patients in a ward for disturbed, "acting-out" children. They were observed by a trained observer, through a one-way mirror, during tutoring sessions in reading and writing with a special teacher. Child C was observed for thirteen such sessions, child D for twelve sessions.

Each session lasted approximately a half hour. While observing, the observer dictated as much of his observations as he could into a recording machine. Immediately after the observation, using his dictation as a mnemonic device to stimulate recall, he wrote out a detailed sequential, timed, phenomenological description of what had transpired during the tutoring session. The first step of the investigation was concluded with the obtaining of these 25 records, specimen records, as they have been called (Barker & Wright, 1955).

The second step consisted of dividing each record into the episodes that were to serve as the basis for the analysis. The behavior episode is defined and illustrated elsewhere in this book (cf. p. 161 & Appendix 1.2), and by Barker and Wright (1955). The reader is referred to these sources for elucidation of the episode as a unit of the stream of behavior. The criteria given by Barker and Wright were carefully followed in identifying the episodes of the specimen records used in this study.

The following excerpt from one of the records illustrates the raw data of the study and its division into episodes. The excerpt is a record of the first forty seconds of D's behavior after entering the schoolroom, ten seconds after 9:19 a.m., December 6, 1956. It contains five episodes, episode #1 overlaps episodes #2 and #3. Within episodes #1 and #4 there are examples of undirected activity or restless movement. In this record J is the teacher, a woman.

9:19 The door is heard opening and J (who is waiting in the schoolroom) walks to the door holding a book.

Entering Room (1)

The door opens and D enters.

He emits a long belching sound.

Ignoring J (2)

Standing in front of him, J greets him, "Good morning, good morning, how are you?"

D doesn't respond.

J holds out the book to him, saying, "Did you ever see this book?"

D walks past her mumbling something. He walks to the center of the room.

J follows him.

Telling Riddle (3)

D turns to J and says, "Why are the prairies so flat?"

J looks at D puzzled and repeats, "Why are the prairies flat? I don't know."

In a matter-of-fact tone D says, "The sun sets on them every night."

J laughs.

D takes a chair and sits down at the center table.

J joins D, sitting down to his right at the table.

D is quite pale and has a blue mark under his left eye. Throughout all this, D's facial expression was coldly neutral, somewhat sullen; it did not change during the telling of the joke-riddle.

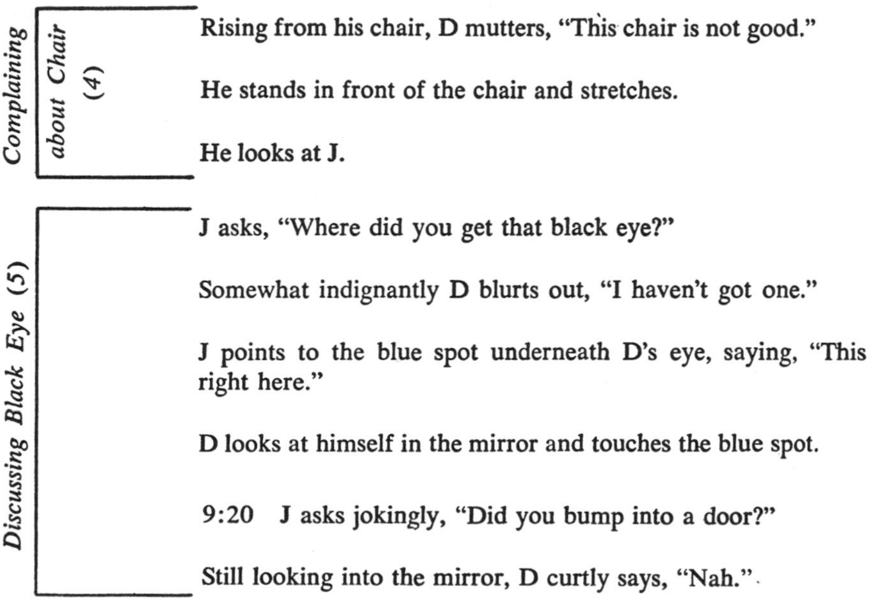

Rising from his chair, D mutters, "This chair is not good."

He stands in front of the chair and stretches.

He looks at J.

J asks, "Where did you get that black eye?"

Somewhat indignantly D blurts out, "I haven't got one."

J points to the blue spot underneath D's eye, saying, "This right here."

D looks at himself in the mirror and touches the blue spot.

9:20 J asks jokingly, "Did you bump into a door?"

Still looking into the mirror, D curtly says, "Nah."

During the period of the observations, November 28, 1955 to April 6, 1956, a change in school policy was instituted. The earlier policy, in effect when the first 6 records of C and the first 5 records of D were obtained, stipulated that the children must remain in the classroom for the half-hour programmed for tutoring, but that they were free, within reason, to do what they liked. The modified policy, in effect when the last 7 records for each child were obtained, stipulated that the children need not spend the time in the schoolroom, but if they wished to stay in the room, after having been brought there, they had to do work relevant to the tutoring objectives.

Number of Behavior Episodes

The duration of each tutoring session and the number of episodes occurring in it are given in Table 10.1. The number of episodes per session can be considered as a fourfold table generated by two factors: individual differences between children and differences in school policy. An analysis of variance, after randomly eliminating one entry from the first cell, shows that differences between the two subjects contributed quite significantly to the variation of number of episodes per session ($p < .005$), but that the change of policy had no noticeable effect on the variance of the episodes,

TABLE 10.1

Dates, Duration in Minutes, and Number of Episodes for Each Tutoring Session for Subjects C and D

	BOY C			BOY D		
	Date	*Duration*	*Number of Episodes*	*Date*	*Duration*	*Number of Episodes*
Initial Policy	11/4/55	24	17	10/28/55	26	25
	11/21/55	29	18	11/8/55	29	23
	12/2/55	26	16	12/6/55	26	39
	12/9/55	28	20	12/13/55	28	25
	12/20/55	30	16	1/3/56	28	25
	1/6/56	28	12			
Subsequent Policy	1/13/56	25	31	1/13/56	31	26
	2/10/56	13	14	1/24/56	30	24
	2/17/56	24	17	2/10/56	30	13
	3/2/56	30	10	2/14/56	27	28
	3/15/56	25	17	2/21/56	18	11
	3/19/56	27	17	2/28/56	30	37
	4/10/56	29	11	4/10/56	29	34

when the children were considered jointly or individually. The number of episodes per minute of observation was 1.6 for subject C and 1.1 for subject D.

Initiation of Behavior Episodes

In *Midwest and Its Children* (Barker & Wright, 1955), analysis of episode initiation is limited to the categories spontaneous, instigated, and pressured. The initiation of an episode is judged to be spontaneous when it appears to originate solely in the acting person, i.e., no change occurs in the environment which acts as an instigator or source of pressure for action. When some change occurs in the environment which appears to "set off" the behavior, the initiation of the episode is considered to be instigated.

In the present research the episode category "instigated" was divided into five subcategories. First, direct instigation was differentiated from indirect. Direct instigation was defined as direct communication to the child by the instigator that the child initiate an activity. Indirect instigation was defined as a change in the environment which attracted the child so that he stopped what he was doing and started a new action. Indirect instigations were subdivided into those resulting from induced and from uninduced changes. An induced change was a change brought about by the instigator in order to attract the child's attention; i.e., it was a technique for the indirect control of behavior. An uninduced change was one which occurred unintentionally. Instigation was further characterized as to the nature of the instigating entity. If it was another person, the instigation was called "social"; if it was an impersonal entity, the instigation was called "object." Instigation accompanied by any form of coercion was called pressured. In practice this category was restricted to verbal threats and physical coercion on the part of another person.

All episodes of the records were, therefore, judged with respect to their initiation on the following categories:

1. Spontaneous initiation
2. Instigated initiation:
   - 2a. Direct social
   - 2b. Indirect, object induced
   - 2c. Indirect, object uninduced
   - 2d. Indirect, social induced
   - 2e. Indirect, social uninduced
3. Pressured initiation
4. Cannot judge

The initial summation of the distribution of initiation judgments showed immediately that only the two categories, (1) Spontaneous initiation and (2a) Instigated initiation, direct social had significant numbers of entries. The other ratings had so few entries that they were pooled as a residual category, *other*. Data are, therefore, reported for spontaneous initiation, direct social initiation, and other types of initiation except where comparisons are made to Midwest data. For these comparisons, the results were regrouped into the categories spontaneous, instigated, and pressured initiation. The ratings "cannot judge" were so few they were excluded from the analysis.

Data are given in Table 10.2 for the total number, and the per cents, of types of episode initiation summated for all records and for both children. Child C had a smaller proportion of spontaneous initiation and a larger proportion of direct social initiation than did Child D. A chi square test shows that the degree of nonindependence found in Table 10.2 falls beyond the .01 level of confidence.

It is of interest to note, however, that both children had almost the same number of episodes with direct social initiation.

Table 10.3 gives the variability of the types of initiation. The distribution of types of initiation in the records of subject C, and of subject D, is characterized by the range of per cents and by the median. For example: for boy C the lowest per cent of spontaneously initiated episodes for a behavior record was 37, the highest was 80, and the median per cent was 46. The median per cents per record are very similar to the per cents of all episodes presented in Table 10.2.

Barker and Wright (1955, p. 296) provide data concerning the occurrence of spontaneous, instigated, and pressured episodes in the day records of twelve Midwest children whose ages ranged from one year, ten months to ten years, nine months, with a median age of five years, seven months. The number of episodes per record, adjusted for different length of days, ranged from 383 to 1,335 and had a median of 853. The range of episodes per record of the present data was from 10 to 39, with a median of 18. Despite these great disparities in age of subjects and number of episodes, it is interesting to compare the two sources of data with respect to relative frequency of the different types of episode initiation.

The episodes of subjects C and D were pooled and recorded to fit the Midwest data. Table 10.4 shows how the data compare. The median per cents are very similar despite the fact that the ranges are systematically larger for the hospitalized children than for the Midwest children. Difference of range is not too surprising, because of the great disparity in the number of episodes per record upon which the per cents are based; a random change of several episodes would effect the Midwest per cents very little, whereas it would have a large effect on the data for subjects C and D. The consonance of the medians is unexpected.

Because the duration of each episode is known, it is possible to sum the durations of the episodes to determine the total time spent in episodes with each type of initiation. The ranges and medians of these distributions are given in Table 10.5.

The medians and ranges for both boys are almost identical. Despite differences in number of episodes, the boys spent about the same amount of time in episodes with each type of initiation. Considering the data for directly instigated activities given in Tables 10.2 and 10.5 we find that the boys spent approximately the same amount of time in the same number of episodes when the initiation was directed by the teacher; i.e., the teacher's instigation was equally frequent and equally lasting for both boys. The differences between the boys are found under conditions of spontaneous instigation of activities. Here D was much "busier" than C, engaging in a greater number of shorter spontaneous actions.

Termination of Behavior Episodes

The same categories used to describe episode initiation were used to describe episode termination, and, in addition, an eighth category, was used. Environmental cessation refers to a cessation of the environmental conditions essential to the continuation of the behavior of the episode. For example: a child is playing ball and loses the ball. He stops, searches for the ball, and finally goes into his house. The episode "playing ball" is terminated by the cessation of the ball.

As with initiation, only spontaneous and direct social termination occurred with sufficient frequency for statistical analysis.

Table 10.6 gives the total number, and the per cent, of types of episode termination summated for all records for both children. There is practically

TABLE 10.2
Types of Episode Initiation, Subjects C and D
Number and Per Cent of Episodes in All Records

SUBJECT	*Spontaneous* *N*	*%*	*Direct Social* *N*	*%*	*Other* *N*	*%*
C	102	50	79	38	25	12
D	189	63	74	25	35	12

TABLE 10.3
Types of Episode Initiation, Subjects C and D
Ranges and Medians of Per Cents of Episodes in Each Record

SUBJECT	*Spontaneous* *Range*	*Median*	*Direct Social* *Range*	*Median*	*Other* *Range*	*Median*
C	37–80	46	10–62	35	6–30	13
D	38–83	66	15–40	26	0–43	8

TABLE 10.4
Types of Episode Initiation, Midwest and Hospitalized Children
Ranges and Medians of Per Cents of Episodes in Each Record

SUBJECTS	*Spontaneous* *Range*	*Median*	*Instigated* *Range*	*Median*	*Other* *Range*	*Median*
Hospitalized children	37–83	55	17–63	41	0–10	0
Midwest children	46–62	49	34–54	41	0–8	3

no difference between the children in proportion of episodes with each type of termination; a test of independence yields a .85 level of confidence. The time spent in episodes with different types of termination is equally similar for the subjects.

Barker and Wright (1955, p. 299) present data for Midwest children regarding frequency of four types of episode termination, viz., spontaneous termination, termination due to environmental cessation, instigated termination, and pressured termination. The episodes of subjects C and D were pooled and recoded to fit the Midwest data.

Table 10.7 shows how these data compare. An outstanding difference is that the "natural" environment in which the Midwest children spent much of their time generated a noticeable number of episodes terminated by environmental cessation, whereas the contrived, therapeutic, classroom milieu generated almost none at all. There, only 7 episodes were judged as being terminated by environmental cessation, and 6 of these were due to the ending of the session and the child having to leave the room. The pattern of termination of episodes as far as total spontaneity and nonspontaneity is concerned was remarkably similar for the Midwest and the two hospitalized children, though directly instigated terminations were more frequent for the hospitalized children. Comparison with Table 10.4 shows that both the hospitalized children and the Midwest children had a greater per cent of spontaneously terminated episodes than spontaneously initiated episodes, and the difference is almost identical in the two sets of data.

Joint Occurrence of Types of Episode Initiation and Termination

Nichols and Schoggen (1956) divided 3,729 episodes from the twelve Midwest day records into four classes: SS (S = self), where both initiation and termination were self-instigated, i.e., spontaneous; EE (E = environment), where both initiation and termination were environment-instigated, i.e., nonspontaneous; SE, where initiation was spontaneous and termination was nonspontaneous; and ES, where initiation was nonspontaneous and termination was spontaneous. Four hundred and ninety of the episodes of the hospitalized children could be partitioned in a similar manner. The two partitions can be put in a 2×4 contingency table as shown in Table 10.8. These data indicate that the Midwest children had a significantly larger proportion of either completely spontaneous or completely nonspontaneous episodes; the hospitalized children had a significantly larger proportion of mixed episodes. When tested for independence by chi square we find that $p < .001$ that the distributions are independent.

Forces Sustaining Behavior Episodes

In addition to the analysis of the initiation and termination of episodes, an analysis was made of the forces sustaining action throughout the episode.

TABLE 10.5
Types of Episode Initiation, Subjects C and D
Ranges and Medians of Number of Minutes
Spent in Episodes of Each Type in Each Record

	Spontaneous		*Direct Social*		*Other*	
SUBJECT	*Range*	*Median*	*Range*	*Median*	*Range*	*Median*
C	4–40	23	0–35	13	0–21	1
D	3–42	21	0–34	11	0–20	1

TABLE 10.6
Types of Episode Termination, Subjects C and D
Number and Per Cent of Episodes in All Records

	Spontaneous		*Direct Social*		*Other*	
SUBJECT	*N*	%	*N*	%	*N*	%
C	137	68	38	19	26	13
D	202	69	59	20	33	11

TABLE 10.7
Types of Episode Termination, Midwest and Hospitalized Children
Ranges and Medians of Per Cents in Each Record

	Spontaneous Termination		*Direct Instigated Termination*		*Environmental Cessation*		*Pressured Termination*	
SUBJECTS	*Range*	*Median*	*Range*	*Median*	*Range*	*Median*	*Range*	*Median*
Hospitalized children	37–90	69	0–53	29	0–11	0	0–20	3
Midwest children	51–67	62	5–11	10	16–26	20	0–6	3

TABLE 10.8

Types of Episode Initiation and Termination, Midwest and Hospitalized Children

Number and Per Cent of Episodes in All Records

SUBJECTS	*SS* *N*	*SS* %	*SE* *N*	*SE* %	*ES* *N*	*ES* %	*EE* *N*	*EE* %
Hospitalized children	181	37	93	19	157	32	59	12
Midwest children	1753	47	298	8	783	21	895	24

TABLE 10.9

Types of Forces Sustaining Episodes under Two Educational Policies, Subjects C and D

Number of Episodes in All Records

TYPE OF FORCE	*First Policy* *C*	*First Policy* *D*	*Second Policy* *C*	*Second Policy* *D*	*Totals*
p (teacher passive)	61	89	76	115	341
po (teacher co-operates)	26	24	24	28	102
p *versus* o (teacher opposes)	9	22	17	27	75

TABLE 10.10

Joint Distribution of Types of Forces Sustaining Episodes and Types of Episode Initiation, Subjects C and D

TYPE OF FORCE	*Spontaneous*	*Direct Social*	*Other*
p	250	33	58
po	12	78	12
p *versus* o	35	27	13

Three categories were discriminated. If the teacher was passive or neutral and the action was sustained entirely by the child, the episode was designated as a "p" episode (p = person); this is conceptually akin to "spontaneity." If the teacher co-operated actively with the child, the episode was designated as a "po" (po = person-other); this is conceptually akin to "instigation." If the teacher opposed the child, the episode was designated as a "p *versus* o" episode; this is conceptually akin to "pressure against." This analysis has no counterpart in *Midwest and Its Children.*

Table 10.9 gives the distribution of the sustaining forces for each child for each educational policy. Of the total of 518 episodes rated, the teacher was either neutral or passive in 341 (p episodes); she actively co-operated with the child in 102 episodes (po episodes); and she opposed the child's activity in 75 episodes (p *versus* o episodes). The entries in the first four columns were placed in a 3 × 4 contingency table and tested for independence; the resulting chi square is significant at approximately the .40 level of confidence. The distribution of sustaining forces did not vary significantly with the children, or with the change in educational policy.

TABLE 10.11

Joint Distribution of Types of Forces Sustaining Episodes and Types of Episode Termination, Subjects C and D

TYPE OF FORCE	*Spontaneous*	*Direct Social*	*Other*
p	243	57	41
po	64	23	15
p *versus* o	40	17	18

Does the distribution of sustaining forces vary with types of initiation and termination? Table 10.10 gives the joint distribution of sustaining forces and type of initiation. A test for independence yields a chi square at a level of confidence less than .001. The four top left cells in this table, those relating *p* and *po* to spontaneous initiation and to direct social instigation, are the only significant sources of variation in the table. If we look at these four cells the pattern is clear. Out of 262 spontaneously initiated episodes, teacher co-operated with child only twelve times; out of 111 episodes initiated as a result of the teacher's direct instigation, the child co-operated in 78 episodes. The teacher actively co-operated in 4.5 per cent of the episodes that the child initiated spontaneously and in 70.2 per cent of the episodes initiated under her suggestion or request.

Table 10.11 gives the joint distribution of types of sustaining forces and types of termination. A test for independence yields a chi square that is significant at the .02 level of confidence. The lower right corner cell relating *p versus o* to *other* is the only cell which contributes a sizeable amount to the total chi square. The meaning of this significant discrepancy between the expected and observed frequencies is unclear since *other* is a residual category which pools together many different kinds of entries. To clarify the meaning of this discrepancy the 74 *other* entries were cross-classified as to whether their termination was pressured or not, and as to whether during the episode the teacher opposed the child or not. The resulting fourfold classification is presented in Table 10.12.

TABLE 10.12

Joint Distribution of Pressured and Not Pressured Episode Terminations and Antagonistic and Not Antagonistic Episode Sustaining Forces among Episodes in "Other" Termination Category

FORCES SUSTAINING EPISODE	*Pressured Termination*	*Not Pressured Termination*
Not Antagonistic (p, po)	2	54
Antagonistic (p *versus* o)	12	6

Table 10.12 shows that 86 per cent of the 14 episodes terminated by pressure were preceded by the teacher's active opposition to the child, whereas only 10 per cent of the 60 episodes not terminated by pressure were so preceded.[1]

Whereas it seems reasonable, on the face of it, to assume that the judgments on the initiation and termination of an episode were independent, the same cannot be said about the judgments of sustaining forces as they relate to initiation and termination. It is quite possible that these judgments were sometimes, if not often, dependent. To be concrete, it is possible that sometimes the cues used by the judge to determine a rating of directed initiation were also used later to determine a rating of co-operative sustaining forces (po), and that the cues which were used to determine a rating of pressured termination were later used to determine a rating of antagonistic sustaining forces (p *versus* o). This is an area for methodological research.

[1] If the reader will compare the marginal distributions of types of initiation and termination in Tables 10.11 and 10.12 with the comparable distributions presented in the earlier tables, he will find that they are not the same, though similar. A slight systematic bias was discovered in the IBM coding of the data and corrections were made by hand tabulation when the types of initiation and termination were discussed proper. These corrections, however, have no significant effect on the interdependencies found in the joint distributions of sustaining forces and types of initiation and termination hence, in order to save time and labor, the raw IBM scores were used for these purposes.

Consequences of the Change in School Policy

The data so far presented indicate that the change of policy which took place after the first week in January seemed to have no effect on episode initiation, termination, and maintenance. This was explored further by testing episode initiation and termination for self-consistency from record to record within the period of policy. A significant effect was found. Only the findings will be reported since the tables demonstrating this effect are complex. Intraindividual variation in distribution of types of initiation from record to record was significant at the .02 level for C and at the .01 level for D while the first policy was in effect. Variation decreased to chance level with the change to the new policy. No effect was found for termination and for sustaining forces.

Discussion: Autonomy and Heteronomy in Behavior

If one judges by results alone, the technique of analyzing the stream of behavior via episodes has proved itself. Striking differences and similarities have been found. Statistical tests of significance have not hovered about the fuzzy penumbra of the 5 per cent level of significance. Either differences were "self-evident" or no tendency could be detected. In addition, the unexpected, albeit puzzling, correspondence of the hospitalized children with the Midwest children with respect to some patterns of spontaneity and instigation supports the impression that one is not dealing with artifacts. As will be shown below, both the differences and similarities that were found are meaningful in terms of some contemporary thinking about behavior and therapy, as well as in terms of naive common sense. However, the findings are discrete and do not point to a basic theoretical pattern which would explain the separate discoveries or why these specific constellations of episode characteristics exist and not others. Probably no analysis limited to the dimensions here studied could yield an organized and integrated pattern; additional analysis along other dimensions is necessary for even an outline of an organized pattern to emerge. It should also be kept in mind that all conclusions and assertions made in the discussion are of a hypothetical nature since the research was not set up to test them specifically.

Analysis of the stream of behavior in terms of spontaneity, instigation, and pressure has established a link between the original work of Barker and Wright (1955), the general problem area of the therapeutic milieu, and some widely used concepts. Using a Lewinian conceptualization one can characterize episode spontaneity, instigation, and pressure in terms of "forces corresponding to own needs," "induced forces," and "impersonal forces" (Lewin, 1951, p. 260); and using Angyal's conceptualization, the analysis can be characterized in terms of "Autonomy," and "Heteronomy" (Angyal, 1941, pp. 32–33).

A striking aspect of the data is the high degree of spontaneity in behavior. Fifty-nine per cent of the episodes of subjects C and D were spontaneously initiated; 68 per cent of them were spontaneously terminated, and in 66 per cent of the episodes the child was the only sustaining force. The Midwest children exhibited a similar degree of self-initiation, and termination. Spontaneity of behavior episodes seems to be the rule. Once this is discovered it seems to be trite. But had we asked ourselves about the occurrence of spontaneity in behavior without the benefit of these data, what answer could we have given?

A host of research questions arise from this new knowledge. Assuming that the distributions of behavior spontaneity are normative, how great deviations in either direction can a person take before it has an adverse effect? What are the variations in these distributions with age, with different people, in different behavior settings?

The similarities between the hospitalized children and the Midwest children are interesting. We can speculate that the therapeutic milieu of the hospital brought about a "normal" distribution of autonomy and heteronomy in the behavior of subjects C and D where otherwise it would not have existed. But, the policy in effect on the ward, based on the concept of hygienic, antiseptic milieu as presented by Redl and Wineman in *Children Who Hate* (1951), did not explicitly consider the variables of autonomy and heteronomy either theoretically or therapeutically. One would have no apriori reason to predict the obtained outcome. Yet the outcome seems to make therapeutic sense since the aim of a therapeutic milieu is to enable the patient to function more normally. Is the attainment of a normal distribution of autonomy and heteronomy a prerequisite for general normal functioning?

The Teacher's Control Over the Child

Table 10.2 shows that the frequency of types of episode initiation differs with the children. Child D initiated a greater number and a larger proportion of episodes than child C. Yet at the same time, if we, following Angyal, consider autonomy as opposing heteronomy, Tables 10.2 and 10.5 show that this "didn't get D anywhere." D spent as many episodes and as much time doing directed activities as did C. Can we say, therefore, that the teacher exercised the same amount of control over both? Table 10.10 shows that initiation was also the single significant determinant of sustaining forces: if the child initiated the activity, the probability of the teacher co-operating with him was very small; if he did what he was told to do, the probability of her co-operating with him was quite great. The withholding of co-operation seemed to be an important technique whereby the teacher established control.

The relationship of overt opposition by the teacher (p *versus* o) to initiation is unclear, its incidence was spread too evenly over the different types of initiation to be amenable to a statistical analysis. Overt opposition by the teacher (p *versus* o) was significantly related, however, to termination. Pressured termination was generally preceded by overt opposition (Table 10.12). One can see a pattern in the teacher's method of handling spontaneous activities. Many of the child's spontaneous activities were irrelevant or in opposition to the tutorial aims of the teacher. Her first line of defense was a passive withdrawal from the child; she withheld her co-operation. If this was insufficient, she then tried to direct him to the activity she wanted. When she was successful, the episode was rated as being terminated by instigation, direct or induced. If she was unsuccessful, she switched to actively opposing the child's action. And the data show that active opposition was generally followed by pressured termination.

The data presented in Table 10.8 offer an additional base for speculation as to the nature of the control in the hospital tutoring setting as compared to the settings of Midwest. These tables show that the Midwest children had a larger proportion than the hospital children of "pure" episodes, that is, episodes which were either both spontaneously initiated and terminated or both environmentally initiated and terminated. Conversely, a larger proportion of the episodes of the hospitalized children were spontaneously initiated and environmentally terminated, and vice versa. How can these data be interpreted?

We assume that the Midwest children lived in an environment comprising settings where the autonomy and heteronomy of the child were rather clearly defined. In an autonomous setting they were free to do as they liked; in a heteronomous setting they did what they were told. The streets and free-play areas of Midwest were probably autonomous settings where the children initiated and terminated episodes spontaneously. The school and organized leisure activity were probably heteronomous settings where both initiation and termination were generally directed by the adult or group leader. In the hospital tutoring setting things were handled differently. As mentioned earlier, many of the activities spontaneously initiated were either irrelevant or in opposition to the tutoring program, hence they probably invited directed termination. The spontaneous termination of environmentally initiated episodes in the hospital tutoring setting also admits to a simple explanation. The teacher, being aware of the difficulties an acting-out child has in controlling himself and his consequent low frustration tolerance, bent over backward to keep down the environmental demands upon the child. When the child did engage in a directed activity she, therefore, let him proceed at his own pace, and stop when he wished, as long as a reasonable amount of work was done.

Environmental determination for the Midwest children was better defined and more overt and circumscribed, whereas the environment of the hospitalized children was fluid, covert, and pervasive.

It may be surprising and disappointing to many that the change of educational policy seemed to have only one effect, that of limiting variation in spontaneity of episode initiation. But this effect may be precisely co-ordinate with the aims of the policy change. The change of policy was introduced because of the clinical judgment that the children could "take it." The children actually did buckle down, after some protest, and did more formal schoolwork. Hence the pattern of their school behavior became more regular, and the variation from record to record disappeared. The limited change may therefore be indicative of the correctness of the clinical judgment.

The analysis presented above shows the strength of a formal analysis of the behavior continuum. It enables an analysis of formal aspects of behavior without becoming enmeshed in the multitude of specifics which comprise the behavior content of the episodes analyzed. But it also shows the weaknesses of a purely formal approach. For example, the change of policy seemed to have little effect. Actually in terms of content, the change of policy had a great effect. Under the first policy very little schoolwork was done, under the second policy the children spent most of their time doing schoolwork. Under the first policy the teacher's pressure on the child generally took the form of: "You'd better not do this because it's not the proper thing to do." Under the second policy it took the form of: "You had better do this or else you will have to return to the ward." The formal classification of "Pressure" hides this significant change in the milieu. Again, Table 10.10 shows that there was not significant difference in the distribution of the "p *versus* o" sustaining forces for types of initiation. Content analysis, however, would show that when the episodes were spontaneously initiated the teacher was the one who generally initiated the opposition, whereas when the episodes were instigated directly, it was the child who initiated the opposition. If someone will argue that this is not a matter of content but a plea for a finer formal analysis, I will not quibble with him. Be that as it may, the present analysis is noticeably incomplete in this respect.

CHAPTER 11

A Method of Measuring the Social Weather of Children

JAMES E. SIMPSON

DR. SIMPSON describes a method of rating the pervasive, over-all social treatment a person receives within a behavior setting. He calls this the *social weather* of the setting. Data regarding the reliability of the ratings are given, and some sample data concerning the social weather of Midwest children are provided. The investigation raises the interesting possibility that a scientifically usable general assessment of the atmosphere of a setting in which a behavior stream occurs may be achieved.

James E. Simpson is Associate Professor of Psychology at Oregon State University; he received the Ph.D. degree from the University of Kansas.

SOCIAL WEATHER denotes the over-all social treatment given a particular individual in a behavior setting. All people propinquitous to this individual may contribute to his social weather in the setting: some may "give him the cold shoulder"; others may "treat him like a king." Social weather includes the totality of social stimuli impinging upon a particular person while he is in a behavior setting.

The major objective of this investigation was to develop a reliable instrument for the measurement of social weather. It has been applied to the day records of 12 Midwest children.

The Social Weather Rating Scales

In the construction of the Social Weather Rating Scales, advantage was taken of the highly developed Fels Parent Behavior Rating Scales, which were designed to measure parents' attitudes and behavior toward their children (Champney, 1941a, b, Baldwin et al., 1945, 1949). Some items were adapted from the Fels scales and other items were devised by the investigator.

The Social Weather Rating Scales measure nine particular aspects of social weather, and together they cover three larger components of social weather. The Warmth component, which describes the emotional tone of social weather, is measured by the three scales: Acceptance, Affectionateness, and Approval. The Tendance component, which describes the direct efforts made for the child, is measured by the three scales: Attention, Assistance, and Communication. The Indulgence component, which describes the freedom allowed the child, is measured by the three scales: Adaptation, Privilege, and Choice. Opposite qualities appear at the ends of each scale; the middle ranges are "neutral" areas. The complete Social Weather Rating Scales and instructions for applying them to specimen record data are given below. The ratings that are marked upon the scales for illustrative purposes refer to the record of Raymond Birch given in Appendix 1.2.

After reading the specimen behavior-setting record the judge rates the behavior of the child's associates toward him by marking an X at whatever point on the scale-line best indicates the main value of that variable in the social weather. Any important variations in the range of that value are indicated on the scale line by dashes (=) above and below the X. Minor variations (i.e., some incidental action by a person whose total influence is insignificant to the over-all evaluation) need not be indicated in the range. An isolated, striking exception in the behavior of a person who is significant to the over-all evaluation or the exceptional reaction of one member of a group is indicated by a diagonal (/) on the scale-line.

In measuring the social weather of a particular child the rater makes himself as nearly as possible a recording instrument to report the characteristics of the behavior pattern directed toward the child by the people in the setting. The rater does this in terms of his own perception of the over-all behavior toward the child without reference to its possible meaning to the child or to the people in attendance. For example, the rater may judge the social weather of a particular child's initial encounter with his first teacher as mainly noncommittal aloofness; the child may see it as cold and rejecting; his mother may see it as warm acceptance; and the teacher may believe she is showing kind impartiality. While the rater judges "objective"; the child may judge in comparison to his warm, indulgent home; the mother may be biased from the PTA reputation of the teacher; and the teacher may not realize that her tacit acceptance of the child is not manifest to him through her professional mien. Social weather, like atmospheric weather, can be judged from various viewpoints, but the psychologist must rate the social weather "objectively." In this case, the rater's evaluative structure is based on standard American values; he shelves his personal standards for the more general attitudes of the U.S.A. He judges the attributes of the behavior setting and expresses his judgments of social weather by means of marks on the descriptive rating scales prepared to represent graphically the cultural values in the social environments of American children.

The closeness of agreement between four raters in their application of the Social Weather Rating Scale was investigated. Two portions of a day's record were selected for testing reliability: one part believed to be of medium difficulty to rate (Sample A), and one part presenting great difficulty (Sample B). These were selected after experience with both the Fels rating scales and the Social Weather Rating Scales. The investigator found that rating difficulty was governed by the number of people in the setting and the length of the occurrence. The social actions easiest to rate were 5-to-10 minute occurrences in which the child's social weather was determined primarily by one person. Social behavior of moderate rating difficulty usually involved about 15-minutes' interaction between the child and two or three other persons. Social occurrences of maximum rating difficulty were those in which four or more people contributed to the child's social weather for 20 minutes or more.

A 20-minute section of the published day record of Raymond Birch (Barker & Wright, 1951a, pp. 372–383) was selected as Sample A for the tests of reliability. The sample describes Raymond and his parents at supper. Because of the length and subtlety of the social action, the occurrence was moderately difficult to rate. Others familiar with the records estimated the rating difficulty of this sample as between percentiles 60 to 75 in a total group of 280 specimen behavior setting records.

Material for Sample B was selected by the six members of the Midwest Field Station staff most familiar with the day records. Each of the six selected the behavior settings in the day records that involved maximally-complex sustained social action. Four setting records nominated by two or more judges were put on a ballot for independent voting by each member of the group. A 23-minute behavior setting record on the school playground from the Raymond Birch record was unanimously selected (Barker & Wright, 1951a, pp. 113–115). In this setting, Raymond's social weather was determined primarily by four schoolmates in the socially-chaotic period of school recess. After rating all behavior settings in the 16 day records, the investigator estimated that less than 5 per cent were as difficult to rate as the setting selected by the judges.

Rigor was added to the conditions of the test by selection of three untrained raters who were, however, trained in child psychology and were familiar with the specimen records. The four raters were provided with copies of specimen records Samples A and B and instructions. The complete instructions will be found in Simpson (1956).

Evidence regarding the investigator's consistency of rating over time was obtained, also. He rated Samples A and B initially, and again after an interval of six weeks. During the interval, the investigator was employed full-time organizing data of 16 day records and rating their social weather.

Results of the reliability tests were evaluated by the use of Kendall's *W* (1948), the coefficient of concordance. This distribution-free statistic is a rank order method of determining the correlation of more than two scores (the nine rating-scale judgments) for two or more judges (the four raters). The nine ratings (n:9) were separately ranked from one to nine for each

THE SOCIAL WEATHER RATING SCALES

I. WARMTH COMPONENT: emotional tone expressing acceptance, affection, and approval of the child.

1. ACCEPTANCE: receiving the child into the emotional warmth of intimacy.
   - —*Avid Acceptance:* constantly, eagerly, warmly reaches out to include the child in intimate association.
   - —*Accepting:* the child warmly accepted but sometimes with reservations and exclusions.
   - —*Noncommittal:* the child neither accepted nor rejected; involvement only potential.
   - —*Resentful:* some resentful and avoidance responses, but the child not openly rejected.
   - —*Rejecting:* the child openly respulsed and rejected.
2. AFFECTIONATENESS: verbal and gestural expressions of affection made directly to the child.
   - —*Affectionate:* ardent expressions of affection.
   - —*Warm:* fond, gentle, tender in expressions.
   - —*Civil:* expressions of affection not used; objective, neutral, matter-of-fact.
   - —*Cool:* chilly, distant, forbidding in expressions.
   - —*Hostile:* icy, hostile, hateful in expressions.
3. APPROVAL: direction of critical reaction to the child's present behavior.
   - —*Praise:* ready, unambiguous praise; shortcomings overlooked or excused.
   - —*Approval:* emphasis on approval; disapproval is sugar-coated.
   - —*Impartial:* balanced criticism as merited by the child's present behavior.
   - —*Disapproval:* disapproves more readily than approves; praise weakened with faultfinding.
   - —*Hypercritical:* severely critical; ignores or belittles praiseworthy behavior.

II. TENDANCE COMPONENT: the direct efforts made for the child by attending, helping, and talking to him.

4. ATTENTION: the division of social attention to the child.
   - —*Fully-focused on the Child:* little attention to anything but the child.
   - —*Child-centered:* though some divided attention to something else.
   - —*Equitable Attention:* proportionate attention to the child and to other demands for attention.
   - —*Minimal Attention:* maximum attention to something else; some divided attention to the child.
   - —*Child-ignored:* even though nothing else in the setting requires attention.
5. ASSISTANCE: amount and kind of aid and protection given the child.
   - —*Babies:* continually helping and sheltering even when the child is capable and willing.
   - —*Overhelps:* helps more than needed; seldom lets the child struggle or risk any possible harm.

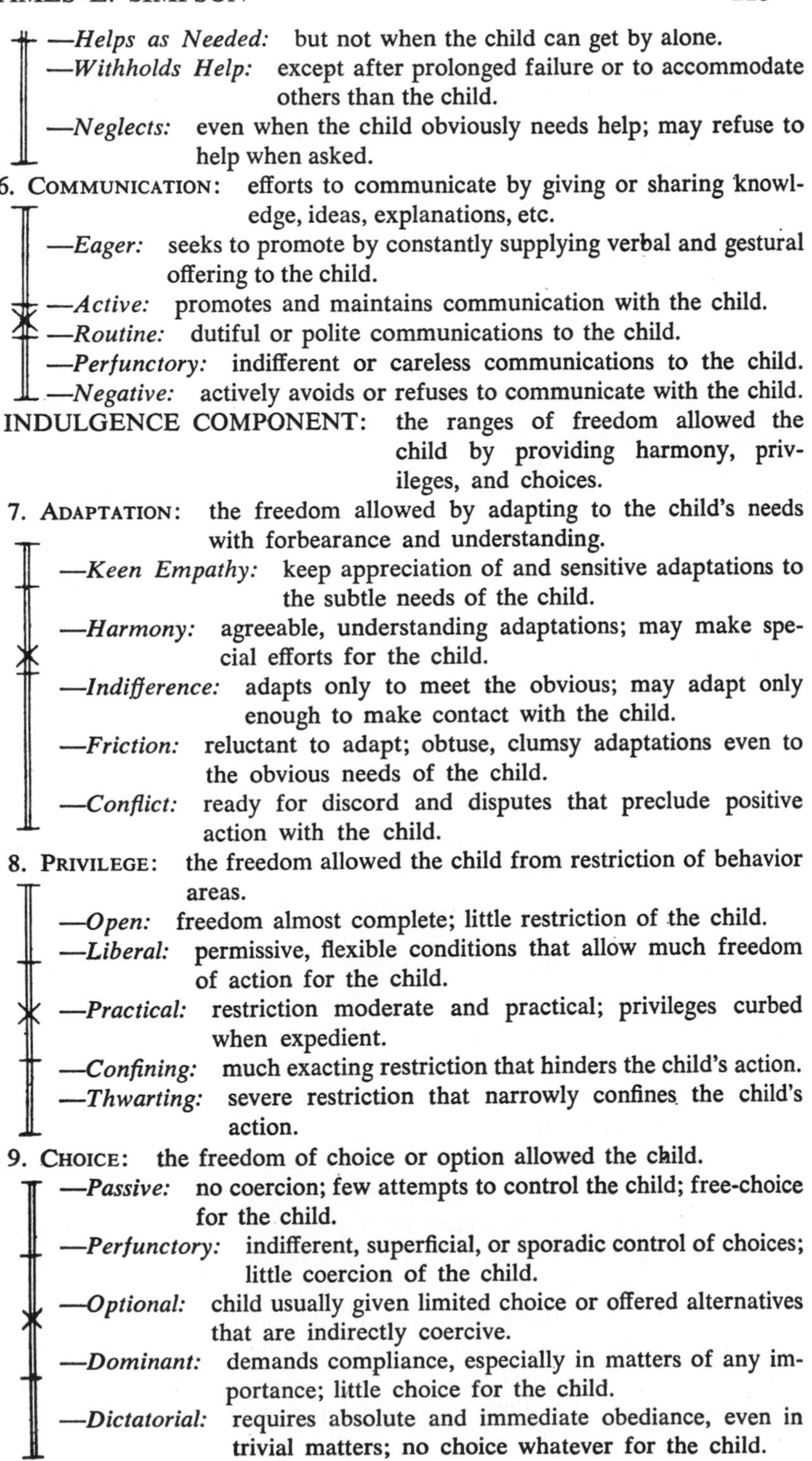

—*Helps as Needed:* but not when the child can get by alone.

—*Withholds Help:* except after prolonged failure or to accommodate others than the child.

—*Neglects:* even when the child obviously needs help; may refuse to help when asked.

6. COMMUNICATION: efforts to communicate by giving or sharing knowledge, ideas, explanations, etc.

—*Eager:* seeks to promote by constantly supplying verbal and gestural offering to the child.

—*Active:* promotes and maintains communication with the child.

—*Routine:* dutiful or polite communications to the child.

—*Perfunctory:* indifferent or careless communications to the child.

—*Negative:* actively avoids or refuses to communicate with the child.

III. INDULGENCE COMPONENT: the ranges of freedom allowed the child by providing harmony, privileges, and choices.

7. ADAPTATION: the freedom allowed by adapting to the child's needs with forbearance and understanding.

—*Keen Empathy:* keep appreciation of and sensitive adaptations to the subtle needs of the child.

—*Harmony:* agreeable, understanding adaptations; may make special efforts for the child.

—*Indifference:* adapts only to meet the obvious; may adapt only enough to make contact with the child.

—*Friction:* reluctant to adapt; obtuse, clumsy adaptations even to the obvious needs of the child.

—*Conflict:* ready for discord and disputes that preclude positive action with the child.

8. PRIVILEGE: the freedom allowed the child from restriction of behavior areas.

—*Open:* freedom almost complete; little restriction of the child.

—*Liberal:* permissive, flexible conditions that allow much freedom of action for the child.

—*Practical:* restriction moderate and practical; privileges curbed when expedient.

—*Confining:* much exacting restriction that hinders the child's action.

—*Thwarting:* severe restriction that narrowly confines the child's action.

9. CHOICE: the freedom of choice or option allowed the child.

—*Passive:* no coercion; few attempts to control the child; free-choice for the child.

—*Perfunctory:* indifferent, superficial, or sporadic control of choices; little coercion of the child.

—*Optional:* child usually given limited choice or offered alternatives that are indirectly coercive.

—*Dominant:* demands compliance, especially in matters of any importance; little choice for the child.

—*Dictatorial:* requires absolute and immediate obediance, even in trivial matters; no choice whatever for the child.

TABLE 11.1

Reliability Tests: Correlations among Social Weather Ratings

RATINGS	*Sample A* W[a]	P[b]	*Sample B* W	P
Four raters	.83	.001	.38	.07
Investigator and median ratings of three untrained raters	.87	.01	.75	.06
Investigator and average ratings of three untrained raters	.90	.01	.63	.08
Investigator's test-retest ratings	.98	.001	.85	.02
Investigator's test-retest ratings and median ratings of three untrained raters	.87	.001	.71	.01
Investigator's test-retest ratings and average ratings of three untrained raters	.91	.001	.69	.01

[a] Kendall's coefficient of concordance
[b] Level of significance by F tests

of the four raters (m:4). The W coefficient indicates the degree of agreement between raters of the nine Social Weather Rating Scales. The coefficient of concordance was also used for evaluations where m:2 so that all coefficients and significance tests are directly comparable. Because there are no tables for W when n:9, the F test (an exact test of significance) was used to determine significance levels of the obtained W coefficients (Walker & Lev, 1953).

Reliability findings are reported in Table 11.1. The social weather ratings by the four raters of Sample A were in high agreement, as is emphasized by the coefficient of concordance, which is .83, at the .001 level of significance. In the case of Sample B, the school playground setting of maximum rating difficulty, the agreement between raters was not so high. Nonetheless, the raters were in fair agreement. Most of the 72 ratings were closely clustered when combined on the scales; there were two deviant ratings. The coefficient of concordance for the four raters is .38 (.07 level of significance). The results indicate that reliable social weather ratings can be made by different raters.

The evidence regarding the investigator's consistence of rating over time is also reported in Table 11.1. Agreement between the test-retest ratings was high. The coefficient of concordance for Sample A is .98 (.001 level of significance) and for Sample B, .85 (.02 level of significance).

Although the medians of the ratings made by the untrained raters (Table 11.1), may be designated the "typical" or middle ratings, they do not fully represent the judgments of the group. If there were many deviant ratings, the median ratings might be the best group measure. Since there are few deviant scores, Kendall's "best estimate" or "best ranking" (Kendall,

1948; Walker & Lev, 1953) was used to represent the "average" ratings of the three untrained raters. These average ratings are computed by ranking the sums of the ranks of the judgments of each rater. The two group measures are but slightly different for Samples A and B (*W* coefficients of median x average ratings are .97 for Sample A and .93 for Sample B). Thus, the two group measures are similar composite ratings that provide additional comparisons with the investigator's ratings. The coefficients in Table 11.1 show the high agreements of the composite ratings and the investigator's ratings.

In short, the reliability tests via both multiple ratings and test-retest ratings indicate acceptable reliability of the Social Weather Rating Scales.

A detailed study of the social weather of Midwest children has been made (Simpson, 1956) but the data are too extensive to be presented here. They indicate that the social weather of six Midwest *preschool* children differed from that of six *school* children in most behavior settings which they shared, and that social weather differed between most varieties of behavior settings. These findings are exemplified in Figures 11.1 and 11.2 for preschool and school children in the behavior settings Home, Indoors and Home, Outdoors. It will be noted that the social weather of the preschool children was less varied within the homes and more varied outside the homes than that of the school children.

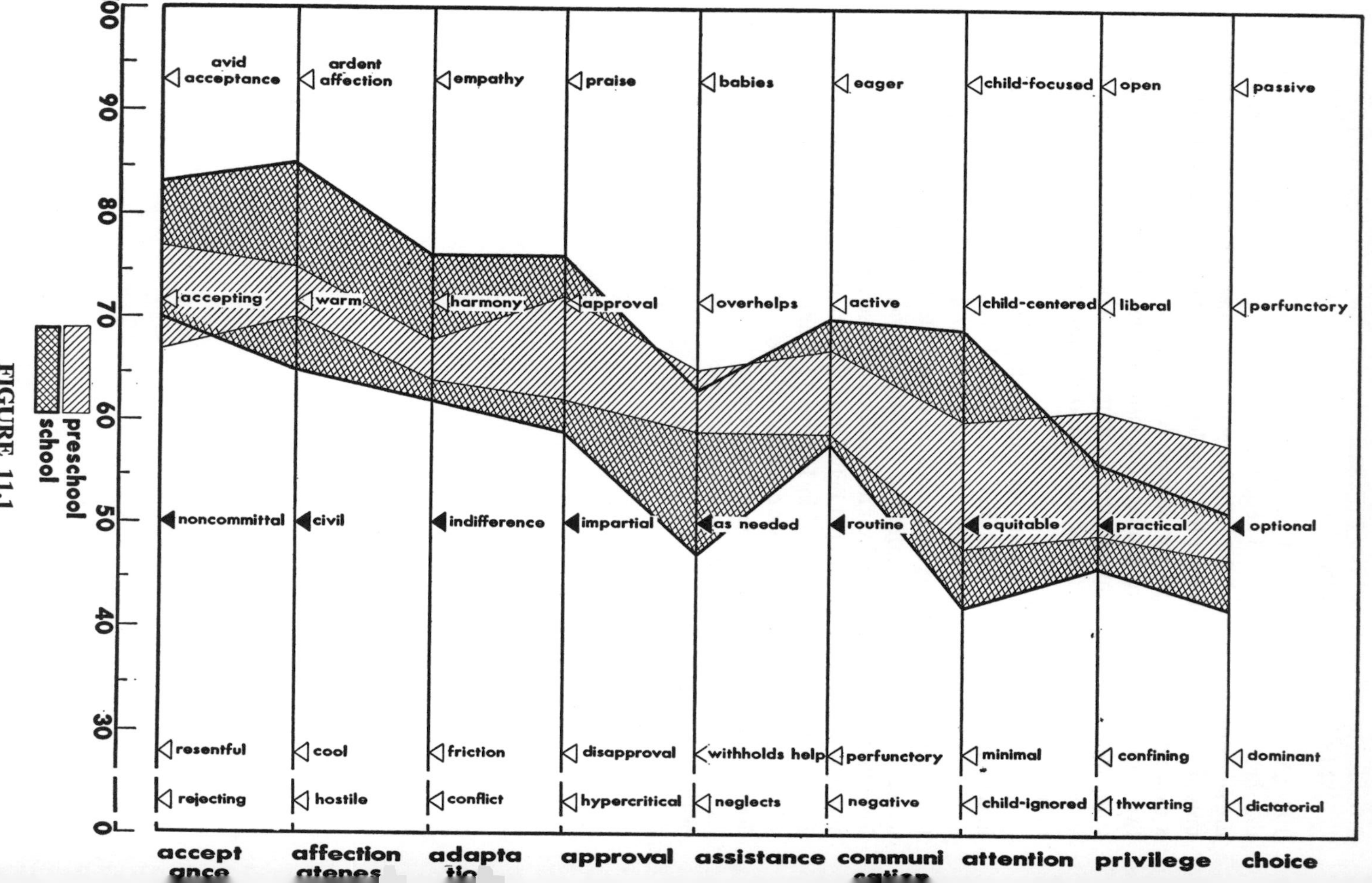

FIGURE 11.1

Range of Median Social Weather Ratings in the Behavior Setting Home, Indoors. Midwest Children: Six Preschool-Age and Six School-Age. Social Weather Scales in Order from Highest to Lowest with Respect to Median Rating (12 Subjects)

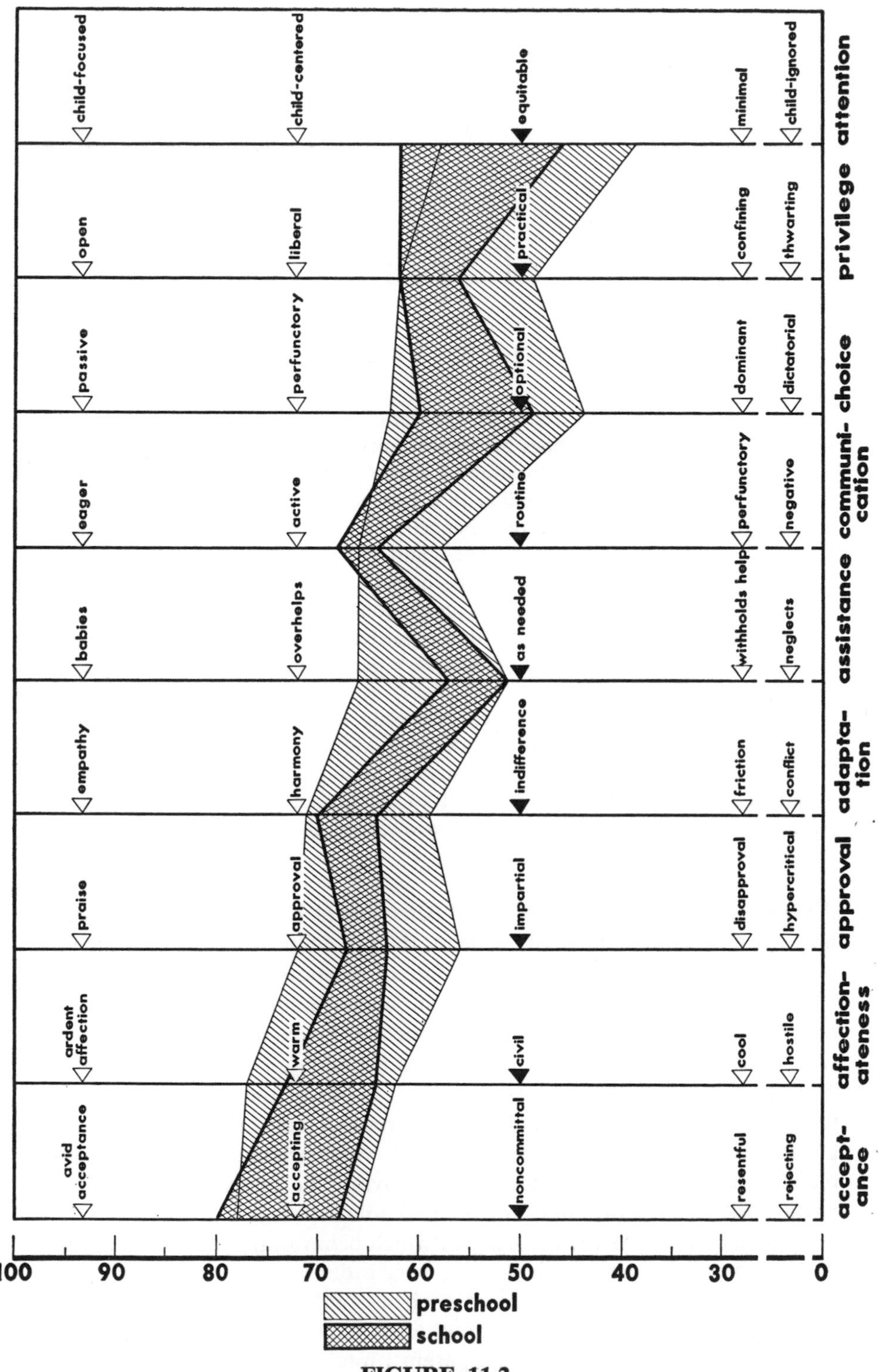

FIGURE 11.2

Range of Median Social Weather Ratings in the Behavior Setting Home, Outdoors. Midwest Children: Six Preschool-Age and Six School-Age. Social Weather Scales in Order from Highest to Lowest with Respect to Median Rating (12 Subjects)

CHAPTER 12

The Study of Spontaneous Talk

WILLIAM F. SOSKIN & VERA P. JOHN

THE EDITOR FINDS *The Study of Spontaneous Talk* a fascinating experience. How infrequently does the opportunity arise to witness from almost the very beginning the exploration of a true scientific terra incognita! And when this unknown is so familiar in a fragmentary and intensely personal way, the fascination is surely enhanced. The authors describe their data as "at once rare and complicated," and comment that this "precluded the formulation of hypotheses at the outset." They liken their problem to that of "going forth to see what a jungle consists of" rather than "making one's way through a jungle to find a particular village." We have here, then, a record of the stream of discovery paralleling the specific study of the stream of talk.

William F. Soskin is Research Associate in the Department of Psychiatry of Harvard University working at McLean Hospital; he received the Ph.D. degree from the University of Michigan. Vera P. John is Assistant Professor in the Department of Anthropology and Sociology at the University of Rochester; she was awarded the Ph.D. degree by the University of Chicago.

AMONG THE conscious and volitional behaviors at his disposal, talk is probably the most common activity of man, the pre-eminent means by which he escapes the basic isolation that is the fate of most other living things.

It is precisely *talk,* rather than speech, language, linguistics, semantics, or communication, that specifies the particular kinds of transitive acts by which the individual creates and manages his minute by minute and day to day associations with other people, and it is out of the talk of those with whom he associates that most of his pleasures and fears and disappointments are fashioned. Of the many approaches by which scientists of different disciplines can examine communicative behavior, the analysis of talk offers particularly rich opportunities for the psychologist.

Spontaneous talk is the modality in which behavioral continuities in man can be observed most effectively. The very ordering of our daily existence, even in the most simply organized societies, naturally precludes intensive observation of one individual by another. A child or adolescent has access only to a very limited part of the parent's total daily experiences; an employer may "know" his employees in a very limited context even after years of association; a husband or wife may claim a broader range of exposure, but for either of them half of every working day is usually beyond the pale of direct observation. Even the five-day-a-week psychoanalyst, the most intensive and sustained trained accumulator of reasonably systematic behavior records on the current scene, has only a second-hand access to the material his patient-subject can recall and is himself witness to only 50-minute samples of predominantly reflective rather than transactional behavior. For all of us, time segments, place boundaries, role definitions, circumscribe each episode of daily life so that we pass successively out of the range of scrutiny of one observer and into that of the next while remaining forever a partial stranger to them all.

It may be for these very reasons that contemporary psychological theory deals so sparingly with behaviors of everyday living. By contrast with the vast accumulation of data about atypical behavior patterns on the one hand, as in the processes involved in severe illness, or of such relatively unidimensional processes as can be isolated and studied by controlled experiment—as in animal learning—we lack even a substantial body of raw material with which to work in this area. For, curiously enough, given the present nature of psychological research facilities, it is far easier to gain access to samples of atypical conditions in man than to study normal behavior.

Provided with the macrosamples that nature has denied us of the continuity of interplay between an individual and his social environment, it should be possible to view the human organism in an entirely new perspective, to note the volume and diversity of its coping behaviors, the vicissitudes of its brief or enduring quests, the common transformations in its system dynamics. This knowledge we need if we are ultimately to develop the more comprehensive psychological theories that Roby (1959) calls for. Such theories and data are needed in psychology to complement the present body of knowledge in the same way that physiologists have found it necessary to study the normal physiological regulating mechanisms as a necessary condition to understanding the organism's mobilization of defensive strategies under extreme stress.

In man, the study of macrosamples of daily behavior will inevitably focus on the character of his talk. A record of one person's talk over a long period of time is a record of the means by which that person tries to achieve, maintain, relieve or avoid certain intrapsychic states through the verbal management of his relations with his social environment. Further than that, if the record extends over long stretches of hours and days it will reveal something of the dynamic character and potential of the social environment itself—how constellations of factors (particular kinds of people, unanticipated external demands, etc.) shape life situations that an individual is called up to cope with, and how the subject himself, by the consequences of his acts successively contributes to the probable future character of his environment. Even more important perhaps, such a record will provide essential data for studying possible relations between events that from the vantage point of either the subject or his associates may seem unrelated.

The remainder of this chapter describes a pilot study undertaken to develop techniques for gathering macrosamples of spontaneous talking behavior in uncontrolled settings and to explore methods of analysis of such samples. It is divided into four main sections, the first describing the way in which the records were obtained, the second presenting a transcribed portion of one of the records, the third discussing some of the early methods used in analysis of such material, and finally some selected preliminary findings with these early methods.

Gathering the Behavior Sample

The behavioral data essential for this kind of pilot investigation are accurate and detailed records of the complete verbal output not only of the subject but of all persons who interact with him. The material must emerge from entirely uncontrolled situations, either those the subject himself creates, or those with which he is confronted by the circumstances of his social environment. If the behavioral records are to be inclusive, it is necessary to have access even to many private settings from which an observer would necessarily be excluded, and the method of gathering the records must not itself impose a serious limiting condition on the range of behavior sampled. Furthermore, if the ambiguity that sometimes inheres in mere transcripts of conversations is to be avoided, it is necessary for later data analysis to have access to the actual voice sound.

Barker and his associates (Barker & Wright, 1951a) had attempted a similar undertaking in recording the behavioral output of a young boy through a single day, but the Barker record has serious limitations for our purposes. Chief among them is that the continuous presence of an observer unintentionally can become a stimulus to incite or inhibit certain behaviors or to modify others, and not only insofar as the subject is concerned. The presence of a "third party" must also inevitably influence the behavior of persons with whom the subject interacts. Equally important, as subsequent experience has shown, it is physically impossible to write verbatim records of many interactions between adults as they occur. The rate of interaction is too rapid, especially in a small-group situation, and there is a tendency for observer-recorders to condense some utterances, completely miss others, overlook inconsistencies, neglect to record grammatical errors, etc. Moreover, it is physically impossible for an observer to record a conversation while the participants are on the move, e.g., from one location to another, just as it would be physically impossible for a single individual to sustain the set of an observer-recorder continuously over a 16-hour day without relaxation and at the same time attend to his own needs. Even less could one maintain such a rigorous observing schedule over a long period of days. The alternative, that of rotating through a series of observers each day, would only expose the subject to an even larger number of individuals with whom he must share his privacy, through whom he must face recurrent reminders of his surveillance.

Taken together, these considerations dictated the choice of a miniature radio transmitter worn by the subject himself as the preferred data-collecting medium. An instrument small enough to be worn continuously for 14 to 16 hours a day and sensitive enough to pick up both the subject's utterances and those of people addressing him, would allow the subject all the freedom necessary. At the same time it would permit collecting records of the desired detail and accuracy merely by tape-recording the entire transmitter output at a receiving station.

Counterbalancing these advantages to some degree is the possible loss of essential descriptive material that an eye witness could gather. Yet, ways can be devised for minimizing some of this loss as will be explained later.

Three main methodological problems were posed for the pilot study: (1) determining whether suitable transmission apparatus could be built which would be tolerable for subjects to wear and at the same time adequately meet FCC regulations covering radio transmission; (2) determining whether subjects could accept and habituate to this continuous monitoring of every aspect of their public and private lives; and (3) determining whether conditions imposed either by the limitations of the apparatus or by the psychological needs of the subjects would vitiate the usefulness of such records for the study of long sequences of behavior.

A year's intensive exploratory work led to the development of a miniaturized radio transmitter that subsequently performed admirably. The transmitter itself was about 1½″ x 2½″ x 5″ in over-all dimension, with a roughly foot-long antenna protruding from the upper end. This small gray metal box was mounted high on the shoulder strap of a brown leather camera case so that in wearing position it hung behind the shoulder blade with the antenna clearly visible slightly off to one side, behind the head. A tiny inch-square microphone was mounted high on the front part of the shoulder strap, the wires from which led along the strap to the transmitter and down to the case containing a mercury-cell power supply. The entire apparatus thus was a single unit and could be slipped on or off with about as much ease as one manages a camera case. Weighing only about three pounds, it could be worn comfortably for several hours. When one was in relatively restricted quarters or immobile for an extended period—e.g., sitting in a room—it could be removed and slung over the back of a chair. Even then it would pick up almost all conversations in the average-sized room.

Subjects in the two pilot runs were two husband-wife pairs. A number of technical limitations of the apparatus necessitated choosing as the site a small town unfamiliar to the subjects. In such a setting, a single adult in a group of strangers might have found himself isolated and bored much of the time, whereas a husband-wife team assured adequate companionship from the outset. Both couples were college-educated and both husbands were graduate students. Both had been married about one year. In both, the husband was slightly over 25, the wife slightly over 20 years of age. The subjects were picked for their willingness and apparent ability to tolerate this kind of experience, as well as for the remoteness of their previous and possible future contacts with members of the research group.

The selection process was obviously a two-way affair, since the subjects were appraising the persons they were about to admit into their private lives as much as the investigators were trying to assess their tolerance of and openness to this kind of new experience. In the weeks preceding the actual run, the principal investigator held several talks with each couple separately during which he tried to give them a full and detailed understanding of the objectives and relevance of the study—in brief, to have them accept the research group as persons with a serious purpose, who would respect confidences later, and in relation to whom the normal events of their private lives need not cause undue self-consciousness. They were also fully informed of the provisions made for safeguarding their anonymity in the subsequent processing of data and in eventual publication. They were assured that with minor deviations, the entire transmitting-recording installations would be manned by the project head and a radio operator and that no other members of the research staff would be regularly present in the station to monitor broadcasts or listen to tapes during their stay.

The main inducement to volunteering was the offer of an expense-free vacation; the project was to be carried out at a large and very pleasant summer resort.

The setting, then, was a resort community in one of the midwestern states, a community that consisted of perhaps 500 or more adults and children, mostly in family groups, and 50 or more college students who worked on the grounds in various capacities. The subjects being reported on here lived for most of their stay in a small cottage at the edge of a very large lake. Their apartment consisted of a single large room and an adjoining bath, the whole designed and furnished very much like the quarters available in a good modern motel. Meals were taken in a community dining room with the other guests. Throughout their stay they had access to all the usual recreational pastimes one expects at a large resort: boating, swimming, tennis, golf, craftwork, fishing, evening concerts, lectures, etc. With certain minor limitations they were free to wander over the entire community and its adjacent golf course, as well as out on the lake. The locus of activity on land was a roughly rectangular area extending about a mile or more in length and about a half-mile in breadth. Near the midpoint of this rectangle a high bluff divided the region into high and low ground. All the many social and residential buildings were concentrated in the lower area along the lake, while on the edge of the bluff above stood the monitoring station surmounted by a high tracking antenna capable of orienting to any point on the grounds. The building was a small permanent structure shielded from view of the lower lake-side sector by a dense growth of trees. Beyond these limits the general topography of the region created difficulties for transmitting.

The subjects were at a slight disadvantage in fitting easily into this community. The college students were in the main a couple of years their junior, were somewhat restricted as companions because of their work schedules, were unmarried, and in any event constituted a more or less well-established social group with its own recreation and living area. Many of the married couples on the other hand, had children, were somewhat older, had different interests, etc. Nevertheless, there were many daily opportunities to mingle with either the "college crowd" or the guests.

Even before their arrival at the resort both couples understood that there was no other expectation of them than that they provide the research group with an opportunity to follow the stream of their behavior over a period of days. They were encouraged to feel free in the choice of their activities,—in a word, to simply regard themselves as on vacation. They were asked not to drive beyond the boundary areas described above, however, in order that they not move out of transmitting range. Aside from daily meetings to replace transmitter battery packs, the research people held contacts to a minimum and the subjects were asked not to visit the receiving station. (During the first week of the first run a series of unforeseen technical difficulties made this impossible. Many discussions and several changes in living arrangements were necessary until these were surmounted.)

Several additional facts are relevant. The transmitters could easily be disconnected and subjects were shown how to do this in the event that they absolutely felt the need for privacy. Neither couple apparently did so during the normal recording day. If any unrecorded communication took place it is most likely to have occurred after midnight when the transmitters were turned off. Also, either husband or wife, and sometimes both, might carry transmitters, although in the latter case only one of the transmitters was actually in operation. Subjects were not told which transmitter was operating; it was felt that if both wore the apparatus neither would feel self-conscious in relation to the other.

Finally a word about the reaction of the community. The directors of the resort were fully apprised of the nature and purpose of the study when initial arrangements were made several months earlier, and they willingly offered considerable co-operation. The guests and student workers were another matter. They were naturally curious about the young couple wandering about the grounds adorned with a strange apparatus, and this curiosity might have led to a continuous flow of questions that could have made social contacts increasingly annoying, thereby spoiling the vacation character of the outing.

Consequently, after the first pair of subjects had lived on the grounds a couple of days the resort director made a public announcement on the matter to the entire community one mealtime. He called everyone's attention to the young couple seen wearing the apparatus on the resort grounds. He identified the apparatus as a radio transmitter and explained that the wearers were the first of two young couples who had volunteered to wear the apparatus while university research workers put it through extensive field trials to study its transmitting characteristics under varying conditions. Inasmuch as the wearers were not engineers and could not explain the working details of the apparatus, and since they, like other guests, were intent on enjoying a vacation, he asked that the community simply accept them as fellow guests and not ply them with questions. The explanation sufficed for all but a few intensely curious adults—who after all, may not have heard the announcement—and some preadolescent boys, whose admiration of Space men apparently made their curiosity impossible to restrain.

The key question was how well the subjects would be able to habituate to the apparatus and the continuous monitoring. This the reader may partially judge for himself in the record fragment presented later in the chapter. It is worth pointing out, however, that self-consciousness seems to vary inversely with the degree of one's involvement with his environment. We have all managed at some time to forget completely, for example, the visible rip in the front of our garment once we become engrossed in conversation, and, as wearers of eye glasses or hearing aids or dental bridges will attest, one comes to terms rather quickly with a new and ever-present appurtenance. The recorded fragment reproduced later in this chapter was chosen especially to demonstrate this point. It is from the very first hour of the first morning of the pilot run. The record dramatically reveals how quickly consciousness of the apparatus recedes as external pressures increase, and then returns some time later.

It is difficult to ascertain how much and under what circumstances behavior was influenced by consciousness of the transmitter. Both pairs of subjects reported afterward that they were aware of such influence at some times and not at others. Both also reported that self-consciousness diminished with the passage of time. We do not know how "representative" is the behavior of our subjects, but for the purposes at hand it need not be representative of anything but the behavior of a young couple wearing transmitters on a summer vacation. There are no data presently available by which to determine how their behavior among strangers, in an unfamiliar setting, when neither had any work responsibilities, might differ from their behavior at home among friends, in their more customary patterns of living. Such comparisons remain as tasks of the future. Nevertheless, the present tapes do contain recordings of a violent argument, of tender expressions of love, of petty behavior, of sober soul-searching, and sheer, exuberant pleasure.

A comment on the description of the situational context is in order prior to presentation of the record fragment. It would seem that much of the essential information in a situation is lost if one has access only to the verbal material. Indeed, it might even seem that much of this material would be incomprehensible without facial expressions and gestures, or without knowing where the subjects were at the time, what the physical environment looked like, who some of the nonsubject participants might be, etc.

Indeed, these are difficulties. It is our firm belief, though one with which many investigators may differ strongly, that while gestures and facial expression do indeed carry significant information in face-to-face communication, such an overwhelmingly large part of the information is carried by the verbal message alone that in a study such as this the loss of facial and gestural information does not seriously jeopardize the usefulness of the records. On the other hand, some interchanges would be quite meaningless without an understanding of behavioral settings, and here foresight born of experience in preliminary field trials proved extremely helpful. Prior to the runs the principal investigator spent many days on the grounds of the resort familiarizing himself with living arrangements, key personnel, the location and function of various buildings, and the general arrangement of major activity areas, so that the interior furnishings, available facilities, etc., could be easily visualized later from the monitoring station. A further and unanticipated aid was the increased auditory perceptiveness that comes as one listens through earphones for many hours while tracking subjects a half-mile away. Familiar sounds, such as the rattle of pans, the ring of a horseshoe against a stake, even the content and quality of background voices, helped quickly to localize activities. Finally, as becomes apparent in the following material, in the preparation of transcripts a knowledge of later developments often enabled the transcriber to add situational detail at the point where it is most helpful to the reader, while the reader himself might well be puzzled as to the source of this information.

A Record Fragment

Following is a sample of the records obtained. The record is from the first hour of the first morning that *Roz* (wife) and *Jock* (husband) wore the transmitters. Shortly before, on this beautifully sunny late-June morning, they had been sitting on the grass with the principal investigator while he reviewed again the general program and objectives of the pilot run, explained various features of the living arrangements in what was to them a completely strange environment, and initiated them in the intricacies of the care and wearing of the transmitter. After the investigator departed, *Roz* and *Jock* set off to explore the waterfront. *Tess,* with whom they are talking as the fragment begins, is the wife of the radio operator. She had been invited to spend several days on the grounds as a social-resource person in case the subjects wanted to contact someone they knew. She was not a member of the research group and had no access to the recording room. After the first day she had very little contact with the subjects.

As this episode begins, *Roz* and *Jock* are down at the swimming pier talking to Tess before going rowing (for other records see Soskin, 1963):

ROWING EPISODE

FRAGMENT FROM HOUR 1: TUESDAY, JUNE 29. 10:30 A.M.

1.	*Jock*	Look, Dear, I knew that before you ever joined the Tri-Y. Now let's go get a boat.	
2.	*Roz*	Girl Scouts sing it too. Bet you didn't learn it there.	
3.	*Tess*	((Look at that dead fish.)) [1]	
4.	*Jock*	Huh?	
5.	*Roz*	That fish, Honey. Get me that little fish.	
6.	*Jock*	Okay. I'll dive in.	
7.	*Roz*	I want it.	
8.	*Tess*	Why?	
9.	*Roz*	'cause there's a cat that walks by our window every. . . .	
10.	*Jock*	Oh! . . .	Roz goes down to try to reach the fish while Jock waits. Meanwhile Tess leaves to go swimming.
11.	*Jock*	Come on.	
			Roz returns and they walk silently about 200 feet to the boat pier where Roz immediately steps into a rowboat.
12.	*Jock*	Yo-ho, heave-ho. You do the rowing.	
13.	*Roz*	Nuts to that idea. You're a big, strong man. Mmmm!	
14.	*Jock*	Yeah, but I have a handicap.	
15.	*Roz*	Yeah, you have a handicap in your head.	
			The attendant in charge of boats comes over.
16.	*Jock*	(*to attendant*) Can we take out a boat?	

[1] Some messages are momentarily unintelligible, for any of a variety of reasons; in this case Tess may have been too far off, with her head turned away from the transmitter. In such cases the content is a guess based on whatever cues can be gleaned from the tape. All remarks that are not clearly audible are enclosed in double parentheses.

17. *Att.* What cabins are you with?
18. *Jock* Huh?
19. *Att.* What cabins are you with?
20. *Jock* I don't know. We're in cabin B-1.

The attendant begins to write identifying data on a register he carries on a clip board.

21. *Roz* We're . . . aren't these . . . Yeah, we're in Cabin B-1.
22. *Att.* Your name?
23. *Jock* Bradley. B-r-a-d-l-e-y.
24. *Att.* Ten after eleven o'clock.
25. *Jock* Ten after eleven. Thirty minutes? Then how do the charges run?
26. *Att.* Twenty-five cents a half-hour.

The attendant walks away.

27. *Jock* Twenty-five cents a half-hour?

Jock shoves off and hops aboard.

28. *Roz* Whoops! Don't get wet.
29. *Roz* You row for a while and then I'll row. Okay?
30. *Jock* All right. ((It's awkward rowing with this transmitter on.))
31. *Roz* Go on. Want me to take it while you're rowing?
32. *Jock* No, it's okay.
33. *Roz* Bet you don't know how.
34. *Jock* Oh, yes I do. I guess I just . . .
35. *Roz* Here, let me change [2]
36. *Jock* I'll just have to set this thing out there.
37. *Roz* . . . Let me take it.
38. *Jock* Okay. It's really a clear lake isn't it?
39. *Roz* It's wonderful. Look, there's ((a big . . . moth)). I wish I had my book with me, then I could tell what kind it was.

Jock hands the transmitter to Roz.

40. *Jock* Here; put it on.

[2] Whenever two people are talking at once their messages are linked by brackets; though presented serially, the remarks occurred simultaneously.

41. *Roz* Like this? I wouldn't want my speech distorted, since I usually have so much to say.
42. *Jock* ((Lengthen the . . .))
43. *Roz* Which? This? Down here?
44. *Jock* Yeah.
45. *Roz* Oh, it won't stay unless I put it over my shoulder.
46. *Jock* Look. Put that thing in back.
47. *Roz* This way?
48. *Jock* Yeah. Now bring that forward.
49. *Roz* Okay.
50. *Jock* Now see if it . . .
51. *Roz* Gad, it weighs a ton.
52. *Jock* (( ))[3] Aren't *those* cabins *nice.*

As Jock rows out from the dock they have a full view of the waterfront and of some large modern cabins beside the water's edge.

53. *Roz* Yes, those are the ones we were supposed to be in. I keep telling you.[4]
54. *Jock* These here?

Jock leans over and peers at the water.

55. *Jock* Look how dark the water is down here.
56. *Roz* You tip this boat over with me in it, and I'll be very upset. Uh, uh, huh, huh, huh.
57. *Jock* I just felt the . . .
58. *Roz* (*laughs*) Jock, I just made a joke . . .

Jock seems completely absorbed in his observation.

60. *Roz* Have you no sense of humor?
61. *Jock* Look how (( )).
62. *Roz* Why are we going way out in the middle? I'll get sunburned.

Roz seems quite apprehensive about being out in a boat.

[3] Empty parentheses indicate that the statement was too inaudible to provide any cues.

[4] Jock and Roz were to occupy one of these, but because of a schedule error one became available only several days later.

63.	*Jock*	(*laughs*) What's the difference whether you're in the middle or not?	
64.	*Roz*	You get more reflection in the middle.	
65.	*Jock*	(*scoffs*) Oh!	
66.	*Roz*	Jock, I know!	
67.	*Jock*	How do you know?	
68.	*Roz*	I can see! You put on your sun-specks before you get a headache, huh?	
			Jock begins rowing vigorously.
69.	*Jock*	No.	
70.	*Roz*	No? Okay. Wanna take your shoes off?	
71.	*Jock*	No.	
72.	*Roz*	(*taunting in a singing way*) Ah, Jock's gonna be sore tomorrow because he insists on showing off.	
			Jock apparently responds by rocking the boat.
73.	*Roz*	No! Now cut that out! You'll ruin this fifty-thousand-dollar equipment.	
74.	*Jock*	Oh, look. ((Boy these are nice oars . . . . . .)).	
75.	*Roz*	You're a good rower, Honey.	
76.	*Jock*	These are very easy to row. Very light.	
77.	*Roz*	Yeah.	
			He rows in close to shore at a point where the shore is undeveloped and heavily wooded.
78.	*Jock*	Look at those waves.	
79.	*Roz*	It's nice to be vacationing.	
80.	*Jock*	You can't slip your oar-locks here.	Jock tries to slip an oar, apparently to measure the depth.
81.	*Roz*	Are you sure?	
82.	*Jock*	Yeah. Uh-oh ((almost lost that)).	
83.	*Roz*	(*chuckling*) You lose an oar, kid, and you're going to swim back.	
84.	*Jock*	That wouldn't be bad. Let's feel the water. Oh, it . . .	
85.	*Roz*	It's wonderful. It's just right. It's like bathtub water.	

86. *Jock*	Feel the waves.	
87. *Roz*	I don't feel it . . . Yeah, I do now.	
88. *Jock*	Getting seasick, Dear? (*laughs*)	
89. *Roz*	Uh-uh. I don't get seasick in boats like this. I get seasick in sailboats. I think . . . I hope! . . . Boy, if I get seasick, I'll be mad.	
90. *Jock*	Here, do you want to feel it sideways?	
		Jock brings the rowboat parallel to the crest of the rolls so that it rocks in the crests and troughs.
91. *Roz*	No, because that'll turn us over. Uh, Jock, uh. This is the way I get seasick.	
92. *Jock*	(*laughs*) ((Like this?))	
93. *Roz*	I don't get sick to my stomach, I get headaches.	
94. *Jock*	Think I can catch up with them?	Jock refers to a passing boat.
95. *Roz*	No, I don't think you're good enough. Show me what a hero you are.	
96. *Jock*	((If you don't know, it's just . . .))	Jock begins rowing faster and his breathing becomes heavier.
97. *Roz*	You're dipping your oars too deep, Dear.	
98. *Jock*	I can't feather them, either.	
99. *Roz*	You should be able to.	
		Jock continues with rapid strokes as Roz chats.
100. *Roz*	He-eave! . . . He-eave! (*laughs*) If you don't stop it, I'm going to.	
101. *Jock*	Where are they? . . . See, we're up to them. We're passing 'em.	
102. *Roz*	You look dissipated, Dear . . .	
103. *Jock*	Huh?	
104. *Roz*	. . . and you're throwing water all over me . . . You're going to bash a sailboat.	
		Jock continues to row vigorously.

105.	*Jock*	((Can you see the waves, there? Look off to the starboard.))	
106.	*Roz*	Undulating . . .	
107.	*Jock*	(*laughs*) What?	Jock causes the boat to rock.
108.	*Roz*	Jock! I don't want to swim right now . . . Here, I'll turn the boat.	Roz is obviously apprehensive. She reaches for one of the oars.
109.	*Jock*	Are you going to . . . You're . . . going to go through the waves again.	
110.	*Roz*	I'm going . . . Turn the boat.	
			Roz takes over one oar and makes the boat swing about.
111.	*Roz*	Okay.	
112.	*Jock*	That sailboat's coming up, I think.	
113.	*Roz*	What? . . . Oh, it's nice to feel water that's so warm you can stand putting your hand in it.	
114.	*Jock*	Yeah, God the lake was cold the last few days.[5]	
115.	*Roz*	I'm kicking, Honey. It goes faster that way.	Roz swings her feet out over the transom and kicks them in the water.
116.	*Jock*	Here, try ((putting 'em that way)).	
117.	*Roz*	(*As if suddenly rejuvenated*) All right. Okay, here we go. Real fast.	She kicks and splashes vigorously.
118.	*Jock*	This way you'll never go anywhere.	
119.	*Roz*	(*laughs*) That's the way. Give me a little help . . .	
120.	*Roz*	(*shifting the transmitter*) Boy, this thing's uncomfortable.	
121.	*Jock*	Hey, hey, be careful! . . . You move up forward.	
122.	*Roz*	Oh, what for? . . . Want me to row a while?	
123.	*Jock*	Yeah, if you want to.	
124.	*Roz*	I'd like to practice a little. . . .	

[5] A lake near their home where they sometimes go to swim.

125. *Jock*	Huh?	
126. *Roz*	. . . It's been a long time since I rowed.	
127. *Jock*	You wrote?	
128. *Roz*	Rowed!	
129. *Jock*	((All right. I'll move over.))	
130. *Roz*	All right. Whoop!	
		Roz starts to take off the transmitter.
131. *Jock*	Change places with me.	
132. *Roz*	Let me get this off first.	
133. *Jock*	No, change places first.	
134. *Jock*	Hold it up and . . . . You can stand up. It's perfectly all right.	She struggles to remove the transmitter while seated.
135. *Roz*	That's the first thing I learned in water safety, Love. Don't stand up in a boat. I don't. 'cause I don't want to fall in . . . 'cause I just ate, and I might get a cramp and drown. (*Exchanging the transmitter equipment*) Oh . . . here . . . uh. Do you want to put your shirt over your shoulder before you sit down.	They exchange seats and Roz takes up the oars.
136. *Jock*	No.	
137. *Roz*	Let's see if I can remember how you do this.	
138. *Jock*	Huh?	
139. *Roz*	Um . . . Which way do I want to go? Like so, huh? Oh, I'm clumsy. Look, see?	
140. *Jock*	Yeah, I see. (*chuckling*) You're also turning us around in a circle.	
141. *Roz*	((I am not.))	
		Jock, seated on the stern, opens a book and begins to read aloud.
142. *Jock*	"I got so downhearted and scared I did wish I had some company. Pretty soon a spider went crawlin' up my shoulder, and I flipped it off and it lit in the candle and before I could budge it, it	

was all shriveled up. I didn't need anybody to tell me that it was an awful bad time . . ."

At this point the recording tape is changed. About 45 seconds are lost during which time a large motorboat comes very close to the rowboat.

143. *Jock* Keep your oars in the water so they can balance us.

144. *Roz* (*softly but apprehensively*) Uh. . . . We're going to be hit.

145. *Jock* (*calmly*) All right, go forward. Push. . . .

146. *Roz* Forward?

147. *Jock* . . . this one. Yeah, push this one.

148. *Roz* Like this?

The power boat passed very close leaving a large wake.

149. *Jock* (*more and more excitedly*) No, no, the other way . . . The other way! Push the . . . That's it. Just put both oars forward. Hey! (*laughs*) No!

150. *Roz* What? (*laughs nervously*)

151. *Jock* Damn it, this way!

152. *Roz* What way?

Although both laugh, they both sound quite concerned.

153. *Jock* With both of them! Oh (*laughs*) that damn boat's going to swamp us, Girl.

154. *Roz* I don't know . . .

155. *Jock* Not that way! Just stop going that way! That's it!

156. *Roz* This way?

157. *Jock* God! Yes! That boat's going to swa . . . all right now just stay straight. Pull on . . . Push with this one.

Now from the other direction a small ferry boat is approaching. Its pilot gives a blast of the horn to warn the rowers, but they don't seem to notice.

158.	*Roz*	(*laughs*) Which one?	
159.	*Jock*	Push. No, the other way. (*laughs*)	
160.	*Roz*	This way?	
			Both laugh nervously as they are tossed about on the waves. Just then the ferry sounds a second blast.
161.	*Roz*	(*giggles nervously*)	
162.	*Jock*	God, here comes another one!	
163.	*Roz*	(*laughing and gasping*) This boat is . . .	
164.	*Jock*	Wait . . . wait.	
165.	*Jock*	All right, just take 'em out.	
166.	*Roz*	(*laughing tensely*) Do you think he'll swamp us?	
167.	*Jock*	Not if you just stay still, it won't. All right, straighten us into it, damn it. (*laughing*) Pull! Pull! That . . . that thing. You'll swamp us!	
168.	*Roz*	(*laughing helplessly*) Oh! Which way?	The wake catches them and tosses the boat around.
169.	*Jock*	(*laughing*) Christ Girl!	
170.	*Roz*	This way?	
171.	*Jock*	(*still laughing*) Yes!	
172.	*Roz*	Oh, all right.	
173.	*Jock*	Directly into it. We're going to get the backwash of that other one!	
			Another wave catches them.
174.	*Jock*	Push, will you! God, you're swampin' me, Girl!	
175.	*Roz*	(*laughs nervously*)	
176.	*Jock*	You *have to* stay directly into them. (*laughs*)	
			Roz succeeds in pointing the bow into the waves.
177.	*Roz*	All right, we're directly into it.	
178.	*Jock*	(*more calmly*) Oh, okay, now is it better?	
179.	*Roz*	I don't know. You got me so scared. I didn't know what was going to happen.	
180.	*Jock*	Well, if you see a three foot wave coming at you . . .	

181. *Roz*	They were only teeny waves.	
182. *Jock*	Yeah, with *caps* on them. That's a big boat. All right let . . . you better learn how to backwater right now.	
183. *Roz*	Well, I don't . . . you only said . . .	
184. *Jock*	Go the other way.	
185. *Roz*	. . . to pull.	
186. *Roz*	All right.	
187. *Jock*	I said push. No . . . !	
		The boat begins to swing as she pulls on one oar.
188. *Jock*	See, you're just turning us. Come on; go straight. All right, let's see you go ninety degrees.	
189. *Roz*	You mean that way?	
190. *Jock*	Yeah, use both oars and go ninety degrees.	
		She tries.
191. *Jock*	No . . . no . . . No! Look, to turn . . .	
192. *Roz*	You want to go this way?	
193. *Jock*	Look, to turn, put one up and one back, and pull.	
194. *Roz*	Oh, you mean do it like that?	
195. *Jock*	Yeah.	
196. *Roz*	Well, you can turn it . . .	
197. *Jock*	Yeah.	
198. *Roz*	You mean like this?	
199. *Jock*	All right, now reverse. You got them reversed?	
200. *Roz*	Hmm?	
201. *Jock*	No, you're not reversing them.	
202. *Roz*	Yes I am.	
203. *Jock*	Now . . . now you are. Okay, now push . . . push on both.	
204. *Roz*	Which way? This way or that way?	
205. *Jock*	No, push.	
206. *Roz*	That's push!	
207. *Jock*	That's pull!	
208. *Roz*	That's pull!	
209. *Jock*	Oh, *this* is push.	
210. *Roz*	What?	

211. *Jock* You pull 'em now. Now push. The other way. Put 'em up. Push. Push out from 'em.

Roz follows his directions.

212. *Roz* That's what I was doing before. Like this. Trying to go backwards.

213. *Jock* That's it. Now watch your oars. I want to . . .

214. *Roz* I can't watch both at once.

215. *Jock* Well, just watch one. You're ah . . . (*laughing*) putting this one in the water and that one isn't . . . I wish that boat'd come around again.

216. *Roz* ((At least, I don't!))

They are rounding a point beyond which they see a large bay.

217. *Jock* Well, this is the end of the lake up here, isn't it.

218. *Roz* Hmm?

219. *Jock* That's the end of the lake up there.

220. *Roz* Yeah . . . Shall we go home?

221. *Jock* No. We've been here ten minutes exactly.

222. *Roz* (*laughing*) Well, I'm worn out. I don't see why you (*laughs*) couldn't row the boat.

223. *Jock* Well, you wanted to. You asked to . . . Gee, when I saw that one coming *straight* for the side of this thing . . . that big . . . that boat couldn't have been more than twenty feet off. (*laughs*) And you were pulling this way towards it. God!

224. *Roz* You said, "Pull, pull, pull!" Then you say "Gee whiskers, you panic in an emergency." Why didn't you say, "Go backwards" or "forwards." What do you think I am, a sailor?

Both are relaxed and amused now that the danger is past.

225. *Jock* Well, I wanted you to stay into the waves, whatever you did.
226. *Roz* Well, why didn't you tell me so!
227. *Jock* Go up that way.
228. *Roz* (*slightly irritated*) "Which way *do* you want to go?
229. *Jock* This way.
230. *Roz* Now let's see. If I . . . If I want to go that way I've gotta go like *this,* don't I? . . . And then like this.

Roz chuckles to herself. She seems to be going in a circle again.

231. *Jock* (*laughs*) Christ. That was pretty good.
232. *Roz* Which way am I supposed to be going?
233. *Jock* The other way.
234. *Roz* Oh. Maybe not.
235. *Jock* You sure are. (*reassuringly*) That's all right, by the end of this . . . our stay here, you'll be able to paddle pretty well.
236. *Roz* (*laughs*) I can paddle pretty well now.
237. *Jock* You sure can.
238. *Roz* You haven't fallen in yet, have you?
239. *Jock* No, but you almost swamped us.

Her oar slips and splashes Jock.

240. *Jock* Hey, Girl!
241. *Roz* I'm sorry!
242. *Jock* Both together, huh?
243. *Jock* Hey (*laughs*) Look! All right, pull on both of them. Just pull on both. — It slips again.
244. *Roz* Which way is pull? Forward?
245. *Jock* That's push? Pull. That's pull.
246. *Roz* Oh, you want me to pull.
247. *Jock* Yeah.
248. *Roz* Well, that's forward.
249. *Jock* Yeah, now . . . Now, look. Don't dig this one in so deep. See you can turn yourself by

		digging one in deeper than the other one when it's shallow. Hey, hey! No!	The oar slips and Jock is splashed again.
250.	*Roz*	Do you want it turned back the other way?	
251.	*Jock*	I want to go out . . . You splash me (*chuckling*) once more and you can sit back here.	It splashes again.
252.	*Roz*	I'm sorry, Honey. Whoops. (*laughs*)	
253.	*Roz*	(*laughs*)	
254.	*Roz*	(*laughs*) Really, Jock, I'm doing the best I can. What do you think I am, after all?	
255.	*Jock*	You told me you could row.	
256.	*Roz*	Well, I could.	
257.	*Jock*	This row's going to start a row.[6]	
258.	*Roz*	(*laughs*) . . . I'll row you right out of the boat.	
259.	*Jock*	Pull on your right . . . You're dipping . . . you're dipping in too deeply, and you're pulling them up too high . . . You're still pulling them up too high.	
260.	*Roz*	Jock, why don't you read your book? That's why I'm rowing—so you can read your book.	Roz' voice sounds as though she's annoyed.
261.	*Jock*	Okay.	
			She splashes a little.
262.	*Jock*	(*laughs softly*)	
263.	*Roz*	Honey, I promise I won't splash you again while you read.	
264.	*Jock*	If you hold your oar up like that it's going to drip.	
265.	*Roz*	Not on you.	
266.	*Jock*	Hey. That way.	
			Jock points out toward the center of the lake.
267.	*Roz*	(*softly but insistently*) I don't want to go way out there.	
268.	*Jock*	Go that way, huh? I want to see around the point.	

[6] Jock puns on the pronunciation.

269. *Roz* (*sighs resignedly*)

270. *Jock* I'll row in. You just go that way.

271. *Roz* You mean I'm going to row all the way over to that point?

272. *Jock* No. (*imploringly*) *This* way. Will you *please* go *this* way? I've asked you five times.

273. *Roz* Oh, you mean you want me to go way out into the middle of the lake? O-o-oh!

274. *Jock* I'm going to shove you in.

275. *Roz* No, you're not going to shove me in. Besides, if you shove me in, they'll have it on tape, and they can get you in court for that.

276. *Jock* Wire tapping's not legal evidence . . . Pull . . . harder, Honey, hmm? You can keep on, just . . .

277. *Jock* It's not too sunny out today, is it?

278. *Roz* I don't know. I feel awfully warm.

Another motorboat is approaching from a distance.

279. *Roz* (*laughs helplessly*) Honey . . .

280. *Jock* Look, you're heading . . . Go over that way. Just . . . this way. Pull. Atta girl. Come on. Come on.

281. *Roz* (*laughs*) Jock, I don't want to join the Navy, and I don't see why you have to think you're my superior officer.

282. *Jock* (*laughing*) All right, now go on, pull on this oar . . . You can't even . . . Hey, there's the observatory. See?

Methods of Analysis

The analysis of macrosamples of talk recorded in completely unstructured situations presents the investigator with data at once both rare and complicated. On the one hand, the volume and diversity of material, its direct and unrestrained quality, in effect, its "naturalness," is enviable yield. On the other hand, because of the absence of behavior controls, these records are unwieldy to say the least. By contrast with investigations in more familiar areas, even learning what to look for becomes a problem. It is the difference between making one's way through a jungle to find a particular village or going forth to see what a jungle consists of.

Four complementary kinds of analyses were considered from the outset and were applied with varying degrees of success to different portions of the pilot-run records.

These different approaches were intended to serve the following purposes: (1) provide systematic descriptions of behavior settings, (2) develop some normative guides for appraising the volume and duration of talking behavior under different circumstances, (3) distinguish major classes of verbal acts in functional terms, and (4) explore concepts and methods for assessing the dynamic aspects of interpersonal relations as influenced by verbal exchanges. The several methods are briefly described under the designations *ecological, structural, functional,* and *dynamic.*

ECOLOGICAL ANALYSIS

Barker and Wright (1955) and Barker (1960), more than any other psychologists, have pioneered in the ecological analysis of human behavior—painstakingly developing methods for the analysis of the complex interlinkages of behavioral episodes and effectively demonstrating the influence of environmental factors on the range and character of social interactions. Useful in its own right, ecological analysis is an essential adjunct to the functional analysis of talk as it provides a systematic means for organizing information on significant features of the psychosocial environment. It also provides a framework within which to organize the large body of transcribed material into sequences of units within which more detailed analyses can be carried out.

The basic ecological unit as developed by Barker and Wright (1955) is the "episode," an organized sequence of behaviors occurring within a specifiable locale and devoted to a particular activity.[7] The episode may be of varying duration, may be interrupted periodically by intervening episodes, may involve the subject with different individuals at different times, etc. For more detailed analyses, an episode may be broken down into subepisodes, each in itself exhibiting distinctive activity-participant characteristics. In the present study an entire 16-hour day of the behavior of Jock (the husband in the record presented earlier) was analyzed into episodes and phases. These were supplemented by movement studies establishing where and for how long and in what order he distributed his activities over the

[7] *Editor's note:* Dr. Soskin's use of the terms "episode" and "phase" differs in some respects from the use of "behavior episode" and "behavior phase" by some other contributors to this book.

main behavior settings. A similar summary took account of the number of individuals and the size of groups with which he became involved. As will be seen in the results section, where a subject spends his time, with whom, and in what kind of activity, influences the functional character of the verbal behavior he produces. Very often the results of functional or dynamic analyses of talk would be quite susceptible to misinterpretation in the absence of ecological data.

STRUCTURE ANALYSIS OF TALK

Relatively little is known about the quantitative aspects of talking in long sequences of uncontrolled situations. Just how much time an individual spends in talk, how this amount may vary among persons in different age groups, of different educational backgrounds, in groups of different sizes, under conditions of altered role relations, in different types of activities, are questions for which little data exist. Indeed, when a suitable measure of the amount of information in an utterance is finally devised, the combined duration-information measure will become an exceedingly powerful tool in the study of sequential talk. Meanwhile, even relatively simple frequency-duration measures are extremely illuminating data.

Three kinds of structural studies have been carried out on various segments of the available records. The first involved determining the absolute and relative amounts of talking time engaged in by the subjects. For the purpose at hand, a unit of speech is defined as the time interval during which *S* is judged to be talking. It may consist of a word, a phrase, or several sentences, and may project beyond the actual production of sound, when content, intonation or context indicate that *S* is still "claiming" the available talking time. From this as the unit of behavior, several useful measures may be developed:

1. *Total talking time* (TTT): the sum of durations of the units produced by all the participants in a particular episode. TTT may not exceed the clocked duration of the episode itself, hence, overlapping units are scored simply as time in use.
2. *Demand for talking time* (D): TTT as a proportion of the clocked duration of an episode. As will be seen shortly, D varies considerably according to the nature of the activity in the episode, the role relations of the participants, etc.
3. *Subject talking time* (STT): the sum of the durations of the units of *S*'s speech in a given episode.
4. *Subject's proportion of* TTT ($S\%$): the proportion $\frac{\text{STT}}{\text{TTT}}$. $S\%$ reveals the extent of the claim that *S* makes on the attention of others in a given episode.
5. *Average unit length* (AUL): STT divided by the number of units *S* has produced in an episode. While suffering from the weakness inherent in

any "average," it reflects gross changes in the character of episodes as will be seen shortly.

The above measures were developed directly from time measurements of the recording tapes.[8] In addition, a series of analyses was performed from the typed transcripts. One of the most immediate problems encountered when dealing with transcribed talk is that of defining *units*. By contrast with well-ordered written language, spontaneous speech occurs in irregular patterns. The sentence is not a meaningful unit for analysis, nor is the single word. In spoken language, stress and intonation reduce sentences to phrases, to units generally larger than a word, but smaller than a sentence. In analyzing talk according to what is being communicated, therefore, one also tends to choose a unit of analysis that is shorter than a sentence. These were called "idea-units," and in our multiple system of scoring, each single unit was scored at the structural, functional, and dynamic level.

Besides measures based on talking time, then, a second structural measure was developed from the unitized typescript by counting the number of utterances of each participant in an episode and expressing this as a proportion of the total number of utterances exchanged. In a classroom situation, for example, the teacher will be likely to speak more often than any individual pupil. In a balanced conversation between two adults, each may be expected to contribute about 50 per cent of the remarks even though one may use more speaking time than the other. In a four-person situation where all participate about equally, each will contribute 25 per cent of the remarks. Departures from such "claims" percentages emphasize the extent of over-under participation of an individual and meaningfully complement the measures of timed speech units.

The third structural study, following the work of Chapple (1940, 1949), Goldman-Eisler (1951, 1954), Verzeano (1951a, b) and others, was an analysis of the distribution of utterance durations. It was a comparison of results obtained from recordings of spontaneous conversations with those of other investigators using interview material, and it was also a careful exploration of some of the problems of curve-fitting with speech duration data. Since a discussion of the issues involved requires considerable space and since some of this work already has been reported elsewhere, it will not be repeated here (Hargreaves, 1955, 1960).

FUNCTIONAL ANALYSIS OF TALK

An elephant, to blind men, is many different things, and for much the same reasons the functions of talk have been described differently by different investigators, each according to his interest. To explain the basis of the functional classification scheme used in the early part of this study, it is necessary that we focus first on a dichotomy, and distinguish between the *relational* and *informational* functions of talk. Talk of the latter type

[8] This work was carried out by William Hargreaves.

consists of objective statements about oneself or (as in Skinner's *tacts,* discussed below) about one's world, and it transmits information from one person to another much as does the newspaper, the dictionary, the textbook, or encyclopedia. Informational messages are those which develop or report what are thought to be facts; they identify, classify, analyze, organize, etc., and are primarily information transfer statements. The scope and subtlety and complexity of informational talk are all markedly influenced by factors of age, intelligence, education, and range of experience.

Relational talk is quite different in character. Much less influenced by such factors as intelligence, maturity, etc., its essential form and content may in fact show marked similarities across such diverse groups as first-graders, primitive tribesmen, college professors, and the mentally retarded.[9] Relational talk encompasses the range of verbal acts by which a speaker manages his interpersonal relations, and it is not often influenced by his social environment. It is the distillate of relational talk that leads to the characterization of individuals as, e.g., selfish, considerate, cold, or dependent. Other things being equal, informational talk is effective to the degree that the relation between participants is relatively stable, whereas the very function of relational talk is the management of the relations themselves. Compare the following examples:

Informational Messages	*Relational Messages*
"That is a Modigliani."	"Oh, I like that!"
"His name isn't Karl Schmidt."	"Now I'm completely confused."
"It's four miles from here."	"Then get going!"

The functional distinction being made here bears similarity to one or another aspect of several better-known dichotomies. Ogden and Richards (1947) describe the function of language as emotive and referential, but if referential and informational are equated, surely emotive and relational cannot be, since the vast majority of relational messages are not emotive. Piaget (1920) long ago distinguished between egocentric and socialized speech, but his definition of egocentric speech is such that its adult equivalent is the readily recognized though somewhat uncommon act of talking to oneself. His dichotomy reduces to a distinction between talking to oneself or to others.

[9] On the other hand, that the subtlety of a relational message will vary from one cultural level to the next is evident from the following roughly graded series of messages, all of which, in the proper setting, will get the speaker a second glass of milk:

1. "Milk!"
2. "Get me some more milk."
3. "I want some more milk."
4. "May I have another glass of milk?"
5. "I'm still thirsty."
6. "Golly, that milk tasted good."

A very close parallel exists between our dichotomy and Skinner's (1957) distinction between functional types of acts, *mands* and *tacts*. The latter are statements about the world; the former are comments about the needs of the speaker and cover such acts as demands, commands, requests, etc. We merely would add that objective statements about oneself and one's experiences also belong in the category of tacts. On the other hand, insofar as the concept of mands emphasizes manifestly directive, regulatory statements it obscures the vast number of statements which, though not manifestly controlling, nevertheless alter interpersonal relations by inducing the listener to take account of and adjust to the state of the speaker. For example, the statement, "I never would have done that," as a form of reproof is nothing more than a statement about one's own operating characteristics, yet under appropriate circumstances it will be a highly potent relation changer.

In any event, a simple dichotomization of something so complex as verbal behavior forms is nothing more than a first step; it merely helps "clear the brush." Much more discriminating are the set of distinctions developed by Charles Morris (1946), by whom we were strongly and profitably influenced at the time the study was undertaken. Morris's two-dimensional classification system is based on distinctions between *modes* of discourse and the *uses* which they may serve. The modes he distinguishes as *designative, appraisive, prescriptive,* and *formative,* the uses as *informative, valuative, incitive,* and *systemic*. The principal value of Morris's effort, from the point of view of the present study, lies less in the identification of 16 forms of discourse—to which his four-by-four classification inevitably leads—than in his singling out some of the major sub-categories around which a relational classification scheme might be built.

Our own examination of spontaneous utterance, leavened by the work of the authors cited above, allowed us finally to distinguish six kinds of utterances. Before defining these it seems essential to state even very briefly certain assumptions with which we approached our task, viz.,

1. that behavior serves the purpose of achieving, maintaining, relieving or avoiding certain physiological—and in the case of humans, psychological—states.
2. that psychological state changes are effected in either of two ways:
   a. by a spontaneous rearrangement of the hierarchy of needs through fatigue, satiation, distraction, sublimation, insight, etc., or
   b. by intentional modification of the relation between the individual and that segment of his environment which seems relevant to the dominant need, through the use of either motor or verbal behavior;
3. that where verbal behavior is used to effect an internal state change (and an interpersonal situation is thereby implied) the function of the verbal message is to structure the environment of the listener so that *his* re-

sponse to *his* newly structured social environment will result in the relation sought by the initiator.

4. that insofar as their relation-changing capacity is concerned, verbal messages may be usefully distinguished as directive or inductive, the former specifying the behavior which will bring about the desired relation, the latter merely providing information, the knowledge of which will induce the recipient to respond with the desired behavior.

This highly abbreviated statement may nevertheless help in understanding the definitions of some message types:

1. *Expressive Statements* (Xp). These are utterances the primary function of which is to discharge immediately experienced tension. They range from "Ouch!" "Wow!" and "Darn!" to more elaborate forms. This type of message almost always has inductive effects on others, in the sense of eliciting some verbal response. From the speaker's point of view, these statements are not aimed at interpersonal communication. They are pure discharge behaviors.
2. *Excogitative Statements* (Xc). These are the verbal acts most commonly described as "thinking aloud." An important, though not sole, function of this type of utterance is verbal exploration of a problem or situation. Others might be confirming statements, questions, etc. In psychotic persons and in children and the aged these occur with greater frequency than in normal persons or the middle-aged. The following, if imagined as spoken to the self, are representative:

   Hm-m-m, what have I done wrong here?
   Oh, I see. . . .
   So that's what they're doing . . .
   I wonder if it would work this way.

Though expressive and excogitative statements are primarily forms of intrapersonal talk, they do tend to have inductive effects when listeners are in earshot; hence both will sometimes fall in the area of relational talk. All other types of verbal messages are explicitly interpersonal. The following three constitute the core of relational talk:

3. *Signones* (S). These are messages that report the speaker's present physical or psychological state, and hence make available otherwise private information that can guide the listener. They include reports on physical sensations, emotional dispositions, needs, hopes, wishes, likes and dislikes, etc. Signones manipulate relations indirectly, and often unintentionally. Needless to say, the same signone can at one time arouse positive responses, at another time negative ones,—which is the risk one takes in not prescribing *O*'s behavior. Its use as a consciously manipulative act seems to be contingent on the degree of confidence *S* has that his social environment is a benign and nurturant one.

Examples are:

I'm cold, tired, hungry, etc.
I'm afraid, disappointed, angry, thrilled, etc.
I wish I could go, too; I hope you'll be able to come.
Oh, Jock, I like that!

4. *Metrones* (M). These are the statements that would fall in Morris's appraisive-valuative cell. They are valuative statements arising out of *S*'s belief system, his interpretation of his environment, etc., and often constitute an attempt to define the environment of *O*. Besides appraisals, the class includes statements of obligation, inferences about *O*, predictions of outcome, etc.
Examples are:

Yours is the best one here.
What a fool I've been.
You shouldn't do that.
I really ought to go now.

5. *Regones* (R). These are regulative statements that take two main forms. On the one hand they control the behavior of *O* by restriction and prescription. On the other hand, they channel *O*'s behavior through creating opportunities for action in specific areas. Hence, they include demands, prohibitions, requests, etc., but also invitations, permissions and some forms of suggestions.
For example:

Why don't you do it right now?
Won't you join us?
Of course you may go.

6. *Structones* (St). These include the entire domain of informational statements which report facts, identify, classify, analyze, explain, etc. As contrasted with metrones, most of these statements have a validity independent of the personal experience of the speaker. Statements about the self are classified as structones if they deal with objective information.
For example:

I weigh 181 pounds.
That fits over the axle.
He was here yesterday.
We couldn't find it.

The informational-relational dichotomy emphasized earlier can now be elaborated into sub-categories of utterance types as follows:

Informational messages:
Structones
Relational messages:
Directive:
Regones
Inductive:
Signones
Metrones
Quasi-relational messages:
Inductive:
Expressive
Excogitative

With these functional categories it was possible to carry out three kinds of appraisals: (1) to study a speaker's over-all distribution of utterance types among these categories, combining results from a variety of situations; (2) to study shifts in distributions of utterance types in different kinds of episodes; and (3) to study changes in distributions sequentially through the several phases of a single episode.

DYNAMIC ANALYSIS OF TALK

Besides analyzing the structural and functional features of a message, an effort was made to assess its psychodynamic properties as well,—a difficult task based on inferences about the emotional state of the speaker at the time the message is produced. Whereas the functional analysis could be carried out directly from the typescript, with only occasional recourse to the original tape recordings in ambiguous cases, the so-called dynamic analysis required working simultaneously with typescript and recording, since voice quality was a critical cue. It was thought possible to distinguish three variables, *state, locus-direction,* and *bond.*

State. Verbal messages are delivered against the background of voice sound which itself conveys information about the state of the speaker as of the time the message is produced. This affective information, an essential part of the spoken message, can be assessed by listening to the recorded voice (Soskin & Kaufman, 1961). A simple six-interval scale was used in making judgments about the affective state of the speaker:

1. a state of joy, glee, high pleasure;
2. a state of satisfaction, contentment, liking;
3. ambivalence;
4. a state of mild apprehension, dislike, frustration, disappointment;
5. a state of pain, anger, fear, grief;
6. neutrality.

These affective states are evident in any of the functional categories, though most excogitative statements and structones will be found to be neutral.

Locus-direction. An attempt was made to score each message for the direction and locus of state-change it would produce from the point of view of a neutral observer. A message might thus have its primary effect on either instigator or recipient or both, and might change the state in an "upward" or "downward" direction on the preceding scale. Nine possible forms of locus-direction change were provided for. In the notation used below, a serif on the left denoted the change in the speaker, one on the right that in the recipient.

Locus-direction	*Examples*
↿	wants, wishes, self-praise
↿ ↾	mutually complimentary statements
↿ ⇂	certain forms of derrogation, reproof, rebuffs which imply the speaker's superiority.
⇃	self-criticism, abnegation
⇃ ↾	apology, certain forms of giving, praise
↾	compliments, permission
⇃ ⇂	mutually unfavorable statements
⇂	accusations, certain forms of derrogation, reproof
0	no inferrable change

Bonds. For a time it was thought possible to distinguish from a combination of vocal and semantic information the degree of intimacy the speaker was willing to tolerate in the relationship. Degree of emotional proximity appears to act as a powerful control on what may or may not be said to another person, and an attempt was made to note changes along this dimension. Either our definitions were poor or intimacy changes occur rather infrequently in a husband-wife relationship; in any event, a satisfactory reliability was never achieved and the results are therefore not reported.

As with the functional material it was possible to make three kinds of analyses, one dealing with over-all summaries based on composites of all situations, another involving comparisons between one episode and another, and the third tracing sequential shifts through various phases of a single episode.

All of the coding performed on these data, with the exception of the work pertaining to the measurement of speech duration units and talking time, was carried out by the same two raters. Reliability checks on a number of independently classified sets of messages ranged between 70–90 per cent for the dimensions reported on in the following section.

Results

The results obtained from a pilot study undertaken to develop apparatus, procedures for data gathering, and methods of analysis are unlikely to contain striking confirmations of bold new hypotheses, yet they may indicate promising lines for future inquiry. Even with the fragmentary records available in this study, it was possible to explore some important features of talking behavior.

ECOLOGICAL ANALYSIS

It will be recalled that ecological data were gathered chiefly to provide a greater understanding of the contexts in which the talking behavior occurred. Since results based on a single subject have little utility beyond their important contribution to the fuller understanding of other analyses, only a few examples will be presented. These are based on the record of Jock's activity during a single 16-hour day—the longest uninterrupted record obtained.

One striking feature of this day is the small amount of time Jock spent alone. A minute-by-minute analysis of his activities shows that he spent only 4.8 per cent of the 16 hours by himself (on the average less than three minutes per hour) throughout a day that began at 8:10 a.m. and ended a half-hour after midnight. During the entire interval he was involved in 51 distinct social configurations that included a total of 47 different children and adults; yet he was also almost constantly in the company of either his wife (57 per cent of the time) or his brother-in-law (42 per cent of the time) or both. Since only 13 per cent of his time was spent in settings that did not include the six-year-younger wife or the roughly ten-year-younger brother-in-law, Jock had maximal opportunity to be the dominant figure.

Jock's day was punctuated by a total of 55 locale changes distributed over 13 different settings. The largest amount of time in any single location was spent in the student employees' recreation center (16 per cent) where, incidentally, he was also likely to be the dominant individual in any social group by virtue of his age and advanced education. Most of the time spent in this location occurred in the late hours of the evening, however, when there was no other organized social activity in which the couple could participate, and when they were not free to "go to town" as many other guests had done.

The second-largest block of time was spent in a forenoon work session at the Crafts Shop where Jock and Roz had been engaged daily in learning to make lanyards and moccasins. Mealtime in the dining hall consumed 13 per cent of his time and another roughly 12 per cent was devoted to fishing off a nearby pier. Although 14 per cent of his day was spent in the cottage, this represented the total time spent there during 10 different "pauses" at home base.

While this particular day is atypical in view of the presence of two of Jock's relatives throughout the afternoon and early evening, it is not grossly unrepresentative. Even on other days Jock was rarely alone. Although he had a great amount of reading to do for an approaching comprehensive examination, relatively little of his time was devoted to study, and when he and his wife were separated Jock usually would find someone else with whom to interact. By contrast, in the same setting a fortnight later, the male in the second pair of subjects behaved quite differently. He rarely visited the student employees' center, he developed few contacts with the students themselves, he never fished, and he spent a considerable amount of time away from his wife, often in relatively solitary activities such as studying, reading for pleasure, playing a round of golf alone, etc.

STRUCTURAL ANALYSIS

How much does a person talk? How often? Questions as simple as these two may be of extreme importance in helping to understand changes in behavior at different stages of development, or in shedding light on the differences in social impact of individuals. Aside from the measures of talking behavior in standardized interviews (Bales, 1950) or in experimentally controlled groups (Chapple, 1940, 1949), we know remarkably little about gross quantitative features of talking behavior, and anything approaching norms seems to lie in the distant future. Nevertheless, with the very fragmentary data at hand it is possible to take a few first steps. The results show that measures of talking time can be quite sensitive indicators of an individual's impact on his social environment.

To facilitate accurate measurement of talking time, the speech signals on the original tapes were transformed electronically into graphic records on moving paper tape, the linear measurements of which could then be converted back into time units. As a reliability check on this method, the same 45-minute sample was analyzed on two different occasions four months apart by the same person. In 107 speech units there was 96 per cent agreement on the definition of units and a correlation of .98 between the two sets of measurements (Hargreaves, 1955).

To develop some quantitative base against which to compare Jock's talking behavior in specific episodes, 11 two-person episodes selected from six different days and representing Jock's interactions with five different people were subjected to detailed measurement. The combined duration of these 11 episodes was 5 hours, 47 minutes, and the participants consumed 32.6 per cent of this time in talking behavior. Jock's claim on available talking time varied considerably, from 29 per cent in a situation where he was being given golf instruction, to 79 per cent in an episode where he was alone with Roz in the cottage. Yet, his total share of talking time across all these situations was 50.6 per cent. By itself this figure means little; it could have resulted from the particular selection of episodes examined.

That temporal aspects of talking behavior vary considerably depending on the size and nature of the group or the freedom for alternative forms of behavior is readily evident from Table 12.1. Here Jock's talking behavior is analyzed in five different situations which included 2 four-person episodes while seated at mealtime, 2 different episodes with his wife in the cabin, and one episode with one of the research workers.

Both of the four-person episodes are "high-demand" situations. In the dining hall the two young couples faced each other across a small table. Talking was the predominant activity, consuming 93 per cent of the time in one instance, 85 per cent in the other. In both instances Jock consumed 36 per cent of the talking time, somewhat more than his share. Even if the other three participants were to divide the remaining time equally, they would have been able to speak only a little more than half as long as he.

TABLE 12.1
Variability in Jock's Talking Time in Five Different Episodes

EPISODE	*Group Size*	*Episode Duration (seconds)*	*D*[a]	*S%*[b]	*AUL*[c]
Breakfast	4	2142	.93	.36	4.0
Luncheon	4	2100	.85	.36	3.1
Packing with wife	2	1719	.33	.45	1.3
Planning with wife	2	977	.25	.69	1.3
Discussion with research worker	2	824	.94	.37	2.8

[a] Demand for talking time
[b] Jock's proportion of talking time
[c] Average speech-unit length in seconds

By contrast with the foursome episodes, demand for talking time was low in the two situations with Roz, undoubtedly because in both of these episodes talk was interspersed with the carrying out of various housekeeping tasks. On the other hand, the third twosome situation with the research worker created as high a demand as was found in the dining episodes. Here talking time was dominated by the research worker who had come to report a change in plans, and then tarried only long enough to report an accident and departed, leaving Jock little opportunity to participate.

When the average unit length is compared with functional analyses, it becomes evident that the longer utterances are predominantly structones, the factual-information-exchanging messages.

By providing measures of the amount of talking time Jock used in different types of situations, the structural analyses corroborate and complement but also qualify the ecological findings. The latter portray Jock as a highly gregarious individual. In the structural analysis it develops that he is also very garrulous under some circumstances though less so in others. Over a relatively large sample of situations he speaks about as much as his co-participant. On the other hand, given an appropriate audience he appears quite ready to take the initiative and to claim considerably more than his share of talking time.

FUNCTIONAL ANALYSIS [10]

The analysis of approximately 1,850 messages spoken by Roz and Jock in six different episodes occurring on three different days constitutes the core of material to be presented here.

Over-all Distribution. Of initial and general interest is the frequency of occurrence of different message types in this selection of episodes. Table 12.2 contains summary distributions of the kinds of messages used by Roz in five different episodes with her husband and by Jock in six—the last one not involving his wife. The over-all distributions for the two subjects are quite similar. Both produced about the same proportions of evaluative statements (metrones) and statements about their feeling states (signones).

TABLE 12.2
Composite Distribution of Utterance Types in Six Different Episodes

UTTERANCE TYPE	*Roz* %	*Jock* %	*t*	*P*
Expressive	8.6	3.8	4.85	<.001
Excogitative	1.1	0.8	0.67	NS
Signone	27.7	24.0	1.85	NS
Metrone	27.1	26.2	0.45	NS
Regone	11.0	13.9	2.05	<.05
Structone	24.5	31.3	3.40	<.001
Total	100.	100.		
N	745	1116		

However, Roz produced significantly [11] more affect-discharging (expressive) messages while Jock used significantly more directive (regone) and informational (structone) statements. A first gross generalization about this young couple, then, might be that the wife was much more explicitly emotive than the husband whereas he tended to be the more active of the two in structuring and directing interpersonal events. Whether these patterns are due to sex differences, age differences, or even the particular selection of episodes remains an open question.

Of more interest and certainly more unexpected in this very general kind

[10] We are especially grateful to Dr. Edward Katz, Aglia Efstathiou, and Jane Ingling for assistance in processing the data in this section.

[11] Throughout this and the following section the words "significant" or "significantly" are used only in the statistical sense and refer to differences where $p \leq .05$ or $\leq .01$.

of analysis is the finding that only about one out of four messages produced in these settings was of the straight information-giving variety (structones) and that nearly two-thirds of all messages by both subjects in this selection of episodes were of the class we have called relation-changing messages. On the face of it, this seems to be an unusually large proportion of high-impact messages for any pair of individuals to endure over a long period of time. There is reason to doubt that so high a proportion of relational messages is standard in the daily interaction of most married couples. The finding suggests a number of tentative hypotheses about the nature of relational acts, viz., that such acts are more frequent between intimates than between strangers; that the frequency of such acts may be positively correlated with some measure of the intensity of a relationship; that the frequency of relational acts is influenced by level of maturity and may diminish with age; that relation-changing messages occur more often in private situations than in public ones, etc. Indeed, the ratio of signones and regones to other types of messages in conversations might be an important component of an index of intimacy or social proximity.

Differences between Episodes. Moving beyond these composite distributions, it is of interest to examine shifts in the production of different types of messages from one kind of episode to another.

For all its advantages as a trial-run setting, the locale of the present study severely restricted opportunities to observe a broad spectrum of any one individual's behavior. For example, Jock was rarely observed in the position of a subordinate; there are no examples of his interactions with male, peer, long-time friends and no episodes approximating work situations. Similarly, for Roz there are almost no examples of sustained interaction with female peers. The range of episodes presently available for comparative study is admittedly limited. For an examination of possible shifts in the uses of message types in different kinds of social settings, we have drawn our material from the same situations on which the preceding composite distributions were based. The general character of these episodes might be sketched as follows:

In Cabin. The early morning hours of Roz and Jock's last full day of their stay constitute this episode. Before they departed for breakfast, their interactions were focused on getting ready for their meal. After their return from the dining hall, they began to gather up their possessions preparatory to packing. In the process they made plans for the remainder of their stay and discussed their return to the city.

Rowing. A major excerpt of the talk occurring in this situation was presented earlier. The segment not available to the reader occurred in the final ten minutes or so in which they slowly rowed back to the boat landing, discussing various sights on the way. The data analysis is based on material beginning with #74 in the excerpt presented earlier.

Craft Shop. This is a portion of a morning episode in the craft shop lasting nearly 2½ hours during which Roz and Jock interacted with a number of different people, though most often with a male and female instructor.

Luncheon. This episode is a foursome conversation in the dining hall with a married couple in their early thirties. The conversation was dominated by Jock who talked about tennis and narrated some personal experiences.

Breakfast. With the same table partners Roz and Jock discussed a lecture on interracial housing heard the previous evening. Both subjects supplemented their joint summary of the lecture by describing interracial housing problems in their home city.

Golf. This material is part of the running conversation during a golf game played at Jock's request so that his companion, an intercollegiate champion, could give him some instruction.

Table 12.3 reports the per cent distribution of types of messages used in each of these various situations. In the first two episodes husband and wife interacted only with each other. In the third they also talked often with each other but there was considerable interaction between Jock and two instructors in the craft shop and Roz had a number of exchanges with a mother and two children working there. The luncheon and breakfast episodes were stable foursome situations. The golf episode is the only example of a sustained interaction between Jock and a like-aged male. The table permits two kinds of comparisons: one concerns intraindividual variability in the output of different kinds of messages from one situation to another; the other involves differences between husband and wife in the production of a given message type in a specific episode. The table reports all instances in which significant differences were found between husband and wife in the per cent of messages of a given type produced in that episode. Significant individual differences from one episode to another are reported in the text.

From the first column, for example, it is quite evident that Roz produced a significantly higher per cent of emotion-venting (expressive) messages than did her husband in both the cabin situation and the rowing incident. In the former the expressive messages were predominantly in the form of happy outbursts, frequent singing, etc. In the latter, as the reader will recall, they were mostly expressions of apprehension or annoyance. Roz' per cent of output of these expressive messages in the twosome situations was significantly greater ($p < .001$) than in the group or public situations.

The so-called exogitative messages in the second pair of columns turned out to provide no interesting leads since there was very little "thinking aloud" done by either subject in the selections under study.

Messages in which one verbalizes his momentary physical or psychological state (signones) varied considerably in frequency both between subjects and from one kind of episode to another. The 13.3 per cent found for Roz in the breakfast situation is significantly lower than that observed in any other passage. Jock also produced relatively fewer signones in the breakfast

TABLE 12.3
Per Cent Distribution of Utterance Types in Each of Six Episodes

EPISODE	UTTERANCE TYPES													
	Xp		*Xc*		*S*		*M*		*R*		*St*		*Total Utterances*	
	Roz	*Jock*	*Roz*	*Jock*	*Roz*	*Jock*	*Roz*	*Jock*	*Roz*	*Jock*	*Roz*	*Jock*	*Roz*	*Jock*
In Cabin	12.7	3.0[b]	1.1	2.0	28.7	27.1	22.8	23.6	15.3	19.1	19.4	25.1	268	199
Rowing	12.7	7.0[a]	1.9	—	31.9	17.2[b]	31.5	25.1	10.8	32.5[b]	11.2	18.2[a]	213	203
Craft Shop	1.0	1.6	1.0	2.4	31.4	40.7	30.4	19.5[a]	10.0	17.9	26.5	17.9	102	123
Lunch	1.1	2.2	—	0.4	23.6	22.7	22.2	23.6	8.3	5.3	44.4	45.8	72	225
Breakfast	1.1	1.3	—	—	13.3	17.9	30.0	34.9	2.2	2.1	53.5	43.8	90	235
Golf	—	2.4	—	0.8	—	30.0	—	29.0	—	9.9	—	28.1	—	121

[a] $p < .005$, [b] $p < .001$: These values apply to differences between subjects; not to differences between episodes.

episode, about the same proportion as he produced in the rowing incident. His 40.7 per cent in the Craft Shop is significantly higher than his output in any other episode. Hence, with regard to signones, there is no clear pattern discernible. Both husband and wife produced relatively fewer in the foursome conversation situations than in the twosome private situations, but both produced a relatively high number in the craft shop where others were present, and the per cent observed for Jock here is significantly higher than in any other episode in which his wife was present.

It may be no coincidence that Jock's two peaks in signone production came in the craft shop and golf episodes, in both of which he voluntarily assumed the role of a pupil in relation to a teacher. In both settings he had considerably less skill than the persons with whom he was associating. During the long craft-shop episode Jock managed to keep one or the other of the two instructors almost continuously engaged with him through frequent expressions of difficulty in mastering the operations in lanyard braiding. Several days earlier he used a similar technique in soliciting a continuous stream of advice and comment from his companion and instructor in the golf game.

The fourth major category of messages, that pertaining to the subject's belief and value systems (metrones), again shows only moderate variability. Metrones comprise between 22 and 32 per cent of all messages produced by Roz in each of the episodes, and there is no significant difference for her from one episode to another. Jock's spread is somewhat larger, from 20 per cent in the craft shop to 35 per cent in the breakfast episode. In this later case where Jock's metrone per cent is significantly greater than that for any other episode except the rowing event, he was decidedly critical of a number of people in the course of his reports about the interracial housing situation in his home community. But, then, so was Roz. Except for the craft-shop episode the per cent of messages that either allocated to metrones was very similar. In that episode Jock's metrone per cent was significantly lower than his wife's, possibly because he was so often engaged in soliciting help from the instructors. In any event, it is worth noting that Roz' metrones were likely to be positive evaluations of the work of other people in the shop or critical remarks about her own work, except for some very pointed critical remarks to Jock during a period when he was annoying her.

Of the directive, regulating, controlling regones, both Roz and Jock produced considerably more in their private interactions than when in the presence of others. Percentagewise, Roz' output of regones in the breakfast episode was significantly lower than in any other behavior sample. For Jock there was no statistically significant difference in regone per cents from one mealtime conversation to the next but his output in these two dining hall episodes was significantly lower than in the other episodes. In all three of the private situations—and for this purpose we classify the craft shop as a private situation because the majority of regones occurred when Roz and

Jock were interacting with each other—Jock's regone per cent was higher than his wife's, but only in the rowing episode was the difference between them statistically significant.

The sixth and last message type used in this analysis was the so-called structone, the straight information-giving type of message. Roz' 11 per cent in the rowing episode was significantly lower than the per cents observed for her in any other episode except the cabin situation. Both for her and for her husband the highest per cent of structones appeared in the dining hall conversations and these per cents were significantly higher than those observed in all other episodes. The only significant difference between subjects in the output of this type of message occurred once more in the rowing episode. Some possible reasons for this difference are discussed later in the chapter.

In summary, there are some distinctively different ways in which each subject varied the production of message types from one kind of situation to another. Roz produced a high percentage of expressive messages whenever the two were out of the public view and became noticeably more controlled in the presence of others. Jock's output, on the other hand, was relatively low throughout. For both, regones tended to appear only in private or semiprivate interactions. With respect to signones, Roz' output was uniformly high in four out of the five situations whereas Jock's was somewhat more variable, his peaks occurring in situations where he had placed himself in the role of pupil. For both, metrone production was least influenced by the private or public character of the setting. Finally, of the six occasions where husband and wife differed significantly in the output of a particular message type, four occurred in the rowing episode. Elsewhere, except as discussed above, the verbal behavior of these subjects had many features in common. For example, their respective distributions are very similar for the breakfast episode, and for both the pattern of verbal behavior was strikingly replicated in the luncheon conversation.

DYNAMIC ANALYSES

The very dimensions by which it was hoped to identify inter- and intrapersonal changes in the sequential development of an episode proved most difficult to isolate. Even though scorers had available both typescripts and the original tape recordings from which to obtain voice cues, the classification of affect state, of locus-direction change, and of bonds was difficult to make. As clues to the regulatory mechanisms alluded to earlier in the chapter, these measures are admittedly crude in their present stage of development. Yet, their application to these records produced some interesting leads.

Locus-Direction Changes. Table 12.4 presents the distributions of messages in which, in the opinion of the judges, the speaker was trying to modify his own disposition or state, and/or that of the person to whom the message was directed. These so-called locus-direction changes were analyzed for Roz and Jock in five episodes. Although the scoring scheme distinguished more types of changes than are shown on the table, some were rarely encountered and the table is abridged accordingly. Frequencies for the least common groups were combined and are reported in the miscellaneous column, while the zero column reports the per cent of messages in which no locus-direction change could be identified.

In only two of the categories were any significant differences observed between husband and wife. It should be recalled that the left-headed dart signifies self-oriented positive messages, those in which the object of the speaker's message seems to have been to elevate or bolster his own status. The per cent distribution of this type of message is reported in the first column. In the morning episode in the cottage Roz produced significantly more of these messages than did her husband. Jock, on the other hand, in this same episode produced a high percentage of precisely the opposite kind of message, *viz.*, one calculated to undermine or detract from the status of the other person.

The circumstances here bear description. Roz had just come out of the shower and was dressing while Jock, who was already dressed and in something of a dour mood, sat in the living room working on his lanyard. In a rather short period of time he pointedly contradicted a casual remark of hers; then he tried to implicate her in a series of errors he had made in his lanyard; and next he refused to help her find a lost lipstick while at the same time criticizing her for her appearance without it. In this sequence Roz, who at first was almost childishly gay and ebullient in the shower, parried his contradiction with an artful display of one-upmanship by subtly exhibiting her superior knowledge of a facet of French history. Next, in the face of continuing criticism she defended herself against his accusation and finally she solicited his help in finding the lipstick and sought his approval for her general appearance.

The very subtle shifts and variations in the way in which these two people attempted to modify each other's states sequentially throughout this episode obliged us to question whether summaries of very long segments of a record reflect the actual sequential dynamics of the behavior in a given episode. In the luncheon episode, several hours later on the very same day, precisely reverse tactics were used and the differences are significant in the opposite direction. Here as at breakfast Jock tended to dominate the conversation. As he warmed up to his role he related a series of personal experiences that would strain the credulity of most listeners. Now while he engaged in ego-elevating behavior, though the second couple listened tactfully to his boasting, Roz directed a number of politely derogatory remarks at him.

When individual differences in the locus-direction characteristics of messages are studied over different episodes, the pattern is somewhat less clear. In so far as the self-elevating, self-displaying types of messages are con-

TABLE 12.4

Per Cent of Distribution of Locus – Direction Changes in Five Episodes

EPISODE	↿		↾		⇂		↿⇂		*Misc.*		○		*Total Utterances*	
	Roz	*Jock*	*Roz*	*Jock*	*Roz*	*Jock*	*Roz*	*Jock*	*Roz*	*Jock*	*Roz*	*Jock*	*Roz*	*Jock*
In Cabin	23	12[b]	4	5	6	22[b]	11	9	9	11	47	41	268	199
Rowing	22	15[a]	5	6	10	8	8	8	2	2	53	61	213	203
Craft Shop	16	26	4	11	6	7	16	14	3	1	55	41	102	123
Lunch	7	44[b]	7	6	13	4[b]	0	0	6	7	57	39	72	225
Breakfast	40	38	6	4	1	2	2	3	2	3	49	50	90	235

[a] $p < .05$
[b] $p < .01$
These values apply to differences between subjects; not to differences between episodes.

cerned, Roz' gaiety and alertness earlier in the cabin continued on into the breakfast episode and here she rivaled Jock in her active discussion of the interracial situation at home. Off to a gloomier start that morning in the cabin, Jock seems to have been stimulated by the presence of an audience at breakfast and the frequency of his self-elevating remarks increased appreciably in the breakfast situation. At lunch, on the other hand, the presence of an audience tended to exert an opposite effect on Roz. At times she seemed embarrassed by her husband's tales. She participated somewhat less in the conversation during this episode while her husband rose to a peak of self-display. This comparison is an excellent example of the objectives of this type of investigation, *viz.*, the study of relationships between episodes separated in time. Still another example is described briefly at the end of the discussion section.

In the second column of Table 12.4, summarizing messages in which the speaker seems intent on enhancing the ego of the other person, no significant differences were found.

Other-directed ego-diminishing messages are summarized in the third column. As has been commented on earlier, the differences observed between Roz and Jock in the cabin and luncheon episodes are statistically significant. No where else in the column is the difference between subjects greater than chance.

In the fourth column the pair of contraposed darts signifies a type of message in which the speaker is regarded as trying to elevate the self while derogating the other or trying to defend the self while refuting the other. Both subjects exhibited significantly more of this type of behavior in private than in public. Differences between the cabin and rowing episodes on the one hand and the dining hall episode on the other were significant at the .001 level. In the two cases where Roz' per cent is highest she was clearly responding to verbal assaults of varying intensity from Jock.

Within this limited range of episodes once more the presence or absence of outsiders emerges as an important dimension influencing verbal behavior. On both available occasions Jock utilized the presence of others to engage in ego-enhancing behavior, while his wife clearly did so in one situation but not in another. Both engaged in more other-oriented ego-manipulating in private than in public, although when Jock had persisted in "being difficult" over several hours in the cabin and craft shop, Roz was not above using a few well-placed barbs at luncheon to bring some of his ballooning tales of exploits to an ignominious public deflation.

Affect Changes. As with locus-direction shift, the assessment of affective state changes met with only marginal success. Yet, as is evident from data in Table 12.5 some differences were observed. A number of earlier observations have foreshadowed the finding reported here about the cabin episode. Roz differed from her husband in producing a larger number of highly positive, ambivalent, or highly negative messages. In fact, the coders saw Roz

TABLE 12.5

Per Cent Distribution of State Scorings in Five Episodes

	STATE[a]												Total Utterances	
	1		*2*		*3*		*4*		*5*		*0*			
EPISODE	*Roz*	*Jock*	*Roz*	*Jock*	*Roz*	*Jock*	*Roz*	*Jock*	*Roz*	*Jock*	*Roz*	*Jock*	*Roz*	*Jock*
In Cabin	6	1[c]	13	13	6	2[b]	13	11	4	1[b]	58	72[c]	268	199
Rowing	0	0	9	8	3	2	38	23[c]	1	0	50	66[c]	213	203
Craft Shop	0	0	2	1	0	0	29	15[b]	2	1	67	83[c]	102	123
Lunch	0	0	1	1	1	0	10	3[b]	0	0	88	95[b]	72	225
Breakfast	0	0	1	0	0	0	3	2	0	0	96	98	90	235

[a] The numbers designate states as follows: 1 = highly positive; 2 = mildly positive; 3 = ambivalent; 4 = mildly negative; 5 = highly negative; 0 = neutral.

[b] $p < .05$, [c] $p < .01$ } These values apply to differences between subjects; not to differences between episodes.

as producing a higher per cent of mildly negative statements than her husband in all five of the episodes, in three of which the difference was statistically significant. By contrast, in all five episodes Jock was seen as producing a higher per cent of neutral statements, and in four of the five episodes the difference between them was significant.

But neither the locus-direction scoring nor the affective state scoring adequately conveys Jock's practice of scattering a series of mildly provocative messages throughout an episode as, for example, his persistence in the rowing episode in urging Roz to row farther out into the lake despite her growing apprehensiveness. While such messages of Jock's were often produced in a tone of voice that led judges to score them as affectively neutral and while they were often sufficiently indirect to earn a neutral scoring for locus-direction change, a series of such remarks or a series of failures on Jock's part to respond to direct or implied requests for help often provoked Roz to a display of negative affect.

Once again in affect change scores the contrast between the twosome and foursome episodes produces significant differences. Both displayed more affect in the former than in the latter, suggesting that the circumstances of mealtime acted as a damper on the arousal or expression of strong emotion.

In summary, when comparisons are based on composites of relatively long sequences of interaction, the differences noted correspond closely to those that might be predicted from normal everyday experience. That is, persons intimately involved with each other tend to relate with less intensity in the presence of quasistrangers than when they are alone. Also, women are usually characterized as exhibiting more emotional lability than men, particularly when alone with their husbands, whereas social custom limits the amount of affectively-toned behavior they display in public.

Instigation-Response Frequency. An entirely different dimension of dynamic analysis has to do with the proportion of instigations and responses a subject produces in verbal intercourse. The study of these records shows that the course of a conversation is directed by the occurrence of strategic instigative remarks. Each new instigation is followed by a succession of responses by either subject so that the next five or six exchanges are controlled by the initial instigation. A high per cent of instigations by both interactants in a conversation could mean that each was preoccupied with his own needs and interests and had little inclination to pursue the interests or concerns of the other. A high per cent of instigation by one speaker and a high per cent of responses by the other would imply that the former was directing the course of the interaction. Roz and Jock differed significantly in the production of instigations and responses throughout several episodes. In the rowing and cabin episodes the proportion of instigations produced by each was quite similar, around 20 per cent of the messages of either speaker in the former episode and 15 per cent in the latter. In the remaining three episodes, however, differences between them were significant beyond the .01 level. Jock was by far the more frequent initiator in the craft shop, a possible reflection of the fact that he was less steadfast or independent in his work orientation than was Roz. He repeatedly sought out instructors to ask questions or came over to examine and comment on his wife's work, or drifted over to observe the work of other persons. Similarly, in the breakfast conversation it was he who took the lead and controlled the topic of conversation. Here 23 per cent of his remarks were instigations while Roz had none. In the luncheon conversation the situation was reversed, roughly 14 per cent of Roz' remarks being instigations while only 2 per cent of Jock's were thus scored. This odd discrepancy seems to reflect the fact that whereas Jock's conversation followed a single theme for some time, Roz on a number of occasions seemed to be trying to shift the conversation to other topics.

PHASE ANALYSIS

From the outset an important aim of this study was to develop a quantitative method for studying the dynamics of long sequences of behavior. A frequency distribution that lumps together behaviors from a whole series of episodes, or even a single frequency distribution summarizing one long episode, obscures many of the subtle shifts that can occur from one phase to the next within an episode. To explore their suitability for the analysis of intraepisode dynamics, the same coding categories were applied to a phase analysis of the rowing episode.

Beginning with message #74, this episode can be divided into five more or less distinct phases as follows:

74–110 The interval in which Jock seemed to be playfully showing off his skill as an oarsman;

110–143 the period in which Roz diffidently undertook to learn to row;

144–179 the encounter with the motor boat and ferry boat;

180–216 the aftermath of the scare during which both were rather angry and argumentative until Jock's easy laughter and change of mood in #215;

217–245 the remainder of the ride up to the point at which they left the dock.

The graphs in Figure 12.1 summarize certain behavior changes for Roz and Jock throughout the five phases of this episode. The top pair of graphs summarize changes in functional types of messages. The middle graphs summarize data on state changes. The bottom graph presents material not discussed heretofore and included now only because of its capacity to illuminate some of the facets of the first graph. Besides their many other encodings, all messages were scored as assertions, assertions in response to

FIGURE 12.1

Phase sequence analysis of rowing episode

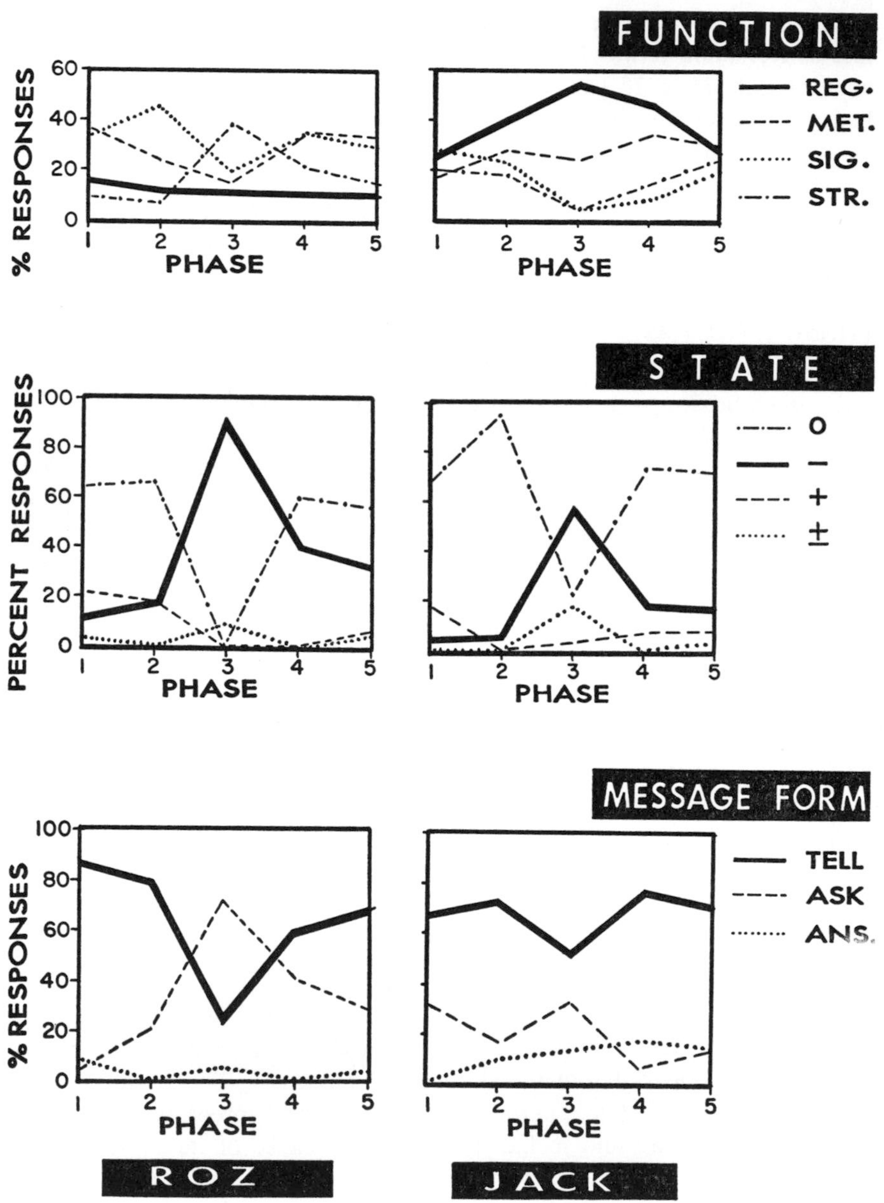

questions, or questions. Here these three dimensions are labeled *tell, answer,* and *ask,* and it will be seen that one of these scorings makes Roz' use of structones somewhat more comprehensible.

The graphs make clear at once that the distribution of functional types of messages changes markedly for the two subjects at different phases in the episode. Roz' output of regones was uniformly low throughout. Her output of signones and metrones dropped markedly in Phase 3—the encounter with the boats—then gradually returned to the former level in Phases 4 and 5. Her use of structones, on the other hand, rose precipitously in Phase 3, then gradually subsided again. For Jock, the pattern of changes is quite different. His output of directive, regulating regones, already rather high in Phase 1, climbed progressively higher throughout the next two phases and reached a peak in the tense minutes of Phase 3 when it seemed likely that the boat might be swamped. Thereafter, regone output subsided and for both subjects there was a fairly high frequency of metrones as each evaluated the other's behavior in the immediately preceding phase.

The state curves are rather similar, although quantitatively they indicate that Roz expressed the greater amount of negative affect, either anger or apprehension, in Phases 3 and 4.

Finally, the third pair of graphs highlights another difference between husband and wife. As soon as Roz took over the oars in Phase 2, her initial assertive, declarative, expressive orientation gave way to increased question-asking. This tendency continued to grow throughout Phase 3. For Jock, by contrast, the declarative, assertive mode was pre-eminent throughout all five phases of the episode.

Comparisons of dynamically scored utterances in Phases 3 and 4 expose an interesting relationship that may illustrate a widespread reaction to stress. Table 12.6 reports distribution of message types in per cent for each subject in each successive phase of the episode, and here the relationship between locus-direction scorings and the scoring of affect states is especially interesting. None of Roz' messages in Phase 3 are of neutral affect and only 23 per cent of Jock's utterances were so scored by the judges. Furthermore, during this phase Jock made very few statements that were scored for locus-direction changes. His major objective, apparently, was the production of regones intended to direct and control Roz' manipulation of the boat. Once the immediate danger was over, however, he reverted to a large number of ego-manipulating messages and the proportion of state-scored utterances dropped sharply. Similar shifts can be observed for Roz in these two phases.

Summarizing this episode, it is evident that in the initial phase Roz was relatively free in providing information about her own internal state and in making evaluative statements. She produced relatively few structones except in response to her husband's questions or in instigations that reported some observation about the environment. Once she took over the rowing, however, self-descriptive state messages increased, reflecting a growing ap-

TABLE 12.6

Comparison of Behaviors in Five Phases in Rowing Episode

	1		*2*		*3*		*4*		*5*	
	Roz	*Jock*	*Roz*	*Jock*	*Roz*	*Jock*	*Roz*	*Jock*	*Roz*	*Jock*
LOCUS DIRECTION										
↿	09	08	28	05	38	—	35	17	18	17
↾	03	—	03	05	—	03	25	07	04	07
⇂	15	08	07	15	—	03	—	03	09	14
↿⇂	—	—	—	—	—	—	05	31	14	10
⇃↾	—	—	—	—	—	—	—	—	02	02
↿↾	—	—	—	11	—	—	—	—	03	01
○	73	85	62	63	62	93	35	42	52	50
FUNCTIONAL TYPE										
Xp	09	15	07	—	19	17	—	—	15	06
Xc	—	—	07	—	—	—	—	—	02	—
S	33	27	45	21	19	03	35	07	29	19
M	36	15	24	26	14	23	35	34	32	28
R	15	23	10	37	10	53	10	45	09	23
St	09	19	07	16	38	03	20	14	13	24
STATE										
1[a]	—	—	—	—	05	—	—	—	—	—
2	21	19	17	—	—	—	—	07	08	07
3	03	—	—	—	10	17	—	—	06	04
4	12	04	17	05	86	57	40	17	30	16
5	—	—	—	—	—	03	—	—	—	—
0	64	66	66	95	00	23	60	76	56	73

[a] The numbers designate states as follows: 1 = highly positive; 2 = mildly positive; 3 = ambivalent; 4 = mildly negative; 5 = highly negative; 0 = neutral.

prehensiveness. At the peak of the crisis in Phase 3 she produced a good many requests for structones in an effort to learn quickly how better to control her environment, but when the crisis had passed, a delayed affective discharge occurred in the form of signones and metrones.

Jock's behavior here, by contrast, is best characterized by the high rate of production of regones. The initially high output continued to rise when Roz took over the oars and reached its peak in the crisis of Phase 3. Yet, even after the emergency had passed, he persisted in telling Roz what to do and attempted to re-create the superior-subordinate relation that existed prior to the crisis. In this situation regones and metrones apparently served two purposes for Jock. At certain points they functioned principally to enhance his ego, and at other times their objective was to control the environment and thus allay his anxiety. Jock's dominant position throughout was also reflected in the relatively low proportion of questions produced in this episode. Finally, Roz' messages about her own physical and psychological state (signones) closely paralleled her output of evaluating messages (metrones). For Jock, by contrast, information about his own physical or psychological state was not often or easily shared with his social environment.

Discussion

The single transcribed fragment presented earlier in the chapter and the statistical summaries of behavior in a few selected episodes hardly succeed in conveying the vividness and diversity with which individual styles of interaction emerge over longer periods of time. From the ecological and structural analyses, Jock stands out as a person who needed to avoid solitude. Although his choice of companions was somewhat limited by the restricted social environment in which this pilot run was carried out, he seemed nevertheless to be quite successful in devising new experiences and in ferreting out new people with whom to interact. By contrast with the male subject in a second couple studied several weeks later, Jock frequently took the initiative in reaching out to strangers in order to satisfy his strong need for continuous social stimulation. In implementing this objective he moved rather freely from place to place, sometimes in accordance with a preconceived plan but always with sufficient flexibility to be able to shift and take advantage of immediately available social opportunities. Roz showed far more capacity to spend the time alone or to be in close physical proximity to a relative stranger without immediately drawing that stranger into her social sphere. In this sense, then, she was considerably more independent, although in fact she made herself available almost continuously as a companion to her husband.

Not only in the episodes recorded here but elsewhere in the record, Jock's verbal behavior was characterized by longer units of speech and by a disproportionally large use of the available talking time. Although his behavior in this respect was quite variable, one tends to remember how easily and how frequently he seized upon available talking time, sometimes quite artlessly assuming the position of the most informed and most interesting member of a social group. Roz, too, showed herself to be a fairly spontaneous person in social situations but with the difference that she was much more sensitive both to her own impact on the group and to the possible interests and needs of other group members. Guided by this sensitivity, she frequently acted as a governor for Jock, often skillfully and tactfully and sometimes not so tactfully attenuating his impact on the group.

While the dynamic analysis highlights Jock's use of group situations to satisfy some of his ego-enhancing needs, only a sociogram would show with what singlemindedness he focused upon the behavior of the relative newcomer or relative stranger. For example, in the long breakfast and luncheon conversations Jock seemed hardly aware of his wife's presence. In this commensal situation theirs was largely a parallel rather than interactional relation as each directed almost all of his messages to the other couple.

One is moved to wonder how this young woman maintained her relatively high-spirited approach to life while under the seeming strain of the continuous claims upon her from Jock. One possible answer is that at least at this stage of her development, Roz tended to handle her moods and many of her needs intrapersonally rather than interactionally. When gay, she exploded with joy so that even the scorers tended to smile while listening to her playful banter, her impulsive demands to be kissed, her comic improvisations of songs, etc. Sometimes it seemed that such behavior was consciously used to change her husband's mood. Yet Roz was no timid sort; although she did "take" a good deal from her husband, she also had her limits of tolerance, as was clearly shown in the rowing episode, and if she gave easy vent to positive feelings, when the occasion warranted she was just as open with negative ones. Thus, her very freedom in expressing and dealing with feelings as they arose might have been one of the methods by which she neutralized the impact of her husband's personality and sometimes insulated herself from him.

Furthermore, seen from a slightly different perspective than is permitted by this particular selection of episodes, Jock was often far less exploitative and often far more considerate than some of these passages suggest. If eager for the admiration and approval of others, he could also be kind and friendly, compassionate and supportive. He exhibited a spontaneity and impulsiveness that, at least at that stage in their lives, complemented Roz' enthusiastic approach to life. Their relationship had its turbulences but also its share of mutually rewarding experiences, and for the turbulences there existed readily available mechanisms for restoring calm, as the following note exemplifies:

One morning Jock stepped into a telephone booth and made a long-distance call while his wife stood at a counter a few feet away purchasing some film. She could hear none of the conversation but *we* could. (As Roz knew, the conversation pertained to his work at home.) It was an annoying and upsetting piece of news he received. When he emerged from the telephone booth and his wife asked him what had happened, he shrugged off the question with a sound indicating irritation and said no more.

Shortly thereafter they proceeded to walk up the hill toward the craft shop where they customarily spent an hour or two each morning. Ordinarily as they walked up the path it was a playful, pleasant saunter. They would tease, laugh, and sometimes one would stop the other and demand a kiss. But on this morning, following the phone call, the walk was different. The playful banter was a little sharp. The gentle jostling or tickling that sometimes went on now took the form of a nudge by Jock that was hard enough to send his wife falling, and when she complained he made only a token apology.

Once at the craft shop where they customarily worked together, he teased her for several minutes, threatening to go off and leave her alone, and when finally induced to stay, he made several ridiculing and disparaging remarks about her handiwork. So the day went, edgy, slightly strained, each interlude of friendliness cut short by some sharp remark by Jock.

A thunderstorm late in the afternoon forced them into the cottage and the interaction there was sufficiently trying for the wife so that a violent argument broke out. At this point I had to leave the monitoring station and drive to an adjoining town and I did so with great reluctance, seriously worried that this outbreak might mean the end of my project. On returning two hours later I rushed into the station and put on the earphones, to hear only silence. It was raining still so that the subjects could not be wandering around the grounds. As I listened more intently for a few seconds there was a quiet rustling and then a soft, low, barely audible whisper. Then some laughter. They were lying on the bed listening to the rain and making the kind of idle talk that intimates often engage in. There was no trace of strain or ill-feeling.

Then the rain subsided and they spent the rest of the evening at a concert. By midnight a beautiful full moon had risen over the lake. They walked down to sit on the docks and gradually there unfolded the husband's apology for his behavior throughout the day.[12]

In trying to account for his behavior during the day Jock made no reference to the morning's telephone call, which the monitor regarded as a critical determinant, and neither did his wife. Nevertheless, the apology led to a long discussion about their relationship, its problems, Jock's needs, their future, etc., and by the time the station was turned off a half-hour later a harmony missing throughout the day was again restored.

The methods of observation of recording and analysis used in this study do effectively delineate some of the coping behavior of ordinary human beings relating to each other in a naturalistic setting. It is evident from the preceding paragraphs, however, that either because of the specific behavior samples chosen for analysis or because of the limited range of episodes included in this study, the important facets of the relationship between Roz and Jock are not adequately illuminated even by these complex methods. Having entered the privacy of our subjects precisely to study the relation between behavior in private and public domains and to study continuities that extend from one into the other, we were not too surprised to discover that their public behavior deviated significantly from their more private interactions. What interested us more was the confirmation that some important dimensions of these different styles of behavior can be operationally specified and quantified.

[12] From Soskin, William F., An approach to the study of social behavior, Unpublished paper read at the 25th anniversary of the Society for the Study of Child Development, Bethesda, Maryland, 1958.

Conclusion

This paper describes some of the preliminary work in a program of research on person-environment interaction as revealed in the analysis of spontaneous talk. It is a study of the syndetic relation between man and his environment, by means of which the former achieves, maintains, relieves, or avoids certain internal states. In one direction the program aims at an extremely general statement of the frequency, duration, and diversity of contacts through which these state changes are effected. In a different direction it seeks to identify the kinds of verbal acts that are produced under various conditions either to instigate change or to adjust to modifications in the social environment.

Talk is the behavior of choice for this kind of study because it is so preeminently the vehicle for effecting relation changes, and also because recent technological developments make it possible to gain access to the totality of a subject's output under nonexperimental conditions over a relatively long period of time.

The analysis of macrosamples of spontaneous talk requires the use of multidimensional tools. Ecological data help identify the resources for and impediments to interaction as well as identifying circumstantial factors that influence the character of talking behavior. Structural analysis provides direct quantitative expression of the frequency of contact, the duration of interactions and the relative accessibility of talking time under different conditions. Functional analyses illuminate the varieties of talk which occur in different social contexts and with changing internal states. To date, the most interesting findings from the functional analyses are that the greatest similarity between the husband and wife appeared in social settings (lunch and breakfast) which call for a relatively heavy reliance on *informational language,* and the greatest difference between the two subjects of this study were in social contexts of greater intimacy where much of their talk consisted of *relational language*. The dynamic analyses reveal two kinds of changes that occur during interaction behavior: (1) a deviation from a neutral affective state which may occur as a result of events external to interpersonal interaction (i.e., phase 3 in the rowing episode) or may occur as a function of more subtle changes of mood, and (2) changes in locus-direction, which consist in one of the interactants' attempting to produce a change of state in himself or the listener by means of talk. These two types of dynamic change seem to function in a complementary fashion: during some phases of an episode messages are characterized by heavy state-loadings; in other phases, the locus-direction categories are of greater utility in characterizing the interaction.

The nature of this study precluded the formulation of hypotheses at the outset. It is only at the conclusion of this exploratory work that the investigators are in a position to suggest certain relationships between social-environmental events and the type, frequency and intensity of talking behavior that are likely to be forthcoming under these conditions. Most of the results in this paper are descriptive in nature. The data are ordered primarily with reference to individual differences and indicate, for example, whether one person is more talkative, labile, or controlling than another. This emphasis on individual differences is somewhat an artifact of the types of analyses carried out in this study. The "stream of talk" was divided into idea-units, analyzed according to the three levels of the scoring system, and summated by episodes. Thus, the grossest and most stable features of communicative behavior characteristic of an individual in a particular social setting are revealed. But the more specific mechanisms of regulatory behavior can only be studied when the data are approached in a more sequential fashion.

These results, then, though interesting for diagnostic purposes, particularly in the light of the great difficulty in accurately predicting or postdicting specific behaviors with existing clinical tools (Soskin, 1959), make only a modest contribution to the understanding of person-environment relations, where the emphasis must necessarily be on *process*. In the preceding results section process is reflected in the shifts that occur in proportions of acts at different stages in time. More important for the understanding of the economics of interactions will be studies of the sequential probabilities associated with different verbal acts.

REFERENCES

Allport, F. H. *Theories of perception and the concept of structure.* New York: Wiley, 1955.

Allport, G. W. *Personality.* New York: Holt, Rinehart and Winston, 1937.

Allport, G. W. The use of personal documents in psychological science. New York: Soc. Sci. Res. Council, *Bull.,* 1942, No. 49.

American Association for Advancement of Science, Annual Meeting Awards. *Science,* 1959, **129,** 138.

Angyal, A. *Foundations for a science of personality.* New York: Commonwealth Fund, 1941.

Ashby, W. R. *An introduction to cybernetics.* New York: Wiley, 1956.

Baldwin, A. L. *Behavior and development in childhood.* New York: Holt, Rinehart and Winston, 1955.

Baldwin, A. L., Kalhorn, Joan, & Breese, F. H. Patterns of parent behavior. *Psychol. Monogr.,* 1945, **58,** No. 3 (Whole No. 268).

Baldwin, A. L., Kalhorn, Joan, & Breese, F. H. The appraisal of parent behavior. *Psychol. Monogr.,* 1949, **63,** No. 4 (Whole No. 299).

Bales, R. F. *Interaction process analysis.* Cambridge: Addison-Wesley, 1950.

Barker, R. G. Ecology and motivation. In M. R. Jones (Ed.), *Nebraska symposium on motivation.* Lincoln: Univer. Nebraska Press, 1960. Pp. 1–49.

Barker, R. G., & Barker, Louise S. Behavior units for the comparative study of cultures. In B. Kaplan (Ed.), *Studying personality cross-culturally.* New York: Harper & Row, 1961. Pp. 457–476.

Barker, R. G., Schoggen, Maxine F., & Barker, Louise S. Hemerography of Mary Ennis. In A. Burton and R. Harris (Eds.), *Clinical studies of personality.* New York: Harper & Row, 1955. Pp. 768–808.

Barker, R. G., & Wright, H. F. Psychological ecology and the problem of psychosocial development. *Child Develpm.,* 1949, **20,** 131–143.

Barker, R. G., & Wright, H. F. *One boy's day.* New York: Harper & Row, 1951a.

Barker, R. G., & Wright, H. F. The psychological habitat of Raymond Birch. In J. Rohrer and M. Sherif (Eds.), *Social psychology at the crossroads.* New York: Harper & Row, 1951b. Pp. 196–212.

Barker, R. G., & Wright, H. F. *Midwest and its children.* New York: Harper & Row, 1955.

Barker, R. G., Wright, H. F., Barker, Louise S., & Schoggen, Maxine. *Specimen records of American and English children.* Univer. Kansas Press, 1961.

Barker, R. G., Wright, H. F., & Koppe, W. A. The psychological ecology of a small town. In W. Dennis (Ed.), *Readings in child psychology.* Englewood Cliffs, N.J.: Prentice-Hall, 1951. Pp. 552–566.

Barker, R. G., Wright, H. F., Nall, J., & Schoggen, P. There is no class bias in our school. *Progressive Educ.,* 1950, **27,** 106–110.

Barnes, R. M. *Motion and time study.* (4th ed.) New York: Wiley, 1958.

Beals, E. W., & Cottam, G. The forest vegetation of the Apostle Islands, Wisconsin. *Ecology,* 1960, **41,** 743–751.

Blatz, W. E., Chant, S. N. F., & Salter, M. D. Emotional episodes in the child of school age. *Univer. Toronto Stud., Child Develpm. Ser.,* 1937, No. 9.

Brim, O. G. The parent-child relation as a social system, parent and child roles. *Child Develpm.,* 1957, **28,** 343–364.

Brunswik, E. The conceptual framework of psychology. *International encyclopedia of unified science.* Chicago: Univer. Chicago Press, 1955, Vol. 1, Part II, 656–750.

Champney, H. Measurement of parent behavior. *Child Develpm.,* 1941a, **12,** 131–166.

Champney, H. The variables of parent behavior. *J. abnorm. soc. Psychol.,* 1941b, **36,** 525–542.

Chapple, E. D. Measuring human relations: an introduction to the story of the interaction of individuals. *Genet. Psychol. Monogr.,* 1940, **22,** 3–147.

Chapple, E. D. The interaction chronograph: its evaluation and present application. *Personnel,* 1949, **25,** 295–307.

Cronbach, L. J. The two disciplines of scientific psychology. *Amer. Psychol.,* 1957, **12,** 671, 684.

Dewey, J. *Psychology.* New York: Harper & Row, 1891.

Dittmann, A. T. Problems of reliability in observing and coding social interactions. *J. consult. Psychol.,* 1958, **22,** 430.

Dyck, A. J. A study in psychological ecology: a description of the social contacts of twelve Midwest children with their parents. Unpublished master's thesis. Univer. of Kansas, 1958.

Fawl, C. L. Disturbances experienced by children in their natural habitats: a study in psychological ecology. Unpublished doctoral dissertation, Univer. of Kansas, 1959.

Festinger, L. Assumptions underlying the use of statistical techniques. In Marie Jahoda, M. Deutsch, and S. Cook (Eds.), *Research methods in social relations.* New York: Holt, Rinehart and Winston, 1951. Pp. 713–726.

Gamow, G. *Matter, earth, and sky.* Englewood Cliffs, N.J.: Prentice-Hall, 1958.

Goldman-Eisler, F. Measurement of time sequences in conversational behavior. *Brit. J. Psychol.,* 1951, 355–362.

Goldman-Eisler, F. A study of individual differences and interaction in the behavior of some aspects of language in interviews. *J. ment. Sci.,* 1954, **100,** 177–197.

Goodenough, Florence. *Anger in young children.* Minneapolis: Univer. Minn. Press, 1931.

Greig-Smith, P. *Quantitative plant ecology.* New York: Academic Press, Inc., 1957.

Gump, P., Schoggen, P., & Redl, F. The camp milieu and its immediate effects. *J. soc. Issues,* 1957, **13,** No. 1, 40–46.

Gump, P., & Sutton-Smith, B. Activity-setting and social interaction. *Amer. J. Orthopsychiat.,* 1955a, **25,** 755–760.

Gump, P., & Sutton-Smith, B. The it role in children's games. *The Group,* 1955b, **17,** 3–8.

Hargreaves, W. A. An investigation of time periods in spontaneous conversation. Unpublished master's thesis, Univer. of Chicago, 1955.

Hargreaves, W. A. A model for speech unit duration. *Lang. and Speech,* 1960, **3,** 164–173.

Heider, F. *The psychology of interpersonal relations.* New York: Wiley, 1958.

Henle, Mary. On field forces. *J. Psychol.,* 1957, **43,** 239–249.

Heyns, R. W., & Lippett, R. Systematic observational techniques. In G. Lindzey (Ed.), *Handbook of social psychology.* Cambridge: Addison-Wesley, 1954, Vol. 1. Pp. 370–404.

Hoffman, M. L. Power assertion by the parent and its impact on the child. *Child Develpm.,* 1961, **31,** 127–143.

Hurlock, Elizabeth B. *Child development.* New York: McGraw-Hill, 1956.

Inselberg, Rachel M. The causation and manifestations of emotional behavior in Filipino children. *Child Develpm.,* 1958, **29,** 249–254.

Isaacs, Susan. *Social development in young children.* London: Routledge & Kegan Paul, 1933.

Jenny, H. Role of the plant factor in pedogenic functions. *Ecology,* 1958, **39,** 5–16.

Kendall, M. *Rank correlation methods.* London: Charles Griffin, 1948.

Ladd, G. T. *Outlines of descriptive psychology.* New York: Scribner, 1898.

Leighton, A. H. *My name is legion.* New York: Basic Books, 1959.

Leeper, R. *Lewin's topological and vector psychology: a digest and critique.* Eugene: Univer. Oregon Press, 1943.

Lerner, D. (Ed.), *Quantity and quality.* New York: Macmillan, 1961.

Lewin, K. *Dynamic theory of personality.* New York: McGraw-Hill, 1935.

Lewin, K. Forces behind food habits and methods of change. *Bull. of the National Research Council,* 1943, **108,** 35–65.

Lewin, K. *Field theory in social science.* New York: Harper & Row, 1951.

Lindsley, D. B. Emotion. In S. S. Stevens (Ed.), *Handbook of experimental psychology.* (Rev. ed.) New York: Wiley, 1951. Pp. 473–516.

Lyons, J. The perception of human action. *J. gen. Psychol.,* 1956, **54,** 45–55.

McCarthy, Dorothea A. Language development of the preschool child, *Inst. Child Welf. Monogr.,* 1930, No. 2. Minneapolis: Univer. Minn. Press.

Mead, Margaret. *Growing up in New Guinea.* New York: Morrow, 1930.

Millen, Clarice. Influence of camp activity-settings on impulsivity in the disturbed child. Unpublished master's thesis, Wayne State Univer., 1958.

Miller, G. A., Galanter, E., & Pribram, K. H. *Plans and the structure of behavior.* New York: Holt, Rinehart and Winston, 1960.

Morris, C. *Signs, language, and behavior.* New York: Prentice-Hall, 1946.

Muenzinger, K. F. *Psychology: the science of behavior.* New York: Harper & Row, 1939.

Murray, H. A. Preparations for the scaffold of a comprehensive system. In S. Koch (Ed.), *Psychology: a study of a science.* New York: McGraw-Hill, 1959, Vol. 3. Pp. 7–54.

Muse, Marianne. Time expenditures in homemaking activities in 183 Vermont farm homes. *Vermont Agriculture Experiment Station Bull.,* 1946, No. 530.

National organizations of the United States. *Encyclopedia of associations.* (3rd ed.) Vol. 1, 315. Detroit: Research Co., 1961.

Nichols, T. F., & Schoggen, P. Children's behavior in terms of episode initiation, termination, and completion. Paper read at Amer. Psychol. Ass., Chicago, 1956.

Ogden, C. K., & Richards, I. A. *The meaning of meaning.* (Rev. ed.) New York: Harcourt, Brace & World, 1947.

Parsons, T. An approach to psychological theory in terms of the theory of action. In S. Koch (Ed.), *Psychology: a study of a science.* New York: McGraw-Hill, 1959, Vol. 3. Pp. 612–711.

Piaget, J. *The language and thought of the child.* New York: Harcourt, Brace & World, 1920.

Pittinger, R. E., Hockett, C. F., & Danehy, J. J. *The first five minutes: a sample of microscopic interview analysis.* Ithaca, N.Y.: Paul Martineau, 1960.

Radke, Marian. Relation of parental authority to children's behavior and attitudes. *Inst. Child Welf. Monogr.,* No. 22. Minneapolis: Univer. Minn. Press, 1946.

Raush, H. L. On the locus of behavior-observations in multiple settings within residential treatment. *Amer. J. Orthopsychiat.,* 1959, **29,** 235–243.

Raush, H. L., Dittmann, A. T., & Taylor, T. J. The interpersonal behavior of children in residential treatment. *J. abnorm. soc. Psychol.,* 1959a, **58,** 9–27.

Raush, H. L., Dittmann, A. T., & Taylor, T. J. Person, setting and change in social interaction. *Human Relat.,* 1949b, **12,** No. 4, 361–378.

Raush, H. L., Dittmann, A. T., & Taylor, T. J. Person, setting, and change in social interaction: II. A normal control study. *Human Relat.,* 1960, **13,** No. 4, 305–332.

Redl, F., & Wineman, D. *Children who hate.* Glencoe, Ill.: Macmillan, 1951.

Ricketts, Agnes. A study of the behavior of young children in anger. *Univer. Iowa Stud. Child Welf.,* 1934, No. 9, **3,** 159–171.

Roby, T. An opinion of the construction of behavior theory. *Amer. Psychologist,* 1959, **14,** 129–134.

Schoggen, P. A study in psychological ecology: a description of the behavior objects which entered the psychological habitat of an eight-year-old girl during the course of one day. Unpublished master's thesis, Univer. of Kansas, 1951.

Schoggen, P. A study in psychological ecology: structural properties of children's behavior based on sixteen day-long specimen records. Unpublished doctoral dissertation, Univer. of Kansas, 1954.

Schoggen, P. Environmental force unit analysis. Unpublished data, Midwest Psychological Field Station, Univer. of Kansas, 1957.

Shaw, Carolyn H. *Book of manners.* McCall's Corp., 1957.

Sidman, M. *Tactics of scientific research.* New York: Basic Books, 1960.

Siegel, S. *Nonparametric statistics for the behavioral sciences.* New York: McGraw-Hill, 1956.

Simpson, J. E. A study in psychological ecology: social weather of children in the behavior settings of Midwest. Unpublished doctoral dissertation, Univer. of Kansas, 1956.

Skinner, B. F. *The behavior of organisms.* New York: Appleton-Century-Crofts, 1938.

Skinner, B. F. *Verbal behavior.* New York: Appleton-Century-Crofts, 1957.

Sorokin, P., & Berger, C. Q. *Time-budgets of human behavior.* Cambridge: Harvard Univer. Press, 1939.

Soskin, W. F., & Kaufman, P. E. Judgment of emotion in word-free voice samples. *J. Communication,* 1961.

Soskin, W. F. Influence of four types of data on diagnostic conceptualization in psychological testing. *J. abnorm. soc. Psychol.,* 1959, **58,** 69–78.

Soskin, W. F. *Verbal interaction in a young married couple.* Univer. Kansas Press, in press, 1963.

Stern, W. *General psychology.* New York: Holt, Rinehart and Winston, 1938.

Tolman, E. C. *Purposive behavior in animals and man.* New York: Century, 1932.

Verzeano, M. Time patterns of speech in normal subjects. *J. Speech Hearing Disorders,* 1951a, **15,** 197–201.

Verzeano, M. Time patterns of speech in normal subjects. *J. Speech Hearing Disorders,* 1951b, **16,** 346–350.

von Hippel, A. Molecular engineering. *Science,* 1956, **123,** 315–317.

Walker, Helen M., & Lev, J. *Statistical inference.* New York: Holt, Rinehart and Winston, 1953.

Walters, J., Pearce, Doris, & Dahms, Lucille. Affectional and aggressive behavior of preschool children. *Child Develpm.,* 1957, **28,** 15–26.

Watson, J. B. *Behaviorism.* New York: Norton, 1924.

Weiskopf, V. F. Quality and quantity in quantum physics. In D. Lerner (Ed.), *Quantity and quality.* New York: Macmillan, 1961. Pp. 53–67.

White, R. W. *Lives in progress.* New York: Holt, Rinehart and Winston, 1952.

Wilks, S. S. *Elementary statistical analysis.* Princeton Univer. Press, 1948.

Wright, H. F. Observational child study. In P. H. Mussen (Ed.), *Handbook of research methods in child development.* New York: Wiley, 1960. Pp. 71–139.

Wright, H. F., & Barker, R. G. The elementary school does not stand alone. *Progressive Educ.,* 1950a, **27,** 133–137.

Wright, H. F., & Barker, R. G. *Methods in psychological ecology, a progress report.* Private printing, 1950b.

Wright, H. F., Barker, R. G., Koppe, W. A., Meyerson, Beverly, & Nall, J. Children at home in Midwest. *Progressive Educ.,* 1951, **28,** 137–143.

Wright H. F., Barker, R. G., Nall, J., & Schoggen, P. Toward a psychological ecology of the classroom. In A. P. Coladarci (Ed.), *Readings in educational psychology.* New York: Holt, Rinehart and Winston, 1955. Pp. 254–268.

APPENDIX 1.1

Sources of Specimen Records

THE SPECIMEN DAY RECORDS which provided some of the primary data for the studies reported in Chapters 3, 4, 5, 6, 7, 8, 9, and 11 are identified in the lists below. Throughout this book all persons and places taken from the records are given the pseudonyms used in the records. Identifying data are reported in the following form: Code name of child (sex, social class, age); date of record; time of record.

Additional information about sixteen of the children and their families (all of the children except Wally O'Neill) is provided in *Midwest and Its Children* (Barker & Wright, 1955) Appendix 1.1 and Appendix 1.2. Additional information about Wally O'Neill is given in Chapter 9 of this book.

The record of Wally O'Neill was made by Paul V. Gump and Phil Schoggen who hold the copyright. The other day records were made by the staff of the Midwest Psychological Field Station. The copyright of the record of Bobby Bryant is held by Roger G. Barker, Herbert F. Wright, and Mariana Remple; that of all other records by Roger G. Barker and Herbert F. Wright.

TWELVE MIDWEST CHILDREN

Mary Chaco, (F, 2, 1–10); October 10, 1950; 7:00 a.m.–9:45 p.m.
James Sexton, (M, 2, 1–11); February 8, 1951; 7:20 a.m.–8:10 p.m.
Lewis Hope, (M, 2, 2–11); November 21, 1950; 7:00 a.m.–9:15 p.m.
Dutton Thurston, (M, 3, 3–10); November 3, 1950; 7:06 a.m.–9:16 p. m.
Margaret Reid, (F, 3, 4–6); June 2, 1949; 8:00 a.m.–10:17 p.m.
Maud Pintner, (F, 1, 5–0); December 5, 1950; 8:26 a.m.–7:44 p.m.
Roy Eddy, (M, 3, 6–2); February 22, 1949; 7:00 a.m.–8:31 p.m.
Raymond Birch, (M, 2, 7–4); April 26, 1949; 7:00 a.m.–8:33 p.m.
Benjamin Hutchings, (M, 1, 7–4); November 23, 1949; 7:33 a.m.–8:00 p.m.
Mary Ennis, (F, 2, 8–7); May 12, 1949; 7:00 a.m.–9:25 p.m.
Douglas Crawford, (M, 2, 9–2); April 18, 1949; 7:28 a.m.–9:45 p.m.
Claire Graves, (F, 3, 10–9); January 28, 1949; 7:20 a.m.–9:40 p.m.

FOUR PHYSICALLY DISABLED CHILDREN

Sue Dewall, (F, 4, 7–1); June 6, 1951; 6:30 a.m.–8:08 p.m.
Verne Trennell, (M, 3, 7–5); June 21, 1951; 7:00 a.m.–9:32 p.m.
Wally Wolfson, (M, 3, 4–3); July 9, 1951; 8:00 a.m.–7:35 p.m.
Bobby Bryant, (M, 2, 7–4); March 26, 1949; 8:35 a.m.–9:42 p.m.

THE SAME CHILD IN DIFFERENT MILIEUS

Wally O'Neill at camp, (M, 2, 9–4); August 17, 1954; 7:23 a.m.–9:03 p.m.
Wally O'Neill at home, (M, 2, 9–4); August 26, 1954; 7:02 a.m.–8:20 p.m.

The specimen behavior setting records which provided the primary data for the study reported in Chapter 7 are in Barker, Wright, Barker and Schoggen (1961). Data identifying and describing the children are reported in this book.

APPENDIX 1.2

Sample Specimen Records Illustrating Some Units of the Behavior Stream: Episodes, Social Contracts, Environmental Force Units, and Social Actions

A MIDWEST AND A YOREDALE specimen behavior setting record are reproduced below with the kinds of behavior stream units used in Chapters 3, 4, 5, 7, 8, 9, 10 marked upon them. These are records Midwest 13 and Yoredale 13 of Chapter 7, Table 7.2. These actual units were not used in Chapters 3, 4, 5, 9, or 10 but the kinds of unit used in these chapters are demonstrated. The actual social action units and episodes marked are part of the data for Chapters 7 and 8.

The following conventions are used in marking the units on these records:

Behavior Episodes. Episodes are identified by the outer tier of brackets on the left side of the record; they are numbered consecutively from Writing Spelling Lesson at Blackboard (1), Midwest 13 and Writing News in Copybook (1), Yoredale 13. Episodes have no other identifications on the records.

Social Contact Units. Social contacts are identified by the inner tier of brackets on the left side of the record. They are identified and numbered consecutively, e.g., Social Contact 1, Social Contact 2, etc.; and in addition there is an identification of the agent of the contact: T = teacher; P = playmate; O = observer. The remaining symbols, e.g., IA1 (contact 1, Midwest 13) identify the *raison d'être* category of the contact; see Chapter 5.

Environmental Force Units (*EFU*) are identified by the brackets on the right margin of the record. They are identified, numbered consecutively, and named, e.g., EFU1 Teacher: Planning Next Activity with Class (Midwest 13). The name of the EFU reports the environmental agent and his action vis-à-vis the subject of the record. For details see Chapter 3.

Social Actions. Each social action is identified by name in italics following its occurrence in the record. See Chapter 7 and Appendix 7.2 for definitions of the social actions identified. The same social action may occur elsewhere in the same record but it is only noted once.

MIDWEST NUMBER 13

Setting: School, Fourth Grade, Academic (Spelling)
Subject: Raymond Birch Age: 9 Yrs. 0 Mos. Sex: Male Class: II
Day and Date: Wednesday, March 7, 1951 Time: 2:41–3:00 p.m.
Observer: Louise Barker
Description of Subject: Raymond Birch is a broad, stocky, round-faced boy. He has a ready smile. On this day he was neatly dressed in jeans and a bright shirt.
Description of Setting: The children had just come in from recess. The work at the board was practice—comparing answers with one's neighbor was entirely permissible. Later, during the test, each child was expected to pay strict attention to his own work.

The room was comfortably warm, the light adequate. It was a cool, bright day. This period immediately follows recess. The children came in from recess, talking and laughing, as they came into the room.

Writing Spelling Lesson at Blackboard (1)

EFU 1 Teacher: Planning Next Activity with Class

TIA1 — *Social Contact 1*

2:41 Mrs. Drouet called them to order very briefly and said, "We've talked it over and decided it might be better to do our practice spelling at the board."

She asked if they would like to do that.

Adult Provides Opportunity for Child

The class in general indicated that they would.

Child Accepts Adult's Control

TIA1 — *Social Contact 2*

She said pleasantly, "All right, then, you may go to the board."

The class went to the board, with the exception of Raymond Pechter, who sat in his seat.

Raymond Birch took a place at the east blackboard between Douglas Kerr and Susy Norman.

Ben Hutchings was at the south end, then Douglas Kerr, Raymond Birch, and then Susy Norman.

Raymond immediately started to number from one to fourteen on the board in two columns.

He wrote very small letters, much smaller than most of the other children and he left only small spaces between his numbers.

Getting New Chalk from Teacher (2)

EFU 2 Teacher: Giving Chalk to Pupils

TIA3 — *Social Contact 3*

Mrs. Drouet said pleasantly from the front of the room, "I think I have some new chalk."

2:42 She said with tolerance, "I suppose everybody will want long chalk if I start to give it to any of you." Many of the children immediately came to get chalk.

Raymond Birch came up eagerly to get his chalk.

The teacher said mildly reproving, "Please, let me take it and give it to you."

I judged that some of them were starting to reach

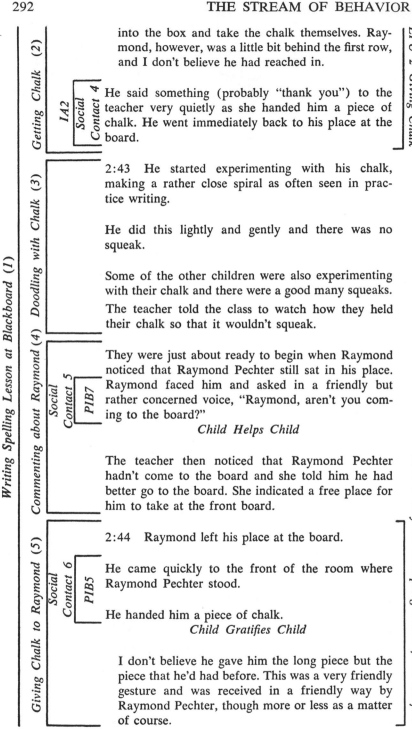

Writing Spelling Lesson at Blackboard (1)

Getting Chalk (2)

EFU 2 Giving Chalk

into the box and take the chalk themselves. Raymond, however, was a little bit behind the first row, and I don't believe he had reached in.

IA2

Social Contact 4

He said something (probably "thank you") to the teacher very quietly as she handed him a piece of chalk. He went immediately back to his place at the board.

Doodling with Chalk (3)

2:43 He started experimenting with his chalk, making a rather close spiral as often seen in practice writing.

He did this lightly and gently and there was no squeak.

Some of the other children were also experimenting with their chalk and there were a good many squeaks.

The teacher told the class to watch how they held their chalk so that it wouldn't squeak.

Commenting about Raymond (4)

Social Contact 5

PIB7

They were just about ready to begin when Raymond noticed that Raymond Pechter still sat in his place. Raymond faced him and asked in a friendly but rather concerned voice, "Raymond, aren't you coming to the board?"

Child Helps Child

The teacher then noticed that Raymond Pechter hadn't come to the board and she told him he had better go to the board. She indicated a free place for him to take at the front board.

Giving Chalk to Raymond (5)

EFU 3 Ray P.: Accepting Chalk from Subject

2:44 Raymond left his place at the board.

Social Contact 6

PIB5

He came quickly to the front of the room where Raymond Pechter stood.

He handed him a piece of chalk.

Child Gratifies Child

I don't believe he gave him the long piece but the piece that he'd had before. This was a very friendly gesture and was received in a friendly way by Raymond Pechter, though more or less as a matter of course.

Raymond then went back to his place at the board. He stood there waiting expectantly for the teacher to say the first word.

He waited only a matter of seconds. He just got back in time for the first word, which was "can't."

The teacher pronounced the word clearly. She said plainly, "can't, can't. It is short for cannot." She then used the word in a sentence.

Adult Manages Child

She followed this procedure with each word.

Raymond wrote the word quickly. He started to write as soon as she gave the word the first time.

Child Complies with Adult

He was ready for the second word as soon as Mrs. Drouet gave it.

The word was "showed." "She showed us her lovely jewelry," was her sentence.

Raymond wrote "showed" very rapidly.

Then he wrote the word "plate" directly under it without instructions.

After he had written "plate" he showed it rather complacently to Douglas Kerr who stood next to him.

He was guessing that "plate" would be the next word.

"Again" was actually the next word, with a sentence to explain it.

2:45 Raymond erased "plate" quickly with no disappointment evident.

He wrote "again" efficiently.

Writing Spelling Lesson at Blackboard (1)

Showing Word to Douglas (6)

TIA1 — *Social Contact 7*

TIA1 — *Social Contact 8*

PIB3 — *Social Contact 9*

TIA1 — *Social Contact 10*

EFU 5 Doug: Noting S's New Word

EFU 4 Teacher: Giving Spelling Words to Class

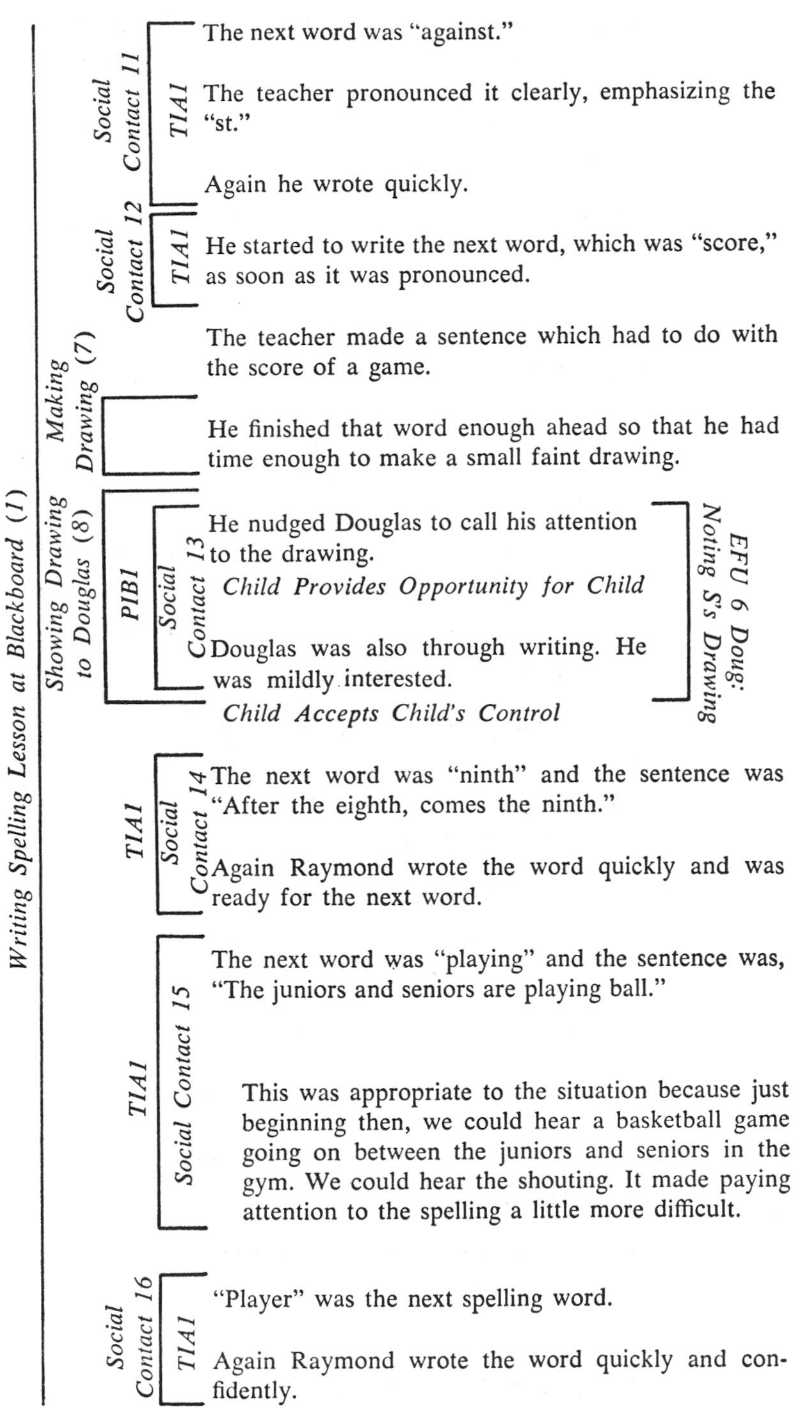

The next word was "against."

The teacher pronounced it clearly, emphasizing the "st."

Again he wrote quickly.

He started to write the next word, which was "score," as soon as it was pronounced.

The teacher made a sentence which had to do with the score of a game.

He finished that word enough ahead so that he had time enough to make a small faint drawing.

He nudged Douglas to call his attention to the drawing.

Child Provides Opportunity for Child

Douglas was also through writing. He was mildly interested.

Child Accepts Child's Control

The next word was "ninth" and the sentence was "After the eighth, comes the ninth."

Again Raymond wrote the word quickly and was ready for the next word.

The next word was "playing" and the sentence was, "The juniors and seniors are playing ball."

This was appropriate to the situation because just beginning then, we could hear a basketball game going on between the juniors and seniors in the gym. We could hear the shouting. It made paying attention to the spelling a little more difficult.

"Player" was the next spelling word.

Again Raymond wrote the word quickly and confidently.

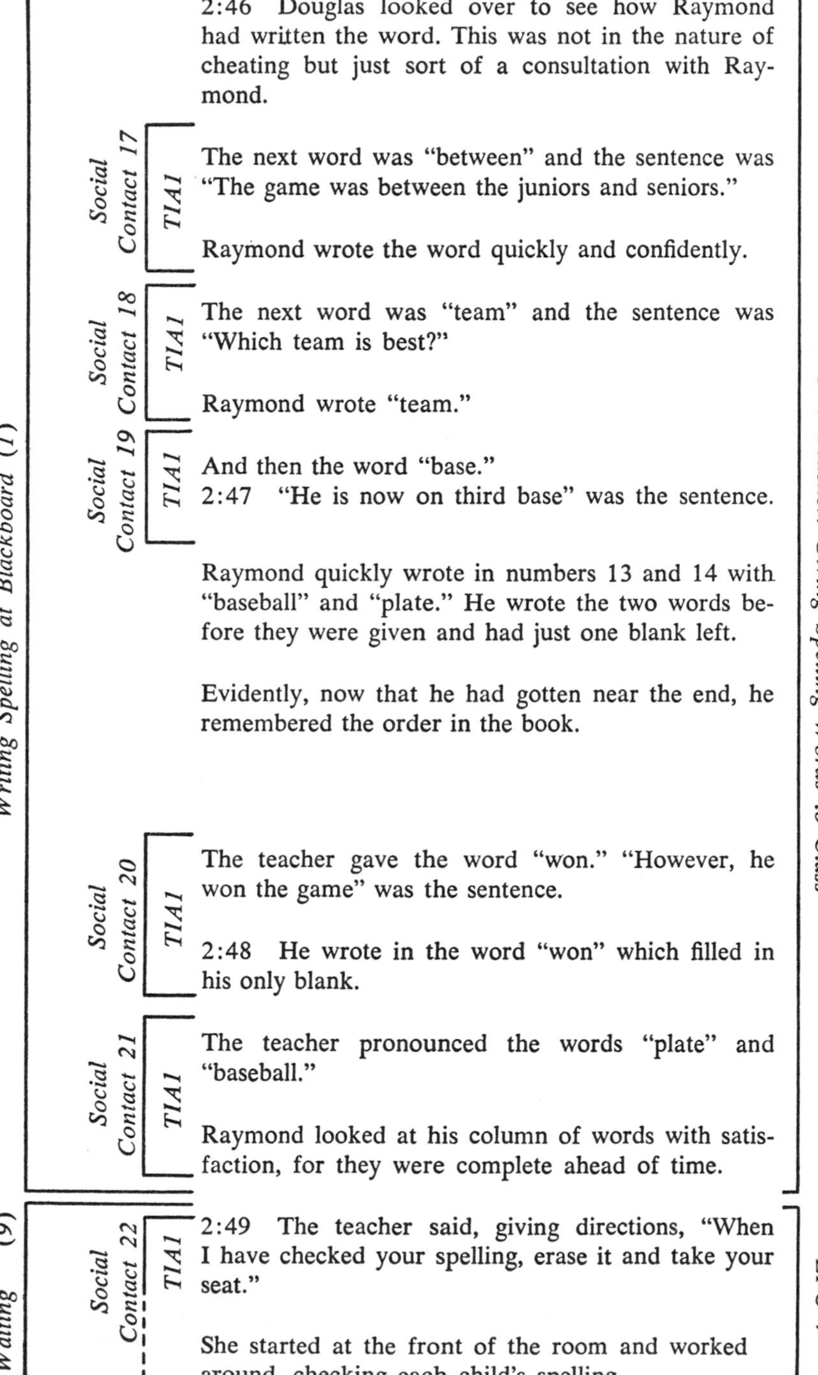

2:46 Douglas looked over to see how Raymond had written the word. This was not in the nature of cheating but just sort of a consultation with Raymond.

The next word was "between" and the sentence was "The game was between the juniors and seniors."

Raymond wrote the word quickly and confidently.

The next word was "team" and the sentence was "Which team is best?"

Raymond wrote "team."

And then the word "base."
2:47 "He is now on third base" was the sentence.

Raymond quickly wrote in numbers 13 and 14 with "baseball" and "plate." He wrote the two words before they were given and had just one blank left.

Evidently, now that he had gotten near the end, he remembered the order in the book.

The teacher gave the word "won." "However, he won the game" was the sentence.

2:48 He wrote in the word "won" which filled in his only blank.

The teacher pronounced the words "plate" and "baseball."

Raymond looked at his column of words with satisfaction, for they were complete ahead of time.

2:49 The teacher said, giving directions, "When I have checked your spelling, erase it and take your seat."

She started at the front of the room and worked around, checking each child's spelling.

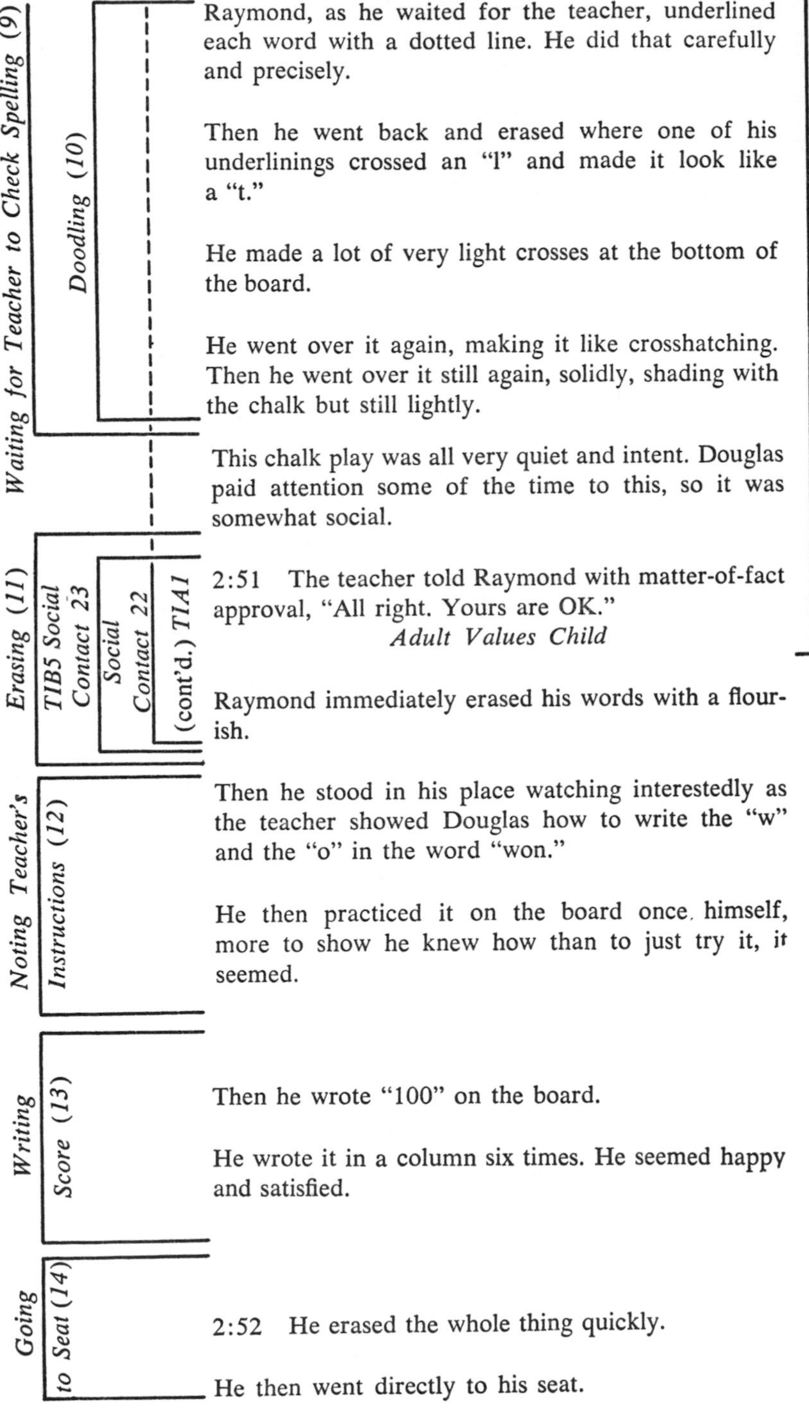

Raymond, as he waited for the teacher, underlined each word with a dotted line. He did that carefully and precisely.

Then he went back and erased where one of his underlinings crossed an "l" and made it look like a "t."

He made a lot of very light crosses at the bottom of the board.

He went over it again, making it like crosshatching. Then he went over it still again, solidly, shading with the chalk but still lightly.

This chalk play was all very quiet and intent. Douglas paid attention some of the time to this, so it was somewhat social.

2:51 The teacher told Raymond with matter-of-fact approval, "All right. Yours are OK."

Adult Values Child

Raymond immediately erased his words with a flourish.

Then he stood in his place watching interestedly as the teacher showed Douglas how to write the "w" and the "o" in the word "won."

He then practiced it on the board once, himself, more to show he knew how than to just try it, it seemed.

Then he wrote "100" on the board.

He wrote it in a column six times. He seemed happy and satisfied.

2:52 He erased the whole thing quickly.

He then went directly to his seat.

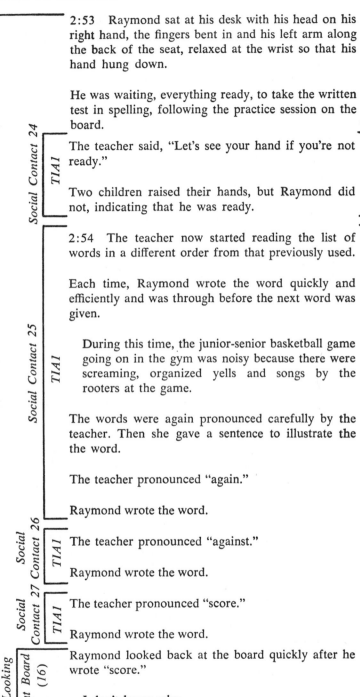

Writing Spelling Words at Desk (15)

EFU 8 T: Asking Pupils Whether Ready

2:53 Raymond sat at his desk with his head on his right hand, the fingers bent in and his left arm along the back of the seat, relaxed at the wrist so that his hand hung down.

He was waiting, everything ready, to take the written test in spelling, following the practice session on the board.

Social Contact 24 — TIA1

The teacher said, "Let's see your hand if you're not ready."

Two children raised their hands, but Raymond did not, indicating that he was ready.

EFU 9 Teacher: Giving Spelling Words to Class

Social Contact 25 — TIA1

2:54 The teacher now started reading the list of words in a different order from that previously used.

Each time, Raymond wrote the word quickly and efficiently and was through before the next word was given.

> During this time, the junior-senior basketball game going on in the gym was noisy because there were screaming, organized yells and songs by the rooters at the game.

The words were again pronounced carefully by the teacher. Then she gave a sentence to illustrate the the word.

The teacher pronounced "again."

Raymond wrote the word.

Social Contact 26 — TIA1

The teacher pronounced "against."

Raymond wrote the word.

Social Contact 27 — TIA1

The teacher pronounced "score."

Raymond wrote the word.

Looking at Board (16)

Raymond looked back at the board quickly after he wrote "score."

> I don't know why.

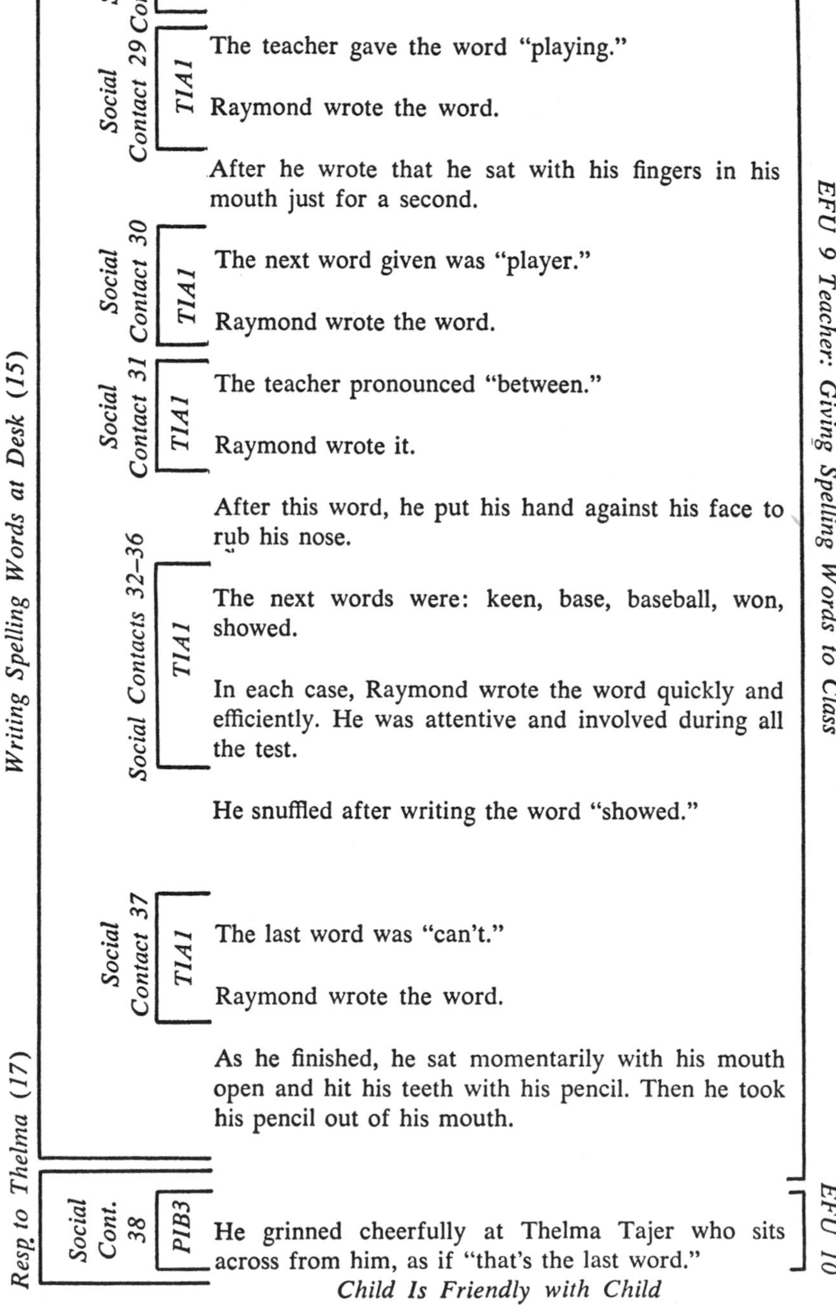

Writing Spelling Words at Desk (15) — *EFU 9 Teacher: Giving Spelling Words to Class*

Social Contact 28 — *TIA1*

The teacher continued with "ninth."

Raymond wrote the word.

Social Contact 29 — *TIA1*

The teacher gave the word "playing."

Raymond wrote the word.

After he wrote that he sat with his fingers in his mouth just for a second.

Social Contact 30 — *TIA1*

The next word given was "player."

Raymond wrote the word.

Social Contact 31 — *TIA1*

The teacher pronounced "between."

Raymond wrote it.

After this word, he put his hand against his face to rub his nose.

Social Contacts 32–36 — *TIA1*

The next words were: keen, base, baseball, won, showed.

In each case, Raymond wrote the word quickly and efficiently. He was attentive and involved during all the test.

He snuffled after writing the word "showed."

Social Contact 37 — *TIA1*

The last word was "can't."

Raymond wrote the word.

As he finished, he sat momentarily with his mouth open and hit his teeth with his pencil. Then he took his pencil out of his mouth.

Resp. to Thelma (17) — *EFU 10*

Social Cont. 38 — *PIB3*

He grinned cheerfully at Thelma Tajer who sits across from him, as if "that's the last word."

Child Is Friendly with Child

Looking at Book (18)

2:57 He got up quickly. He walked down the outside aisle to the bookcase at the back of the room. He picked up a book, "Mother Makes Christmas," that lay on the west end of the shelf.

He went back to his seat with the book.

2:58 He opened the book. He leafed through the pages.

> The teacher, in the meantime, repeated certain words when a child raised his hand and asked her to read the ninth or sixth word or whatever it was that he'd missed.

EFU 11 T: Giving Pupils Directions

When the questions were all answered, the teacher said, "As I check your papers, get your things ready for music."

Most of the children got out their things for music, as the teacher checked the spelling papers.

Raymond continued to look at his book, turning pages rather rapidly.

2:59 He turned quickly in his seat.

Looking for Another Book (19)

He went quickly back to the bookcase.

He put the book back on the shelf.

Then he opened the bookcase door.

He began pulling out one book and then another as if he were looking for a particular book, or at least a book that interested him.

Getting Ready for Music Class (20) / *Social Contact 39* / *TIA1* / *EFU 12 Teacher: Dismissing*

The teacher said, although she had not finished checking the spelling, "I expect Mrs. Madison is waiting for you now, so put your spellers away and get out your music things and be ready to go. Rise." Each child got a tonette from his desk.

Raymond came back without a book from the bookcase. Efficiently he got out his little plastic tonette and a folded piece of paper from his desk.

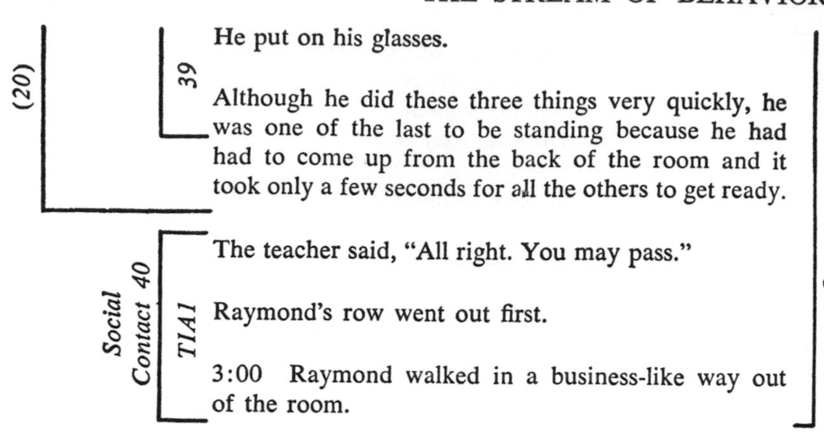

He put on his glasses.

Although he did these three things very quickly, he was one of the last to be standing because he had had to come up from the back of the room and it took only a few seconds for all the others to get ready.

The teacher said, "All right. You may pass."

Raymond's row went out first.

3:00 Raymond walked in a business-like way out of the room.

The whole spelling lesson seemed to be an opportunity of showing what he knew. He seemed to have a good time, feel secure in knowing how to spell the words, and in general to be very relaxed and pleased about the lesson.

YOREDALE NUMBER 13

Setting: County School, Lower Juniors, Academic (Writing)
Subject: Clifford Matthew Age: 8 Yrs. 6 Mos. Sex: Male Class: II
Day and Date: Monday, June 24, 1957 Time: 10:54–11:17 a.m.
Observer: Louise Barker
Description of Subject: Clifford Matthew is a sturdy, pleasant-faced boy with blue eyes and blond-brown hair. He is active in school and on the playground. His father is a government employee for the district. His mother teaches a one-room school. His younger sister, Alice, is in Miss Rutherford's class. Up till this year his best friend was Steven Dover who is now in a private preparatory school.
Description of Setting: From the older children in Miss Rutherford's room through Miss Culver's class the children write daily in their diaries, or news book. Each child writes his own news. The purpose is to get some fluency in expression. Miss Culver takes the spelling words she teaches from the words used in the children's writing. She will also put on the board any word a child asks for so that they will not be too hampered in their writing by their inability to spell. The writing is all done with a steel pen and ink in copybooks. Errors are placed in parentheses. At the beginning of this observation Miss Culver had already announced that it was time to write their news. Clifford is in Group Two in Miss Culver's class.

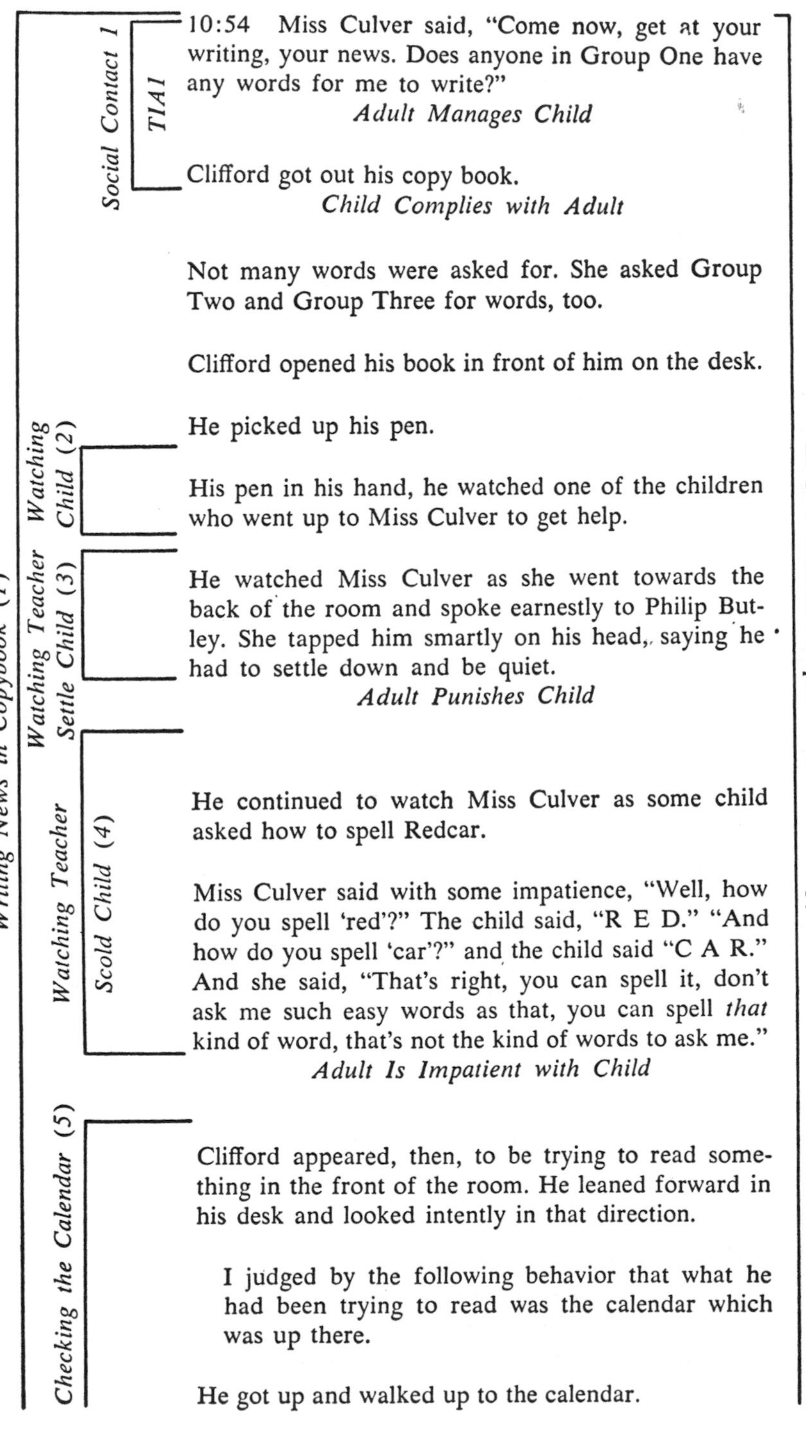

10:54 Miss Culver said, "Come now, get at your writing, your news. Does anyone in Group One have any words for me to write?"

Adult Manages Child

Clifford got out his copy book.

Child Complies with Adult

Not many words were asked for. She asked Group Two and Group Three for words, too.

Clifford opened his book in front of him on the desk.

He picked up his pen.

His pen in his hand, he watched one of the children who went up to Miss Culver to get help.

He watched Miss Culver as she went towards the back of the room and spoke earnestly to Philip Butley. She tapped him smartly on his head, saying he had to settle down and be quiet.

Adult Punishes Child

He continued to watch Miss Culver as some child asked how to spell Redcar.

Miss Culver said with some impatience, "Well, how do you spell 'red'?" The child said, "R E D." "And how do you spell 'car'?" and the child said "C A R." And she said, "That's right, you can spell it, don't ask me such easy words as that, you can spell *that* kind of word, that's not the kind of words to ask me."

Adult Is Impatient with Child

Clifford appeared, then, to be trying to read something in the front of the room. He leaned forward in his desk and looked intently in that direction.

> I judged by the following behavior that what he had been trying to read was the calendar which was up there.

He got up and walked up to the calendar.

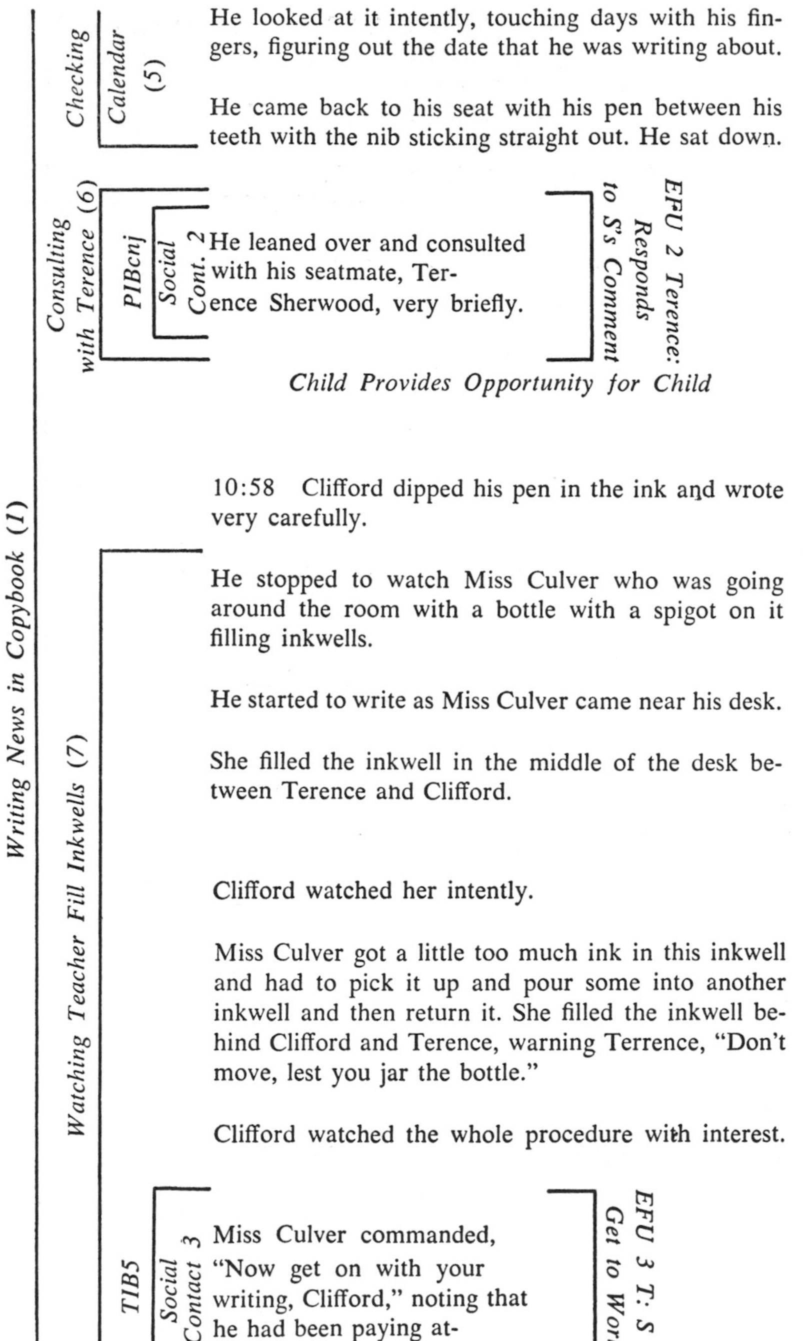

He looked at it intently, touching days with his fingers, figuring out the date that he was writing about.

He came back to his seat with his pen between his teeth with the nib sticking straight out. He sat down.

He leaned over and consulted with his seatmate, Terence Sherwood, very briefly.

10:58 Clifford dipped his pen in the ink and wrote very carefully.

He stopped to watch Miss Culver who was going around the room with a bottle with a spigot on it filling inkwells.

He started to write as Miss Culver came near his desk.

She filled the inkwell in the middle of the desk between Terence and Clifford.

Clifford watched her intently.

Miss Culver got a little too much ink in this inkwell and had to pick it up and pour some into another inkwell and then return it. She filled the inkwell behind Clifford and Terence, warning Terrence, "Don't move, lest you jar the bottle."

Clifford watched the whole procedure with interest.

Miss Culver commanded, "Now get on with your writing, Clifford," noting that he had been paying attention to the inkwell filling.

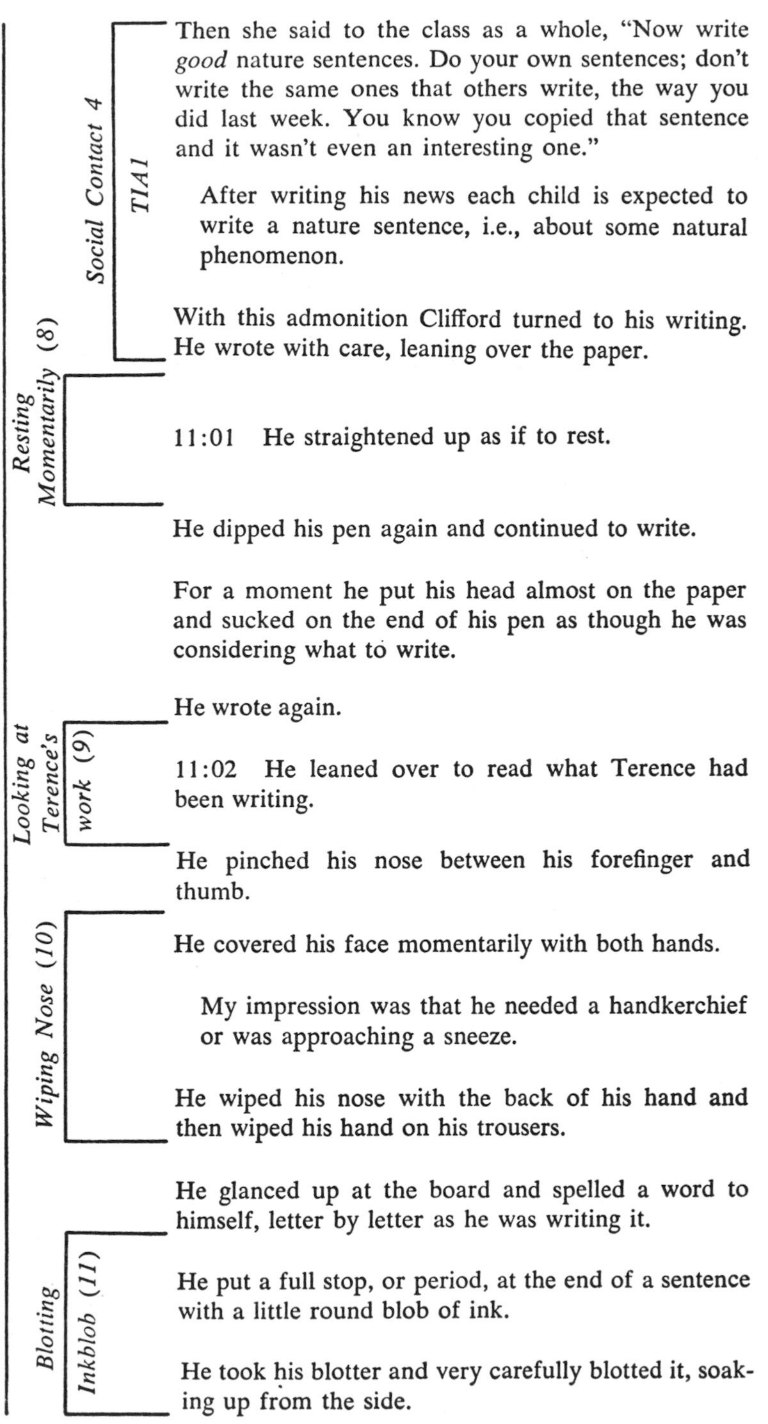

Then she said to the class as a whole, "Now write *good* nature sentences. Do your own sentences; don't write the same ones that others write, the way you did last week. You know you copied that sentence and it wasn't even an interesting one."

> After writing his news each child is expected to write a nature sentence, i.e., about some natural phenomenon.

With this admonition Clifford turned to his writing. He wrote with care, leaning over the paper.

11:01 He straightened up as if to rest.

He dipped his pen again and continued to write.

For a moment he put his head almost on the paper and sucked on the end of his pen as though he was considering what to write.

He wrote again.

11:02 He leaned over to read what Terence had been writing.

He pinched his nose between his forefinger and thumb.

He covered his face momentarily with both hands.

> My impression was that he needed a handkerchief or was approaching a sneeze.

He wiped his nose with the back of his hand and then wiped his hand on his trousers.

He glanced up at the board and spelled a word to himself, letter by letter as he was writing it.

He put a full stop, or period, at the end of a sentence with a little round blob of ink.

He took his blotter and very carefully blotted it, soaking up from the side.

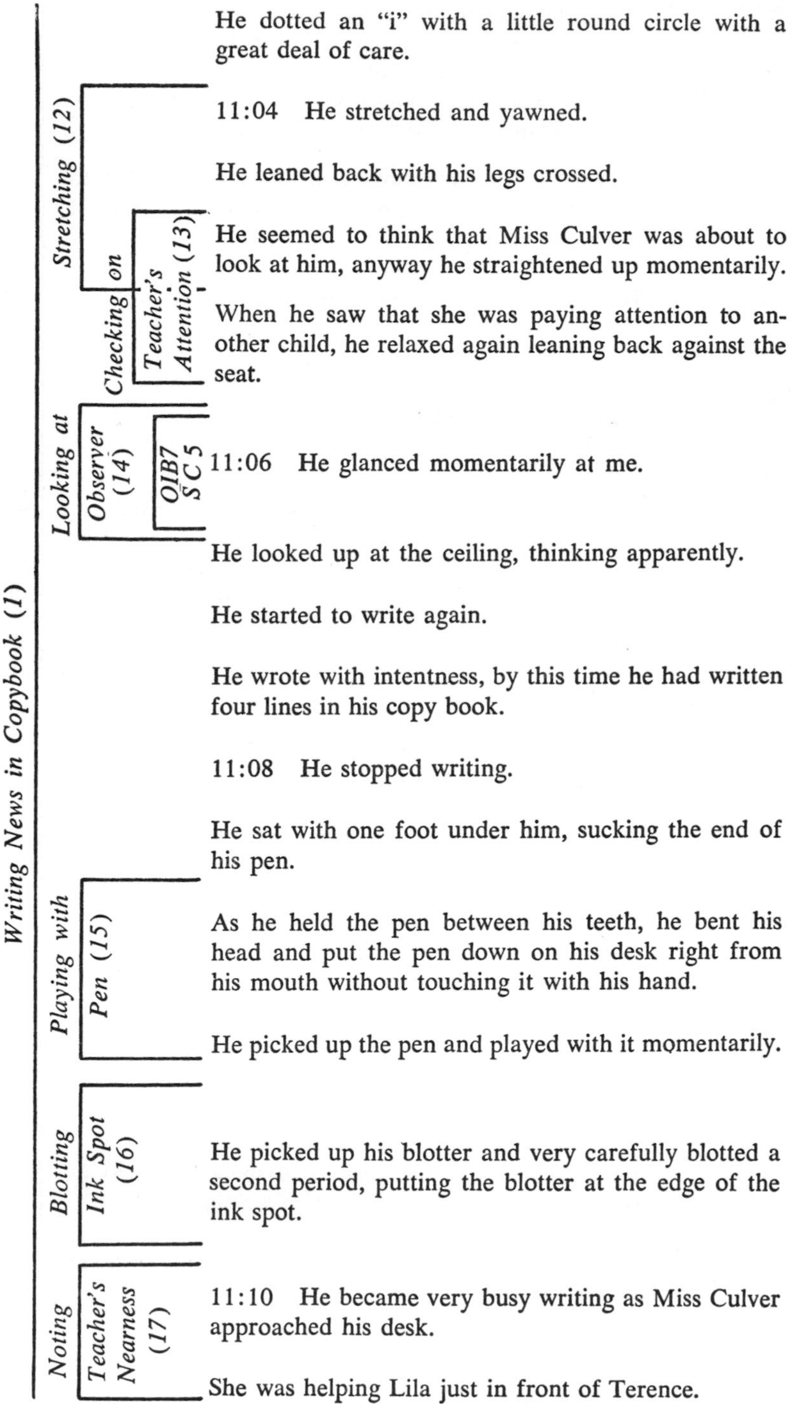

He dotted an "i" with a little round circle with a great deal of care.

11:04 He stretched and yawned.

He leaned back with his legs crossed.

He seemed to think that Miss Culver was about to look at him, anyway he straightened up momentarily.

When he saw that she was paying attention to another child, he relaxed again leaning back against the seat.

11:06 He glanced momentarily at me.

He looked up at the ceiling, thinking apparently.

He started to write again.

He wrote with intentness, by this time he had written four lines in his copy book.

11:08 He stopped writing.

He sat with one foot under him, sucking the end of his pen.

As he held the pen between his teeth, he bent his head and put the pen down on his desk right from his mouth without touching it with his hand.

He picked up the pen and played with it momentarily.

He picked up his blotter and very carefully blotted a second period, putting the blotter at the edge of the ink spot.

11:10 He became very busy writing as Miss Culver approached his desk.

She was helping Lila just in front of Terence.

Writing News in Copybook (1)

EFU 1 Teacher: Pupils to Write in Copybook

Watching Teacher Help Terence (18)

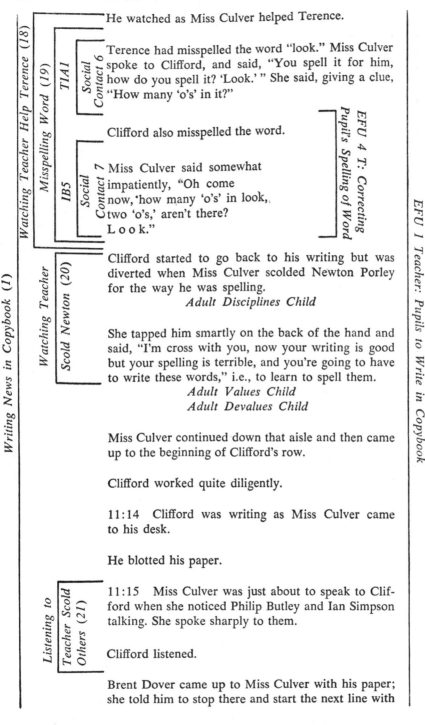

He watched as Miss Culver helped Terence.

Misspelling Word (19)

TIA1 — *Social Contact 6*

Terence had misspelled the word "look." Miss Culver spoke to Clifford, and said, "You spell it for him, how do you spell it? 'Look.' " She said, giving a clue, "How many 'o's' in it?"

EFU 4 T: Correcting Pupil's Spelling of Word

Clifford also misspelled the word.

IB5 — *Social Contact 7*

Miss Culver said somewhat impatiently, "Oh come now, how many 'o's' in look, two 'o's,' aren't there? L o o k."

Watching Teacher

Scold Newton (20)

Clifford started to go back to his writing but was diverted when Miss Culver scolded Newton Porley for the way he was spelling.

Adult Disciplines Child

She tapped him smartly on the back of the hand and said, "I'm cross with you, now your writing is good but your spelling is terrible, and you're going to have to write these words," i.e., to learn to spell them.

Adult Values Child
Adult Devalues Child

Miss Culver continued down that aisle and then came up to the beginning of Clifford's row.

Clifford worked quite diligently.

11:14 Clifford was writing as Miss Culver came to his desk.

He blotted his paper.

Listening to Teacher Scold Others (21)

11:15 Miss Culver was just about to speak to Clifford when she noticed Philip Butley and Ian Simpson talking. She spoke sharply to them.

Clifford listened.

Brent Dover came up to Miss Culver with his paper; she told him to stop there and start the next line with

Writing News in Copybook (1)

Responding to Teacher's Corrections (22)

EFU 1 Teacher: Pupils to Write in Copybook

EFU 5 T: Correcting S's Spelling

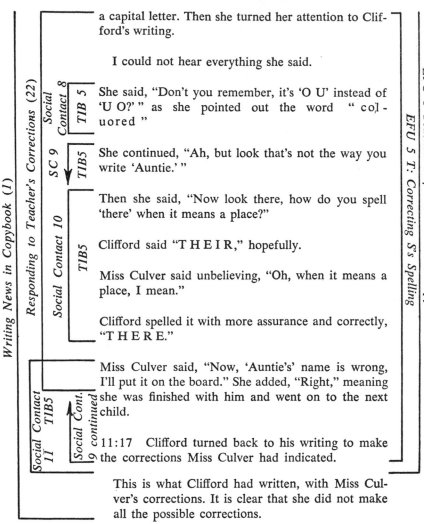

a capital letter. Then she turned her attention to Clifford's writing.

I could not hear everything she said.

Social Contact 8 — *TIB 5*

She said, "Don't you remember, it's 'O U' instead of 'U O?'" as she pointed out the word " co|l - uored "

SC 9 — *TIB5*

She continued, "Ah, but look that's not the way you write 'Auntie.' "

Social Contact 10 — *TIB5*

Then she said, "Now look there, how do you spell 'there' when it means a place?"

Clifford said "T H E I R," hopefully.

Miss Culver said unbelieving, "Oh, when it means a place, I mean."

Clifford spelled it with more assurance and correctly, "T H E R E."

Social Contact 11 — *TIB5*

Social Cont. 9 continued

Miss Culver said, "Now, 'Auntie's' name is wrong, I'll put it on the board." She added, "Right," meaning she was finished with him and went on to the next child.

11:17 Clifford turned back to his writing to make the corrections Miss Culver had indicated.

This is what Clifford had written, with Miss Culver's corrections. It is clear that she did not make all the possible corrections.

24th June 1957 Monday

On Wed. 19th my only auntie came with a uncle
Auntie
bab/y called Ann. /Ante/ Con has a col(uo)red film/e in her (.) camera. On Saturday we had a film show and there were 8 people (ther) th/e/r. Today it is 62° in this classroom.

A drawing in pencil of racing cars and crowd of people.

The / marks and ○ were put in by Miss Culver when she corrected the writing. The sentence "Today" etc., is the nature sentence assigned. It was written after the observation ended.

APPENDIX 2·1

Description of Behavior by Phases First Behavior Grouping Test

THE ASTERISK INDICATES points at which there was significant agreement that a natural break in the continuum had occurred.

1. Selma and Arnold walked down the road together.
2. Selma said, "George is going to be a farmer when he grows up. He's going to raise buffaloes."
3. Arnold replied sagely, "The buffaloes will all be killed, I know, my father killed them."
4. Selma retorted, "They aren't all dead, anyway that's what George is going to be when he grows up."
5.*Arnold said, "When I grow up I'm going to be a soldier and shoot all the time." He raised the stick he was carrying and made shooting noises. He covered a semicircular area with his shooting and ended up with the stick pointing at Selma. "I'll be fierce," he concluded.
6. Selma replied, "I'm going to be a WAC and I'm going to shoot more than you do because I'm older." She said this in a superior tone of voice, bobbing her head up and down as she spoke.
7. Arnold retorted vehemently, "No you won't, you're a girl."
8. Selma replied knowingly, "Girls can shoot just as well as boys."
9.*Arnold stopped suddenly and pointed to the side of the road.
10. He shouted, "Lookie!" and pointed to a rock upon which a squirrel was sitting, eating a nut.
11. Selma looked at the squirrel a moment and said very deliberately, "When I'm a WAC I'm going to pull out my gun—" as she spoke she drew back her arm.
12. Arnold cut in, "WACS don't have guns."
13. Selma repeated, "I'm going to pull out my gun and go bang! just like that," and she threw the rock she held at the squirrel.
14. The squirrel toppled off the rock.
15.*Selma was surprised and immediately sorry. She said, "Oh! Oh!" plaintively as she walked toward the squirrel.
16. Arnold walked over to the squirrel and knelt down beside it. He said, "You sure killed him, Selma, you killed him dead."
17. Selma knelt down by the squirrel, she said mournfully, "I didn't mean to."
18. She cried as she stroked the squirrel's fur, "It was just pretend," she wailed.
19. Arnold replied casually, "Shucks it was only a red squirrel, they're bad."
20. "But he wasn't doing anything bad," Selma sobbed. "He was just eating his dinner and I picked up a rock and I almost never hit where I aim."
21.*The children came running up to the house.
22. Selma shouted, "We're home Ma."

23. Her mother replied, "Ring the dinner bell and then you and Arnold go wash."
24. "All right Ma," Selma replied.
25. Both children ran for the bell.
26. They arrived at the bell at the same time, both grabbing for the rope.
27. Arnold said, "You should let me pull it."
28. "Why?" Selma asked.
29. "Because I'm the guest," Arnold replied.
30. "But you always pull it when you're here," Selma said.
31. "That's because I'm always the guest," Arnold countered.
32. "Oh, all right," Selma replied, and she let go of the rope.
33. Arnold looked up at the bell and pulled the rope, ringing the bell as Selma looked on.
34.*Martinius, who was working in the field, stopped his horses. He waved his arm in recognition and began to unhitch the horses to come in for lunch.
35.*Selma put her hand on Arnold's arm and said, "That's enough, come on."
36.*Both children ran to the pump.
37. They both arrived at the same time and each grabbed the pump handle.
38. Selma said, "I'll pump for you first."
39. Arnold relaxed his hold and went to hold his hands under the spout.
40. Selma pumped vigorously.
41. Suddenly Arnold protested, "That's too hard."
42. Selma stopped pumping and replied, "I'm sorry."
43. She began pumping again—easier this time.
44. Arnold scrubbed his hands and daintily dabbed a little water on each cheek.
45. Selma let go of the pump handle, wiped her brow, sighed and said, "Now you pump for me."
46. Arnold took the pump handle and worked it vigorously while Selma washed her hands.
47. Her mother stepped out on the back porch and said, "Your face too, Selma."
48. Selma replied, "But I didn't touch anything with my face."
49. Then she sighed and said, "Oh, all right."
50. She scrubbed her face vigorously.
51. Her mother shook her head slightly, smiled, and walked back into the house.
52.*Martinius came around the corner of the barn, leading a team of horses.
53. Selma shouted, "Yoo hoo Pa."
54. Martinius replied, "Yoo hoo Yentemi."
55. The children ran to meet him.
56. Martinius put his arm around Selma's neck as they walked toward the gate into the barnyard.
57. Selma said eagerly, "We're having pancakes for dinner, Pa, with honey!"
58. The father said, "That's fine, you love that don't you."
59. When they came to the gate, the children climbed up on the fence.
60.*Martinius led the horses to the watering trough as the children looked on.
61. Then he turned and walked back toward them.

62. He put his pipe in his mouth, took out a handkerchief, and wiped the perspiration from his face and neck and the inside of his hat.
63.*Selma, from her perch on the fence, said questioningly, "Pa?"
64. "Yeah?" Martinius replied, walking up to the children.
65. Selma continued, "Red squirrels are bad, aren't they?"
66. Her father replied, "Oh I don't know as they're so bad."
67. "But they eat crops and steal bird's eggs and rob farmers, don't they?" Selma queried.
68. Martinius took his pipe from his mouth and said, "I never saw one stealing bird's eggs, of course they do eat, but I never mind a red squirrel getting himself a square meal off my place." "Why Yentemi, what's the matter?" he asked.
69. Selma said sadly, "Oh, Pa, but I just killed a red squirrel."
70. Arnold said quickly, "She picked up a rock and killed him dead."
71. Selma's father looked at her kindly, smiled, and said, "Yes, but you really didn't mean to do it, did you?"
72. He put his hand on her arm to comfort her.
73. Selma replied stoicly, "It isn't what you mean to do—it's what you do."
74. Her father looked at her thoughtfully and said, "Well there's enough trouble Yentemi, without grieving over something that can't be helped."
75*He looked up at her and said, "Come," beckoning with his arm.
76. Martinius lifted Selma down off the fence.
77. The children took hold of Martinius' hands and began walking toward the barn.
78. Martinius said, "Now I've got something in the barn that I think you'll like."
79. "For me?" Selma queried.
80. Martinius hesitated a moment and then said, "Why, it's a present."
81. Arnold said quickly, "Well what is it?"
82. Martinius replied, "Well it's something brand new, it just came today."
83. They walked into the barn and turned to a stall just inside the door.
84. Martinius pointed toward the stall.
85. Arnold squatted down to look between the boards.
86. Selma stood holding her father's hand and looking between the boards of the stall.
87. Then she climbed upon them and looked in.
88. In the stall stood a cow licking a damp, newly born calf.
89. "Jeepers!" Selma exclaimed, "Is it my calf, my very own?"
90. "Your very own," Martinius affirmed.
91. "You mean I can take care of it too?" she queried.
92. Her father replied, "Well if a girl's got a calf, she has to take care of it."
93. Selma looked at her father smilingly and said, "Oh, Pa, I'm so very happy."
94. Martinius put his hand on his daughter's head and replied gently, "It's good to be happy."
95. "Pa," Selma queried thoughtfully, "Do you think when I was killing the squirrel the calf might have been born right about then?"
96. Her father hesitated a moment, then replied, "It—it probably was, Yentemi."

97. Selma looked back toward the calf with a pleased expression on her face.
98. The cow continued to lick the calf.
99. Arnold queried, "How's that calf ever gonna get dry if she keeps on licking it?"
100.*From the house the mother called "Dinner."
101. Martinius put his hand on Selma's head and said gently, "Come on Selma."
102. Selma slowly climbed down from the board fence and started for the house with her father.
103. She took a fleeting glance back at the calf again.
104. She glanced at Arnold and said, "Got pancakes, Arnold."
105. Selma and Martinius went on to the house.
106.*Arnold looked at the calf a moment, stood up, and said philosophically, "It sure is wet."
107. Then he too started for the house.
108.*Martinius, Selma and Arnold were seated around the table, eating dinner.
109. Selma's mother put a platter of pancakes on the table and sat down at her place.
110. Martinius took an extra large bite of pancake.
111. Arnold watched him closely.
112. Then he too speared a large piece and started it toward his mouth.
113. Selma's mother warned, "That's too big a bite, Arnold."
114. Arnold held the pancake in mid air a moment, then countered, "Uncle Martinius takes big bites."
115. Selma's mother replied teasingly, "Well, your Uncle Martinius has a big mouth."
116. Martinius glanced at his wife momentarily.
117. She smiled back victoriously.
118. Arnold put the pancake down and began to cut it. (Selma made no comment about this interchange though she was aware of it.)
119.*Selma questioned eagerly, "Do I get to feed my calf tonight, Pa?"
120. Martinius answered, "Well, we'll have to wait three or four days and then we'll teach him to eat out of a bucket."
121. Selma looked at Arnold and said, "Gee, it's nice to have a calf all your own."
122. She began eating again, very heartily.
123. Arnold replied, "If I had a calf it would be bigger than yours, only I haven't got a calf."
124.*Selma's mother broke in, "Well," she laughed, "Selma doesn't either, really."
125. She reached across the table for a pitcher and put a little milk in Selma's glass.
126. Selma immediately said, "I have so, Pa said I did."
127. Martinius affirmed this with a "hmmm."
128. Arnold commented dryly, "Sure is funny how I keep on not getting a calf."
129. Selma's mother said, "Well, Selma's Pa meant it was just pretend it was Selma's calf."
130. Selma, hurt and defensive, retorted, "But Pa didn't say it was pretend, he said it was really mine."

131. Her mother explained, "Well, everything on the farm is all yours, Selma, yours and ours. The clothes that keep us warm, the food we have."
132. She continued, "It couldn't belong to any one of us any more than the—sunshine—or these pesky flies," she added, sweeping her arm across the table.
133. "I'm sure that's what your Pa meant," she went on, "Isn't it, Martinius?"
134. Martinius replied hesitantly, "Well, that may be what I meant to say but I did tell her it was all hers."
135. Selma looked up hopefully for a moment.
136. Martinius continued, "Maybe your Mother's right, Selma, maybe we ought to figure it like she said instead of like we spoke about."
137.*Selma looked very crestfallen, she lowered her eyes and was about to cry.
138. Her mother intervened saying, "Land sakes, Martinius, you can't take it away from her if you gave it to her like that."
139. She continued, speaking to Selma with renewed enthusiasm, "Maybe it's a good thing, I think your Pa's right."
140. Turning her head toward Martinius she said, "She needed something like that."
141. Selma beamed happily.
142. Her mother continued, "She'll have work to do just like a grown-up."
143. Arnold commented wryly, "I wonder if that calf knows who he belongs to."
144. Selma, smiling broadly, took a drink of milk and continued with her meal.

APPENDIX 2.2

Description of Behavior by Phases Second Behavior Grouping Test

THE ASTERISK INDICATES points at which there was significant agreement that a natural break in the continuum had occurred.

1. Selma and her father were riding down the road in an old car.
2. Suddenly Martinius pointed to a new red barn in the distance and said, "There it is!" and then continued with obvious admiration, "Well, there's a barn, Yentemi."
3. "Jeepers!" Selma exclaimed.
4.*Mr. Bjornsen and Arnold were working on a wagon when Selma and Martinius drove up.
5. Mr. Bjornsen wiped his hands on a cloth and came over to the car as it drove up.
6. "Good day, Martinius," said Mr. Bjornsen pleasantly.
7. "Good day, Mr. Bjornsen," Martinius replied.
8. Mr. Bjornsen acknowledged Selma with a "Good day, little Selma."
9. Selma responded quickly, "Good day, Mr. Bjornsen!"

10. Martinius also greeted the man who was working on a wagon in the shop.
11.*Then Martinius turned to Mr. Bjornsen and said, "We're going to town for a load of salt and thought we'd drop by and have a look at the barn."
12. "Oh yeah! yeah! come on," said Mr. Bjornsen eagerly as he opened the car door for Selma.
13. Selma and Martinius climbed out of the car and gazed at the new barn.
14. "Ah fine, fine," said Martinius.
15. Mr. Bjornsen replied, "Yeah to have a big barn is a fine thing when a man is old."
16. Mr. Bjornsen stooped to wash his hands in a bucket of water.
17. "But to have it paid for!" "Ah it's hard to believe a man could be so lucky," he continued.
18. He dried his hands quickly on a towel hanging near the bucket.
19. "Paid for to the last truss board in that haymow," he continued with pride.
20. "It's not luck, Mr. Bjornsen," Martinius commented, "you've worked hard."
21. "Ah, everybody works hard," Mr. Bjornsen replied, throwing the towel back on the post.
22. He put his hand on Martinius' shoulder and said eagerly, "Come on!" "Come on, we go inside."
23. The three of them started for the barn.
24.*Mr. Bjornsen opened the door and the three stepped inside and stood looking at the new barn and the cattle.
25. Martinius drew a deep breath, "Ahh," he sighed, "can still smell the new wood, no finer smell on earth."
26. "Yeah," Mr. Bjornsen replied, "makes me see home; when I smell new wood I'm a boy again."
27. "Were you a boy very long, Mr. Bjornsen?" Selma asked inquisitively.
28. Martinius bent over to put his finger to his lips to shush Selma.
29. Mr. Bjornsen laughed and replied, "Not nearly long enough, little Selma."
30. Both he and Martinius laughed.
31. The three of them walked down the aisle between the two rows of stanchioned cows.
32. Martinius pointed approvingly at the small signs above each cow.
33. Mr. Bjornsen explained, "A sign painter came through—a fellow from Kenosha."
34. "Yeah," Martinius affirmed.
35. "I guess it's kind of foolish but I always wanted name plates for each cow and now I got 'em," Mr. Bjornsen continued, gesturing proudly toward the plates.
36. Martinius laughed good-naturedly and commented, "This place must have cost you a lot of money!"
37. "All I had," Mr. Bjornsen replied seriously. "Fifty years but I got my barn."
38. Martinius gave silent affirmation to Mr. Bjornsen's comment.
39. Then he turned and put his hand out to Selma and said, "Well, Selma," indicating it was time to go.

40. The three turned and walked back toward the barn door—Martinius with his arm around Selma.
41.*Martinius and Selma were back in the car on their way to town.
42. Selma asked inquiringly, "Do you want a new barn, Pa?"
43. "Every man wants a new barn," Martinius replied seriously.
44. "Then I'll pray for one," Selma said.
45. Martinius chuckled and replied, "That's fine but it will take considerable praying, Yentemi."
46. "Well, gosh," Selma commented seriously, "What's one more barn to God?"
47. Martinius looked down at Selma and laughed appreciatively.
48.*Selma and her mother were sitting on the back porch.
49. The mother was doing some sewing.
50. Selma was sitting on the step, apparently in deep thought.
51. Suddenly she said, "Ma?" quietly.
52. "Hm?" her mother replied.
53. "Why don't you want Pa to have a new barn?" she asked seriously.
54. Her mother replied, "I'd like him to have a new barn, Selma; I'd like anything that would make your Pa happy."
55. "But new barns aren't easy," she continued with a sigh—"sometimes they take too much out of a man like your father."
56. Selma moved over next to her mother.
57. Then she said, "But if you'd like him to have a new barn, then why do you always talk like you didn't?"
58. "Well," said her mother with a sigh and putting her hands gently on Selma's, "What you'd like people to have and what people are able to have, those are two different things."
59. "Right now your Pa's out in the barn mending some harness when he should be here with us getting some rest."
60. "With the old barn he works more than any man should; to pay for a new one he'd be working longer—he'd never be able to stop a minute."
61. She furrowed her brow and continued quietly, "Just growing older and dreaming at night about his debts."
62. She fingered Selma's hair gently and sighed again. "Oh, it's better, Selma; it's better never to have a thing than to have it and be afraid," she said seriously.
63. "Some of these days when you're older"—then she stopped suddenly and looked around.
64. She patted Selma's hands, straightened up, and said, "Shh, it's your Pa, isn't it?"
65. Selma nodded her head and straightened up too.
66.*Martinius came walking up to the house, wiping his hand on his handkerchief.
67. "Well, that's done," he said tiredly.
68. His wife moved some sewing from a chair beside her and said, "Why don't you sit here, Martinius?"
69. Martinius replied as he turned and sat on the steps, "No, Broda, this will be all right."

70. Selma got up from her chair and walked over by her father.
71. His wife rubbed his back affectionately.
72.*Martinius looked up in the sky and said, "Did you ever see so many stars?"
73. "Pa?" Selma said questioningly—"do people live on the stars?"
74. "They do if you want them to," Martinius replied casually nodding his head.
75. "Why is that?" asked Selma.
76. "Well because nobody can be sure they don't," answered Martinius matter-of-factly.
77. "I wonder if the people who live on the stars have free barns?" Selma conjectured.
78. Martinius looked down at Selma and answered, "Why, of course, Yentemi."
79. He pointed skyward and said, "Up there every man has a new red barn and a fine herd of cows," and then he added lightly, "It's guaranteed with his birth certificate."
80.*Selma's mother laughed and got up from her chair.
81. "Five more minutes until bed time," she said to Selma; "I'll turn down your covers," she continued as she went into the house.
82. "All right," Selma assented.
83.*She said thoughtfully, "I guess that's why they call it the milky way, isn't it?"
84. "Naturally," Martinius replied.
85. He pointed upward—"See the big dipper."
86. Selma peered intently in the direction he pointed.
87. "Almost running over with milk," Martinius continued.
88. Selma continued to peer intently skyward.
89.*Suddenly a car pulled up in front of the house.
90. "Evening, Martinius," the man in the car called.
91. "Evening, Peter," Martinius replied.
92. "Going to the Grange meeting tonight?" Peter inquired.
93. "No, not tonight, I guess," Martinius replied.
94. "Well, just thought I'd stop and pick you up," Peter said.
95. "Well, thank you," Martinius answered.
96. They exchanged goodnights and Peter drove away.
97.*Selma and Martinius remained silent for a moment.
98. Then Selma inquired, "Why didn't you want to go, Pa?"
99. Martinius answered, "Oh, I don't know—on a night like this, with a lot of people around, I—I get lonesome."
100. "Can you get lonesome with people?" Selma asked quietly.
101. "Sometimes," Martinius replied.
102. "Are you lonesome now?" Selma continued.
103. Martinius looked down affectionately and said, "No."
104. Selma pointed toward herself and said, "But I'm people."
105. Martinius sat down and put his arm around Selma and said, "No, Yentemi, you're my daughter."
106. Selma smiled and climbed onto her father's lap and hugged him affectionately.

APPENDIX 2.3

TABLE 1
Subdivision of Modal Units

NUMBER SUBJECTS	NUMBER SUBDIVISIONS
1. *Modal Unit (a)*	*Phases 1 to 20 ± 1*
7	0
8	1
16	2
2	3
4	4
	5
	6
Total 37	
2. *Modal Unit (b)*	*Phases 20 ± 1 to 35 ± 1*
12	0
11	1
4	2
6	3
1	4
	5
	6
Total 34	
3. *Modal Unit (c)*	*Phases 35 ± 1 to 51 ± 1*
23	0
6	1
2	2
3	3
	4
Total 34	
4. *Modal Unit (d)*	*Phases 51 ± 1 to 62 ± 1*
14	0
8	1
5	2
1	3
	4
Total 28	
5. *Modal Unit (e)*	*Phases 62 ± 1 to 74 ± 1*
25	0
3	1
	2
	3
Total 28	

Subdivision of Modal Units–Cont'd

NUMBER SUBJECTS	NUMBER SUBDIVISIONS
6. *Modal Unit (f)*	*Phases 74 ± 1 to 99 ± 1*
6	0
8	1
4	2
5	3
	4
Total 23	
7. *Modal Unit (g)*	*Phases 99 ± 1 to 107 ± 1*
11	0
10	1
5	2
	3
1	4
	5
Total 27	
8. *Modal Unit (h)*	*Phases 107 ± 1 to 118 ± 1*
19	0
8	1
	2
2	3
	4
Total 29	
9. *Modal Unit (i)*	*Phases 118 ± 1 to 144*
11	0
3	1
9	2
3	3
1	4
1	5
2	6
	7
	8
	9
	10
2	11
Total 32	

APPENDIX 2.4

TABLE 1
Agreements on Occurrence of Units Test 1 (38 Subjects)

Beginning & Ending Phase Numbers of Units	NUMBER OF AGREEMENTS	*Beginning & Ending Phase Numbers of Units*	NUMBER OF AGREEMENTS
1	5	59	3
1–4	7*	59–62	4
1–8	9*		
1–9	3	60–62	5
1–20	4	61–74	2
1–14	3	63–74	15*
2–4	3	63–75	4
5–8	6*		
5–14	2	75–82	3
		75–87	2
9–10	4	75–94	3
9–13	3	75–99	5
9–14	6*	75–107	3
9–19	2	76–77	2
9–20	3	78–99	2
14–19	3		
15–20	13*	83–99	2
20–33	3	88–99	2
20–35	3	95–97	5
20–51	2	98–99	4
21	3	98–107	3
21–22	3	100	4
21–24	6*	100–105	6*
21–25	3	100–107	7*
21–33	2	101–104	2
21–34	2	101–105	2
21–35	5	104–105	2
22–33	2	106–107	11*
		108–109	6*
25–33	2	108–110	3
25–34	3	108–118	19*
25–35	2	108–144	5
		110–118	7*
34	8*	111–118	2
35	7*	118	2
35–51	6*	119–120	2
35–50	2	119–121	2
36–51	16*	119–122	3
		119–123	7*
46–51	4	119–128	3
47–50	2	119–144	11*
47–51	2		
		124–125	2
51	4	124–137	3
52–54	2		
52–55	2	128	3
52–56	2	129–135	2
52–58	4	129–136	3
52–59	6*	137	2
52–60	2	137–144	5
52–62	9*	138–144	7*
52–74	5	143	4
55–58	2	144	6*

* Indicates agreement at .05 level.

APPENDIX 2.5

TABLE 1
Agreements on Occurrence of Units Test 2 (17 Subjects)

Beginning & Ending Phase Numbers of Units	NUMBER OF AGREEMENTS	*Beginning & Ending Phase Numbers of Units*	NUMBER OF AGREEMENTS
1	2	41–47	12*
1–3	7*	42–47	2
1–10	3*	48–50	2
2–3	2	48–64	3*
4–23	4*	48–65	10*
6–10	2	65–88	2
11–23	3*	66–88	5*
24–26	2	72–79	3*
24–40	8*	80–82	5*
27–30	2	83–88	6*
31–35	2	89–96	11*
36–38	2	89–106	3*
39–47	2	90–96	2
41	2	97–106	12*

* Indicates agreement at .05 level.

APPENDIX 5.1

Criteria for Marking the Social Contact

1. THERE IS ONLY *one* agent per contact. Where two or more agents are successively interacting with the subject, even if it is for the same reason, the subject is said to have a contact with each agent. Whenever two or more agents are simultaneously interacting with the subject, a judgment is necessary as to whether the agents are acting as one unit or as individual agents. Two agents singing a vocal duet while the subject listens would usually qualify as one agent unless there is evidence that the subject is not responding to their duet as such. When the subject recites before his classmates or addresses two or more of his friends collectively (as, for example, in the expression "Hey fellows!"), we also can consider the classmates or friends as one agent so long as the responses of the subject support such a judgment. As soon as the subject's interaction with two or more agents forming one group shifts to interaction with one of these agents in the group, or with some different combination of agents within the group or with some other agent or group of agents, a new contact has begun for the subject.

2. There is only one *raison d'être* per contact. The expression *"raison d'être"* literally means "reason for being" and, when used to refer to a characteristic of a social contact, it means that which the agent or subject says or does which has the effect of originating a response or set of responses such that social interaction, as we have defined it above, takes place. Twelve different types of activities which serve to "touch off" or originate social interaction have been specified; five of these are associated with agent origination, seven of them with subject origination. Each time there is a change in the *raison d'être* of social interaction as defined by these twelve specified types of activities, a new social contact begins.

In identifying units by means of the *raison d'être* criteria, we first distinguish between contacts originating with the agent and those originating with the subject.

The numbering used is the same as that used in Dyck's M.A. thesis (1958). Under Roman numeral I are all the ratings which have to do with the originating ground or *raison d'être* of the contact. The capital letter A is used to denote those contacts which originate with the agent, and the capital letter B for those which originate with the subject.

IA, IB. *Origination*

A contact originates with the agent where one can judge that the behavior of the agent does not originate from the immediately perceived action, state, or wish of the subject. Thus, for example, waking up the subject in the morning follows from the expectations or wishes of the agent and not from the state of the subject, i.e., the fact that he is asleep. Waking the subject is an activity that the agent has in mind each morning and agents will even come to wake a subject and find the subject already awake; this is sure evidence that the agent is not responding to the state of the subject in waking him up. Should a subject fall asleep at the table, however, waking him up would be a response to the subject's perceived state. Here the agent's behavior would be evoked by the immediately perceived state of the subject and the agent's activity is not a "planned," or premeditated action in such a case.

When the agent reacts to something at the time that it occurs (that is, something the subject is doing, about to do, saying or about to say), and is within communication distance of the subject, the agent is, of course, not the originator of the contact even though the agent may speak first. For example, should Johnny be on the verge of kicking someone and the agent acts to prevent him, the subject here originates the contact. But where the agent is making inquiry of the subject about something he has done in the past (past in the sense that it is finished), and there is nothing the subject is saying or doing that specifically calls for such a contact from the agent, the agent is the originator of the contact. It makes no difference for this rating whether the subject's past activity occurred on the day of the record or on some previous day. Thus, for example, the agent may ask the subject, while he is eating, what he is going to do with a certain crate with which he has been playing. Here, this inquiry, when it is not evoked by a conversation or action of the subject in the present, originates with the agent who can be said to have "something in mind" in respect to the subject. (The agent may wish to express interest in the subject's activities, etc.) Should the subject "bring up" his intentions to do something with this crate, while eating, the agent, in speaking about the crate, would be responding to the subject and the contact then would originate with the subject.

Five categories of agent-originated *raisons d'être* have been specified and designated IA 1-5 as follows:

IA 1. *Seeking an activity on the part of the subject*

a. This must meet the criteria for agent origination.

b. Clearly every contact with the subject, in so far as it is a contact, involves some activity on the part of the subject. However, the category here refers to an effort on the part of the agent to bring about or prevent an activity on the part of the subject under the conditions which meet the criteria for agent origination and which cannot be described as falling into any of the categories IA 2, IA 3, IA 4, or IA 5 as specified below.

An example of IA 1 would be that of a mother coming to a boy who is playing and telling him to wash up for lunch.

IA 2. *Seeking an activity with the subject*

a. This must meet the criteria for agent origination.

b. To be an activity with the subject, the activity must involve both agent and subject participation. For example, an activity like playing a game of ping-pong, baseball, etc. Going for a walk together qualifies as an activity with someone.

c. The activity of agent and subject must be shared in the sense of being similar or equivalent as it is in walking together or in playing a game requiring two or more people.

Therefore, when Ben Hutchings' mother tries to get Ben to practice his piano lessons and sits down with him at the piano, this is not an activity with Ben since Ben practices and the mother criticizes, encourages, demonstrates, suggests, etc., but does not also practice the pieces—Ben does the practicing. The mother is with Ben, not sharing his activity, but rather sharing with him her ideas, influencing his activity, etc. Thus also, being with a child in the bathroom to help him wash or see that he washes is not an activity with the subject but is a matter of being with the subject, for whatever reason, when the subject is engaged in a given activity.

d. Activity with the subject may not involve similar or equivalent simultaneous activity such as occurs in walking together, but activity with the subject must then involve a common focus maintainable only as long as there are two simultaneous participants. Thus, for example, reading to a subject, or listening to a subject read is activity with the subject, for sharing the story depends upon the simultaneous listening and reading of the participants. Where the focus is upon the performance of one of the participants in a joint activity, it is no longer an activity with the other participant, for such a focus is not then common or shared. When, therefore, a teacher has a student read, she focuses not on sharing a story but upon the reading performance of the subject, i.e., the activity of the child. (That the story is shared is incidental.) When a teacher reads a story to the student and is not illustrating how to read or any such thing but is sharing the story, this is an activity with her students.

Returning to the example of Ben Hutchings practicing on the piano, we see that it also fails to meet the criterion of a common focus maintainable only by two simultaneous participants. Practicing with Ben was focused on Ben's performance (this was no duet—which would have been activity with Ben).

Eating together is not IA 2 because any common focus that might be cited in connection with it does not depend upon two simultaneous participants. Eating behavior or practicing does not stop when one of two participants quits eating or practicing, but sharing a story does stop when one of two participants no longer reads or listens.

IA 3. *Seeking to express oneself to the subject*

a. This must meet the criteria for agent origination.

b. Expressing oneself may be manifested by the agent in:

(1) Sharing his own experiences with the child, e.g., Raymond Birch's father tells him to look at the antics of the cat that are a source of amusement to the father;

(2) Telling the subject how he feels, e.g., "I certainly feel tired today";

(3) Telling the subject about the agent's own activities, e.g., relating what happened at work that day and in this way giving the subject some picture of what the agent does, what people he meets, etc.;

(4) Making evaluative comments about the subject to the subject, e.g., "I'm proud of you today" or "You're a bad boy";

(5) Saying hello or goodbye to the subject;

(6) Showing affection to the subject, e.g., hugging or kissing the subject, taking the subject up in one's arms, patting the subject's head, etc.;

(7) Telling the subject a joke, making a humorous comment, etc.

(8) Communicating one's needs, wants, attitudes, opinions, etc., to the subject, e.g., "I like red" or "We have good schools." (Here no

immediate activity is expected of the one to whom one is communicating. That is the agent does not say "I want that box" meaning "Get that box for me now." Such a case is judged a IA 1);

(9) Volunteering information for the sake of giving out information. In other words, information is given to the subject which is not evoked by any specific perceived need for it in the immediate situation.

c. In rating "seeking to express oneself" the rater should keep in mind that the agent contact can only be rated thus when there is no evidence: (1) that the agent-expression is evoked by the subject in the immediate situation; (2) that the agent expects some "immediate" action from the subject (i.e., action during that very day at least) for that is rated IA 1 (see above); (3) that the agent is trying to elicit an expression from the subject (see "seeking an expression on the part of the subject" IA 4 below).

d. The rater must bear in mind, then, in rating IA 3 that the focus here is not upon the response that will be elicited from the subject (as it is in IA 1 and IA 4) but upon the fact that the agent wishes to communicate something to the subject. Of course, that does not mean that the agent doesn't expect the subject to listen, laugh, or return a greeting when the agent expresses himself (IA 3) but simply that the agent is not making any specific demand for a response, at least there is no evidence that he is doing so.

IA 4. *Seeking an expression on the part of the subject*

a. This must meet the criteria for agent origination.

b. The agent here is manifestly in some way trying to get the subject to respond in one of the ways that has already been described under "expressing oneself" [see IA 3, (1), (2), (3), (4), (5), (6), (7), (8), and (9)]. In respect to IA 3 (9), the information that the agent is seeking from the subject here is strictly information about the subject and his own activities. Seeking information about other subjects and matters of knowledge in general is to be rated as IA 1 (seeking an activity on the part of the subject). When there is evidence that an agent's inquiry into the subject's own activities is put in such a way that one can judge that the agent is not seeking information about them, but rather is seeking to influence or induce the activities or suggest new ones, this, of course, is to be rated as IA 1 (seeking an activity on the part of the subject), e.g., Raymond Birch's mother asks him whether he has brushed his teeth. The mother's interest in Raymond's activity here is much more likely that of seeing that he gets it done rather than simply showing an interest in having him communicate or share his activity so that this inquiry is rated IA 1. An example of IA 4 is that of Raymond's mother asking what he shot with his BB gun today or asking him in the morning whether he wanted an egg for breakfast.

c. The rater must remember that in rating IA 4 the focus is upon the fact that the agent wishes to know the needs or wants of the subject or wishes to satisfy an interest in what he does or wishes him to share or communicate his needs, wants, opinions, evaluations, feelings, etc.

IA 5. *Expressing oneself about the subject to someone other than the subject*
a. There must be evidence that the subject responds or has a definite opportunity to choose not to respond before one can mark a contact as IA 5, e.g., Raymond's father tells the observer about the fact that Raymond caught a fish and he, the father, did not. To this Raymond responded with a smile.
b. This contact is considered agent-originated unless the subject should specifically request the agent to talk about him and then the contact would be rated IB 1 (a request of the subject for activity on the part of the agent).

Seven categories of subject-originated *raisons d'être* have been specified and designated IB 1-7 as follows:

IB 1. *Responding to a request of the subject for activity on the part of the agent*
a. Origination is straightforward here because the subject asks the agent to act, e.g., Raymond calls to his mother "Mommie, come here."
b. The rater must not use this rating where the agent is responding only to the subject's request: (1) for an activity with the agent (IB 2); (2) for permission for some intended activity (IB 5); (3) for information from the agent (IB 6).
c. When a subject says, for example, "I want peaches" and this requires the agent to act if the want is to be fulfilled, this is a request for activity on the part of the agent.

IB 2. *Responding to a request of the subject for activity with the agent*
a. Origination is again straightforward because the subject specifically requests the agent's response.
b. Activity with the agent is defined already above (see IA 2) and examples of such instances have been cited.

IB 3. *Responding to the overt expression of the subject*
a. This must meet the criteria for subject origination.
b. The term "overt expression" takes in the whole list of acts that are given above (see IA 3) for "expressing oneself." In this case, however, it is the subject who tells the agent of his activities, his feeling, his needs, etc. The rater must remember that when the subject says "I want that" the subject may mean "You get me that" which is a case of IB 1 as specified above.
c. The "overt expression" of the subject may or may not be directed to the agent but it must be explicitly directed to someone or something. Verbalized expressions are always overt expressions. Expressions that are directed at someone or something are always considered "overt" where one can explicitly judge that they are directed, e.g., the subject hugs his brother (or his doll) and the mother responds to this in some way.

IB 4. *Responding to the state of the subject*
a. This must meet the criteria for subject origination. Here, however, the fact that the subject originates the contact is not explicit or self-evident. The agent will always make the first move and say the first word in this particular contact, for in responding to the state of the subject, the agent does so without an explicit request or an evidently directed outburst on the part of the subject.

b. Responding to the state of the subject may take the form of:

(1) Responding to the perceived need or desire of the subject (in the ongoing situation) where the subject has not explicitly and overtly expressed such a need or desire, e.g., all instances of passing food to the subject at the table (e.g., passing potatoes) are responses to the state of the subject provided that: (a) the subject has not said "I would like some potatoes, please" (IB 1); (b) the subject has not been straining to reach for the potatoes (IB 5); (c) the subject has not said to the agent "Please pass me the potatoes" (IB 1); (d) the agent does not first ask (before passing) whether or not the subject wants the potatoes and expects some answer before passing them, for this would be rated IA 4;

(2) Responding to the appearance of the subject, e.g., Raymond's father exclaims that the boy has toothpaste on his face and simply laughs. Raymond's mother tells Raymond he looks tired or his shirt is dirty, etc.;

(3) Responding to the subject's mood or feeling or to some muttered or muffled expression that cannot be judged to be directed to someone, e.g., the subject may be asked why he looks so dejected. This is not IA 4 because there is evidence that the agent is responsive to the immediately perceived "feeling state" of the subject;

(4) In general, responding to the immediately perceived "state of being" of the subject, e.g., "Say, you look happy."

IB 5. *Responding to the activity of the subject*

a. This must meet the criteria for subject instigation.

b. This may be a response to ongoing activity whether or not the subject is perceived as needing the contact with the agent. The subject, of course, makes no request for the agent's response; the agent responds to the subject's activity as such, e.g., Raymond's father takes his fishing rod away from Raymond who is trying to disentangle it.

c. This may be a response to an intended activity. The subject may be heading for the door and to this the agent responds in some way (e.g., "You're not going out just now"). Raymond's father hears Raymond ask his mother about using something and tells him that she wouldn't let him use it the other day.

d. This may also be a response to an activity for which the subject requests permission whether directly or indirectly. This is just like responding to an intended activity but it is mentioned separately to point out that any time the agent gives his approval or disapproval of an activity one should not confuse this with answering a subject's request for sheer information which is not perceived to be for the purpose of some immediate or explicitly anticipated activity on the part of the subject. The agent's response to the subject's asking "When can I go outside?" is not rated IB 6 but rather IB 5.

e. When a subject says "I like that there a lot" and the agent responds by saying "Don't say 'that there,' it's incorrect," the response of the agent is not to the "overt expression" of the subject as such (IB 3) but is rather a response to an incorrect use of the language. This is an example, then, of a IB 5.

IB 6. *Responding to a request for information*

a. This must meet the criteria for subject origination.

b. This must be a response to a request for information for information's sake, e.g., the agent may respond to the subject's question as to how old someone is or how far it is to the moon, etc.

IB 7. *Failing to respond*

There must be evidence that: (1) the subject is seeking contact with the agent; (2) the agent is aware of this; (3) when a subject's request is simply repeated without intervening contacts, the agent does not comply even after such repeated request.

3. There is only one topic per contact. Social interaction involves many shifts with respect to its agent and its *raison d'être* ratings. The social contact unit, therefore, can very often be discriminated by means of either of these criteria. However, there are instances where one agent continues to interact with a subject without a change in the *raison d'être* of such interaction and how much of this social interaction is to be included within the boundaries of one social contact is judged by means of the criterion now under discussion, namely, that there must be only one topic per contact. We have stated previously that the unity of a topic depends upon its being presented or reacted to as a unit. The examples that follow, and the discussion that accompanies them, are designed to clarify the conditions under which one topic, and hence one contact is marked.

a. As a rule, whatever the agent or subject says or does in a temporally continuous manner is considered as one topic, and therefore this action and the reaction to it will constitute one social contact. A mother, for example, may say to the subject "Sit up straight and get your elbows off the table" and subsequent to this, the subject responds in some way. The commands of the mother and the subject's response to them comprise one social contact. In examples such as these, there is no need to specify or name the topic of this mother-subject interaction, but only to judge that it is one topic whatever the topic may be. The basis for judging that this segment of interaction is indeed one contact having one topic is that the person presenting something to someone else does so in a temporally continuous manner, that is to say, he does so without a response on the part of the responding person which either interrupts or comes "between" what is being presented. (One should keep in mind that our example is also judged to be one contact because the interaction within its boundaries involves no changes in respect to its agent or *raison d'être*.)

b. For the most part, whatever the agent or subject says or does in a temporally discontinuous manner is considered as involving at least more than one topic. For example, a mother may say to the subject "Sit up straight" and the subject responds to this in some manner. The mother then follows this by saying to the subject "Get your elbows off the table." This example of mother-subject interaction constitutes two topics and hence, two social contacts. The command to sit up straight and the response to it is the one contact; the command to get your elbows off the table and the response to it is the second contact. Without specifying what the topics are, one judges that there are two because what the one person is presenting is temporally segregated by the response of the responding person. (One should note that the portion of interaction given in this example involves no change in agent or *raison d'être* but does involve a change in topic.)

Temporal discontinuity is not always obvious in that the intervening response to whatever the agent or subject is doing or saying is sometimes "understood." For example, a teacher declares that she wants silence before she begins the lesson (the subject here is a member of the group addressed) and, after her call for silence, she tells the class to get out their arithmetic books. The subject may make no visible response to the call for silence except to hear what is said but because even this response is separated by the teacher from the other response she wishes, the requests of the teacher are to be considered as temporally discontinuous and therefore as two contacts (two topics).

Of course, one should not neglect to notice the instances of a change in topic which occur in a one-sided conversation, i.e., in a conversation in which one person carries on at length while the other listens. "Let me tell you something else that happened to me" or "I don't want to change the topic but . . . ," or "So much for our science lesson, let us now review last week's arithmetic" are all remarks which serve as explicit evidence that the topic is being changed and the point at which the topic changes during social interaction marks the beginning of another social contact.

c. One condition for temporal discontinuity, that is to say, one of the conditions under which more than one topic occurs in an interaction sequence, should now be qualified. When, for example, an agent says or does something to which the subject responds and, then this same agent says or does something else to which the subject responds, one is justified in marking this interaction sequence into two social contacts because the "topic" (in this example what is presented to the subject by the agent) is temporally discontinuous in so far as a response comes "between" that which the agent presents. The exception to this general rule about temporal discontinuity occurs when an interaction sequence is simply repetitive. The following example illustrates what is meant by a simply repetitive interaction sequence: The subject asks his mother for permission to go somewhere and the mother refuses; the subject immediately asks again for permission to go to this same place and the mother again refuses. This whole interaction sequence constitutes one social contact because the topic does not at all change but is simply repeated. (It is also one social contact in so far as the agent and the *raison d'être* do not change.) However, and this is important, it is also one social contact because the responses of the mother (in this example) are not such that they threaten the continuation of ongoing social interaction as such. Had the mother refused the subject's request and then walked away, the action of walking away would have made the continuation of the ongoing interaction appear doubtful. This activity of walking away is said to be unrelated to the interaction preceding it in so far as the activity threatens or interrupts the flow of social interaction. Thus, for example, when a mother who is reading a story to a subject gets up to obtain a drink of water, she will often assure the subject that she will continue her reading (should she plan to do so), because otherwise the subject will be in doubt as to whether or not the reading will be continued. In such a case, getting a drink of water has interrupted the reading interaction, and the point at which the mother and subject resume the reading interaction marks the beginning of another contact concerned with reading. Should a mother call the subject to come for supper, and there is evidence that the subject heard the mother but goes outdoors, the subject in so doing would be indulging in an activity unrelated to the interaction instigated by the mother. Therefore, should the mother call the subject again to come for supper, this call for supper would initiate another contact. Now all the essential conditions for simply repetitive interaction to be included within the scope of one social contact can be briefly summarized. Interaction is simply repetitive as long as the interaction continues (1) without a change in the agent involved, (2) without a change in the *raison d'être* involved, (3) without a change in the topic involved, and (4) without an activity on the part of the subject or agent that is unrelated to the interaction in progress.

d. It is possible to get a situation in which a given contact overlaps with another or a number of other contacts. In such a situation, the topic, the agent, and the *raison d'être* of the larger, overlapping contact are being simply repeated, and there is no activity on the part of the agent or subject between repetitions which is unrelated to the ongoing, continuous contact. Thus, for example, when a subject asks specific questions about various matters in a story the mother is reading, each differing question constitutes a contact. However, such contacts do not "threaten" or cast doubts upon the continuation of the reading contact and each time the mother resumes reading is not considered a contact, provided that at least one reading contact has been marked before the questions about the story were asked. Should the agent, for example, Maud's mother, talk about what kind of book she is reading and how Maud should look after it, this is a contact to be marked and to be distinguished from that of reading but it is not a contact that interrupts the reading. Such a contact is considered simultaneous and related to the reading. The resumption of reading after a simultaneous and related contact does not justify the marking of a new reading contact. A related contact, as opposed to an unrelated contact, does not cast doubt upon the continuation of the contact in the midst of which it occurs.

APPENDIX 5.2

Criteria for Rating the Ritual-relatedness of Contacts

THE DESCRIPTION OF CONTACTS in respect to situations involving common cultural ritual follows:

Five "situations" have been specified as being common to all Midwest homes and as having certain ritual connected with them. These are: (1) Getting up and ready for the day; (2) Breakfast or the morning meal; (3) Lunch or the noon meal; (4) Supper or the evening meal; and (5) Getting ready for and going to bed. The contacts that occur within the boundaries of these situations are to be judged as to whether or not they are related to the "ritual" (the activity perceived as appropriate, necessary, and fitting to the situation in question). All contacts that occur outside the boundaries of these specified situations are by definition rated as not related to the ritual of these situations.

a. Specifying the boundaries of these situations is usually accomplished by the agents in them and the rater need only follow their fairly self-evident cues. Meals begin with the first contact that specifically has reference to the very meal that is about to take place (e.g., Raymond Birch's mother asks whether or not he wishes an egg for breakfast), and end with the last contact that just immediately follows the meal and has to do with the completion of the ritual specifically connected with that meal (e.g. Raymond helps his father put away the breakfast dishes—when that is done breakfast ritual has ended). Where there are no contacts before or after the meals, the meals begin when the child is seated at the table, and end when the child leaves the table and does not return while anyone else is still at the table. Breakfast is sometimes contained within the getting-ready boundaries but it makes no difference for the rating whether washing before and/or after breakfast is judged as related to breakfast or getting ready. The getting-up beginning is obvious; the end to getting ready comes when the child is fully enough dressed and groomed to get no more agent comments about it before the child leaves for school, in school-age records, and by the end of clearing away the last remnants of the breakfast, in the preschool records. Getting ready and going to bed should be fairly obvious when begun by contacts aimed at this. Where there are none, it begins with the child undressing or washing (not immediate after-supper washing), and ends where the specimen record ends (which is usually when the child is asleep).

b. Judging the relatedness of contacts to the ritual associated with the cultural situations specified involves two kinds of relatedness: (1) Actions or comments which actually serve to facilitate and accomplish the behavior perceived as required or fitting within the boundaries. Such comments, for example, as "Pass me the potatoes" or "Bring me a fork" or "Don't use your hands"; (2) Actions or comments which have as their subject matter that which pertains to some aspect of the ritual. For example, Claire Graves' mother, while getting Claire ready for the day, comments that Claire has not done an adequate job of combing her hair.

c. The rater must bear in mind that a contact is only rated as ritual-related if it occurs within the boundaries of the very ritual situation to which it has reference. Thus, for example, talking about lunch at breakfast time is not a ritual-related bit of conversation because it does not refer to the situation in which the comment is made. Raymond's mother, during supper time, tells Raymond (who responds with pleasure) that he can have potatoes tomorrow for "dinner" (supper): this is not ritual-related.

APPENDIX 6.1

Instructions for Marking Units of Disturbance

Disturbance Units

I. *Distinguishing a Unit of Disturbance*

A. A unit commences when

1. the child first indicates a conscious *state of disturbance*[1] which has been
2. *evoked by a discernible referent.*[2]

B. The unit continues so long as the child remains disturbed with respect to the evoking referent. It *ceases* when the child is judged to be *no longer disturbed with respect to the evoking referent.*

II. *Duration and Intensity of Units*

A. As long as the disturbance experienced by the child fulfills the requirements of disturbance specified below,[1] a given unit of disturbance may be

1. *very brief,* even momentary (as well as much longer, although long units of disturbance likely are rare since it is expected that it would be difficult to fulfill the criteria over a long period of time), and it may be
2. *very mild* (as well as intense, of course).

In other words, a given unit must be reasonably definite, but it may be very brief and/or mild.

B. Units vary in intensity from very mild to very strong. There is no a priori requirement concerning the frequency distribution of the various degrees of intensity. All units theoretically, but hardly conceivably, could be rated "very mild" or "very strong" or any combination falling between these extremes. See Table 1 for criteria designed to serve as *guides* for rating disturbance intensity. The scale is so constructed that it may be converted to a three-point scale if desired.

III. *Differentiation of Units.* This refers to the problem of the number of units in a given section of the record where it already has been established that there is at least one unit.

A. An additional unit of disturbance is marked when, as seen by the child, a *different referent evokes* disturbance and becomes a referent of the disturbance in its own right.

1. Example illustrating *two* units.

A boy already disturbed as he searches in vain for a favorite toy is also disturbed by his mother calling him to supper.

It might be argued that the disturbance with respect to the mother is really due to the already existent frustration regarding the toy, and that he simply is taking out his troubles on her; or that both the in-

[1] See "Concept of Disturbance" below.

[2] See "Concept of Referent" below.

ability to find the toy and the being called to supper are barriers to the same goal ("playing with favorite toy"), hence only one unit. But the fact remains that a different referent *has* evoked a new disturbance, which is all that is needed for marking a second unit of disturbance.

a. It must be kept in mind that the second referent must in some way actually *evoke* disturbance and not simply be an object of hostility aroused by the original referent. (See discussion of this point under "Concept of Referent.")

B. Even without a change in referent, an additional unit of disturbance is marked if between two incidents of the section in question there is a *definite interval,* not less than 30 seconds in duration, in which the child is judged to be virtually *completely devoid of disturbance.* This assumes that

1. there is very good evidence, such as absorption in a pleasant task, for making the judgment of nondisturbance, and that
2. the two incidents being considered otherwise qualify as units of disturbance, namely, evidence of disturbance evoked by a discernible referent.
3. Examples, illustrating *two* units.

a. Where essentially the same referent is repeated. A young girl reading a magazine is called by her mother to put away the toys in her room. After a brief but definite manifestation of disturbance, the girl *avidly resumes her reading* without putting away the toys. *A minute or two later* the mother repeats her order, and again the girl is disturbed.

b. Where the referent remains constant. A small child is disturbed when he enters his house and fails to find his mother. His dog comes bounding into the room at this time, and the boy *plays happily* with the dog, forgetting as he does the absence of the mother. Several minutes later, however, her absence again enters his awareness, and he becomes disturbed again.

C. Since a unit continues as long as there exists disturbance with respect to the referent which evoked it, and since a different unit commences when disturbance is evoked by a different referent irrespective of the child's relation to the original referent, there exists the possibility of *overlapping* and *interrupted* units.

1. Example of two units *overlapping* with one another. Before a young girl completely gets over her anger at being pushed roughly by one boy, another boy adds to her troubles by calling her an insulting name. For a while she is simultaneously angry at both of them.
2. Example of one unit of disturbance being *interrupted,* but not ended, by a second. A boy already upset by being refused a cookie accidentally bumps his head and cries. He is disturbed by the latter event only briefly, however, and then resumes his plaintive pleas for the cookie.

TABLE 1

Criteria To Be Utilized as Guides in Judging Intensity of Disturbance

INTENSITY	*Duration of Incident*	*Importance of Incident to Child*	*Number of Indications* of Disturbance*	*Is child "emotionally upset"?*	*Does incident last beyond initial reaction to evoking referent?*	*Can effects of disturbing incident be detected in subsequent acts not directly related to evoking referent?*
VERY MILD	Usually very brief, even momentary	Very minor	Usually just one	Never	Almost never	Never
MILD	Usually very brief	Minor	Sometimes more than one, but more often not	Never obviously upset even mildly	Usually not	Virtually never
LOW–MODERATE	Unpredictable	Moderate	Usually more than one	Definitely, but mildly	Perhaps half of the time	Sometimes, but not usually
HIGH–MODERATE	Unpredictable	Moderate	Almost always more than one	Definitely, and moderately	Usually	Perhaps half of the time
STRONG	Never momentary; longer on the average	Major	Virtually always several	Definitely, and greatly	Almost always	Usually
VERY STRONG	Never momentary; longer on the average	Exceptionally important; major	Virtually always several	Definitely, and greatly. Degree suggested by term "temper tantrum"	Virtually always	Almost always

* Examples of "indications" are: "He looked annoyed," "He plaintively replied . . . ," "He stormed out of the room." If these statements all occurred within the same unit of disturbance, then there would be three "indications" for this incident.

Concept of Disturbance

Disturbance is used here as a construct of the behaviorally-inferred process of experiencing. It may be characterized as an

unpleasant disruption
in the ongoing feeling tone
of conscious experience.

In essence, we wish to detect those incidents in which the child actually *feels* disturbed—a disturbance with an *emotional tinge* to it.

PRACTICAL CONSIDERATIONS IN THE INTERPRETATION OF DISTURBANCE

1. There must be *some behavioral evidence* of disturbance. This evidence can vary from explicit and overt (e.g., "He slammed the door and cursed his brother") to subtle and covert (e.g., "He gave the appearance of being afraid," "She frowned when scolded by the teacher," "He said aggressively, ...") *Circumstances alone* do *not* suffice as a basis for interpreting disturbance. For example, the fact that the teacher scolds the child may lead one to expect that the child would be at least mildly disturbed; but if the record gives absolutely no behavioral indication that he or she actually was disturbed, then no disturbance can be assumed.

2. One must not confuse a *signal* of *potential* disturbance with the manifestation of an active disturbance. The disturbance we are concerned with usually is *in reaction* to some change that has taken place in the child's life space (the psychological environment of which he is a part). Thus, when a child "whiningly" or "plaintively" requests permission to go outside, this act in and of itself, can be considered no more than a signal that disturbance *may* result if permission is refused. This is significantly different from a whining request which is *in reaction* to being informed that he cannot go outside; this *would* be evidence of disturbance.

3. The individual child's habitual style of behaving and expressing himself frequently must be taken into consideration in evaluating his specific acts. Virtually the same act may indicate disturbance for one child but not another. This is particularly true of aggressive and vigorous acts. It should be kept in mind that acts manifesting disturbance *deviate from the individual's habitual behavior* and/or manner of expression.

Along this same line, one must distinguish actual disturbance from pretended disturbances (pretended for purposes of play, or pretended as a technique for obtaining something desired). Usually, however, this distinction is not difficult to make.

4. Any act best described as effort or striving or conation, even though intense, is *not* to be considered as disturbance in and of itself. In order to qualify as disturbance, affect must be detectable in conjunction with the conation.

5. An expression of mere dislike also is *not* to be considered as disturbance in and of itself. There must be a detectable affective component to the expression in order that it qualify as disturbance.

6. The disturbance we are investigating in this study is *"experiential" disturbance* and not *"behavioral" disturbance* (interruption in the smooth flow of behavior), even though behavior is the basis from which experiential disturbance is inferred. A child blocked in his progress toward a goal may be positively excited by the challenge which the barrier presents, or he may simply unemotionally choose a readily available alternative path to the goal. In either case there is no disturbance as we have defined it. Behavioral disturbance *may* produce experiential disturbance, but not necessarily.

7. Whereas incidents of mild disturbance are to be included in the study, an incident must be *devoid of positive effective connotation* for the child in order to be included. An incident in which a child is "embarrassed but somewhat pleased," for example, would not be included.

8. In order to avoid certain practical difficulties, it is required that the disturbance be *consciously* experienced by the child; thus, we exclude incidents in which (a) the child is only half awake (the tossing and turning of a child as he is about to awaken, for example) and also incidents in which (b) an unconsciousness is postulated as the level upon which the disturbance is felt. To be included, the child must be *aware* of his unpleasant state.

9. *Physical pain and/or discomfort.* Feeling and sensation, while very closely related, are not one and the same. An intensely painful sensation virtually always is accompanied by negative feelings (at least with children), but this is not always true of mild sensations of pain and/or discomfort. One can stub his toe and say, "Ouch!" (and mean it) but then let the whole matter pass without any emotionally tinged feeling of disturbance. On the other hand, if one reacts to this event by calling out demandingly, "Why doesn't someone turn on the lights around here!" then there is reason to believe that feelings are involved. In summary, therefore, one must always look carefully for evidence of whether or not the unpleasantness of any given physical sensation actually disturbs the child in our sense of the word.

10. *Boredom* is another phenomenon that may or may not involve a *feeling* of disturbance, and furthermore, a dividing line is difficult to draw. Certainly if the child is *thoroughly* bored he probably also feels disturbed. Boredom of this degree involves *satiation* with the task of situation at hand. Satiation is manifested by frequent pauses, fluctuations in the speed of performing the task (if a task is involved), nonfunctional [3] variations in the manner of performing the task, as well as more direct and obvious expressions of experienced discomfort. On the other hand, an occasional pause, unconscious restlessness, occasionally attending to distractions, etc. are obviously indications of a lack of interest; but these signs, in and of themselves, can only support an interpretation disturbance: they cannot be the sole basis for such an interpretation. *Boredom that is synonymous with indifference or simple lack of interest does not qualify as disturbance.*

JUDGING BORDERLINE CASES

Sometimes it is difficult to determine whether or not even mild disturbance has taken place. For these cases, the following operations are indicated:

[3] Nonfunctional as far as the objective requirements of the task or situation are concerned.

1. Is there sufficient reason for the child to be disturbed? That is, does it "make sense" (common sense, not theoretically "interpretive sense") that the child be disturbed? Is it understandable? This does not rule out the requirement of behavioral evidence of disturbance; rather, it is a question to be asked when the behavioral evidence is not entirely clear.

2. Is an observer's use of a specific, key word weighted correctly? Some words (e.g., angry) clearly imply disturbance in almost any context, but many others (e.g., puzzled, shy, impatient, disgusted, troubled, concerned, firm, whining, plaintive, *et alia*) are much more dependent upon context. Whenever a word of this type is used in a crucial spot of the reporting of an incident, *substitute for it a synonym or phrase* that fits the context supplied by the observer. Do *not* reinterpret the incident: merely rephrase it. The point is that in doing so, since words have a range of meaning, the judge will be less likely to be influenced by a single word and more likely to understand the observer's intended meaning.

3. Does the material leading up to, and especially following the incident, provide clues that might have a bearing on the section of the record in question? It might even happen, although this would be unusual, that later, as one proceeds through the record, one would come across information having relevance for a much earlier incident.

4. After taking the above three operations into consideration,
   a. the incident is to be included if one's confidence for doing so is greater than that for excluding it, and
   b. excluded if one's confidence for doing so is greater than, or equal to, that for including it. Ties mean exclusion.

Concept of Referent

DEFINITION OF TERMS

Referent. "The object, event, or abstraction [or situation, too, it might be added] that is pointed to by a word or other symbol." [4]

Referent of disturbance. The concrete object, event, or situation about which a person is disturbed. The referent is what the person is disturbed about; the "thing" to which the disturbance is attached.

A referent may be physical (e.g., accidental damage to a favorite toy), social (e.g., the hostile act of another person), or personal (e.g., lack of ability to reach a desired goal, injury to one's body). Also, a referent may be individual (e.g., a given other person) or collective (e.g., a group of people perceived as a whole).

Another person as a referent almost invariably is in conjunction with an act, or acts, of that person. See "Change in Referent" below.

Evoked by a discernible referent (I-A-2 of outline). This refers to the fact that an event, object, or situation has in some way given rise to disturbance. The evoking referent, however, need not be the "real" cause of the disturbance; it simply must "trigger-off" the disturbance. Thus in the outline example under III-A-1, where a boy is disturbed by being called to supper, the disturbance

[4] English, H. B. and English, Ava C. *Dictionary of Psychological and Psychoanalytical Terms* (New York: Longmans, Green, 1958).

might not have occurred at all had it not been for the fact that he already was disturbed by his inability to find his favorite toy. Nevertheless, being called to supper, as a referent, did evoke additional disturbance.

By "discernible referent" we simply mean that there is something which can be identified as the referent. To put it negatively, we wish to exclude those disturbances for which the referent is entirely unknown. Thus a "bad mood" which apparently is completely private to the child would be excluded. Disturbances for which there is not discernible referent are very rare in these records, however.

DISTINCTION BETWEEN A REFERENT THAT EVOKES DISTURBANCES AND A REFERENT OF DISPLACED HOSTILITY

This is a distinction which one seldom needs to make, but nevertheless one of some importance. Hostility can be thought of as a conative aspect of disturbance. *Displaced* hostility is this conative aspect of disturbance which is transferred from the referent which evoked it to a different inert *recipient* of hostile (aggressive) behavior which it has had no part in producing. An example would be the boy who kicks his sleeping cat when he, the boy, is frustrated in his efforts to construct a tunnel in the sand. Had the cat done something (i.e., had the hostile act of the child been in reaction to the cat, other than the cat's mere existence), such as clawed the boy or even just been in the boy's way when the boy started to step from the sand box, this would have been significantly different; then a new unit of disturbance would have been required.

The point is, therefore, that for this study one must take care to distinguish a referent which evokes disturbance from one which is only the recipient of hostility. The former can inaugurate disturbance; the latter cannot.

CHANGE IN REFERENT

By our definition above, a change in referent, the primary condition under which units of disturbance are differentiated as outlined under III-A above, is a change in the "object, event or situation about which a person is disturbed." Usually such a change is obvious except when the referent is the same person engaged in a series of acts. As mentioned above, a person as a referent almost invariably is accompanied by an act or acts. Occasionally the question arises as to whether or not each act in a series constitutes a referent of disturbance in and of itself or is simply a part, or subunit, of a single referent. The determining factor in such a case (assuming temporal contiguity of acts) is whether or not the child is judged to perceive a constant direction of the disturbance being evoked by the individual acts of the other person. Let us say that Child A is disturbed by the teasing of Child B. The fact that the teasing may be composed of several successive acts on the part of B (e.g., B calls A a sissy, then calls him another name, then mimics him) is not to be taken as proof of a change in referent since all of these acts likely are seen by A as being in the same direction of derogatory teasing. Had Child B become physically aggressive with intent to do physical harm, or had B ceased his teasing and asked a favor of A which A took offense to, then a change in direction would be in evidence.

APPENDIX 7.1

Titles of Books Used in Study of Social Actions in the Behavior Streams of American and English Children

AMERICAN BOOKS

Author	Title	Publisher	Date of Publication
Bell, Margaret	*Ride Out the Storm*	Morrow	1951
Brink, Carol Ryrie	*Family Grandstand*	Viking	1952
Caudill, Rebecca	*The House of the Fifers*	Longmans	1954
Cleary, Beverly	*Henry Huggins*	Morrow	1950
de Angeli, Marguerite	*Bright April*	Doubleday	1946
Enright, Elizabeth	*The Saturdays*	Rinehart	1941
Enright, Elizabeth	*Thimble Summer*	Rinehart	1938
Estes, Eleanor	*Ginger Pye*	Harcourt, Brace	1951
Faulkner, Georgene and Becker, John	*Melindy's Medal*	Messner	1945
Friedman, Frieda	*Dot for Short*	Morrow	1947
Gates, Doris	*Blue Willow*	Viking	1940
Gorsline, Douglas	*Farm Boy*	Viking	1950
Haywood, Carolyn	*Betsy and the Boys*	Harcourt, Brace	1939
Hunt, Mabel Leigh	*Miss Jellytot's Visit*	Lippincott	1955
Krumgold, Joseph	*And Now Miguel*	Crowell	1953
McCloskey, Robert	*Homer Price*	Viking	1943
Stolz, Mary	*Ready or Not*	Harper	1953
Weber, Lenora	*Beany Malone*	Crowell	1948

ENGLISH BOOKS

Author	Title	Publisher	Date of Publication
Barne, Kitty	*Visitors from London*	Dodd	1940
Barne, Kitty	*She Shall Have Music*	Dent	1938
Brown, Pamela	*The Swish of the Curtain*	Nelson	1941
Edwards, Monica	*Spirit of Punchbowl Farm*	Collins	1952
Garnett, Eve	*The Family from One End Street*	Muller	1937

ENGLISH BOOKS

Lloyd, Marjorie	*The Farm in Mallerstang*	Methuen	1956
Lyon, Elinor	*Wishing Water-Gate*	Hodder & Stoughton	1949
Mayne, William	*A Swarm in May*	Oxford	1955
Mayne, William	*The Member for the Marsh*	Oxford	1956
Pearce, Philippa	*Minnow on the Say*	Oxford	1955
Ransome, Arthur	*Swallows and Amazons*	Lippincott	1931
Severn, David	*Forest Holiday*	John Lane	1946
Streatfeild, Noel	*Family Shoes*	Random House	1954
Streatfeild, Noel	*Circus Shoes*	Random House	1939
Treadgold, Mary	*Left Till Called For*	Doubleday	1941
Trease, Geoffrey	*No Boats on Bannermere*	Heinemann	1949
Tring, Stephen	*Penny Dreadful*	Oxford	1949
Tring, Stephen	*Barry's Exciting Year*	Oxford	1951

APPENDIX 7.2

Definitions of Social Actions in Study of the Behavior Streams of American and English Children

1. X dominates Y. X applies maximal personal pressure on Y.
   X dictates to Y, bosses Y, decides issues for Y, determines Y's behavior, demands action from Y. Evidence of maximal pressure: X speaks loudly, definitely, confidently; X shows determination but does not show threatening emotion or use physical power.
   Example: See Yoredale sample specimen record (p. 302).
2. X manages Y. X applies medium personal pressure on Y.
   X supervises Y, teaches Y, regulates Y, leads Y, cautions Y. Occurs when X has greater competence, when X knows the way, when X is older; includes the leadership of an elected president, chairman, or acknowledged leader in games.
   Example: See Midwest sample specimen record (p. 293).
3. X influences Y. X applies routine personal pressure to Y.
   X makes requests of Y; asks advice, aid, information of Y; gives Y advice, aid, information.
   Example: See sample specimen record (p. 8).

4. X provides opportunity for Y. X increases positive valence or removes obstacle for Y.

   X promises reward, removes barrier. X makes no direct pressure on Y; X influences Y indirectly by changing the situation. In limiting case, X merely "goes along with" Y, giving Y moral support; includes conversation interesting to both X and Y.

   Example: See Midwest sample specimen record (p. 291).

5. X asks favor of Y. X makes own need explicit to Y.

   X appeals to Y for a gift, for help, for attention, for love. X controls Y indirectly by revealing his (X's) lacks to Y; asks aid because of inability, helplessness; seeks pity.

   Example: Geoffrey came to the front of the room and requested that the teacher tie his shoes for him. (Midwest specimen record #3, Barker et al., 1961, p. 11.)

6. X punishes Y. X determines Y's behavior by his authority plus actual punishment.

   X sends Y away, deprives Y of something of value, shakes Y, strikes Y as punishment.

   Example: See Yoredale sample specimen record (p. 301).

7. X disciplines Y. X determines Y's behavior by his authority plus threat of worse to come.

   X scolds Y, admonishes Y, rebukes Y, threatens Y. To X's authority is added (1) threat of physical action against Y, or (2) emotionality by X which indicates that "I am likely to become dangerous," "I am exasperated."

   Example: See Yoredale sample specimen record (p. 305).

8. X accepts Y's control. X completely accepts Y's influence.

   X identifies with Y, says in effect, "You are right." Includes expected compliance to elected president, chairman, captain; and also conversational interchange where one person gives way or follows another's lead.

   Example: See Midwest sample specimen record (p. 291).

9. X complies with Y. X accepts Y's authority realistically.

   X accepts Y's supervision without enthusiasm, is pupil of Y, is under Y, answers Y, obeys Y as a matter of course. Occurs when Y has the knowledge, knows the way, has the power, and X accepts this as a fact of life.

   Example: See Midwest sample specimen record (p. 301).

10. X surrenders to Y. X complies under Y's duress.

    X does as he is told while protesting, accepts Y's order reluctantly. X is forced to accept Y's authority, obeys unwillingly.

    Example: Miss Culver said, "We'll do *My Little Pony,* each 1A girl can get a boy." There were only two 1A girls. Claire asked Gideon. Gideon refused Claire. Claire appealed to Miss Culver saying, "Gideon said he won't." Miss Culver said definitely, "Gideon, there is no such word as 'won't' in this class." Gideon came down off the work bench to be a pony for Claire to drive. (Yoredale specimen record #29, Barker et al., 1961, p. 225.)

11. X resists Y. X does not comply with Y's efforts at domination.

    X refuses Y, defies Y, is unbending to Y, ignores Y's request.

Example: See X surrenders to Y, "Gideon refused Claire."

12. X disagrees with Y. X engages in verbal opposition to Y.

X delays his compliance, while he disputes with Y, argues with Y, is blunt with Y. Does not include objective discussion from different viewpoints.

Example: Mrs. Briggs stared at her son. 'Well, I never did,' she said at length. 'Fancy you getting mixed up in a fight. I never thought you were that sort of boy at all.'

'Don't be silly, Mum,' Barry urged, rather crossly. 'I'm not "that sort of boy." Everybody has a bit of a fight sooner or later. It—it just happened, that was all.' (*Barry's Exciting Year,* p. 25.)

13. X exploits Y. X uses his power over Y to benefit himself.

X has Y give him information, answer his questions, run errands for him, wait on him, do his work; X copies school work from Y. Indirectly and finally this may be for the "good" of Y, but here it is evaluated for the present.

Example: Shirley leaned over to look at Hilda's arithmetic paper. Hilda said indignantly to her, "Stop looking, you're copying off me." This was said, although quietly, with a good deal of feeling. Shirley looked unhappy but didn't say that she hadn't been copying. Hilda, looking resentfully at Shirley, took her blotter and held it in such a way that she covered her answers as she wrote them. (Yoredale specimen record #16, Barker et al., 1961, p. 199.)

14. X gratifies Y. X gives to Y without request or effort on Y's part.

X waits on Y, makes present to Y, indulges Y, is unselfish with Y, does more for Y than was expected.

Example: See Midwest sample specimen record (p. 292).

15. X helps Y. X adds his power to Y's efforts.

X assists Y, encourages Y, boosts Y, lends a hand to Y, inspires Y. In all of these, X is an accessory; the main effort is Y's.

Example: See Midwest sample specimen record (p. 292).

16. X co-operates with Y. X joins with Y in common task.

Task and goals are jointly held, and planned. The distinction from *helps* lies in the fact that here there is a joint or common goal which X and Y share; X is not an accessory, but a partner. Games played by rules mutually agreed upon are rated *co-operates* as well as *competes.*

Example: Mart threw his ball back. He made a very good throw, a nice straight one that was easily caught and thrown back. Mart caught it and threw it back. This meant that he had thrown twice in succession and Metcalf said, "Give someone else a turn, Butley." Ian Metcalf caught the next ball. Mart watched as Metcalf threw and said, "Good catch." The ball was thrown back. Mart and Ian Metcalf both went for it. Ian Metcalf ran into Mart Butley. Ian Metcalf said, "Sorry," to Mart. This was just routine politeness. (Yoredale specimen record #42, Barker et al., 1961, p. 243.)

17. X accommodates his behavior to Y. X adjusts his behavior, including his thinking, to Y.

X tries to behave (think) by standards of Y, makes his behavior appropriate to Y, aspires to behave like Y. Differs from *helps* and *co-operates* in that here X does not join Y toward a definite goal. X makes the general pattern of his behavior harmonious with Y's. In rating child's interaction with adult, the question is asked: Is the child trying to behave by adult standards? In rating adult's interaction with child, the question is asked: Is the adult really trying to behave in harmony with the child? In this respect accommodates refers to the degree of juvenilization of adult behavior, and to the degree of maturization of child behavior.

Example: (C accommodates to A.) That evening Homer was taking care of the gas station and helping his mother while his father was in the city. In between cooking hamburgers, and putting gas in cars, he read the radio builders' magazine and looked at the pictures in the mail-order catalogue. (*Homer Price,* p. 21.)

Example: (A accommodates to C.) "Let's see. He needs two hundred and twenty-eight more. It shouldn't take long to catch them," Mr. Huggins said to Mrs. Huggins. "After all, he promised. Let's help him."

So Henry and his mother and father bent and pounced together. Henry felt a little uncomfortable to see his mother catching worms, but he was very, very glad when the one thousand three hundred and thirty-first worm was in the jar. (*Henry Huggins,* p. 76.)

18. X comforts Y. X consoles Y when Y is sad or hurt.

X feels for Y, soothes Y.

Example: Miss Culver suddenly noted that Shirley was crying. She put her hands out to Shirley and said consolingly, "Now, now, Shirley, what's the trouble?" Shirley came up to Miss Culver and Miss Culver put her arm around her and said kindly, "What is it, did they say you killed the frog?" (Yoredale specimen record #12, Barker et al., 1961, p. 187.)

19. X defends Y. X is protective of Y.

X shields Y, guards Y, stands up for Y.

Example: Miss Culver said emphatically, "That's nonsense, that's a very unkind thing to say, why she didn't kill the frog." She continued indignantly, "Why Ian Simpson, I saw you teasing Shirley." And Miss Culver reiterated how unkind it was to say this kind of thing and comforted Shirley by saying she wasn't responsible and that it was all right; she turned Shirley around and with a comforting pat sent her back to her seat. (Yoredale specimen record #12, Barker et al., 1961, p. 187.)

20. X forgives Y. X overlooks faults or misdemeanors of Y.

X excuses Y, condones Y, pardons Y, makes allowances for Y, is patient with Y, is tolerant of Y.

Example: Mum had observed in life that men were foolish enough to fight over nothing; so she presumed, sadly, that boys were probably the same.

'Who won?' she inquired next.

'Well, I'm not sure. I suppose I did in a way.'

'That's something. If you've got to fight, you may as well win.' (*Barry's Exciting Year,* p. 25.)

21. X deprives Y. X withholds or withdraws something of value from Y.
X neglects Y, does not take care of Y, takes away from Y (not as punishment), dispossesses Y, is selfish with Y, is stingy with Y.
Example: Gideon appeared to hand out the pencils that had the better point or were longer to the children he liked. He handed a pencil to Harold. Harold fussed about it, objected to the kind of pencil that Gideon had given him. But Gideon ignored Harold and against Harold's objection went on. Gideon went down the next aisle. Harold got up and followed him and again objected, "I can't sharpen this." Gideon completely ignored this. He went right along handing out pencils. Harold continued to argue quietly. Gideon continued to ignore him. (Yoredale specimen record #27, Barker et al., 1961, p. 222.)

22. X hinders Y. X tries to prevent Y from reaching Y's goal.
X discourages Y, delays Y, disheartens Y, slows down Y, places a damper on Y, restricts Y, thwarts Y, restrains Y. X prevents Y from copying school work.
Example: See X exploits Y (p. 340).

23. X competes with Y. X tries to win over Y.
X wants more than Y, promotes own behavior to detriment of Y, plays competitive game with Y.
Example: She looked the crowd over and then said with finality, "Wasson, Wasson is 'it.' " Wasson smilingly went out to take his place to be "it." Immediately and abruptly the groups of children began running, shouting, "Black Man," as they ran. Wasson tried to catch several children but was unsuccessful as the children streamed across in wild confusion. (Midwest specimen record #40, Barker et al., 1961, p. 124.)

24. X is antagonistic to Y. X tries to inflict maximal injury of which he is capable on Y (not as punishment).
X tries to hurt Y, fights with Y; X has the intention of injuring Y.
Example: The sound of furious argument came to their ears long before they reached the trap; it's occupants seemed to be disagreeing with each other at the top of their shrill voices. The pony was rearing and backing and grew more and more restive, the more punishment it received. There were two girls and a boy in the trap, Michael saw as they came nearer, and the boy held the reins and was shouting furiously at the pony and slashing it with his whip. One of the girls, she had red hair he noticed, was shouting just as angrily and was trying to stop the boy by force, but the other girl was holding her back. They were all of them in a savage temper and at the moment the pony and the girl

with red hair seemed to be getting the worst of it. What a jolly party! Michael thought as they came running up. (*Forest Holiday,* p. 152.)

25. X is impatient with Y. X inflicts medium injury on Y.
X is angry with Y, finds Y a nuisance, is annoyed with Y, assaults Y verbally.
Example: See Yoredale sample specimen record (p. 301).

26. X teases Y. X inflicts minimum injury on Y.
X baits Y, bothers Y, pesters Y, badgers Y, nettles Y.
Example: Some of the Lower Junior Girls were playing hopscotch. Catherine threw her stone, a small piece of slate, into the third square successfully, i.e., not on any line. She turned to start hopping. Heather Simpson ran from leaning against the wall and hit the stone out of the hopscotch pattern completely. She did this quickly and mischievously. Catherine went right over to Heather. She pummeled her with both fists, not very hard, good-naturedly rather than hostilely. (Yoredale specimen record #39, Barker et al., 1961, p. 23a.)

27. X is affectionate to Y. X shows by explicit behavior that he loves Y.
X kisses Y, hugs Y, tells Y "I love you."
Example: Now there was no question of what Dot must do. She must recite the speech so well that the audience would remember her words long after they had forgotten what a failure she had almost been. She straightened her shoulders, stood her very tallest, and turned to face the audience. Her eyes looked straight into Mommy's and Mommy nodded lovingly. (*Dot for Short,* p. 68.)

28. X is friendly with Y. X shows medium affection for Y.
X is kind to Y, is congenial with Y, befriends Y, likes Y, is glad to see Y, welcomes Y.
Example: See Midwest sample specimen record (p. 298).

29. X enjoys Y. X shows by specific expressive action that he is pleased to interact with Y.
X has fun with Y, is merry with Y, feels good because of Y, is entertained by Y.
Example: Mart had been listening with great interest. He not only had been following in the book as the other children read, but had quietly pantomimed the action. Now he read with a good deal of pleasure. (Yoredale specimen record #21.) See also sample specimen records (p. 9).

30. X values Y. X makes specific positive evaluation of Y.
X rewards Y, praises Y, compares Y favorably with others, puts Y at the top of the list, congratulates Y. X approves Y with no application of pressure.
Example: Miss Graves asked, "Does anyone have twenty right?" Claire raised her hand and Miss Graves said, "Well done, Claire." Then she asked, "How many missed only one?" Heather and another child had hands up. She asked, "How many missed

two?" Gregory raised his hand, Miss Graves said, "Very good, Gregory." She said, "Gregory is in the fourth group, that's very good for him." (Yoredale specimen record #5, Barker et al., 1961, p. 175.)

31. X hates Y. X expresses maximal negative emotion toward Y.
X loathes Y, detests Y, can't stand Y.
Example: Janey nodded, never dreaming that Bounce could mean anything unpleasant.

"Well, it's a good thing Danger spotted you before you found the hen house. Now get off the place and stay off of it, if you know what's good for you. We don't want people snoopin' around here."

Now Janey knew what he meant. He thought her a thief, the kind of person who would sneak into a chicken house and steal whatever she could find there. (*Blue Willow,* p. 77.)

32. X is unfriendly to Y. X expresses medium negative emotion toward Y.
X is unkind to Y, does not care for Y, dislikes Y, turns his back on Y, rebuffs Y.
Example: "Can you tell us how to find Wishing water?"

"Wishing water?"

"Yes, or any caves or anything. Have you ever found any?"

"No," they said both together, and their frowns were quite fierce. (*Wishing Water-Gate,* p. 22.)

33. X is distressed by Y. X is grieved by Y.
X is saddened by, is embarrassed by Y.
Example: *Bright April* is about a little negro girl who is a member of a Brownie Scout troop. In this excerpt she represents her troop at an outing and supper party.

When it was time to go to the table, April was last to find a seat.

"Here, child, sit here!" called Mrs. Green as April hesitated, not being sure where to go.

She went to the table, and just as she stepped over the long bench to sit down, the little girl sitting in the next place turned around. It was Phyllis! She looked at April and started to get up.

"I'm not going to sit there next to—" She got no further, for there was Mrs. Green who had followed April to help her find her seat.

Mrs. Green did as Mrs. Cole had done once before, clapped her hands over Phyllis's thoughtless mouth, and at the same time helped her to rise, then led her away into the house, where Griz quickly followed. Mrs. Cole was near at hand too. She gently led April down the hill out of sight of the others, who were so busy chattering they hadn't heard what Phyllis said.

"Dear child," she said as they walked together, "remember

D.Y.B. [do your best]. It means allowing for the thoughtlessness of others as well as trying to be thoughtful yourself. It means being forgiving because someone else doesn't know what she is saying."

Mrs. Cole smoothed April's hair as she talked and with her quiet voice and gentle way helped April to swallow the lump in her throat and to feel sorry for Phyllis when Mrs. Cole told her that she had no mother. (*Bright April,* p. 78.)

34. X devalues Y. X makes specific negative evaluation of Y.

X criticizes Y, deprecates Y, compares Y unfavorably with others, puts Y at bottom of the list, belittles Y, jeers at Y.

Example: See Yoredale sample specimen record (p. 305).

35. X understands Y. X has insight into reasons for Y's behavior. X analyzes Y's problem, considers serious explanation of Y's behavior, sees Y's motives.

Example: He said, still in a whisper, no, he had not seen their old dog; and furthermore, he said he had an enormous dog himself, and this dog was so ferocious Wally had to keep him locked up with heavy chains. So they better not come knocking at his door any more, see?

Jerry and Rachel hurried away from there. "Maybe he did not have any Thanksgiving dinner," said Rachel, who was always ready to make excuses for anybody, even the unpleasantest people. (*Ginger Pye,* p. 129.)

36. X is baffled by Y. X does not have insight into Y's behavior.

X is confused by, does not understand Y.

Example: Mr. Andrews, like all men who have gone through the ordeal of dressing-up to go out, was inclined to be testy.

'What the deuce is that stamping noise?' he asked suddenly.

The stamping noise ceased, but nobody offered an explanation of what it was.

'What was it?' Mr. Andrews repeated. 'Something wrong with the car?'

'It was only me,' Penny said a little nervously.

'You, Penny? What on earth were you stamping for?'

'I wasn't exactly stamping. I was a charger pawing the ground before the trumpets sounded for a cavalry charge.'

'My God!' her father said crossly. 'I don't know what they teach girls at school nowadays. You don't seem to have a thought in your head except horses and nonsense like that.' (*Penny Dreadful,* p. 74.)

37. X plays with Y. X enters into game with Y, not as a supervisor or official, but as a player.

X recreates with Y, jokes with Y, engages in light, playful acts with Y.

Example: "But here we sit at the table wasting time," interrupted Mike O'Dea. "If you and I are to have any fun, Trish, we had better get at it. Whether or not you agree to be my daughter, I'm determined to be your papa. Of evenings Katie and I often used to play ball. So come along. Let's have a game." (*Miss Jellytot's Visit,* p. 109.)

38. X works with Y. X engages in serious activity.

X makes arrangements with Y that are seen as serious by X and Y, X does adult work with Y.

Example: Every ten or fifteen minutes the two men slid open the metal door with a piece of lead pipe; the clanging sound shattered all the dark gathered stillness of the woods. For a few moments you could look into the brilliant heart of the fire as Mr. Freebody and Mr. Linden, staggering a little, lifted the big logs to feed it. . . .

Jay was busy too. He helped the men with the logs, and slid open the glowing door for them. (*Thimble Summer,* p. 36.)

39. X is distant from Y. X appears indifferent to Y.

X is perfunctory with Y, is inattentive to Y, makes light of Y, is casual with Y, disregards Y. (Rated for A-C and C-A only)

Example: The Head (master) was towering above me. . . .

He swung round on the small fry. "You have all, no doubt, been brought up in the sentimental modern idea that the younger you are, the more you matter?"

"Yes, sir," they all babbled, not because they understood a word, but because it sounded like a question.

He chuckled. "This school is extremely old-fashioned. The younger you are, the less you matter. You are all so young that as yet you hardly matter to anyone except possibly yourselves and your mothers." (*No Boats on Bannermere,* p. 84.)

40. X is polite to Y. X shows proper forms of conduct with Y.

X is courteous to Y, is well-behaved with Y. (Rated for A-C and C-A only.)

Example: Alice said, "Please Miss, I have a new T-shirt." Miss Rutherford suggested that she take off her cardigan so that they could all see it. Alice did this with great pleasure and showed her new yellow and white striped T-shirt. (Yoredale specimen record #1, Barker et al., 1961, p. 164.)

INDEX